THE CHANGING FACE OF CHINA

THE
CHANGING
FACE OF
CHINA

From Mao to Market

JOHN GITTINGS

UNIVERSITY PRESS

OXFORD
UNIVERSITY PRESS

Great Clarendon Street, Oxford OX2 6DP

Oxford University Press is a department of the University of Oxford.
It furthers the University's objective of excellence in research, scholarship,
and education by publishing worldwide in

Oxford New York

Auckland Cape Town Dar es Salaam Hong Kong Karachi
Kuala Lumpur Madrid Melbourne Mexico City Nairobi
New Delhi Shanghai Taipei Toronto

With offices in

Argentina Austria Brazil Chile Czech Republic France Greece
Guatemala Hungary Italy Japan Poland Portugal Singapore
South Korea Switzerland Thailand Turkey Ukraine Vietnam

Oxford is a registered trade mark of Oxford University Press
in the UK and in certain other countries

Published in the United States
by Oxford University Press Inc., New York

British Library Cataloguing in Publication Data

Data available

Library of Congress Cataloging in Publication Data

Data available

ISBN 0–19–280612–2

1 3 5 7 9 10 8 6 4 2

Typeset by RefineCatch Limited, Bungay, Suffolk
Printed in Great Britain
on acid-free paper by
Biddles Ltd, King's Lynn, Norfolk

Acknowledgements

On 1 October 1949, Mao Zedong looked over the balcony of Tiananmen Square, where the crowds had assembled to hear him proclaim the People's Republic of China, and called out 'Long Live the People'. Unhappily, that slogan fell quickly into disuse and was replaced by the obligatory 'Long Live Chairman Mao', yet the history of China is the history of its people, and it is their help above all which I acknowledge. In writing *China Changes Face* (1990), I benefited from the opinions of the scholars and students who in the first post-Mao decade persisted in asking difficult questions about their country's past and future and often suffered for doing so. Since the trauma of Tiananmen Square, the face of China has continued to change much more radically and its society has become much more diverse. In bringing the story up to date now for these pages, I have relied on a wider spread of opinions heard in towns and villages throughout the country over the last decade. Although communication with Chinese officials remains stilted and frustrating, talking to the Chinese people has become easier and more rewarding. Their thoughts are far more 'liberated' than those of their leaders: even their faces are more interesting (as I have sought to illustrate in the photographs for this book). I am grateful to editors and colleagues on the *Guardian* for giving me the extended opportunity to range around China and to set up the newspaper's bureau in Shanghai. I am grateful to my family for its invariable support and for putting up with my periodic disappearances to a distant world. Further back in time, I owe a huge amount to the distinguished scholars who taught me at the School of Oriental and African Studies and at Oxford University, while later I learnt much from my fellow-teachers at the Polytechnic of Central London. But I must acknowledge my greatest debt by saying, once again, Long Live the People of China.

John Gittings
March 2005

Contents

List of Illustrations

All photographs taken by the author, except for nos. 8 & 14.

1

Introduction

The new 'New China'

After a period following the Transition to Ownership by the Whole People, the Productive Forces of Society will be expanded even more greatly; the Products of Society will become extremely Abundant; Communist Ideology, Consciousness, and Moral Character of the entire people will be raised immensely, and Education will be Universal and raised to a Higher Level.

(*Red Flag*, editorial on Great Leap Forward, 1 Sept. 1958)

On the basis of economic growth, efforts should be made to increase income for urban and rural residents, constantly improve their living conditions, including food, clothing, housing, transport and daily necessities, improve the social security system, and medical and health facilities, with a view to bettering their life. When some people and some regions Get Rich First, others will be brought along . . .

(Jiang Zemin, speech on eightieth anniversary of Chinese Communist Party, 1 July 2001)

Just over half a century after Mao Zedong established a new Chinese state led by the Communist Party based upon 'the alliance of workers and peasants', the influential Academy of Social Sciences in Beijing issued a report which would have made the Chairman turn in his mausoleum. China was no longer a nation of workers and peasants, it said in December 2001, and the definition of these classes 'clearly does not conform to China's realities today'. Mao had famously proclaimed that 'we should rely on the workers in everything', but the social scientists now believed that China needed fewer workers and more managers, professional people and entrepreneurs. The peasants who traditionally made up 80 per cent of the population were now less than half of the population. Yet this peasant stratum, once the mainstay of the revolution, was also judged by the Academy to be 'still too big'.

And what about Communism, the ultimate goal to which society should progress via the 'socialist transition'—so every Chinese had been taught at school—under the leadership of the Party? In November 2002 Jiang Zemin, who had succeeded Mao's own successor, Deng Xiaoping, only mentioned the word once in his speech to the Party Congress, with a passing reference to the 'ideal of Communism'. Now the only ideal which counted was to build China into a 'reasonably well-off society' (defined as average GDP at current value of US$2,000 a year) by the year 2020. China would be an industrialized country with 'a more open and viable economic system'; there would be a high rate of employment, and 'people will have more family property and lead a more prosperous life'.

Mao's passionate pursuit of the road to socialism (which, he insisted, could also include some early 'sprouts of Communism') had reached its ultimately disastrous peak with the Cultural Revolution (1966–76) and ended with his death. Important elements of this attempt to speed up the 'socialist transition' were dismantled in the 1980s—particularly the rural People's Communes which had been set up earlier in the Great Leap Forward (1958–61) when Mao insisted—against most of his colleagues—that China's peasants were ready for collectivized production. As the door opened wider to the West in the 1980s and Chinese society grew more diverse, serious strains emerged between those who clung to the Maoist vision and those who searched for a new course. In many respects China had already changed face, but the outlines of its new features were still shifting and confused. This brew of tension and uncertainty boiled over explosively at the end of the decade, with the bloody suppression of the student and workers' protests in the Beijing massacre of June 1989.

For a while it seemed possible that the Chinese government would revert to an ossified Maoism leading to further unrest and the collapse of the Communist Party. Instead, in 1992 Deng Xiaoping kick-started the economic reforms back to life, and into a higher gear, prompting a sustained burst of expansion. Midway through the first decade of the new millennium, the road ahead is no longer hazy: the Party has reinvented itself as the guarantor of the people's 'economic livelihood' and defender of China's position in the world, thus entitled to be the 'ruling party' (now the preferred term). Although China's political culture still contains elements of the socialist past, these aims are essentially the same as any other great power in the twenty-first century. The methods by which they should be achieved have nothing identifiably in common with socialism: competition and private enterprise are encouraged, corruption and inequality have grown worse, while China roars ahead in the global market, becoming the world's premier manufacturing base. Party theorists even justify exploitation. Xie Chuntao of the Central Party School, had a ready answer when challenged in an internet discussion staged by the *People's Daily* to celebrate the Party's eightieth anniversary. 'What about reducing the gap between town and country and ending exploitation?', he was asked. Xie responded that 'in order to achieve future prosperity for everyone, we should maintain and even expand some things which traditionally have been regarded as exploitation'.[1] China's features are no longer confused: state socialism has become state capitalism.*

The magnitude of this shift is often underestimated by Western (and particularly American) critics who persist in putting the Chinese leadership in a special category because it is still formally 'communist'. Chinese officials themselves reject the charge of capitalism, clinging to Deng's formula of 'socialism with Chinese characteristics' although they are hard pressed to define what those characteristics are. The most common explanation is that socialism looks after the welfare of ordinary people, as if this could not be achieved under any other system. In reality China is now a much more competitive place where many of the social safeguards of the past, such as virtually free health and education, have been abandoned. Most Chinese are in no doubt that the economic relationships which form the basis of their society have changed irretrievably and that socialism is a dead word. To

* Terms such as these are subject to endless debate: It has often been argued that China under Mao (and also the Soviet Union) were already 'state capitalist' societies in which the surplus value generated by workers and enterprises was in the main appropriated by state bureaucrats and the political elite. For China at any rate, this ignores the degree to which such surplus value was redistributed in favour of the working classes and the underlying socialist ethic of the 1950s and 1960s. Some analysts now regard the current system as a version of 'state corporatism' in which an authoritarian government controls and regulates economic activity through those social organizations (e.g. the 'All-China' national labour union) which it allows to exist. Although a useful concept when applied to the earlier post-Mao years, it does not adequately explain the China of today where both the exploitation of a large section of the working force and the accumulation of private capital have become such significant factors.[2]

many—such as private entrepreneurs making big money, young professionals entering the new middle class, artists and (to a lesser extent) writers enjoying more freedom, urban women deciding to remain single, students surfing the net and aspiring to study abroad, journalists able (sometimes) to tackle sensitive issues, migrant workers sending money home to their villages, criminals making money from drugs and prostitution—it has changed for the better. To many others—such as laid-off state industry workers, overtaxed farmers with hardly any cash income, the seriously ill who cannot afford hospital bills, rural women trapped by a resurgence of feudal attitudes, those evicted from their homes for new luxury housing schemes, those whose land or water is poisoned by industrial pollution, migrant workers who do not get paid on time or at all, women and children sold to brothels or as house-slaves, and the victims of other crimes in a now less peaceful society—it has changed for the worse.

As Party-led political culture loses dominance, there is more space for the emergence of a civil society which is partly autonomous and fast gathering confidence. Sociologist and dissident Liu Xiaobo writes that 'the concepts of "public" and "national" have surrendered much of their status to the concepts of "popular" and "personal" ', and that 'the debased status of the public sector has been accompanied by a rise in prestige for people or organisations with populist tendencies'. They include religious study groups, environmental and AIDS organizations, academic institutes, think tanks, and bookshops which offer venues for informal discussions often on sensitive issues. The Communist Party, though still alarmed if an organization seems likely to turn into a national pressure group, and while continuing to exercise control through a system of registration, is becoming more tolerant of what are often called 'Chinese NGOs'.[3]

China, by virtue of its endless supply of cheap labour and because of the—at least potential—attraction of its own market was able to attract huge sums of inward investment even during the Asian economic crisis of the late 1990s. However, the massive export surpluses, the rise in average incomes, and the transformation of urban China were not cost-free. By the early 2000s, there was increasing concern at the widening gap between rich and poor, the failure of disadvantaged rural areas to advance, the growth of unemployment among laid-off state workers (often after the industries in which they work had been asset-stripped unscrupulously), and the shaky financial basis for many wasteful prestige projects. A new 'fourth generation' of leaders headed by President Hu Jintao—the first to grow up since the

revolution—appears to take the threat of social and environmental dislocation more seriously. Unless proper action was taken, Premier Wen Jiabao has
warned that China's migrant workers might end up 'in a miserable plight as
described in the novels by Charles Dickens and Theodore Dreiser'. For the
first time these concerns, articulated at the highest level, seem to be more
than words.[4]

All of this means that the 'New China' proclaimed by Mao in the 1950s has
become a 'new "New China" ' of an entirely different character. It has
become much harder too to sum up this new more complex society in the few
phrases which once seemed sufficient to describe the old New China. In the
words of the writer Wang Meng, 'you can make any number of statements
about China and they are all true: Things are good, things are bad; China is
quite developed, and yet also underdeveloped. China has so many luxury
hotels, malls, department stores, and restaurants . . . And yet at the same
time, it is also possible to say that China is one of the poorest countries in
the world'.[5] Almost no one has been left unaffected by this transformation:
the exceptions are usually found in remote mountain valleys and other out-
of-the-way places, or among the elderly who have been left behind by the
modernizing tide. To illustrate this new diversity, here are some individual
examples:

• Wang, aged 51, now an investment banker based in New York and
Hong Kong, who specializes in buying up the assets of non-productive loans
from Chinese state banks. Sent to a remote north-west province in the
Cultural Revolution, Wang had been trained as a 'bare-foot doctor' with
sufficient skills to set bones and deliver babies (and once was faced with a
much more serious challenge—a local outbreak of plague).

• Liu, aged 47, son of an army officer who became a civil servant in
Shanghai after 1949. His father's income was 28 yuan (then equivalent to
£9) a month, although they had free housing in a Shanghai lane. In recent
years Liu has developed connections with Japanese businessmen based in
the city, and now runs a drinking bar (with hostesses) patronized by them.
He is investing in property and plans to open a Korean restaurant.

• Chen, aged 38, graduated from law school in 1988 and was 'assigned' to
the legal department of the province. He expected to rise slowly through
the bureaucracy and retire at 55, as millions of Chinese 'cadres' had done
before him. In 1992 he was sent abroad for further training on the understanding that he would go back to his job. While he was away, the department

was downsized, and he returned to set up an independent law firm serving foreign clients.

• Sun, aged 37, the daughter of parents in the army headquarters in Beijing who was brought up in a military compound and was expected to join the service. Instead she studied English at university, worked for a multinational company, and learnt computer skills. Now she runs a website which specializes in dating services. Much to the disappointment of her parents, Chen intends to remain single although she would like to have a child. She drives a Pajaro and spends Chinese New Year in Thailand.

• Li, aged 45, who with her husband had jobs for life in a factory in Hefei, two children, and free accommodation. The factory was asset-stripped by its managers and closed down: the pension fund was used to pay off creditors. Li has been retrained by the city labour department and now sits in a shopping centre mending clothes, sewing buttons, etc. for passers-by. Her husband is unemployed and plays cards with his friends.

• Cui, aged 28, a migrant worker from a lakeside village in Jiangxi, recruited to a Shanghai building site by his uncle who subcontracts labour gangs. Chen was tempted by the foreign goods he could see from the site in a neighbouring house rented by a Taiwanese businessman. He broke in one night and stole a video recorder and laptop computer: he left his fingerprints behind and has been jailed for five years.

• Zhou, aged 21, lured by an aunt from her village in Guiyang province to work in a textile factory in the Shenzhen Special Economic Zone. The accommodation address she was given was a centre for traffic in women and children: she was beaten, raped, forced to work as a prostitute, and has already contracted HIV-AIDS.

• Tang, aged 26, a migrant worker in Guangzhou who returned after two years to his native township in Guangxi province. With the money he had saved, he set up the town's first modern unisex hairdressing shop and is driving the old barbers, who shave with a broken mirror in the market place, out of business.

• Dai, aged 18, a student in Shanghai studying business administration. Her ambition in life is to take a marketing course abroad, and then come home to work for a well-known company like Kentucky Fried Chicken. She reads the Chinese edition of *Elle* and her favourite pursuit is shopping.

In spite of the increasing diversity of Chinese society and the huge material gains for the majority, politics in the new millennium still lags far behind.

This is true both of the country's ruling institutions which have barely changed in the past three decades, and of elite political culture which remains crippled by the traumas of the 1960s and 1970s.

The annual National People's Congress (NPC)—China's parliament—still meets behind doors to discuss an agenda and to make appointments already determined in secret by the Party leadership. Delegates are still quartered in hotels and guesthouses to which the public is denied access. The proceedings of the Chinese People's Political Consultative Conference, a mainly non-Party sounding-board for professional and academic opinion, which overlap the NPC are only slightly less formal. The Party's own leadership is chosen by a process of bargaining between rival factions—a topic for backstreet rumour but never for media report. Proposals in the 1980s for a more democratic Party have been shelved. Party office remains a source of privilege, more frequently abused now in a new age where the rewards of corruption and patronage have become vastly greater. Elections in both State and Party organizations remain indirect and their results are mainly determined in advance. The only reform has been to allow rural villages to choose their own leaders by direct ballot: attempts to extend this process to the next administrative level—the rural township—have been consistently blocked.

Psychologically the ruling Party is still unable to come to terms—in the popular phrase to 'settle accounts'—with its own past. The official verdict on Mao Zedong has not progressed from the trite conclusion, already reached in 1981, that he had 'made mistakes in his later years'. The famine induced by his adventurist policies in the Great Leap Forward, which increased mortality across the nation (estimates vary between 16 and 30 million 'excess deaths'), is only discussed in a few academic institutions. The standard formula here is that 'the Great Leap Forward plus natural calamities severely affected the development of the national economy'. The Cultural Revolution was formally condemned in 1981 as 'ten years of chaos' but remains a sensitive area. It is permissible to mourn the fate of those senior Party leaders such as former Head of State Liu Shaoqi who were victims of the high-level purge, but not that of the millions of ordinary people caught up in everyday violence. The cannibalism in some areas of Guangxi when, at the height of factional fighting in 1968, rival groups ate body parts as an act of revenge, remains a state secret. The unofficial cemetery on a hillside in Chongqing where dozens of worker Red Rebels lie buried is only known to relatives and survivors. Mao Zedong still lies in his mausoleum, imperfectly preserved, on Tiananmen Square. A bold appeal in 2004 by a group of intellectuals for the corpse to be removed to Mao's native home was ignored.

The June 1989 Beijing massacre remains by far the most neuralgic spot. A decade and a half later, no Chinese leader including Jiang had yet publicly departed from the official line that a 'turmoil' had been 'justifiably quelled in order to maintain social stability'. The only exception was the accidental publication in February 2004, on the *People's Daily* website, of an item from a foreign news agency referring to the 'violent crackdown' of 1989: the mistake was immediately corrected. Chinese dissidents who called for a reappraisal of the Party's verdict, circulating petitions or issuing statements to the foreign press, were harassed and sometimes charged with subversion. The ousted Party leader Zhao Ziyang, who had opposed the armed suppression, was kept under virtual house arrest until his death. A group of mothers in Beijing who had lost relatives in the massacre were also frequently harassed for demanding a public inquiry and full accounting of the deaths.

There have been some gains: Chinese media is far more diverse than before and older journalists stress the positive side. A Shanghai editor recalls the excitement when his newspaper was first allowed to report local disasters (he can remember the exact subject—a trolley bus had overturned in a central shopping street) and publish its own commentaries on foreign news. New evening tabloids are more popular than the familiar broadsheets. 'The youth don't read our Party papers', a Chongqing media official confesses. 'The tabloids have already overtaken us.'

Yet many younger journalists chafe at the restrictions and seek training abroad, hoping for better times. 'Our papers are full of empty talk, jargon and prejudice,' says a junior editor in Beijing. 'The government does not allow us enough leeway to explore such issues as laying-off workers, family violence, women trafficking, and the urban groups being marginalized in the cities.' Some of these problems are tackled by a few more adventurous newspapers, with the Guangzhou-based *Southern Weekend* as the outstanding example in spite of periodic purges. In 2002–3 *Southern Weekend* carried critical discussions on the widespread use of the death penalty, the suppression of bad news, and the practice of detention without trial.

The electronic media has more freedom than the printed press. Though Beijing has spent hundreds of millions of dollars on sophisticated surveillance equipment to police the internet, and blocks the most obvious external sites such as Amnesty International and Radio Free Europe, it cannot keep up with the spread of information. When Beijing sought in spring 2003 to conceal the spread of the SARS virus, millions of Chinese turned to their keyboards and cell phones to access banned foreign reports and censored domestic information.

However, more than twenty journalists and civil rights campaigners were detained on charges such as 'using the internet to subvert state power' in 2002–3 and several were jailed for up to ten years. Local campaigners are the most vulnerable. In a typical case the Hunanese independent writer Chen Shaowen was jailed for publicizing on the web the plight of a group of laid-off workers in Lianyuan city who drove three-wheeled motor cabs for hire: their crime was to set up a self-help association when the authorities banned their vehicles from the roads.

Censorship by the Party's propaganda apparatus remains unaccountable and unpredictable across the media. As one magazine editor describes it, 'You don't know where is the bottom line. You can find anything in the bookstores but as an editor you must be careful. If your publishing house is suspended for a year, who will pay the workers?'

The difficulty of reaching a balanced judgement on China today is exacerbated by our own prejudices and misperceptions. As a semi-academic journalist who first visited China in 1971 and has been writing for more than three decades, I am only too well aware of the defects in our own vision. The difficulty lies partly in China's sheer complexity and size and the challenge of its formidably long history and culture, but especially since 1949, the task has been further complicated by an international context in which governments—both Western and Chinese—seek openly or covertly to influence public perception. As Professor Colin Mackerras has concluded in a thoughtful study of this problem, 'the main determinant of Western images of China is the West itself . . . [and] the major power-concentrations have usually exercised a significant, and often determining, influence'.[6] The major power for the past half-century has been the US, and while some of the best scholarship and reporting on China is American, a large quantity has been influenced consciously or otherwise by cold war and anti-communist attitudes.

To this we should add a range of orientalizing stereotypes that date much further back in which China and the Chinese are seen (often inconsistently) as devious and inscrutable, violent and rebellious, elaborately polite and immensely cultured, natural philosophers in the Confucian tradition, callously ready to accept the loss of human life. The list descends into bathetic comment about the alleged willingness of all Chinese people to 'eat anything' and their stubborn refusal to 'lose face'. The Chinese government under Mao did its best to present a countervailing image of a peaceful society united in struggle to tame nature and build a new paradise on earth. Sympathetic foreign observers were given the flattering description of 'friends of China' and encouraged to take China's side against a hostile outside world. 'If China did not exist,' exclaimed one European academic after visiting China during the Cultural Revolution, 'we would have to invent her!' I must admit that some of my own reports from China after that first visit fell into this category.

Though the ideological divisions between the West and China have now almost disappeared, there is still a tendency to see the Chinese in terms of black and white—or rather red and black. Admitted fundamental weaknesses in the banking sector and the widening gap between rich and poor—problems not unfamiliar in other large developing countries—give rise to predictions of the 'coming collapse of China'. The repression of dissent of the state apparatus is presented as the operation of an all–powerful totalitarian regime, ignoring its patchy nature and the constraints imposed by more vocal public opinion.

Too often the complexities of life in China are reduced to what may be called the 'babies-in-ditch' cliché. Babies, especially unwanted female ones, do get abandoned: they also get sold. Yet babies also get rescued from ditches and from the dealers, by passers-by and by dedicated welfare officials and police. Many of them get adopted too—often by couples who 'want a girl'. In a village outside Beijing, disabled children from a city orphanage are fostered by rich farming families who do not really need the modest subsidy. Once the kids reach 16, they are supposed to go back to the city, but the house mothers have a different idea. 'They've become part of the family now: we can't let them go!'

The foreign media exposes—rightly—the plight of the millions of Chinese workers laid off with miserable benefits from failing state-owned industries. Yet for years Western diplomatic sources, quoted by the same media, have insisted that China's readiness to dismantle its 'unprofitable' state industrial sector is a key test of its 'commitment to reform'. We have drawn attention—correctly—to the pitiful state of China's rural medical services which would be quite unable to cope if an epidemic like the 2003 SARS virus spread deep into the countryside. Yet when China took the quasi-capitalist road under the rule of Deng Xiaoping, there was widespread applause for its wholesale rejection of the socialist values of the past—

including the rural 'barefoot doctors' whose absence is now deplored. Western manufacturers (and consumers) benefit from the comparative advantage of cheap Chinese labour, while shaking their heads when another sweatshop with barred windows catches fire and a dozen more workers die. We frown on the ugly glossiness of the new urban China, with its extremely rich who build replicas of the White House on their estates and squander millions in the casinos of Asia. Yet they are merely copying, in a cruder form, the lifestyle of Western counterparts whose wealth is celebrated in popular Chinese magazines.

In judging Chinese foreign policy too, Beijing's 'rationality' is too often measured by a partisan pro-US yardstick. In 1999 it was accused of stirring up xenophobia when many Chinese objected loudly to the American bombing of their embassy in Belgrade. Their genuine anger at the US spy-plane episode in April 2001 was also said to have been orchestrated. The real surprise should have been the speed with which Beijing patched up the dispute with a new US administration that had already sounded an unfriendly note towards China. On the night of September 11, China was accused of reacting callously because the state TV did not carry live coverage from New York. In reality China joined the US-led 'war on terror' very quickly, and kept its criticism of the subsequent Iraq war strictly muted. The only Chinese demonstration against the war was squelched by police, while a march by foreign residents was tolerated for just twenty minutes.

Many Chinese who are critical of their own government still find Western coverage unbalanced. 'I object strongly to the persecution of the Falun Gong and other human rights abuses,' says a graduate from an MBA programme in the US, 'but I simply did not recognize my country in the one-sided reporting there.' Chinese officials tighten a vicious circle of misunderstanding further by blocking the kind of access that would give a more balanced picture. A foreign NGO working in Yunnan province on HIV-AIDS tried for nearly a year without success to get permission for coverage of its project. 'The irony is that the authorities there are doing really good work,' said the project director.

The question of where China is heading—Whither China?—has been asked insistently since the final decades of the Manchu empire, and the debate was only stifled when the task of national survival against Japan assumed a higher priority. From 1949 until Mao's death the question was answered by the confident assertion that China was heading from socialism to Communism. In the quarter of a century since then, the terms of the debate have changed entirely: no one is interested any longer in -isms, and the questions now being asked within and outside China focus much more sharply on the strengths and weaknesses of China as it exists today, and may evolve tomorrow, rather than on any long-term projection.

Today as in the past, opinions range right across the spectrum. At one end there is admiration for China's progress in the past two decades and confidence that it will continue. The world now faces the reality of a 'huge, rapidly modernizing, but still relatively poor economy, operating at full throttle in global markets, increasingly able to perform economic tasks that formerly could only be handled by the wealthiest and most advanced industrial economies,' says Dr Robert Kapp, President of US–China Business Council.[7] At the other end there is the deeply dystopic view of those who believe that China is on the verge of catastrophe. 'All the experts acknowledge that the People's Republic faces serious challenges: failing state-owned enterprises and banks, rising corruption, a deteriorating environment, a slowing economy, and growing ethnic and religious unrest,' argues Gordon Chang, author of *The Coming Collapse of China*, accusing us of being deluded by the 'wonderful statistics' produced by Beijing.[8] In between these two poles there is a more moderate view—held particularly by Chinese whose judgement may be more balanced—that China does face serious but not insurmountable problems. As argued by Minxin Pei, 'the challenges confronting the Chinese government today are primarily economic, although weaknesses in the political system make potential solutions more elusive'.[9]

China has surprised us too often in the past half-century to be so confident now of our predictive powers. If we can make a reasonable forecast as to where China will be within the next decade, steering between the extreme interpretations, that will already be an achievement.

• *Will the Communist Party continue to rule China?* In spite of the precedents of the Soviet Union and Eastern Europe, hardly anyone expects the Party to collapse suddenly, and very few critics of the regime even among dissidents abroad call for such a collapse or believe it would be desirable. As Liu Qing (president of the US-based Human Rights in China organization) has argued, the struggle for human rights and democracy has to be paced 'into stages without seeking total success in one great step . . . to undertake a highly risky cause, especially a cause concerning the fate and even the lives of human beings, the responsible strategy should be conservative'.[10] Many ordinary people freely express their contempt for the Party and their admiration for multiparty systems abroad, yet at the same time they are nervous of the 'chaos' (*luan*) which they fear would result from a sudden overthrow or upheaval. Many younger Chinese hope, with varying degrees of confidence, that the Party will evolve over time in the direction of more internal democracy and less interference in everyday government. 'We are prepared to let these old fellows take their time,' says a young business executive, a graduate of Beijing University. 'The main thing is that they should go smoothly. Many of my friends in business are quietly building up links with the younger party people—those who will move into power in ten years' time. That's when we expect to see real change.'

Within the leadership, there is a search for new ideas: As described at a conference in 2002 by Li Junru, an influential Party adviser, 'the Party faces two problems: (*a*) how to stay in power, and (*b*) how to promote its own reform'. Li argued that the Party needs to develop a more mature 'political civilization', which will enable it to 'withdraw from government and guide by rules and norms'. While a revolutionary party is justified in monopolizing authority, a ruling party should be more detached from government.[11]

Those with longer memories recall that similar reforms, particularly focusing on the separation of powers between Party and government, were publicly argued in the 1980s but have hardly been heard since the 1989 Tiananmen crackdown, and they are also aware that successive leaderships since then have backed away from making changes. There is general agreement on one point: if the Party is to remain the sole or principal source of authority, it needs to stop saying that 'the time is not ripe', and to initiate serious reforms within the next few years. And there is regret that so far every new leadership has failed to live up to its initial promise.

• *Will the peasants and workers rise up in rebellion?* There is no shortage of predictions that the Chinese government could face a revolution in the countryside, which would then link up with alienated workers who have lost their jobs in the towns. Every change of dynasty, it is argued, has started with rural rebellion and if the Party fails the peasants, it could happen again. Many such warnings come from foreign observers: Gordon Chang claims that 'peasants riot and workers go on the rampage, hundreds of times a day'. However, as early as 1993, peasant protests at excessive taxation in Renshou County (Sichuan) caused alarm in Beijing: Deng Xiaoping warned that 'if economic trouble occurs in the 1990s, it is very likely to be in agriculture' and this would 'severely affect' the social situation. After repeated failures to

tackle the root causes of unrest, three scholars in 2002 published an influential article entitled 'Sounding the Alarm' which asserted that China 'is again
entering a period of social instability' and that the plight of the laid-off
workers and deepening crisis in rural China were key causes. In 2004 discussion of a book by two investigative journalists reporting the exploitation of
Chinese farmers was banned by the Party propaganda department.[12]

The 'rebellion of the masses' scenario is certainly possible, but it is less
likely to have the revolutionary consequences of peasant risings in the past.
There is still a tendency among disadvantaged communities to blame local
officials rather than the national leadership. Most protests are directed at
specific grievances and the officials often manage to defuse them by making
limited concessions. Increased social mobility and the freedom (denied in
the past) to seek jobs elsewhere also provide alternatives to rebellion. Those
who suffer most—the old, the young, and the women left in the villages, and
the middle-aged laid-off workers—are less likely to persist in resistance.
Finally, the central government still commands substantial forces of repression such as the *wujing* armed police who are frequently sent in to suppress
protests. However, the most significant mitigating factor is the escape route
offered by migrant labour for the rural unemployed, and by informal
employment for laid-off workers, in the booming cities. If the Chinese
economy were to suffer a protracted downturn, either because of global
economic problems or because of domestic overheating, then the knock-on
effect upon migrant labour and the informal sector could trigger unrest on a
much larger scale.

• *So might the Chinese economy burn itself out?* Chinese industry's voracious
appetite for energy and raw materials, the rising consumer demand for
finished products, the rolling programmes of investment in infrastructural
development—roads, railways, ports, public buildings, upgrading of communications and other utilities—had not flagged at the time of writing
(2004) since the new economic leap forward was launched more than a
decade before. Chinese oil consumption grew by 30 per cent in the four
years 1999 to 2003 and was expected to double between then and 2015.
The Chinese economy both impresses with its visible power and terrifies
with its potential weakness. It rode out the Asian financial crisis of 1997–8
defying predictions that it would become 'the next domino' after Thailand
and Malaysia. It was helped in this by its low ratio of foreign debt, the
momentum generated by five years of rising exports to the industrialized

world, and the protection afforded by its still largely non-convertible currency.[13] While the little Asian tigers slithered (Malaysia, which also imposed currency controls, was the exception), the big Asian dragon continued to breathe fire. Yet the Chinese economy was already sending out danger signals in other fundamental areas. A series of high-profile corruption cases (notably the massive Yuanhua scandal on the southern coast, centred on Xiamen, which involved a national deputy justice minister and the wife of a Party Politburo member) threw light on the dark world of nepotism and graft with which foreign business ventures had to contend. The State Owned Enterprises (SOEs) continued to soak up large quantities of credit while productivity declined and assets were stripped. These loans combined with other 'special arrangements' added to the build-up of non-performing loans granted by the state banks, over whom the People's Bank of China only exercised weak supervision.

The total of such loans was conservatively estimated in 1997 at US$200 billion or about one-quarter of total GDP. China's relentless economic growth also began to arouse fears of overheating when in 2003, in spite of government pledges to rein it back, GDP surged by 9.1 per cent. Much of this growth was based upon programmes of infrastructural investment designed to reduce unemployment but also prone to corruption. China in 2003 consumed more than half of the world's cement production and about a third of its steel. The surge also put energy production under further pressure: in Shanghai during the sweltering summer of 2004 manufacturers were ordered to work by night to ease the burden. China had imported 100 million tons of crude oil in 2003, 20 per cent more than the previous year, and the official press began to talk of an energy crisis.[14] In spite of rising wages, retailers were finding it harder to move consumer products such as fridges, freezers, electric heaters, and air conditioners which piled up in the warehouses. Was China then becoming a 'bubble' economy in 2004, as Japan had become a decade earlier, and if so would this result in a hard or a soft landing? The experts could agree at least that the collapse of an economy of China's size, if it occurred, would create instability on a global as well as a national scale.

• The final, most important, question to be asked about the future is this: *Can China's natural resources cope with escalating demand?* Environmental degradation and rising pollution (as described in the conclusion to Chapter 13, pp. 284–9) represent a far more serious threat to the Chinese people than political or economic instability. Every Chinese knows, and frequently tells the foreign visitor, that 'our population is too large, and our natural resources too limited'. The Chinese leadership still believes with Chairman Mao that man can tame nature, and continues to launch projects on a vast scale—such as the Three Gorges Dam and the South–North Water Transfer scheme—to address the shortages, but critics fear such projects will have hidden costs for the environment. The nightmare scenario for China is not a collapse of the Party or of the banks, or that the rural masses will once again surround the towns as they did in the revolution. It is that China will run out of water.

In conclusion, everyone can agree that there have been huge achievements as set out in this report on an international conference on poverty reduction held in Shanghai:

Since opening its economy in 1978, China has accounted for three-quarters of all the people in the world lifted out of abject poverty.

According to the World Bank, the number of Chinese people subsisting on less than $1 a day has fallen from 490 million in 1981 to 88 million. During this period the country's output has increased more than eightfold and the average income has risen by 7 per cent a year, passing $1,000 (currently £551) for the first time in 2003.

With factories opening and the ports booming, China is now the world's fourth biggest trading nation and the main draw for foreign investment.

'This will go down as one of the most remarkable feats in human history,' the prime minister, Wen Jiabao, said in his opening address. 'We are here to establish a new economic and political order.'[15]

Yet halfway through the new millennium the balance sheet remained very mixed. In global trade the world might be 'dancing to a Chinese tune' (*Financial Times*, 7 Dec. 2004) to the point where a Chinese company could buy the personal computer business of IBM. However, candid officials in Beijing admitted that real poverty remained far too high and warned of environmental disaster. Politically, the rigid handling of Zhao Ziyang's death (January 2005) showed a continuing failure to come to terms with the past while the new Hu-Wen partnership disappointed expectations by stepping up political repression. A National People's Congress resolution sanctioning the use of force if needed against Taiwan (March 2005) was a reminder of the continuing threat of US confrontation with China. The Chinese miracle is a precarious one: the leadership, whether it calls itself a ruling or a Communist Party, only has a few years to get it right, and it can only hope to succeed with the support of the Chinese people.★

* In writing this general account of modern Chinese history since the Communist revolution, I have sought to give full value to the ideas and goals of the period when Mao was in power as well as charting the huge changes which have taken place since his death amd particularly since the early 1990s. There is a tendency among younger Chinese today to dismiss Maoist ideology as 'political stuff' of no great interest, just as the Cultural Revolution is labelled as nothing but 'ten years of chaos' (a formula which also allows the current communist leadership to suppress serious questioning about the Party's responsibility for it). Yet a full appreciation of the Maoist period, acknowledging its ideals which millions at the time shared as well as its fatally destructive weaknesses, remains essential for any serious attempt to understand how China has since developed. The failures of this period also help to explain why 'socialism' has been so comprehensively discredited except in the most formal rhetorical sense. With the ending of the cold war and the growing chronological distance from the Maoist decades, there has also been a shift in the perception of those years by many scholars outside China, challenging or revising judgements which were widely shared before particularly in two areas. First, there has been a tendency to devalue the importance of Mao's theoretical arguments, and to take a much harsher view of his personality and his dictatorial behaviour. There is no question that we know now much more about Mao's despotic behaviour and that it reflects very badly on him, even if there is room for argument over the reliability and veracity of some memoirs and recollections. However, I continue to believe that Mao was an original thinker whose arguments should be taken seriously and that the history of post-1949 China cannot be understood if he is regarded simply as a 'monster' or as a despot only interested in his exercise of supreme power. Similarly, I do not think that it is helpful to dismiss the Cultural Revolution simply as 'ten years of chaos' attributable to power-hungry opportunists who exploited Mao's cult. As I have sought to show in this book, it was a much more complex affair in which high aspirations played a part as well as vicious ambitions, and serious ideas contended (though they could not prevail against) sterile dogma. Some of those ideas have also influenced the growth of dissent and democratic argument in more recent times. Second, the opening of many diplomatic archives in the former Soviet Union, plus the publication of a much smaller amount of formerly secret Chinese documents, has provided some evidence for a different view of Mao's diplomacy in the late 1940s and early 1950s. In particular, it is argued that US support for Chiang Kai-shek and failure to respond to various overtures did not after all amount to a 'lost chance' to establish relations with Mao's China at a much earlier date. In this interpretation, such a chance was ruled out by Mao's revolutionary world-view and by his respect for Stalin as a world leader in spite of all the difficulties between them. My own view remains that even in the area of ideology, circumstances can alter cases—as indeed was shown by the speed with which Mao responded when the US eventually sought détente with China in the 1970s. Beijing's earlier efforts to open a diplomatic dialogue with the US in the mid-1950s also need to be accounted for. I remain convinced that 'Western' (effectively American) hostility to a communist-led China was an important contributory factor in the growth of Maoist extremism in the late 1950s and 1960s. This relationship still needs to be better investigated and understood at the present time when US–China relations are emerging again as a critical factor, for better or worse, in the unfolding twenty-first century.

2

Search for Socialism
From Liberation to Utopia

Scene: A village somewhere in north China, 1952.

Party Secretary Wang left the old Taoist temple where the village council had been installed, and walked out into the fields where the peasants were working late on their newly distributed plots of land. Under the chestnut trees on the hillside, next to a few graves, there was still enough light to sit and read. Today he had organized the Poor Peasants to start digging a new well, and he had personally gone down the shaft to shift the largest stones. Chairman Mao said that every Party cadre should Plunge Deep into Construction and play an Exemplary Role among the Masses.

But Party cadres were also expected never to lose sight of the long-term goal—Communism. Now, at the end of the working day, there was just time for half an hour of self-study. Secretary Wang took a creased pamphlet out of his pocket, and squatted down with his back against a pile of brushwood. The contents were simply arranged for the barely literate reader. The main text was written in large characters, setting out the eight main tasks of the model Party member. Each sentence was followed by a longer explanation in smaller type just like the old commentaries on Confucius and the classics. Wang found his place at a line drawing of Stalin, surrounded by factory chimneys and other signs of material progress, and began to read:

> *The final aim of the Chinese Communist Party is to establish Communism in China.* Socialism is only the first step towards Communism.

In this stage, those who don't work don't eat, and the system is 'From each according to his ability, to each according to his work.' But when Communism has been attained, class distinctions will disappear. Production will develop greatly. Both agriculture and industry will have been electrified and mechanized. One person will be able to support several tens of people with his work, or several hundreds—or even several thousands. The working people will have a high cultural and technical level. The differences between workers, peasants, and intellectuals will have disappeared. Everyone's needs will be fully satisfied, and the system will be based on 'From each according to his ability, to each according to his needs.'

The textbook went on to say that when Communism was reached, the state itself would be abolished, including the government, the law courts, the army, and the police. Imperialism would have been defeated, everyone would live as one big family, and there would be Great Harmony in the World. Secretary Wang found this rather puzzling—especially the bit about the state withering away. Besides, it was getting too dark to read, and the storekeeper in the village below had promised him a special bottle of liquor, not available across the counter. With a little belch of anticipation, he set off down the track.[1]

The Communist vision

Between the ultimate vision of Communism and the immediate tasks of rebuilding the Chinese nation, shattered after nearly four decades of internal strife and external war, lay a vast theoretical void which the Chinese communist leadership made no attempt to fill for nearly a decade. There was no shortage of theory on the subject of the revolution which had just been successful. 'The Way of Mao Zedong' was advertised (much to Stalin's irritation) as the right path not only for the Chinese revolution but for all the other 'colonial and semi-colonial countries', especially in Asia, which still had to throw off their burdens of 'feudalism and imperialism'. But the path ahead remained undefined. There was not the slightest echo of the lively debate on the role of the state, the Party, and the army which had followed the Soviet revolution, and to which Lenin had contributed passionately and extensively. Mao showed no signs of even having read Lenin's *The State and Revolution*, in which the Soviet leader discussed the

means by which the state apparatus would 'wither away' during the transition to Communism (although the text was a prescribed document for
study by all Party cadres). In this long essay—the most utopian of his writings—Lenin expounded (according to the historian E. H. Carr) 'his vision
of a society in which, after the destruction of the bourgeois state and the
ending of class antagonisms, the coercive functions of the state would wither
away . . .'. He also argued in some detail how the bureaucratic and coercive
functions of the state could be replaced quite speedily by the voluntary
participation of its citizens in running their own affairs, and forecast that this
might be achieved 'in ten years or perhaps more'.[2]

The other classic texts on the subject of the transition to Communism,
Marx's *Critique of the Gotha Programme* (1875) and Engels's *Anti-Dühring*
(1878), are also ignored by Mao in his *Selected Works*. Mao did predict the
eventual withering away of the state, and with it the Communist Party, in
his 'On the People's Democratic Dictatorship', published three months
before Liberation. But he did so briefly and polemically, and without
beginning to raise any of the questions about the transition to Communism which had so exercised Lenin at the time of the October
Revolution.

Communists the world over are wiser than the bourgeoisie, they understand the
laws governing the existence and development of things, they understand dialectics,
and they can see further. The bourgeoisie does not welcome this truth because it
does not want to be overthrown . . . But for the working class, the labouring
people, and the Communist Party the question is not one of being overthrown, but
of working hard to create the conditions in which classes, state power, and political
parties will die out very naturally and mankind will enter the realm of Great
Harmony.

It was characteristic of Mao to use a traditional term, which dated back to
the fourth-century BC philosopher Mozi, the *da tong* or Great Harmony, as a
euphemism for Communism. The term had been adapted by the late-
nineteenth-century reformer Kang Youwei to serve his own argument
attempting to persuade the Manchu emperor to work towards an age of
Great Harmony by promoting reform. Mao's purpose in using it was not to
speculate on the future withering away of the state, but to stress the present
need for unconditional leadership by the Chinese Communist Party, and to
mock the defeated Nationalists for being unwilling to accept their own
much more imminent demise. There was some confusion as to what he

meant by Great Harmony. Some texts (including the one read by Secretary Wang on the hillside, quoted above) explained it as 'World Communism'. A later footnote in Mao's *Selected Works* offered a less internationalist definition, loosely embracing both Marx and Mozi: 'It refers to a society based on public ownership, free from class exploitation and oppression—a lofty ideal long cherished by the Chinese people. Here the realm of Great Harmony means communist society.'[3]

The 'Common Programme' adopted in September 1949, which served as China's constitution until the first National People's Congress (NPC) was held in 1954, did not even mention the word 'socialism'. Premier Zhou Enlai (Chou En-lai) explained that it would be 'proved to the entire people through practice', and therefore did not need to be put into writing. Mao told the drafters of the Common Programme that China would only enter the socialist stage some time in the future, 'unhurriedly and with proper arrangements when our economy and culture are flourishing, when conditions are ripe, and the transition has been fully considered and endorsed by the whole nation'.

Mao's reticence can be explained partly by political caution. The Common Programme was adopted by the Chinese People's Political Consultative Conference, a non-Party body through which the communists were seeking to mobilize the middle-of-the-road political forces that had long ago written off Chiang Kai-shek and were prepared to give the new regime a chance. The Communist Party needed the support of the 'national bourgeoisie'—the factory owners, businessmen, and intelligentsia of the urban areas—although it could already dispense with the rural landlords (who would before long be deprived of their land and often executed to satisfy 'the wrath of the masses'). But Mao after all did not hesitate to proclaim that Communism was the ultimate goal, nor that in foreign policy the new Chinese government intended to 'lean to one side' (that is, to enter into an alliance with the Soviet Union). The most compelling reason for uncertainty was that Mao and his colleagues simply had not thought about the future. 'Mao was very practical', a Chinese political scientist has explained. 'At that time China was still in the period of New Democracy which lasted in theory until 1956. And if Mao did not think about the theory of socialism, then no one else would.' If China had already been reasonably well developed and the international environment had been less threatening, this lack of theoretical clarity could have resulted in a long period of gradual change (as seemed at first to be the case). But China's circumstances encouraged impatience and innovation. The combination of a well-defined end (Communism) and an ill-defined means (socialism) would have a profound effect upon the politics of the next four decades. The utopian objective created a constant pressure to find new and better means of making progress towards it. It was necessary, then, to reshape theory in order to justify changes in practice. At any one time there was only one correct 'line' which supposedly reflected a universal truth or 'law'. Yet in reality the underlying doctrine had to be improvised to meet changing political needs. Socialism changed its meaning, as this chapter will demonstrate, no less than seven times between 1949 and 1989, and in doing so became increasingly less credible to the majority of the Chinese people.

Peach-blossom socialism

Socialism meant something very simple at first. The two mountains of feudalism and imperialism, described by Mao in his famous adaptation of the parable of the Old Man who Moved Mountains, had been levelled by the revolution. Now it was time to 'revive the nation'—a phrase familiar from the earlier twentieth century—and to bring about the social and economic well-being which it had been denied by nearly forty years of warlord struggles, war with Japan, and civil war. 'We promote socialism', said Mao—not yet concerned with more complex definitions—'because we want to develop our country, develop a national economy and culture that is better than the system of private ownership, and to ensure our national independence.' People were proud of China and confident about their future. The mood was conveyed by Song Jingling, widow of the 1911 Chinese republic's founding father Sun Yat-sen, in a triumphant statement published on the first anniversary of the communist liberation of Shanghai:

This has been a year of learning. We have learned about ourselves. We have learned about our city. We have learned about our future . . . We have discovered that the Chinese people have a mountain of strength, bursting vitality, and a genius that can competently meet any problem and overcome any difficulty . . . We are going to bring prosperity to our city and to China, the likes of which our long history has never recorded . . .[4]

In the backstreets of Shanghai, socialism had a more practical meaning in the sanitation campaigns which were launched to clean up the rubbish and the drains. Lanes and neighbourhoods competed for red pennants in the Sanitation Campaign. The Family Women's Organization got to work:

We'll get some powdered lime to sprinkle around the drains and damp and shaded places and along the house walls and fences. We've already contracted with a plumber to clean the drains twice a month and we'll share the cost . . . Besides cleaning up all places—where [rats] can nest, we should use traps and bait to catch them. Then we'll send them to the police station. We get credited with every rat we turn into the police.[5]

The mood was above all one of getting things done which had been obstructed in the past by the heavy burden of oppression, extortion, and ignorance. Simple improvements led to rapid and visible progress in many areas. The mortality rate fell from 25 per thousand before 1949 to 17 in 1951 (and 10.8 by 1957) mostly as a result of simple sanitation measures. Those who knew Shanghai's factories before the revolution were astounded to find labour regulations enforced, machines protected with guards, exits cleared of rubbish, and anti-dust fans installed. 'In the old days the machines came first', explained a worker, 'and we were their servants. Now we are the masters, we make them work for us.' The 505 km-long railway from Chongqing to Chengdu, planned for over forty years without a start being made, was completed within two years. Civil servants retained from the old regime knew they had to work conscientiously to keep their jobs. Others were replaced by new officials who made up for lack of experience by enthusiasm to 'serve the people', taking up their posts wherever they were assigned. The county magistrate no longer prayed in front of the City Temple God for rain: he mounted his bicycle and rode to meetings, listening to the people who asked for electricity, piped water, a new cinema.[6]

In the countryside the vast majority of peasants benefited from redistribution of land and worked hard to improve it. There were stories of peasants who went out to their new land in the middle of the night to check if it was still there. These innocent expectations of future material wealth were attached to the new idea of socialism. Chin Chaoyang, a young writer eager to record the optimism of the peasants among whom he had worked before Liberation, reports the words of a fruit-grower describing the benefits of the new co-operative which was now organized in his district:

Now at last the people in the whole of our mountain district were getting firmly rooted. The roots that they were growing were the roots of socialism! And socialism means that our mountain district will be clothed with trees, that peach-blossom and pear-blossom will cover the hillsides. Lumber-mills will spring up in our district, and a railway too, and our trees will be sprayed with insecticide from aeroplanes, and we will have a big water reservoir! . . .

Can we cover more and more of the mountains in the whole district with green trees, and make the streams clearer each year? Can we make the soil more fertile, and make the faces of the people in every village glow with good health? Can we make this mountain district of ours advance steadily on the path to socialism? If you ask me, I tell you it can be done! We have heart, and we have hands! It can be done![7]

Socialism Soviet style

The vision thus conjured up, expressed in hundreds of woodcuts and oil paintings showing the first tractor being welcomed by joyous villagers, was based on the experience of the only state to call itself 'socialist' so far—the Soviet Union. 'The Communist Party of the Soviet Union is our very best teacher', Mao had already written in his 1949 essay, 'and we must learn from it.' Only a few years earlier Mao and some of his colleagues had been tempted by a very different vision of a post-war China seeking Western—particularly American—technology and investment. Their invitation, extended to American visitors, including some US diplomats, was part of an unsuccessful effort to win US neutrality during the 1946–9 civil war. Even in spring 1949 the new communist government made private approaches to continue diplomatic relations with Washington. But the 'loss of China' had by now become a political issue, and Washington would only deal with a China that refrained from close relations with the Soviet Union. In spite of Mao's differences with Stalin, the Soviet Union on balance was still preferred if China had to choose sides. (The opportunity for an opening to the West would not recur for another twenty-five years, when President Richard Nixon visited Beijing.) Cut off from Western trade and finance by American containment—a deliberate policy of isolation which began before the Korean War but intensified as a result of it—the Chinese were soon obliged to rely on the Soviet Union for credits, equipment, and education. During the 1950s, at least ten thousand Soviet advisers (some estimates suggest up to twenty thousand) worked in China, and more than eighty thousand Chinese engineers and researchers were trained in the Soviet Union. Knowledge of policy differences with Moscow was confined to the highest levels: the general public was expected to respond without reservation to Mao Zedong's call in February 1953 for 'a great nationwide upsurge of learning from the Soviet Union in order to build up our country'. Only two years later Mao would hint that not everything about the Soviet Union was worth learning, but for the time being socialism meant the Soviet Union, as the head of the Chinese Publications Administration explained:

Without the moral and material assistance of the Soviet Union, the nationwide victory of the Chinese revolution would have been inconceivable, so it is not surprising that there is an upsurge of interest all over the country to study the Soviet Union and her advanced socialist experience . . . Since we are on the threshold of large-scale economic construction and a readjustment of curricula is under way in our universities, we now stand in urgent need of large numbers of translated works that introduce us to advanced Soviet scientific theory and technique and which will take the place of the stale and outworn texts cribbed from bourgeois writers and scholars which in the old days were used for the education of Chinese students.[8]

It was China's misfortune to catch the Soviet model in its last and intellectually most stultified years of Stalinism. The theoretical debates of the early 1920s in the Bolshevik Party about the nature of the transition to Communism had long ago been reduced to bland assertions that the Soviet Union was well on the way. At the end of 1953 Stalin's successors appointed a new ambassador to China, the philosopher P. F. Yudin, whom they hoped would strike an ideological chord with Mao. (The Chinese later said scornfully that the appointment had brought to Beijing someone who might be better able to 'study Mao Zedong's Thought'.)[9] Yudin's work on the transition to Communism was already a familiar source-book, making it sound reassuringly simple. All that was required for the Soviet Union, he wrote in *On the Nature of Soviet Society* (1950), was to complete the nation's main economic task: 'To overcome and outstrip the principal capitalist countries in the main items of industrial production.' These had already been defined (by Stalin in 1946) with what Yudin called 'scientific precision': 50 million tons annually of pig iron, 60 million tons of steel, 500 million tons of coal, and 60 million tons of oil. 'Once the productive forces reach this level of development', concluded Yudin, 'it will then be possible to pass over to Communism in the USSR. This task will be carried out by further developing heavy industry, especially the iron and steel, machine-building, and chemical industries and power supply . . .'. China also set specific tasks in the First Five-Year Plan (1953–7 but only fully worked out in 1955): Lenin had said that the foundation of socialism was 'large industrial development', and heavy industry was to be allocated 58 per cent of total investment in the

Plan (actually a larger proportion than the 49 per cent allocated in the first Soviet Plan of 1928–33), while state investment in agriculture at 8 per cent was less than half the Soviet figure (19 per cent).[10]

The pressure to 'be modern and Soviet' was overwhelming for a while after the ending of the Korean War and not unwelcome to many young Party cadres searching for a way to overcome China's economic backwardness. With China set on its feet again, the Soviet emphasis upon heavy industry as the key to development of light industry and then agriculture, and as the prerequisite for socialism, seemed to guarantee results of an impressively tangible nature. It made good sense too, when translated into terms which could be understood by the Chinese peasant. Wide publicity was given to the remark of an 85-year-old peasant on viewing his first Stalin-80 tractor, that 'Twenty oxen ploughing for a day can't do as much as this iron ox in one shift.' The distinguished economist Chen Hanseng, author of several famous studies of Western economic penetration and rural backwardness before the war, produced an imaginative historical argument to demonstrate the need for giving priority to heavy industry:

In many lands, where agriculture was ruined by war, pestilence, or depopulation, it perished for lack of large-scale mechanical means to restore it. That was the cause of the downfall of the Babylonians in Iraq, the Incas in Peru, the Mayas and Aztecs in Mexico, and the Uighur civilization in our southern Sinkiang [Xinjiang] province. The development of heavy industry and modern engineering—plus socialism— makes it possible to reclaim vast areas of wasteland. This has been shown in the Soviet Union, and it means much to us because we have huge tracts of unused land.

China's main task, wrote Chen, was to build a heavy industry which would enable it to become a semi-industrial nation by 1957, the end of the First Five-Year Plan. It would then be 'well on the way to socialism'.[11]

The gradual road

To make political progress towards socialism in China conditional on economic advance was not merely a response to Soviet dogma. The country was exhausted after four years of civil war preceded by eight years of war against Japan and, before that, over two decades of internal instability. As William Hinton (author of *Fanshen*, the classic eyewitness account of early land reform) later recalled, after 1949 the prospect of a prolonged stage of New Democracy—collaboration between the Communist Party and all social forces prepared to accept its leadership—was 'consensus politics' in

Beijing.[12] In the rural areas where the revolutionary process of land reform was still in progress, the consensus was only reached after three years (1950–2) of frequently savage struggle in which the poor peasants settled scores with their oppressors, landlords and their agents who had often raped and killed on behalf of the Japanese or Guomindang. Some 700,000 of them now paid the price. But once the redistribution of land was completed, the Party encouraged only the most cautious social reorganization in setting up 'mutual-aid teams' and, later on, low-level co-operatives. In urban life, the mixed economy extending from state to private ownership was intended to persist for many years. The reality was sometimes different, partly because of a new siege mentality brought about by foreign isolation and the pressure of the Korean War. But after that war was concluded, the general mood was peaceful as the Chinese people enjoyed the absence of conflict for the first time in their modern history. Chinese leaders now restated their gradualist view of the transition: before any further radical change in the 'relations of production'—for example, setting up rural co-operatives on a large scale and completely abolishing private commerce—the level of the 'productive forces', particularly the country's industrial base and the mechanization of agriculture, should be greatly raised.* This process, said the head of state, Liu Shaoqi, at the Eighth Party Congress in September 1956, would take between five and ten more years. The Congress's resolution stated that socialism had been basically established in China, that class struggle now belonged mostly to the past, and that the main contradiction was between the people's aspirations for a better life and their material backwardness. As Liu explained:

Of course, our people still have to struggle to liberate Taiwan, to complete the socialist transformation [of industry and trade] and to eradicate finally the system of exploitation. We must also continue to struggle to purge the remnant forces of counter-revolution . . . Nevertheless, our main internal contradiction is now between the people's demand to build an advanced industrial state and the reality of

---

* The 'productive forces' comprise the 'means of production'—land and farm implements, machinery, and plant—and human labour itself together with the 'human resources' (like housing and hospitals) which will make that labour more productive. The 'relations of production' refer to the sets of relationships between the producer and the productive system, including (a) ownership (private, collective, or state), (b) distribution of rewards (i.e. pay, share-out of produce, and so on), and (c) management or 'human relations' (how production is planned and work organized and assigned). The 'productive forces' and the 'relations of production' together form the 'material base' available to a given society. That society's political complexion, as well as its vital resources of education and culture, form the 'super-structure', which thus includes political parties, armed forces, police, and civil service.

our backward agriculture. It is between the people's need for rapid economic and cultural development and the actual situation where our economy and culture cannot satisfy their demands.

Liu Shaoqi also spoke approvingly of the need to 'enlist the services of the bourgeois and petty-bourgeois intellectuals in building socialism', and he proposed that political movements and 'struggles' should be phased out and replaced by a well-defined legal code. Meanwhile, Deng Xiaoping, the Party's General Secretary, made a tactful speech taking its cue from the de-Stalinization under way in Khrushchev's Soviet Union to condemn the 'cult of the individual', although he still argued that 'love for the leader' who had been chosen by the Party was acceptable. More to the point, the Thought of Mao Zedong was dropped from the new Party Constitution. Mao probably accepted the need to depersonalize his leadership in view of what was happening in Eastern Europe, although many years later in the Cultural Revolution Liu and Deng would be charged with sabotaging his Thought. On the pace of change, Mao was ambivalent, and we shall see that he had already moved to speed up rural co-operativization. But there is no evidence that he opposed the demotion of class struggle. Within a few months, he had launched the Hundred Flowers campaign to encourage non-Party criticism of the bureaucracy with a speech (February 1957) which in its original version implied that class struggle had come to an end. 'Now we have entered a different kind of battle . . .', he said. 'When class struggle is over, we declare war on nature.'[13]

The mid-1950s would later be widely regarded as golden years, characterized by a high degree of social harmony and shared enthusiasm for the future. The Party's heavy hand was only shown intermittently: many educated Chinese felt this was a small price to pay for having a government genuinely committed to reducing poverty, raising health and education standards, and defending the national interest while apparently remaining free from the pervasive corruption of the Chiang Kai-shek regime. Others, especially those intellectuals who had a 'bourgeois' past or had trained abroad, were more wary. After a literary witchhunt in 1954 against the famous poet and critic Hu Feng in which his private letters were judged to be proof of 'counter-revolutionary crimes', the writer Hsiao Ch'ien concluded that 'if you absolutely have to write [letters], stick to routine business . . . Writing diaries and memos that might provoke a dispute [with the Party] is particularly taboo.' (Hu had been singled out for criticism by Mao after calling for more intellectual freedom and remained in jail till 1979.

Later the episode would be seen as an early example of Mao's obsession with ideological struggle which led to the Cultural Revolution.)[14]

However, with the vast majority of Chinese either benefiting directly from the 'new China' or prepared to give the Party the benefit of the doubt, there was a general sense of participation in building a new and better society while the more pleasant traditional features of everyday life remained more or less unchanged. The British journalist Alan Winnington, one of the very few foreign residents in Beijing at the time, would later recall that

Beijing was vivid, kaleidoscopic, optimistic. If you went into the clay-walled *hutongs* where its real life pulsed, the city's ordinary activity was an exciting pageant, bright with the genius by which the Chinese can make the simplest everyday things attractive.

Makers of everything, sellers of everything announced their presence and their wares and services: the taps of second-hand dealers, the clash of knife grinders, trumpet calls, and whistles were all part of the daily scene. Moslem priests went round to slaughter sheep in the ordained manner. Falcons sat hooded on their owners' wrists. Women gossiped as they stitched shoes, spun noodles, cooked wonderful simple meals on home-made clay stoves in a single pan. At every corner there was something delectable to eat, costing pennies. Life had vastly improved since those days when we had marched in as liberators.[15]

Poor is beautiful

Yet the inner compulsion of a still-revolutionary process must be to fulfil its goals in the shortest possible time. Gradualism was grounded more in caution than in theory, and it had no effective defence against the politics of optimism, especially when the leading optimist was Mao. Preoccupied in the early 1950s by the Korean War and China's edgy relations with the Soviet Union, Mao had left pronouncements on socialism and the economy to the Head of State, Liu Shaoqi. Returning to the subject, Mao looked carefully at the countryside where the pressures from below for 'continuing the revolution' were far greater than in urban China. Where Mao chose to intervene, he would always prevail. Early in 1955 a group of Party officials who visited Confucius's birthplace at Qufu—a pleasant spot with ancient cypress trees and a comfortable guesthouse—but failed to take in a neighbouring rural co-operative received a pointed reprimand from Mao:

[Confucius] didn't care much about the economic aspects of the life of the people
. . . Now the people in his home town have set up socialist co-operatives. After three
years of co-operation, the economic and cultural life of the people, who were poor
and destitute for over two thousand years, has begun to change. This demonstrates
that the socialism of our time has indeed no parallel in history. Socialism is infinitely
superior to the Confucian 'classics'. I would like to suggest to those interested in
visiting the Temple and Tomb of Confucius that on their way they might well go
and have a look at the co-operative . . .

Mao now launched a full-scale propaganda campaign, going over the heads
of his Politburo colleagues to speed up the establishment of 'socialist'
agricultural co-operatives in which all the land, tools, and other means of
production were collectively owned and the profits were shared on the basis
of work-points, not according to the amount of land or equipment originally put into the collective. Poorer peasants who had gained less from the
original land reform generally supported the pooling of labour and
resources in the new co-operatives. Less poor 'middle' peasants and the rich
were naturally more dubious. The Party's own Rural Work Department was
sceptical, and Mao accused it of 'tottering along like a woman with bound
feet'. Reports of local success stories were edited by Mao with sharp comments on the obstructionism of local cadres, and circulated to the delegates
of a full Central Committee meeting in October 1955 which endorsed the
speed-up. Mao the journalist proudly told the delegates that he had spent
'eleven days behind my closed study door' making his editorial selection,
and—with another dig at Confucius—that he had travelled more widely in
spirit than had the sage in his wanderings.[16]

  Though the theory was not yet fully spelt out, Mao had already begun to
break with the orthodox view that the 'productive forces' must be fully
developed before further change could be made in the 'relations of production'. For agriculture this view—later attributed to Liu Shaoqi—meant
'mechanization before co-operation'. Mao argued on the contrary that only
co-operation could provide the collective infrastructure and produce the
surpluses necessary for mechanization. He also contested the belief that the
peasants were not sufficiently educated to run co-operatives. Perhaps not at
first, but co-operatives would provide both the framework for communal
literacy classes and the incentive (through the need to keep collective
accounts) for education. Underlying Mao's advocacy was the belief that the
socialist enthusiasm of ordinary peasants was itself a potential productive
force waiting to be unleashed. Mao dramatized his faith in the masses with a

phrase soon to become famous. China suffered, he said, from being poor, but poor people possessed the advantage of 'wanting revolution'. China suffered too from being 'blank' (uneducated), but this too had its advantage. Holding up a sheet of paper, on one side of which he had scribbled some notes, Mao turned it over dramatically. On the other blank side, fine words could be written (and fine pictures drawn, he added later).[17] Although twenty years later the co-operatives campaign was judged to have been 'over-hasty', for many peasants at the time, especially the younger ones, it opened up the possibility of translating the vision of socialist plenty into a reality where the peasants played their part rather than passively waiting for urban industrialization.

The novelist Zhou Libo put their enthusiasm into the character of a young secretary of the Youth League in a mountain village in southern China with big plans for the future:

After the co-operative is established, I'm going to propose that we do away with all the ridges between the fields, and make small plots into large ones. With large fields, the Iron Buffalo [tractor] can go into the water . . .

When we've built a reservoir, all the dry fields in the village will be irrigated, and even after paying tax we shan't be able to eat all the grain we grow. We'll send the surplus grain to help feed the workers in industry. Won't that be wonderful! Then they, all smiles, will come in their jeeps to the countryside, and say to us, 'Hello, peasant-brothers, would you like to have electric light here?' 'Yes, paraffin lamps are really too inconvenient and wasteful.' 'Very well, we'll install it. Do you want the telephone?' 'Yes, we want that as well' . . .

With electric light, telephone, lorries, and tractors, we shall live more comfortably than they do in the city, because we have the beautiful landscape and the fresh air. There'll be flowers all the year round and wild fruit, more than we can eat . . .[18]

Another later element of Maoist theory was also implicit in the collectivization campaign—the fear that failure to move ahead in restructuring social and production relations would increase the danger of a move backwards. Land reform, Mao maintained, had led to 'a vast sea of ownership by individual peasants' which, unless quickly raised to the co-operative level, would polarize the countryside, as the better-off peasants strove to get rich while the poorer fell into debt. There was merit in the argument, but it was overstated and expressed in language which hinted at political storms far ahead. Mao talked of a 'foul atmosphere' which was now being dispelled by a tidal wave of popular enthusiasm 'sweeping away all demons and monsters' (a familiar Red Guard slogan ten years later). Political work was 'the lifeblood of economic work', and hard struggle would be needed to oppose 'spontaneous tendencies towards capitalism'.[19]

Great Leap socialism

Although the 1955 co-operatives movement led directly to the establishment of the People's Communes in the Great Leap Forward of 1958, this had not been planned. Mao expected the co-operatives to develop in time directly into state-owned farms rather than collectively owned communes (essentially, agglomerations of many individual co-operatives). Both the structure of the new communes and the theoretical basis for them were at first improvised, indicating that in spite of later criticism there was a degree of spontaneity in their origins. The starting-point was a vast campaign for water conservancy and land improvement in the slack 1957 winter season, for which co-operatives joined forces with their neighbours. It was an impressive effort: by January 1958, said the Chinese press, one out of every six people was out 'digging the fields and hacking the hills'.[20] The defects of this crash campaign, which included not only shoddy construction but disastrous effects upon water tables and soil cohesion, were as yet unperceived. A modernized folk-song from Shandong, one of hundreds published at the time, conveys something of the mood:

> A Girl's Reply
> We were under the trees when I asked with a sigh:
> 'You still won't take up with a sweetheart, now why?'
> Her checks became flushed with a mantle of red
> And after some light-hearted banter she said:
> 'I won't be a wife till the hills are reclaimed,
> I won't leave my home till the river's been tamed.
> Green hills and green water for bride-chair I'll take,
> For my dowry the orchards and fields that we'll make.'[21]

Romantic poems were not uncommon in the new style, and were not always as trite as might be expected. The following example was written by a worker at the Liaoyang Textile Mill:

> The Girl Checker
> The dark eyes of the girl checker are sharp:
> Not a single defect in warp and woof escapes them.
> Some I know are afraid of these eyes

> But still more are fascinated!
> I send her the cloth I have woven myself,
> And my heart that can stand any test.
> I hope she will take the keenest look at them
> With her beautiful eyes![22]

Henan province in the north took the lead, claiming to have doubled its irrigated acreage, and under the leadership of its first Party Secretary Wú Zhipu (a student of Mao's thirty years before) its agricultural co-operatives began to merge forces, at first spontaneously and then as a party-guided experiment. In the first issue of a new theoretical journal, *Red Flag*, Mao Zedong leapt into a bold generalization based on the achievements of a Henan co-operative which had 'removed the threat of flood and drought' from its land. 'Throughout the country', wrote Mao, 'the spirit of Communism is surging forward. Political consciousness among the masses is rising rapidly. Backward sections among the masses have roused themselves energetically to catch up with the more advanced . . .'. Reiterating his 'Poor and Blank' thesis, Mao said that heaven was sending down 'talented men of every kind' who emerged from the ranks of the masses. The quote was from a poem by Gong Zizhen of the Qing dynasty:

> Let thunderbolts rouse the universe to life.
> Alas that ten thousand horses should stand mute!
> I urge heaven to bestir itself anew
> And send down talented men of every kind.

The *People's Daily* ran a new feature called 'Greatness from small beginnings', introducing the lives and work of Chinese and foreign inventors who had contributed to science in spite of their lack of formal education. The Chinese peasant personified the spirit of new China as a whole, now expressed in the rejection of the Soviet economic model, and the determination to 'catch up and overtake' the Western world by very different means.[23]

Though the mood was clear, the theory was improvised. Mao did not use the term 'commune' in his first *Red Flag* note. He spoke instead of a 'large, public community' (*da gong she*). The phrase 'large and public' (*yi da er gong*) would become a standard description of the advantages of the commune, Maoist both in its brevity and ambiguity. The actual term 'People's Commune' was first used two issues later by Chen Boda, editor of *Red Flag*, Mao's close ideological adviser and later head of the Cultural Revolution

Group. Chen envisaged the setting up of agri-industrial co-operatives which would break down the historic barriers between town and countryside and between mental and manual labour. Foreshadowing the 'all-round' approach of the Great Leap, which soon led to the mostly useless smelting of steel in rural backyard furnaces, Chen wrote under the heading 'Brand-new society, brand-new man'.[24] Mao endorsed the 'all-round' approach after a provincial tour in August 1958. 'It is better to run People's Communes,' he pronounced. 'Their advantages lie in that they can merge industry, agriculture, trade, culture and education, and military affairs into one entity, and make it easier for leadership.' The agro-industrial co-operative had become the new basic unit of social organization; urban society too was supposed to be organized into communes in the first wave of Great Leap enthusiasm. This notion of the 'many-handed peasant' is caught in a photograph from Shucheng County in Anhui. The local peasants are packed on to a parade ground in front of a thatched village with low wooded hills behind. Four large cartoons are displayed on posts among them, showing a small blast furnace; a resolute peasant; a student clutching two books marked respectively 'Marxism-Leninism' and 'College Graduate' in one hand and the atomic symbol in the other hand; and a militiaman with rifle and broad-brimmed hat.[25]

The improvisation of theory led at first in some interesting directions. A *Red Flag* editorial described the commune 'not only as the primary unit of our present society but the primary unit of the future communist society'. This implied a rejection of the hitherto orthodox progression from collective to state ownership. The commune enthusiasts spoke instead of a transition from collective to 'by the whole people' ownership. The latter phrase was not (as in the Soviet Union and previously in China) interchangeable with state ownership, but suggested instead a continuation into Communism of self-management by the community. *Red Flag* also briefly revived the notion of the withering away of state power: 'The function of the state will only be to deal with aggression from external enemies; it will no longer play an internal role.' (Even this external function would be modified by the communes' new military role in which a greatly expanded People's Militia would play a vital part in national defence.) Yet the theoretical uncertainties of the Great Leap and the People's Communes prompted no great debate. The only argument was with the Soviet leader Nikita Khrushchev, who mocked the whole affair, accusing the Chinese of 'skipping over a stage' and indulging in 'egalitarianism'. Mao had vaguely proposed that every Chinese province should have its own *Red Flag*, with licence to publish on 'all matters under the sun'. In reality Mao's ad hoc pronouncements in the central journal rapidly became dogma which precluded real discussion among the Party rank and file, let alone among the 'masses'. The only debate which did take place was a deeply divisive one within the upper ranks of the leadership, as the Great Leap veered from enthusiastic excess to demoralizing disaster. Disillusion began to spread within the Party, where some wondered if the leadership really knew where it was heading. News of the disgrace of the Minister of Defence Peng Dehuai for daring to criticize the Great Leap spread with the announcement of his replacement by Lin Biao in October 1959. Many local cadres, obliged to meet impossible targets, either alienated the peasants by dragooning them into collective work or offended their superiors by refusing to falsify the figures. A sense of losing the way filtered through to the non-Party masses as well, though there was still a fund of great enthusiasts. A character in Wang Meng's short story 'The Barber's Tale' recalls the mood:

In the late fifties we celebrated the construction of new factories, electric power stations, bridges, and the victory of the socialist reformation. But at the same time many unusual things happened. One day we'd hear that a certain high-ranking person was a wolf in sheep's clothing; the next that one-fourth of China's arable land would be growing flowers. Or that China would realize Communism very soon. Incredible announcements, conferences, and deeds were all too frequent.[26]

Rethinking the transition

The early 1960s were a time for reflection, as Mao contemplated both the collapse of the Great Leap Forward and the worsening of the Sino-Soviet dispute. With Chen Boda beside him, Mao retired to his study. First he picked up the latest edition of a standard Soviet textbook on political economy, and wrote a set of critical reading notes which were then circulated among cadres (but not published until long after his death). In these notes Mao provided retrospective justification for the Great Leap, filling out his instinctive view that the poor and the blank could more easily achieve the transition to socialism. There were a few insights too into the flawed political relationships which had been concealed by the formal apparatus of the socialist state—privilege, nepotism, and the dictatorial behaviour of Party cadres. The Notes (1961–2) were still mainly concerned with ways and means of raising the level of social ownership and collective work (the relations of production) in order to stimulate economic growth (the productive forces).

But as this attempt to hoist China into Communism by a rapid advance in productivity failed, and met with opposition both at home and abroad, Mao broodingly turned away from the 'material base' to focus on the 'super-structure' of politics and culture. With the assistance of Chen Boda and a large team of researchers, Mao produced a series of fluent anti-Soviet polemics (the *Nine Critiques*, 1963–4) which concluded with the claim that capitalism had been restored in the Soviet Union under Khrushchev's leadership. It followed that in China too it was essential to be on one's guard.

In an important passage of the *Notes*, Mao challenged Lenin's statement that 'The more backward the country, the more difficult is the transition from capitalism to socialism.' On the contrary:

Actually, the transition is less difficult the more backward the economy is, for the poorer they are the more people want revolution . . . Countries of the East, such as China and Russia, had been backward and poor, but now not only have their social systems moved well ahead of those of the West, but so does the rate of development of productive forces. In the development of the capitalist countries too, the backward overtake the advanced as America overtook England, and as Germany later overtook England early in the twentieth century.

But what was the nature of this transition? In the Soviet textbook (and in Stalin's 1952 essay 'Economic Problems of Socialism in the USSR', on which Mao had also commented), socialism was a relatively well-defined system with its own economic laws. Its society was unified except for a few malevolent forces and free from internal contradictions. Its economy was proceeding smoothly to the point where the productive forces would be sufficiently developed for the breakthrough to Communism to be achieved. Cultural levels were rising steadily; so was the growth of 'communist consciousness'. Mao took exception to the orderliness of this view, and now drew together the threads of the alternative perspective which he had begun to construct patchily in the 1950s. First, contradictions not only persisted in a socialist society but were the 'motive force for social development'. This was true both in human terms, where the tension between the backward and advanced could be harnessed to mobilize popular enthusiasm, and in economic terms, where it was a mistake to believe that there could or should be a perfectly planned balance. Mao wrote of the 'wavelike advance of the development of socialist production' which could never be 'perfectly linear and free from dips' (the setback after the Great Leap was one of those dips). Planning was the attempt to regulate the 'objective laws of imbalance', but if a perfect balance was achieved then there could be no progress. 'Balance is relative,' wrote Mao, 'imbalance absolute. This is a universal law which I am convinced applies to socialist society.'

Mao's second theoretical innovation was to spell out the need for developing the social organization of production *ahead of* the productive forces. (Although this had been done during the Great Leap, Chinese theorists had continued to pretend that orthodoxy was still being observed, claiming that the productive forces were far more developed than they were in reality, and therefore that it was the relations of production which were belatedly catching up.) Mao now deployed exactly the reverse argument as another universal law: 'We must first alter the relations of production', he wrote, 'before we can possibly develop social productive forces on a grand scale.' After all, the revolution itself had not waited for China to reach a higher level of productivity before embarking on its transformation of society. The revolution started with Marxist-Leninist propaganda to win over public opinion, then destroyed the old political superstructure and thus created a new set of production relations. Only then was it possible to set in motion a revolution in technology. Moreover, just as in the revolution, material incentives were not an adequate form of motivation. People still had to be inspired to work for socialism. Over-reliance on incentives, Mao argued, was a futile attempt to 'beat capitalism at its own game'.

[The textbook] should put stress on hard and bitter struggles, expanded reproduction, and the future of Communism. It cannot emphasize personal material interests, and lead people into the private pursuit of 'a wife, a dacha, a car, a piano, and a TV set'.

A third, much less well-articulated, area of theoretical innovation in Mao's musings of the early 1960s was his attempt to identify some of the social tensions which persisted in spite of the formal labels of state ownership and government 'by the people'. He wrote in the *Notes* that 'much remains to be written about human relations in the course of labour, e.g. concerning the need for the leadership to adopt egalitarian attitudes and to change certain [restrictive] regulations and established practices'. If industrial cadres did not change their attitudes, Mao continued, then the workers would never look on the factory as their own. 'Do not think that under socialism creative co-operation between the workers and the leadership of the enterprises will emerge all by itself without the need to work at it.' Mao also touched on the emergence of new vested interests in the state socialist system, particularly among cadres. Village cadres, for example, would be reluctant to surrender their power when their production brigades were eventually merged into larger communal units. Among the ordinary peasants, those who earned more under the system of differential work-points would object to a loss of earnings when a more egalitarian system of sharing out the proceeds of labour was adopted. 'The human animal is queer indeed,' Mao pondered. 'No sooner do people gain some superiority than they assume airs . . . it would be dangerous to ignore this.' Mao also noted the emergence of a new form of privilege which would only be generally recognized after his death:

The children of our cadres are a cause of discouragement. They lack experience of life and of society, yet their airs are considerable and they have a great sense of superiority. They have to be educated not to rely on their parents or martyrs of the past but entirely on themselves.[27]

The rethinking of the early 1960s should have led to a much broader discussion on how to move forward. But theory was the exclusive preserve of Mao and his closest colleagues, who were if anything further to the left than he. (Chen Boda wrote an article early on in the Great Leap calling for the abolition of 'commodity production' and the 'law of value'. Mao criticized him at the 1959 Beidaihe conference for advocating what would have amounted to the creation of a society where prices had no meaning.) The only serious theoretical challenge came from Sun Yefang, director of the Institute of Economic Studies, who advocated a return to farming on a family basis and more attention to the 'law of value' so that costs could be properly compared. In 1960–1 the commune system was modified, restoring the basic-level village or 'team' (shengchan dui) as the main unit for planning and production, restricting the role of the intermediate-level 'brigades' (da dui), and reducing the size of many communes by creating new ones. These reforms were more a response to events than to argument. The political scientist Su Shaozhi, one of the most independent thinkers of the 1980s, has recalled how willingly he and his colleagues in the 1960s followed the changing line: 'What I wrote then was often explanation of policies or interpretation or elaboration of talks by Party and government leaders, fettered by personality cult.' Su describes how he wrote an article explaining why the basic accounting unit in the People's Communes should be the dui or 'brigade', according to the official formula at the time. He then learnt that the word dui in the formula now referred to the 'team'—and promptly wrote another article explaining why this was more appropriate. Sun Yefang became the target of a criticism campaign organized by the Party's Central Propaganda Department.[28]

Return to class struggle

The Great Leap Forward had taken for granted the enthusiasm for socialism of all but a tiny percentage of the population, and it charted a future road along what was still an essentially materialist path. The attempt to hoist China into Communism by a rapid elevation of collective ownership and product-ivity failed. Convinced that China's enemies within were far more numer-ous than had been thought, Mao turned away from the 'material base' of production and producers to the intellectual and bureaucratic 'super-structure' of politics and culture, which he regarded as lukewarm if not hostile to continuing the revolution. His conviction was strengthened by events in the Soviet Union where, he believed, the leadership had now abandoned not only the 'sword of Stalin' but the 'sword of Lenin'. Nine research groups were set up to compile volumes of material to prepare the *Nine Critiques* against the Soviet Union which were then produced by smaller writing teams and edited by Mao or his closest colleagues. The research group on 'war and peace' alone produced five large books summar-izing the views of Marx, Engels, and Lenin, of Mao himself, of the 'revisionist' Soviet Union, and of the 'imperialists' and Yugoslavia.[29]

Khrushchev's crude attempts to force China into line by withdrawing Soviet aid and manoeuvring against Mao in the international communist movement brought the dispute into the open. The origins of the dispute were primarily concerned with international diplomacy. Tension between China and the Soviet Union was to be expected as China emerged from its dependence of the early 1950s. Mao strongly opposed the Soviet search for détente with the US (which was hardly in China's interest since it could only further isolate Beijing) and complained of lukewarm Soviet diplomatic support. Soviet reluctance to help China become an independent nuclear power enraged the Chinese. But Mao, with his own recent memories of heavy-handed Soviet guidance, also reacted sharply to Khrushchev's disapproval of the Great Leap, and regarded Soviet society as a model of what he sought to avoid. He saw in the Soviet Union a privileged stratum of bureaucrats which, although already in existence under Stalin, had since degenerated to become a 'new bourgeoisie'.

The members of this privileged stratum have converted the function of serving the masses into the privilege of dominating them. They are abusing their powers over the means of production and of livelihood for the private benefit of their small clique. The members of this privileged stratum appropriate the fruits of the Soviet people's labour and pocket incomes that are dozens or even a hundred times those of the average Soviet worker and peasant. They not only secure high incomes in the form of high salaries, high rewards, high royalties, and a great variety of personal subsidies, but also use their privileged position to appropriate public property by graft and bribery. Completely divorced from the working people of the Soviet Union, they live the parasitical and decadent life of the bourgeoisie.

Mao regarded Khrushchev as leader of a 'revisionist clique' which had rejected Marx and Lenin along with Stalin and was now paving the way for the 'restoration of capitalism'. Not far below the surface of Mao's anti-Soviet critique lay his growing dislike of China's own bureaucracy (which he believed had largely sabotaged the Great Leap) and mistrust of most of his own colleagues, whom he also suspected of 'revisionism'. Already in 1962 Mao had responded to their veiled criticisms of the Great Leap by producing a new call to action, 'Never forget class struggle!', at the Tenth Party Plenum in September. The more moderate economic policies in 1960–1 were now condemned for 'painting the picture too black', encouraging the peasants to 'go it alone', and seeking to 'reverse the verdict' on Peng Dehuai and other 'anti-Party' figures. The opposition of the bourgeoisie was more than a remnant from the past. As long as the transition to socialism continued, the opportunity existed for 'new bourgeois elements to be produced'. The struggle was protracted, and one could not even be certain about its outcome. What one should do was to 'talk about class struggle every year, every month, and every day'. The external and domestic stimuli to Mao's rethinking of theory had now converged, and the ninth *Critique* concluded with a fifteen-point statement on how to prevent the 'restoration of capitalism' which was intended to apply as much to China as to the Soviet Union:

Socialist society covers a very long historical period. Classes and class struggle continue to exist in this society, and the struggle still goes on between the road of socialism and the road of capitalism. The socialist revolution on the economic front (in the ownership of the means of production) is insufficient by itself and cannot be consolidated. There must also be a thorough socialist revolution on the political and ideological fronts. Here a very long period of time is needed to decide 'who will win' in the struggle between socialism and capitalism. Several decades won't do it; success requires anywhere from one to several centuries.

Mao had now arrived at the Stalinist conclusion that the class struggle would intensify rather than diminish as the socialist transition progressed further. Like the waves of the sea, it might be calm at one time but turbulent at another, and it was this struggle that would decide the fate of a socialist society. (After his death, the 1981 Party Resolution would censure him above all for having 'widened and absolutized the class struggle' at the 1962 Tenth Plenum.) Mao's response was less Stalinist. The solution, the fifteen points went on to explain, was to 'train and bring up millions of successors who will carry on the cause of proletarian revolution'. It was they who would do battle with the 'capitalist-roaders' who, unless checked, might one day cause China to 'change colour' and 'become revisionist or even fascist'.

Basing themselves on the changes in the Soviet Union, the imperialist prophets are pinning their hopes of 'peaceful evolution' on the third or fourth generation of the Chinese Party. We must shatter these imperialist prophecies. From our highest organization down to the grass-roots, we must everywhere give constant attention to the training and upbringing of successors to the revolutionary cause.[30]

Early in 1965 Mao wrote in a document setting out guidelines for the 'Socialist Education Movement', which was designed to clean up the countryside, that the chief target was to be 'those Party persons in power taking the capitalist road'. The ground was now prepared for the Cultural Revolution— which in spite of the toppling of Mao's rivals and the extreme violence employed was not simply a Stalinist purge but a much more complex affair which mobilized millions of activists to defend one man at the top and his version of the road to Communism.

3

Mao Zedong versus the Party
From cult to Cultural Revolution

It had been a heated argument in the Hall of Embracing Benevolence, built by the Empress Dowager for five million silver dollars after the Boxer Rebellion. For two days (14 and 16 Feb. 1967) the new Cultural Revolutionary leaders wrangled with the old guard. Did the Cultural Revolution need the Communist Party's leadership? Should veteran cadres be overthrown? Should the struggle by Red Guards and Rebels be extended into the armed forces? In the afternoon of the second session, the Minister of Agriculture Tan Zhenlin put on his coat, picked up his documents, and prepared to walk out:

Tan: You lot carry on, I'm going. Chop my head off, put me in jail, expel me from the Party, I'll still go on fighting!

Foreign Minister **Chen Yi**: No, don't go, Stay and fight them here!

Yu Qiuli (in charge of planning): What a way to treat old cadres! If the Planning Committee does not apologize, I won't criticize myself!

Li Xiannian: Now they've made it a nationwide confession [for old cadres]!

Tan: I never cried before but I've cried three times. Only I can't find anywhere to cry in private, because of my secretaries and children.

Li: I've cried a lot too.

Tan: Just look at my record from the Red Army on Mt Jinggang-shan right up to now. When have I ever opposed Chairman Mao?

The ultra-left leader Zhang Chunqiao hurried to Jiang Qing with a report on the proceedings, which she conveyed swiftly to Mao. Two days later Mao convened the Politburo and bitterly denounced the veteran protesters. Seven more sessions were held to criticize them for seeking to 'restore' (capitalism) and 'reverse' (the verdicts on Peng Dehuai and other disgraced officials). The Politburo then ceased to meet at all.[1]

Origins of the cult

In January 1965 Mao, by his own account, took the decision that Liu Shaoqi must be removed from office, and in the same month he was interviewed by the American journalist Edgar Snow, an old friend from their first meeting at Mao's revolutionary base in 1936. Snow had noticed a marked increase in the glorification of Mao since his last visit in 1960. At the climax of a performance of the song-and-dance pageant *The East is Red*, Snow saw a portrait of Mao copied from a photograph taken by him in 1936, blown up to about thirty feet high. 'It gave me a mixed feeling of pride of craftsmanship and uneasy recollection of similar extravaganzas of worship of Joseph Stalin seen during wartime years in Russia.' He put the question to Mao when they met again: was there a basis for the Soviet criticism that a cult of personality was now being fostered in China?

Mao replied that perhaps there was. It was said that Stalin had been the centre of a cult of personality, and that Khrushchev had none at all. The Chinese people, critics said, had some feelings or practices of this kind. There might be some good reasons for some more. Probably, he concluded, Khrushchev fell because he had no cult of personality at all.

Almost unobserved (for Snow did not grasp the significance of what Mao was saying—he had to be reminded of it when he met the Chairman again five years later) Mao had demolished the alibis offered on his behalf for the cult. He was not unaware of its extent, nor was it enlarged against his will by sycophantic followers. It served a precise political purpose at a time when he was preparing to launch the Cultural Revolution. (Yan Jiaqi, author of China's first scholarly account of the Cultural Revolution, begins the whole tale with Mao's remark to Snow.)[2] It had served a similar purpose in support of Mao's leadership for more than two decades.

Mao Zedong was a hero to many millions of Chinese, but more particularly he was a hero to himself. This dimension of his self-image became more pronounced as he grew older. The heroes of the revolution in his early poems were 'the soldiery of heaven' (*tianbing*), the Chinese workers and peasants who soared through the high clouds punishing the corrupt and the bad. By the 1960s there was only one hero: the wonder-working Monkey King celebrated in the classic novel *Journey to the West*. Monkey, wrote Mao in a 1961 poem much quoted later by Red Guards in the Cultural Revolution, 'wrathfully swung his massive cudgel, and the jade-like firmament was cleared of dust'. Mao was once observed by the British writer Robert Payne watching an episode from the *Water Margin* epic on the stage in wartime Yanan. There was no doubt in anyone's mind, wrote Payne, that this drama of peasant heroism in the Song dynasty was a morality play: the leader of the peasant forces in his dragon-painted gown represented Mao, and the white-faced feudal landlord represented Chiang Kai-shek. As for the real Mao, enjoying the performance from the front row of the audience, he had 'deliberately or undeliberately modelled himself on the old Chinese heroes', believing that democracy and socialism were 'the essential aims of heroism' in the modern age. Edgar Snow was also convinced that Mao modelled himself on the peasant chieftains of the *Water Margin*. 'He certainly believed in his own star and destiny to rule.'[3]

Mao saw himself as the commanding officer of the Chinese revolution, just as he recognized Stalin as playing the same role for the world revolution. Without a Stalin, he asked in 1939, who would give orders? Who would be the good commander and ensure that the soldiers of the revolution were properly looked after? Many years later, while acknowledging Stalin's 'mistakes' and the hard bargain which he had driven with China in the 1950 negotiations, Mao still insisted that the revolution needed its heroic leader as well as its collective leadership. In his 1958 speech 'On the problem of Stalin', Mao argued that a cult of the individual—or at least of the 'correct side' of an individual—was justified in so far as such a person 'represents the truth'. Marx, Engels, Lenin, and 'the correct side of Stalin' all held truth in their hands, so why should they not be revered? Party historians have since described the effect of Mao's formulation upon his own cult: 'Some Party comrades developed a confused understanding of this question. Even at the Chengdu Conference [in 1958, where Mao spoke on the Stalin problem] some responsible cadres raised the slogan: Believe in the Chairman to the point of blind faith, obey the Chairman to the point of following him blindly.'

The official view, which describes how Mao's cult escalated in the 1960s until he 'became arrogant' (in the words of the 1981 resolution on Party history) and led China into the Cultural Revolution, glosses over or ignores the early appearance of the Mao myth during the authentic revolution of the 1940s. This had soon elevated 'Mao Zedong Thought' to the guiding doctrine which laid down 'the correct path in the entire course of China's liberation movement—past, present and future . . .'. The triumph of Mao's Thought came at the end of the 'rectification campaign' (1941–2) in which Mao destroyed the influence of the Moscow-trained 'returned students' faction, defining the characteristics of the Chinese revolution as the 'sinification of Marxism'. It also coincided with the reduction of Soviet interest in China to its lowest point, as Moscow became overwhelmingly preoccupied by war with Germany. To some extent the myth of Mao also responded to a not dissimilar effort on the Chinese Nationalist side to promote its cause through Chiang Kai-shek's ghost-written book *China's Destiny*. The need to promote Mao's own thought was accepted by most of his colleagues and particularly by Liu Shaoqi, whose hagiographic speech in July 1943 first introduced the concept to the public. (Liu's involvement has since become an embarrassment to Chinese historians.) Liu again took the lead at the long-delayed Seventh Party Congress held in April 1945, calling Mao 'not only the greatest revolutionary and statesman in Chinese history, but also the greatest theoretician and scientist . . .'. Visiting Yanan in 1946, the American journalist Theodore White observed that, although Mao was supposed to be first among equals, 'his will was perhaps even more dominant in the Communist Party than Chiang's in the Guomindang. At public meetings it was not unusual for other members of the Political Bureau, men of great rank themselves, to make ostentatious notes on Mao's free-running speeches as if drinking from the fountain of knowledge.'[4]

Limits of Great Democracy

Was Mao's semi-feudal relationship with his colleagues in some way offset by a greater concern than theirs for popular democracy? During the Cultural Revolution this was a popular explanation of Western sympathizers who argued that Mao had turned to the 'masses' in order to clip the wings of Party bureaucracy. Mao did combine an autocratic style of leadership with a 'mass line' which sometimes paid more attention to popular opinion than many of his colleagues allowed. However, it was never a question of submitting problems to arbitration by the masses, but at the most of allowing them to 'make suggestions' (*ti yijian*, a phrase which implies a carefully restrained element of criticism). Mao demonstrated the limits of this approach in discussing the 'suggestions' which were offered on the draft new Constitution in 1954.

They are of three kinds. The first consists of suggestions that are incorrect. The second consists of suggestions that are not so much wrong as unsuitable and that had better not be adopted . . . The third consists of those suggestions that have been adopted. These are of course very good and necessary.[5]

An anecdote told by Mao to the second session of the Eighth Central Committee reveals both his concern for what he called 'great democracy' to combat growing bureaucracy, and the limits which he placed on it. Several years previously, he said, an airfield was to be built somewhere in Henan province, but no proper arrangements had been made to provide alternative accommodation for the peasants displaced by it. 'So the local people set up three lines of defence: the first line was composed of children, the second of women; and the third of able-bodied young men. All who went there to do the surveying were driven away and the peasants won out in the end.' What Mao meant by winning was simply that the authorities were compelled to give 'satisfactory explanations' to the peasants. They were then relocated, and the airfield was built according to plan.[6]

Mao grew increasingly concerned by the problem of state—people mediation when events in the Soviet Union and Eastern Europe, echoed to a lesser extent in China, showed just how wide the gap could grow. It was in this context that Mao in 1956–7 advocated 'democratic methods' to resolve what he now defined as 'contradictions among the people'. Such contradictions were not 'among the people' in the sense that they expressed the rival demands of different interest groups whose relative strengths should be weighed and adjudicated by the government. They were, rather, those differences between the ruling stratum and the ordinary people which were judged (by the former) to be relatively benign and open to discussion—although always on the assumption that it was the leadership which held the correct view. Mao was chiefly concerned in such situations to ensure that the leadership used persuasion and education rather than coercive measures to enforce its policies, on the pragmatic grounds that 'regulations alone will not work'.

In a revealing comment during the Great Leap on the experiences of a village which had persisted in running the (often unpopular) communal dining-halls, Mao quoted from Sun Yat-sen: if men with 'foresight and vision' carried out that which conformed to the 'heavenly truth' (*tianli*) and answered the people's desires (*renqing*) then the cause would not fail. But how could one establish what the people really wanted? In a crucial argument in defence of the Great Leap Forward in 1959, Mao used statistical sophistry to convert the minority who did support the communization of the countryside into an absolute majority:

At least 30 per cent of them [the peasants] are activists, another 30 per cent are pessimists and landlords, rich peasants, counter-revolutionaries, bad elements, bureaucrats, middle peasants and some poor peasants, and the remaining 40 per cent will follow the main stream. How many people are 30 per cent? It's 150 million people. They want to run communes and mess-halls, undertake large-scale co-operation and are very enthusiastic . . . For the followers of the main stream, it does not matter whether these programmes are carried out or not. Those who are not willing to carry on constitute 30 per cent. In short 30 per cent plus 40 per cent is 70 per cent [in favour of the Great Leap, if it is handled correctly]. (speech of 23 July 1959)

The Great Leap demonstrated Mao's growing unwillingness to 'listen to opinions' unless they conformed to his definition of what was correct. Peng Dehuai, Minister of Defence and a blunt critic at the Lushan Plenum (July 1959) of unrealistic targets and the exaggerated 'wind of Communism', sought to offer his views in a private letter to Mao. The Chairman—always a master tactician of inner-party manoeuvring—had the document circulated as a 'Letter of Opinion', and then denounced it as a 'programme of an anti-Party nature'. Mao (or perhaps those closest to him) insisted that Peng had formed a 'Military Club' which constituted an anti-Party clique, maintaining this definition even though Peng sought to have the letter withdrawn and made a self-criticism. Two months later Peng was replaced as Minister of Defence by Lin Biao (later to become Mao's 'chosen successor' and chief sycophant in the Cultural Revolution). The political thread of internal Party struggle which would be publicly unravelled in the Cultural Revolution can thus be traced precisely to Mao's obstinacy in the Peng Dehuai affair. Liu Shaoqi and Deng Xiaoping did not support Peng at the time, but by advocating more cautious policies later they retrospectively, and for Mao woundingly, validated his critique of the Great Leap. Liu spoke out in favour of Peng's rehabilitation in 1962, when Peng himself sent Mao an 80,000-character letter of justification. A group of Party intellectuals in the capital wrote veiled attacks on Peng's dismissal, including the famous play *Hai Rui Dismissed from Office* by the writer and deputy mayor of Beijing, Wu Han. These became the first targets of the literary polemics written by the ultra-left group now congregating around Mao, with which the Cultural Revolution was launched. The political chain led directly first to the mayor of Beijing, Peng Zhen, who had sought to protect Wu Han, and then to Liu Shaoqi, who sent 'work teams' of Party cadres to try to silence the first Red Guard agitators. A separate thread of connections leading back to Peng Dehuai was unravelled in the People's Liberation Army (PLA), where Lin Biao first disposed of the Chief of Staff Luo Ruiqing, and then neutralized most of the military leaders of his generation.

Discipline and dissent

Mao's growing authoritarianism was assisted by the preference of his colleagues, most of whom were to suffer in the Cultural Revolution, for discipline at the expense of democracy. The Party's highly vertical structure had been taught by Soviet advisers in the 1920s (who also helped the Guomindang establish a similar model). Soviet manuals on Party discipline were required reading. As Liu Shaoqi wrote in his famous 1941 lecture 'On Inner-Party Struggle', the Chinese had the advantage of being able to take the Soviet CPSU as its 'living example', and 'the majority of our Party members can recite from memory the organizational principles of the Bolshevik Party'. On the eve of Liberation Mao had called on the People's Liberation Army (PLA), which would provide large numbers of cadres for civilian life, to turn itself into 'a great school', and urged the party to behave modestly, shunning the 'sugar-coated bullets of the bourgeoisie' by which it would be tempted. Yet these provisos were outweighed by the belief that the Party's right to rule had been validated beyond further question by the sacrifices of the revolution. In his classic text 'How to be a Good Communist', Liu Shaoqi quoted approvingly from the philosopher Mengzi (Mencius): 'When heaven is about to confer a great office on any man, it first exercises his mind with suffering, and his sinews and bones with toil.' The members of the Communist Party, he continued, now faced 'the unprecedentedly "great office" of changing the world'. This Confucian belief in the 'superior man' dovetailed neatly with the Leninist concept of the 'vanguard party' and the Stalinist example of the 'great leader'.

The emphasis upon unity masked the reality of chronic disunity. The history of the Party had been punctuated by damaging internal conflicts which were designated as 'struggles between two lines [sets of policies]'. Political handbooks listed these in chronological order, starting with the 'line struggle against Chen Duxiu's rightist opportunism' in 1924 (Chen was the founder of the Party). The eleventh 'line struggle' would be designated briefly as that against Deng Xiaoping's 'right deviationism' in 1976, soon to be replaced by the struggle against the Gang of Four's 'anti-Party clique'. These episodes only increased the pressure for conformity. The Party Constitution contained provisions for 'inner-Party democracy' including the right (variously worded at different times) to appeal to higher authorities. Those who did so ran the risk of being identified as oppositionists. As the wartime Constitution warned, care should be taken that this right would not open the way for 'any conspirator, renegade or factionalist to utilize the principle of democracy to injure or divide the activities of the Party'.

Lower-level Party cadres were thus always under pressure to validate policies decided above by demonstrating that they worked below among the 'masses'. Mao himself acknowledged this danger during the Great Leap, yet deterred honest reporting by his own treatment of the Peng Dehuai opposition. Many writers of the late 1950s were labelled as 'rightists' precisely because they identified this harmful practice. The novelist Wang Meng made his name—and was exiled to the countryside—after publishing a short story in which complaints about a domineering factory director are answered with the warning to 'respect the leadership and strengthen unity'.[7] The journalist Liu Binyan wrote a fictionalized report, 'On the Bridge Site', showing how a disaster was caused while officials waited for 'higher instructions' instead of taking decisions during an emergency. Liu too was labelled a rightist. So was the young engineer who dared to make decisions on his own and provided the model for Liu's story.[8]

In 1956 the Party had held its Eighth Congress after an interval of eleven years since the Seventh. The delay could be explained by civil war and the struggle for post-war reconstruction, and the congress seemed to mark the completion of a return to normal Party life. The main congress speeches were published in full. Central Committee meetings were then held at least once a year until the Tenth in 1962. There followed a prolonged gap until the highly irregular Eleventh in August 1966, which officially launched the Cultural Revolution. The Ninth Congress, which should have been convened in 1960 at the required four-year interval, did not meet until 1969. This progressive 'abnormalization' of Party activity reflected Mao's increasing suspicion of the bureaucracy and preference for operating through ad hoc meetings such as 'working conferences' of provincial and national officials.

His colleagues, led by Liu Shaoqi and Deng Xiaoping, did not clamour for a resumption of internal democracy, but seemed happy to manipulate the system from within. Their policy differences with Mao were confined to the highest level, and they made no attempt to mobilize the Party rank and file. Mao was a better tactician in Party warfare, as he had been in guerrilla warfare. While circumventing the Party's democratic rules, he targeted the Party bureaucracy for his criticism, appealing to the less privileged and more resentful cadres. In December 1963 he wrote that 'large numbers of fine comrades are frustrated by those comrades who are highly placed with fat emoluments and live in style, who are conceited and complacent and are only too glad to stick to the beaten track, and who are addicted to bourgeois metaphysics; in other words, these fine comrades are frustrated by the bureaucrats'.[9] Provocatively, he argued on another occasion that

There are always people who feel themselves oppressed; junior officials, students, workers, peasants, and soldiers who don't like big-shots oppressing them. That's why they want revolutions. Will contradictions no longer be seen ten thousand years from now on? Why not? They will still be seen.[10]

But cadres within the Party in the early 1960s who sought to criticize bureaucracy were likely to harm their promotion prospects and to attract negative reports in their personnel files. In extreme cases they were sent to prison or to mental hospitals. Many denunciations of higher officials in the Cultural Revolution were fuelled by the real resentment of their juniors. Whole government ministries would be taken over by 'rebel' cadres who published exposés of the bureaucratic style and the privileged existence of their superiors. This happened most notoriously in the Ministry of Foreign Affairs, where the young chargé d'affaires from the embassy in Indonesia, Yao Tengshan, gained temporary power by denouncing the 'shameless behaviour' of Liu Shaoqi and his wife on their 1963 visit to Indonesia. 'Rebel' junior diplomats, interpreters, and trainees seized truckloads of classified documents and published exposés in Red Guard magazines. Senior diplomats were accused of revelling in foreign luxuries: 'They prefer everything foreign, even including foreign-made paper napkins . . . Many . . . are known to have brought back dozens of trunks of foreign merchandise, such as radios, television and stereo sets, tape recorders, cameras . . . in addition to sizeable bank balances.'[11]

Anatomy of ultra-left

Many people supported the ideals of the Cultural Revolution with a genuine conviction that they belonged to the 'true left' which was working for the creation of a 'socialist new man'. Their commitment was fatally tarnished by the usurpation of power at the apex of the Party by leaders who combined ultra-left rhetoric with an autocratic style and the acceptance of luxurious privilege. Though labelled retrospectively as the Gang of Four, the ultra-left was a more complicated phenomenon with its own internal divisions. It included serious though dogmatically inclined theorists; others who rose from the Party ranks through opportunism or zeal; and a few thugs and criminals. The Gang of Four was a shorthand expression, originally used by Mao in a private memorandum, which only became common after his death. Three of the group, Jiang Qing (Mao's wife), the Shanghai-based Party leader Zhang Chunqiao, and the polemicist Yao Wenyuan, had worked closely together to foment the Cultural Revolution. They were sometimes known contemptuously as the 'ten-eyed three' (because two of them, Jiang and Zhang, wore glasses). The fourth, Wang Hongwen, was an ex-worker from Shanghai, promoted to high Party office in 1973 in order to bring new blood into the leadership. A much larger group of ultra-leftists was briefly active in 1966–8, working through the Cultural Revolution Group with Chen Boda, Mao's intellectual confidant, as its head (and Jiang Qing as a deputy leader). Most of this group discredited itself in 1967 by openly attacking Premier Zhou Enlai and by seeking to stir up revolution within the armed forces. Chen himself was denounced in late 1970 as a 'sham Marxist political swindler'. His disgrace was followed by the much more sensational exposure of Mao's 'chosen successor' Lin Biao, Minister of Defence since 1960, in September 1971, when his alleged plot to assassinate Mao was exposed and he died in an aircrash while fleeing the country. Jiang Qing herself, although closely involved with the discredited groups, managed on each occasion to distance herself sufficiently to retain her influence, although this dwindled considerably in 1971–3. The period 1974–6 then saw a second struggle between a new ultra-left coalition, now owing total allegiance to her group, and the moderate forces led by Zhou Enlai and his de facto deputy, Deng Xiaoping, who was rehabilitated in 1973.

Mao was well aware of the dubious quality of the ultra-left forces on which he relied to launch the Cultural Revolution, but regarded them as a lesser evil than the Party bureaucracy. Transcripts of meetings show his impatience at sycophantic interjections by Lin Biao. Mao objected to a speech by Lin (18 May 1966) warning against a *coup d'état* and flattering Mao as a 'genius' of modern Marxism-Leninism. In a letter written in July 1966 and published internally in September 1972, Mao had already told Jiang Qing not to become 'dizzy with success', but to keep in mind her 'weak points, shortcomings, and mistakes'. But, he added, his criticisms could not be made public because it would mean 'pouring cold water on the leftists'. He added prophetically that they might not be published until after his death, when the rightists would probably 'use my words to hold high the black banner'.

Although Jiang Qing enjoyed lavish material privileges as the Chairman's wife, she resented the disapproval of his colleagues which had excluded her from active political life since Liberation. (It was said that they only approved her marriage with Mao in 1938 on condition that she should refrain from political activity.) When Mao showed his growing concern with class struggle and the reform of the superstructure—the world of politics and culture—she seized the chance. In March 1967, speaking to a group of Red Guards, Jiang gave a revealing account of her rise to power, claiming that it was she who from the early 1950s had encouraged Mao to criticize 'revisionist' tendencies in literature and art. Though Jiang's account was self-serving, it illustrates that even Mao's wife needed to secure his validation (although at first it seems to have been half-hearted) for her actions. Jiang's concern, verging on an obsession, with the reappearance of 'feudal' culture from the past meshed with Mao's own fear that the cultural superstructure had been taken over by his opponents.

In the last seventeen years [since 1949] there have been some good or fairly good works in literature and art reflecting the Workers, Peasants, and Soldiers. But most things were Famous, Foreign, or Fabled, or else they distorted the people's real image. As for education, it all seemed to belong to Them, plus a whole lot of stuff from the Soviet Union. So in literature and art we produced some Old Artists, and in education we produced even more intellectuals than before who were completely Cut off from the People, Proletariat and Production. Without the Cultural Revolution, who would ever manage to change things? They wouldn't budge if you hit them!

I thought it very funny then, all those Hong Kong films we were getting stuffed with, so I did my very best to shove them away. But They said something like 'Oh, we must pay attention to the needs of the National Bourgeoisie'. I really was on my own then! You can't have Peaceful Coexistence in this area of ideology. You Co-exist, and They'll Corrupt you.

Jiang Qing then launched a sidelong barb at Zhou Enlai (who appears to have been at the same meeting with her). It was Zhou, she said, who argued that China should subsidize the patriotic films made in Hong Kong 'as long as they're not anticommunist'. She then revealed that while she was 'ill for several years' the doctor advised her to 'Participate in Cultural Life', apparently as a form of therapy. She soon discovered that there were some Big Questions in Literature and Art, with mostly 'bourgeois and feudal stuff' on the stage and the screen.

I think it was in 1962 that a whole heap of Hong Kong, imperialist and revisionist films appeared. And so many new opera companies! I'm a great fan of Beijing Opera although I know it's been on the decline. Well, they used the Ministry of Culture to set them up everywhere—even down in Fujian there was more than a dozen! So everywhere you could see Lords and Ladies on the stage! I come from Shandong, and when I was a child they used to call the Hebei Clapper style the 'Big Opera'. I went to investigate and found that the Big Opera was now mostly Beijing. There were forty-five Beijing Opera companies, not counting illegal ones and amateurs. Shanghai opera had also spread all over the country in the same funny way. But they never put on stage the Rich Achievements of our People, or the Long March, *or* the Red Army, or the Anti-Japanese War. They never put on all those heroic things. Films had the same problem. So I gradually became aware of this problem. In 1962 I talked about it with four ministers or deputies from Propaganda and Culture, but they wouldn't listen to me.

Jiang Qing then explained how she and her confederates 'took a big risk' in preparing the article by Yao Wenyuan (which eventually launched the Cultural Revolution) without Mao's approval. She gathered some information on the 'Problems' in literature and art, but did not show it to her husband because he was 'too tired'. She admitted that Mao at first rejected her criticism of the play by Wu Han which allegedly was a covert defence of Peng Dehuai. But she relied on a tortuous interpretation of Mao's response to claim she was justified in pursuing the matter further.

. . . the Chairman turned me down. He said he wanted to read it [Wu Han's play] and that we should protect some of the historians like Wu Han. I only realized later that this was Mayor Peng Zhen's idea; he said I was completely negative about the world of history, which was actually a distortion of what I thought. So I said to the Chairman, 'Can I stick to my opinion?' And the Chairman said 'Stick to it if you like'. At that time Peng Zhen was doing everything to protect Wu Han. The Chairman must have seen it all clearly but he didn't speak out. It was because he allowed me to stick to my views that I felt entitled to organize that article and keep it a secret.[12]

The loyal opposition

Control of the Cultural Revolution in the first 'Red Guard' period (1966–8) was vested in a special group, run by Chen Boda with Jiang Qing as adviser, and responsible only to the Politburo's much smaller Standing Committee. Zhou Enlai's authority in the Cultural Revolution was based on a decision taken when it began that he should be 'in charge of the daily work of the Politburo and . . . of handling the routine affairs of the Party, government, and army'. The distinction was vital: Zhou could explain and interpret policy but he could not initiate it, nor is there any evidence that he sought to. His overriding concerns were to keep the state apparatus functioning and to save as many senior figures as possible from victimization. Legalisms were still vital amid the chaos. After receiving a note from Mao asking him to intervene on behalf of an old friend, Zhou felt entitled to draw up a 'protection list' of senior officials who should be saved from the Red Guards. An article mourning Zhou's death bore the title: 'A towering huge tree guards China heroically.' Many stories tell of his efforts—not all successful—to mitigate the worst consequences of Red Guard violence and Gang of Four vendettas. (Sometimes Zhou's countermanding order arrived too late, and when an investigation had been ordered only Mao could authorize release from prison.)

Yet Zhou gave the impression at the time to all of those who met him of being firmly convinced by the basic theory behind the Cultural Revolution, while struggling to protect it from manipulation by the ultra-left. Deng Xiaoping later tried to give an explanation for this. Premier Zhou, he said, 'was in an extremely difficult position then, and he said and did many things that he would have wished not to. But the people forgive him because, had he not done and said those things, he himself would not have been able to survive and play the neutralizing role he did, which reduced losses. He succeeded in protecting quite a number of people.'[13] Ten years after Zhou's death, the People's Daily for the first time admitted that he might have meant some of the things that he said. Zhou's understanding of the Cultural Revolution, it explained, was 'restricted by historical conditions'. Since its 'true nature' had not yet been revealed, he still hoped that the movement would produce 'good results'.[14]

Respect for Mao remained an important factor for many of his colleagues. Zhou's semi-official biographers explain that 'Mao had been right so many times before. If he decided that the Cultural Revolution was good for the Party and the country . . . Zhou went along without much question.' When it seemed to be leading to disaster, Zhou's first reaction was to reproach himself for failing to understand Mao's underlying strategy.[15] Yet Zhou did not believe in Mao unconditionally. Mao should not be regarded, he had said in a speech on the eve of the 1949 Liberation, as a demigod or a leader impossible to emulate—that would amount to isolating him from his people. Mao was 'a people's leader born of the experience and lessons of a history of several thousand years, of the revolutionary movements of the last hundred years, and of direct struggle over the last thirty years'. Young people should follow Mao's own example and 'seek truth from facts'—a concept later to become the catchphrase for the post-Mao regime of Deng Xiaoping.[16]

Other leaders were deterred more by respect for Mao's power than for his ideas. 'None of us could say this [criticize the rebels] to Chairman Mao', the veteran Marshal Xu Xiangqian was to observe. 'Influenced by the awesome power of Chairman Mao, none of us could do anything about it!' Their opposition in the early months of the Cultural Revolution was blustering and ill-organized. A sympathetic account of the famous 'February [1967] Revolt' of the senior marshals depicts little more than a bad-tempered wrangle over whether or not the Cultural Revolution should be extended into the armed forces. Marshal Ye Jianying is said to have struck the table with such force that he cracked one of the bones in his hand. 'We don't read books or newspapers,' he told Chen Boda sarcastically, 'and we don't understand the Principles of the Paris Commune. Please explain what they are! Can there be revolution without party leadership and without the army?' The ultra-left compiled a damaging dossier and promptly reported to Mao. It included verbatim remarks by the Minister of Agriculture Tan Zhenlin:

The masses, it's always the masses, what about Party leadership? It's all day long without the Party, the masses Liberating themselves, Educating themselves, Making Revolution. What's it all about? It's Metaphysics!

Your aim is just to overthrow the old cadres and clean them out one by one. Once you've fixed all the old cadres, forty years of revolution will be smashed like a broken family . . .

Jiang Qing wants to have me Rectified as a Counter-Revolutionary—she said so to my face! [A leftist supporter objects that Jiang Qing only wants to 'protect' Tan.] I don't want her to protect me! I work for the Party, I don't work for her![17]

Protesting his loyalty to Mao, Tan wrote an ill-advised letter to Lin Biao accusing Jiang Qing of being worse than the notorious Tang empress Wu

Zetian. Lin promptly showed the letter to Mao, who summoned a special Politburo meeting to castigate the dissenters. More than four years passed before Mao fully relented, choosing to regard the 'February adverse current' as a protest against Lin and Chen Boda, who by this time had been disgraced.

Meanwhile Deng Xiaoping, the ultimate survivor in the 1966–76 power struggle, refrained from shouting across the table. Named as the Number Two Person in Authority Taking the Capitalist Road (Liu Shaoqi was Number One), he was insulated from the savage treatment which led to Liu's death from pneumonia in 1969. Deng had always had a complicated relationship with Mao, which now may have saved him. In 1954–5 he had loyally conducted the purge of the Gao Gang–Rao Shushi faction, and then actively led the 'rectification' campaign against dissenting intellectuals which followed the 1956–7 Hundred Flowers liberalization. At the 1956 Party Congress Deng had criticized the cult of personality—ostensibly referring to de-Stalinization in the Soviet Union—in terms which Mao later resented. However, Deng (like Liu Shaoqi) kept quiet at the Lushan Party Plenum in July 1959 when Mao rejected criticism of the Great Leap Forward. (According to one version Deng pleaded illness and left early, claiming he had injured his leg playing ping-pong.) Mao respected Deng's talents. 'See that little man there,' he told Khrushchev in 1959, according to the Soviet leader's memoirs, 'he is highly intelligent.' But later Mao claimed that Deng had for years failed to keep him properly informed as Chairman of the Party. 'He treated me like his dead ancestor,' Mao complained.

In October 1966 Deng made a prudent self-criticism which helped him to withdraw from the leadership struggle and sit out the worst of the Cultural Revolution. He acknowledged that together with Liu Shaoqi he represented the 'bourgeois line' and had tried to suppress the mass movement. 'What I need to do', he concluded ambiguously, 'is to reflect on my past actions . . . Though I have gone astray on the road of politics, with the radiance of Mao Zedong Thought lighting my forward path, I should have the fortitude to pick myself up and go on.' (Liu Shaoqi's 'confession' was more courageous—he maintained that everyone in the leadership, including Mao, was open to criticism.)

In matters concerning class struggle and struggle within the Party, I have consistently shown rightist tendencies . . . I have become accustomed to lording it over others and acting like someone special, rarely going down among the people or even making the effort to contact cadres and other leaders so as to understand their working situation and problems . . . Rarely did I ask for help or advice from other comrades or the people. Worse still is that I have rarely reported to and asked advice from the Chairman. Not only is this one of the main reasons for my errors, but it is also a serious breach of Party discipline. In late 1964, Chairman Mao criticized me for being a kingdom unto myself.[18]

In 1971 Deng was working in a 'May Seventh Cadre School' when he heard about the death of Lin Biao. Correctly perceiving that this had altered the balance at the centre in Zhou Enlai's favour, he wrote to the Central Committee saying that he was eager to get involved in the campaign to 'criticize Lin Biao'. He hoped that the Party would give him some work while he remained in good health. Soon afterwards Mao attended the funeral of former Foreign Minister Chen Yi. He informed his widow that Chen had been a 'good man', that Lin Biao's purpose had been to overthrow all of their generation, and that the cases of Liu Shaoqi and Deng Xiaoping were not counter-revolutionary but belonged to the more benign category of 'contradictions among the people'. Zhou Enlai saw his chance, and arranged for Chen Yi's family to quietly spread Mao's words. In 1973 Deng was restored to his previous post of Vice Premier.[19] There is a story that at the end of 1973, Mao sent Deng and the young Wang Hongwen, who had just 'helicoptered' to power, to make inspection tours of the country. On their return, Mao asked both men: 'After I die, what will happen in China?' Wang replied that 'The whole country will certainly follow Chairman Mao's revolutionary line and carry through the revolution to the end!' Deng replied that 'Civil war will break out and there will be confusion throughout the country!' Mao preferred Deng's reply, and appointed him Chief of Staff of the People's Liberation Army (PLA). But that was by no means the end of the story as the great leader, by now so stricken with Parkinson's disease that he was barely able to communicate, allowed a final destructive bout of factionalism to break out.[20]

4

The Rebel Alternative
From 1919 to the Red Guards

In the early 1960s, a very junior clerk called Chen Lining became convinced that the Head of State, Liu Shaoqi, was a 'revisionist' and traitor to Mao's line. He wrote—as the Party Constitution allowed him to—a letter to the Central Committee. The case was promptly referred back to Chen's superiors who locked him up, at first in prison and then in a mental hospital. Three years later his case came to the attention of the ultra-left intellectuals running the Party journal *Red Flag* under the head of the Cultural Revolution Group, Chen Boda. Chen Lining was transferred first to a Beijing hospital and then—with a set of new clothing—back into society. He was sent on a lecture tour to tell the tale of his persecution. A hostile account later reported that,

Thrusting forward his small belly and swaggering, he put on airs of a 'hero' and demagogically deceived the masses. This counter-revolutionary element delivered 48 reports to an audience of more than 200,000. Still more people heard the playing back of his recordings, and read the materials carefully forged for him. Each day many people called on him because they admired his 'fame' and two men [were appointed] to receive the visitors . . .

A play was written about Chen with the title 'Madman of the New Era'—a conscious echo of the famous story 'Diary of a Madman' written by Lu Xun in 1918 describing the alienation of a young man from China's semi-feudal society. The hero, thinly disguised, was given the name 'Chen Weidong' ('Chen Guards the East') and was played by Chen himself in some performances. It was said to have inspired 'even more brazen plays', including one called 'Angry Flames of a Madman' performed in Shijiazhuang by a Red Guard troupe called the Madman Commune.

Chen's fame was shortlived. The ultra-left *Red Flag* leadership was disgraced for attempting to extend the targets of the Cultural Revolution to include the armed forces and Premier Zhou Enlai. Chen Boda abandoned the group to save his own position. Chen Lining was investigated after a performance of his play at a literary festival in Tianjin which had been banned by the army authorities. He was declared to be 'not a madman but a counter-revolutionary', and sent to jail, where he disappears forever from sight.[1]

Making trouble in Heaven

Order and disorder, obedience and rebellion, are recurring themes in Chinese political culture, sometimes opposed to each other but as often yoked together. In Mao's philosophy they assumed a quasi-Marxist dialectical relationship, as in the phrase 'There is no construction without destruction.' In his later years Mao was apt to put it more colloquially: 'Do not be afraid to make trouble', he advised Party members in 1959. 'The more trouble you make and the longer you make it the better. Confusion and trouble are always noteworthy. It can clear things up.'

For generations of Chinese the concept of trouble-making instantly recalls the tale of Monkey, the troublesome hero of the Ming dynasty novel *The Journey to the West* by Wu Chengen, who leads his master, the Monk Tripitaka, through countless dangers to bring back the holy word of Buddha. 'It is clear', wrote Arthur Waley in his translation, 'that Tripitaka stands for the ordinary man, blundering anxiously through the difficulties of life, while Monkey stands for the restless instability of genius.' Monkey began his career by 'making trouble in heaven'—theme of many an opera, folk ballad, and comic book—but then adopted the Great Faith and distinguished himself by 'the subjugation of monsters and demons'. After many adventures in which more than once he saved his master from wandering into death or defeat, Monkey with his companions ascended into heaven and was rewarded with the title of Buddha Victorious in Strife.

During the Cultural Revolution these metaphors of struggle became the everyday language of wall-posters and manifestos. The targets of the Red

Guards were those monsters and demons—the 'capitalist-roaders'—who, lurking in the shadows behind foolish monk-like leaders who had lost the way, sought to subvert the quest for the Holy Sutras of Communism. One of the earliest manifestos from the Red Guards at the secondary school attached to Qinghua University in Beijing ends with this triumphant claim:

Revolutionaries are Monkey Kings, their golden staffs are powerful, their super-natural powers far-reaching, and their magic omnipotent, for they possess Mao Zedong's great invincible Thought. We wield our golden rods, display our super-natural powers, and use our magic to turn the old world upside down, smash it into pieces, pulverize it, create chaos, and make a tremendous mess—the bigger the better! . . . Long Live the Revolutionary Rebel Spirit of the Proletariat![2]

Mao had evoked this spirit of rebellion in very similar terms throughout his political career—a spirit which has always lain close to the surface of the well-regulated face of Chinese society (and which is still reflected in the rural farmers' riots and the protests of the urban unemployed in the 1990s and 2000s). The deportment of the Confucian man, wrote Mao in an early essay on the importance of physical exercise (published fifty years before the Cultural Revolution), may be cultivated and pleasing, but the Chinese nation needs people who are 'savage and rude'. They should have the ability to 'leap on horseback and to shoot at the same time; to go from battle to battle; to shake the mountains by one's cries, and the colours of the sky by one's roars of anger'.[3] This concept of revolutionary 'rudeness' evoked both the legendary Chinese generals who featured in romances such as *The Tale of Three Kingdoms* and the anonymous heroics of peasant rebellion. Scholars have debated how far in theoretical terms Mao credited the peasantry with a leading revolutionary role. But there is no doubt that he identified emotion-ally with their sufferings, and approved of the measures to which they were driven by oppression.

As a young man, Mao had tried to emulate China's first great historian Sima Qian, who in the second century BC chronicled the exploits of actors and beggars as well as kings and generals, by travelling through the country-side. In the summer vacation of 1916, Mao and a friend set out on a 'travel study' tour not only dressed as beggars but actually begging for their food. (Half a century later, the Red Guards were encouraged to travel across China 'exchanging experiences' and 'learning from the peasants'.) 'Having seen for himself the tragic suffering of the peasants . . .', wrote an official biographer of Mao, 'how could he remain calm? How could he bury his head in the library?'

Ten years later, Mao returned to his home province of Hunan as the Communist–Guomindang alliance came under strain on the eve of the Northern Expedition led by Chiang Kai-shek to unify China. Once again Mao shouldered his pack and set off for a month-long inspection tour of five counties near the provincial capital of Changsha. He found a thriving movement of 'peasant associations' which in the revolutionary atmosphere had seized village power and made life unendurable for the local gentry and rich landlords. They had stepped on the ivory beds of the landlords' daughters, said Mao, paraded the gentry in tall paper hats like criminals, and turned everything upside down.[4] The report which Mao produced, *The Peasant Movement in Hunan*, defended the peasant associations against the complaints not only of the Guomindang but also of urban communists whom they had alarmed by 'going too far'. The associations were largely led, said their critics, by the village riff-raff who 'go around in wornout shoes, carry broken umbrellas, wear blue gowns and gamble'. Mao did not deny much of this—though he did explain that most of them had actually stopped gambling and given up banditry! In refuting the charge of 'going too far' Mao produced what remained until the end of his life his most famous revolutionary judgement:

A revolution is not the same as inviting people to dinner or writing an essay or painting a picture or embroidering a flower; it cannot be anything so refined, so calm and gentle, or so 'mild, kind, courteous, restrained and magnanimous' [as were the virtues of Confucius]. A revolution is an uprising, an act of violence whereby one class overthrows the authority of another . . . If the peasants do not use the maximum of their strength, they can never overthrow the deeply rooted, age-old authority of the landlords . . . To right a wrong it is necessary to exceed the proper limit; the wrong cannot be righted without doing so . . .

Peasant rebellion

Within a year after his report on the Hunan peasant movement, Mao found himself on the wooded mountain slopes of Jinggangshan in south-east China, patching together a rag-tag army labelled 'Soviet', with mostly peasant recruits who included at least two groups of bandits. The united front between the Guomindang and the communists, which helped to unify China and liquidate most of its warlord regimes, had been broken by Chiang Kai-shek in a vicious blood-letting against the communists once they had served their purpose. At the time, Mao and the other surviving communist guerrillas seemed not so different from the outlawed scholar-officials of imperial times who had taken to the hills to mobilize peasant rebellion. The tale of the *Heroes of the Water Margin* (a favourite of the youthful Mao) contains many examples of educated gentry and minor officials who, victimized by corrupt authority, take to Mount Liangshan. Though the disaffected scholars might have formed only a tiny percentage of the rebels, their skills and leadership were essential. But like the 'social bandits' analysed by E. J. Hobsbawm in his study of primitive forms of social protest, the leaders of China's peasant revolts possessed an ideology well described by him as one of 'revolutionary traditionalism'.[5] In the last analysis according to Jean Chesneaux, an authority on rural rebellion, the Chinese revolts only served 'to confirm the Confucian theory of the Mandate of Heaven, consolidating the traditional political system by purging it when this became necessary'.[6] The great Taiping Rebellion (1850–64), led by a would-be scholar who had been frustrated in the imperial examinations, produced a regime which professed support for elections and recall of officials, equal distribution of necessities, and equality between the sexes, but which rapidly established a pseudo-imperial hierarchy with fatally destructive internal divisions. The memory of the failure of this movement of 'social bandits' was still fresh in Mao's rural China.

The Chinese communist leaders consciously set out not to take over the existing order but to establish a new one and disprove the old saying that 'He who fails becomes a bandit, he who succeeds becomes a king!' The Leninist concept of the vanguard Party was handily available; Mao attributed the previous failure of peasant rebellions largely to the lack of 'correct leadership' by an 'advanced political party'. Mao's insistence upon strict Party control over the revolutionary armed forces, enunciated early on in the Gutian Resolution (December 1929), has rightly been regarded as crucial. Yet there was a paradox: In rational terms the communists argued for the dominance of the educated vanguard (Liu Shaoqi wrote of 'the rather low cultural level of the masses of the Chinese peasantry and other sections of the people, except for the intelligentsia'), but mass radicalism based upon traditional revolutionary culture had an appeal which was hard to resist, especially by local cadres who feared the accusation of 'stifling the masses' initiative'.

After publication in October 1947 of the first serious land reform programme in the communist-held areas, many peasant associations were dominated by the poor, who settled scores not only with landlords but with those defined as 'rich' or merely 'middle' peasants. Party officials tended at first to support them, reasoning as Mao had argued in Hunan that the most poor must be the most revolutionary. 'Their life is most bitter,' proclaimed the government of one communist-led area; 'they are oppressed and exploited and pushed around. Hence they are the most revolutionary . . . This is determined by life itself.' But this revolutionary spirit from below led to dangerous demands for a share in the Party's political and military power, as in this open letter from the peasant association in the Shanxi–Suiyuan border region:

We peasants have the right to supervise and reform all departments and organizations, all working groups, schools, factories, or publicly owned shops whether they
belong to the Party, the government, army, or the people . . .

You have not only the right to examine all cadres and organizations, you have
also the right to reform and improve all organizations. You can improve the
peasants' organizations, revive their constitutions and qualifications for membership.
Democracy must be fully developed . . . In this way, all Party, government, military,
and public organizations can be firmly built.

Hence we suggest: bear your share of responsibility for the people's army. This is
the peasants' own army . . . Military force must be in the hands of the peasants. The
people's militia must be under the direct control of the peasants' associations so that
it will really be the armed force which protects the peasants.[7]

The 'excesses' of this movement were vigorously criticized by Mao in a whole series of policy directives (much later in the Cultural Revolution, Liu Shaoqi would be improbably criticized for the ultra-left line of this period). Mao again stressed the leadership of the Party and the need to involve a broad spread of society in the 'revolutionary united front'—but not to share power. There was no word of approval now for 'going too far'. Instead, Mao condemned 'serious errors' which included the indiscriminate use of vio-lence against landlords and rich peasants, 'sweep-the-floor-out-the-door' confiscations, and an obsession with unearthing the landlords' hidden wealth. Yet the revolutionary spirit made excess almost unavoidable, and junior cadres could also object that their 'errors' had at first been encouraged from above, as William Hinton showed in *Fanshen*, his first-hand study of land reform in a Shanxi village. The local Party secretary Chen condemned 'absolute egalitarianism', arguing that even if every peasant was given an exactly equal share today, inequalities must re-emerge until Communism was realized. It was wrong to say that Left was better than Right. But Chen himself was reminded that he had sent work-teams to carry out land reform with the instruction that 'If you can't find any poor peasants you had better not eat'—an invitation to leftist excess—and he was obliged to accept 'primary responsibility' for the errors. It would take another three decades until after Mao's death before the long-term effect of the Chinese revolution's rural-based bias towards 'adventurism' was generally acknowledged.

After Liberation, the 'poor' peasants became a political spearhead for rural change, first breaking a lifetime of silence to denounce the power of the landlords (and often, with the Party's encouragement, demanding their execution), and later persuading the better-off peasants, by argument and example of their own efforts, to join the new co-operatives of the mid-1950s. There were also daunting physical challenges. The great floods of 1954 were contained (in contrast to the devastation of the 1931 floods) by vast voluntary armies of collective flood-fighters. Mass campaigns for literacy and public health demanded the support of rural activists. Within ten years, most peasants had acquired a basic reading knowledge, although standards fell off again in the 1960s. Public sanitation greatly improved and endemic diseases such as schistosomiasis (which requires immense physical effort to eradicate the breeding-places of the snail carrier) were brought at least partially under control. The Great Leap Forward, while bewildering many peasants with its millenarian aims, did absorb the energy and mobilize the enthusiasm of a large activist minority.[8]

During the hard years of 1960–1 when the Great Leap failed, millions of people died prematurely for lack of food. Nevertheless, underlying support for the collective principle persisted, and rural activists could still be found to lead the Socialist Education Movement (1962–4) in the countryside. Yet peasant rank-and-file enthusiasm was beginning to wane. Already in the early 1960s the Party had become concerned by a revival of the 'three evil tendencies' of 'capitalist' practices such as moneylending, 'feudalist' customs such as bride-sale, and 'extravagance' in the shape of lavish spending and local corruption.[9] The scaling down of the People's Communes after the Great Leap created a more sensible balance between collective and private interest, in which accounting and the organization of production were carried out usually at the level of the local village or 'team', and 'private plots' were allowed. However, the prestige of the Party had been seriously weakened, and away from the main towns and lines of communication there was still widespread hardship, while the social and economic fabric of rural life had been undermined. Gu Hua, in his novel *A Small Town Called Hibiscus* (1981), describes the dislocation caused to the rural market, hub of a previously thriving community:

In 1958, the year of the Great Leap Forward, as everyone had to smelt steel and boost production, the district and county governments restricted village markets and criticized capitalist trends; so that the Hibiscus markets were reduced from one every three days to one a week, finally to one a fortnight. By the time markets disappeared, it was said, they would have finished socialism and entered Communism. But then Old Man Heaven played up and they had bad harvests, on top of which the imperialists, revisionists, and counter-revolutionaries made trouble. It wasn't so bad their failing to make the great leap into Communism; but instead they came a great cropper, landing back in poverty with nothing but vegetable soup in the communal canteen, and nothing in the market but chaff, bracken-starch, the roots of vines and the like. China and all her people developed dropsy. Merchants stopped coming to the market, which was given over to gambling and prostitution. Fighting, stealing, and kidnapping spread . . . Then towards the end of 1961 the county government sent down instructions to change the fortnightly market into one every five days to facilitate trading. However, so much damage had been done that Hibiscus market could no longer attract all those merchants from far away.[10]

The May Fourth spirit

Student rebellion was a much more modern strand in Chinese revolutionary tradition. Mao and other communist leaders had first been radicalized in the 'May Fourth Movement' which, in 1919, voiced youthful disillusion with the warlord takeover of the first Chinese republic, and particularly with China's humiliation at the hands of the Great Powers. Students in the 1920s were fired more by patriotism than by a particular ideology, but the betrayal of the nationalist revolution by Chiang Kai-shek in the 1930s drove many sympathetic young intellectuals closer to the communists. Hundreds made their own long march to Mao's north-west base at Yanan. Most were chastened by the rectification campaign in the early 1940s after a few had criticized the first emerging signs of Party bureaucracy and privilege. But by the late 1940s, the Party's defects were hugely overshadowed by the oppression of the Guomindang and its secret police operating on university campuses in nationalist-held China. In 1949 the great majority of intellectuals welcomed the prospect of a 'new China'. Their welcome was reciprocated by the Party, which urgently needed a stock of young educated people to provide teachers, administrators, and cadres for an entire country.

In the first years after Liberation many responded to the demand, accepting their 'job assignments' without question, and eagerly joining the Youth

League and the Party. The writer Lu Wenfu catches their enthusiasm in his retrospective political parable 'The Gourmet':

When my turn came [to be assigned] I made a mess of things . . . I didn't have any particular skills and couldn't even sing properly [the previous student has just been assigned to join a 'cultural troupe'].

The man asked impatiently; 'You don't know anything at all?'

'Yes, I do, I know how to buy special foods for people, and I know all the eating places in Suzhou.'

'Right, go to the commercial department. Suzhou is known for its food.'

'No, no, please, I hate eating.'

'You hate eating? All right. I'll tell the cook to starve you for three days. Then we'll discuss it again. Next . . .'

Alas, my future was settled amidst general mirth. But I wasn't depressed, nor would I think of disobeying orders![11]

There was a hunger for education: in Beijing the students would climb the trees to read their textbooks by the light of streetlamps. Thousands joined the Communist Youth League, hoping to prove themselves worthy candidates for eventual membership of the Party. But the strength of idealism gave their support a conditional character and the tradition of student protest revived at Beida (Beijing University) in the Hundred Flowers movement (1956–7). In retrospect, the most striking feature of their criticisms was that they anticipated by two decades the analysis of China put forward in the democracy movement of the late 1970s and partly adopted then by Party reformers. There was a 'Democracy Square' in 1957 at Beida. Most of its wall-posters—more than three hundred in one day alone—accepted the socialist goal but challenged its dogmatic distortion by the Party cadres and their routine adulation of all things Soviet. Rene Goldman, who was studying at Beida at the time, recalls how the Hundred Flowers movement briefly stimulated student enthusiasm. The walls were covered with slogans like 'Think Independently' and 'Storm the Fortress of Science', which allowed discussion of Western science. 'Their thirst for learning was admirable and they sometimes dreamed up fantastic plans of research.'[12]

Students demanded a more liberal cultural and educational policy but almost no one advocated a change of regime. Khrushchev's secret speech on Stalin to the Soviet Twentieth Party Congress was translated into Chinese by students of the Beida Physics Department from the version published in the United States. Students in the department of history complained of being taught that the Russo-Swedish war was a 'just war' because it gave Russia an outlet on the Baltic Sea. Lin Xiling, a 23-year-old student training to become a cadre at the People's University, had previously defended Stalin. Now she argued in terms which would lead to a campaign against 'Lin Xilingism' in the rectification which followed the Hundred Flowers. Her analysis of the feudal elements in Chinese and Soviet state socialism also anticipated the arguments of the late 1970s:

The problem of Stalin is not the problem of Stalin the individual; the problem of Stalin could only arise in a country like the Soviet Union, because in the past it had been a feudal, imperialistic nation. China is the same, for there has been no tradition of bourgeois democracy. This could not happen in France. I believe that public ownership is better than private ownership, but I hold that the socialism we now have is not genuine socialism; or that if it is, our socialism is not typical. Genuine socialism should be very democratic, but ours is undemocratic. I venture to say that our society is a socialist one erected on a feudal foundation; it is not typical socialism, and we must struggle for genuine socialism!

The analogy between Stalin and Mao now came close to the surface. Student speakers quoted the figure of 770,000 deaths during the land reform and other campaigns of the early 1950s from Mao's own 'secret speech', which had launched the Hundred Flowers and was only published in a revised version after the rectification began. The Party and its leader, they argued, belonged in Marxist terms to a backward political 'superstructure' which had not kept pace with the socialization of the country's economic 'base'. Mao had argued in his speech that 'contradictions among the people' which persisted under socialism could, if not correctly handled by the Party, become 'antagonistic'. Lin Xiling responded that such contradictions were those between 'the leadership and the led', and reflected an objective law that all ruling classes have their limitations. 'Men in different positions', she said, 'have different points of view. He who was the ruled before but who has now climbed to the ruling position (from worker to head of a factory) speaks a different language; everything has changed.'[13]

This early flowering of a student democracy movement was soon extinguished, and left no visible mark as the policies of rectification and the Great Leap led to the beginnings of the 'revolution in education' which would culminate in the Cultural Revolution. Admission policies shifted to favour students from peasant and working-class families. Students helped with revived enthusiasm to build the Ming Tombs Reservoir, and joined the campaign to set up blast furnaces for steel in the suburban communes of

Beijing. The educational institution, announced the president of Qinghua University, should become 'not just a school, but at the same time a research institute, factory, designing institute, and building concern'. But some officials soon became concerned at the effect upon educational standards and at the haphazard results of the 'half-work half-study' campaign. The new President of Beida, Lu Ping, warned that 'lofty revolutionary ambitions' should be combined with 'the good academic tradition of learning with realism and perseverance'. He expressed alarm at the number of injuries to Beida literature students who had been sent to work in primitive coal mines west of Beijing. In 1963 all the students were brought back from work assignments, and examinations were reintroduced. Anyone who failed in two subjects had to withdraw from college and was assigned to be a secondary school teacher—frequently back in the countryside. Many of these came from the same poor 'worker-peasant' background which had been preferred during earlier student enrolment. Staff promotion once again encouraged those with ability in teaching or research, while political activity declined. These shifts in policy reflected growing divisions in China's educational establishments which provided much of the social basis for student activism in the Cultural Revolution. The Beida lecturer Yue Daiyun has described the realignment of Beida's three constituent groups in her remarkable memoir of this period:

One group was composed of those already established as faculty members and administrators before Liberation, people educated under the old system . . . A second group was composed of people like me, who were educated largely after Liberation, who often had participated enthusiastically in the underground movement, but who had been influenced by the older generation of intellectuals and shared some of their ideals. The third group was composed of workers, peasants, and soldiers, many of whom had worked in the 'red', or rural, areas of the country during the revolution, people who had come to Beida after Liberation to receive an education and stayed on as teachers and Party cadres. It was this group that Chairman Mao had hoped would change the character of the universities.[14]

These tensions now began to be manipulated by rival groups in the national leadership—the 'behind-the-scenes backers' as they would become known in the Cultural Revolution. In 1964 an investigatory 'work-team', sent to Beida by Mao's security chief Kang Sheng, condemned the University as a 'reactionary fortress' under Lu Ping. Within months a rival team had been sent to Beida by the mayor of Beijing, Peng Zhen, and the head of the city's Party Committee, Deng Tuo (both would be among the first targets of the

Cultural Revolution in 1966). This team called a conference at the International Hotel in the centre of Beijing, busing nearly three hundred faculty members—both supporters and critics of Lu Ping—for discussions which lasted seven months and (it was later claimed) cost 200,000 yuan (£50,000) in hotel bills. The pro-Mao radical delegation to this conference was led by Nie Yuanzi, a former cadre from one of the post-war revolutionary bases who had become Party secretary of the Beida Philosophy Department. It was Nie's wall-poster attacking Lu Ping on 25 May 1966 which was to launch the Red Guard movement. Mao, it was said, soon 'heard about it'— not surprisingly, since it was probably instigated by people close to him. Describing it as 'the first Marxist-Leninist big-character poster', Mao ordered it to be broadcast over the radio and published nationally.

The ageing American writer Anna Louise Strong, uncritically sympathetic to the Red Guards, described Nie as a 'slender, friendly woman who . . . showed no pretension to power . . . she was approachable and intelligent, the qualities of a teacher'.[15] Yue Daiyun, watching Nie carried on Red Guard shoulders at the first chaotic meetings, had the opposite impression. ' "Chairman Mao has said that I am the first red banner," she would cry, "so anyone who opposes me opposes Chairman Mao himself!" How arrogant she is, I thought; how curious that sometimes history pushes to the forefront someone so completely undistinguished.' Yue guessed that Nie had become friendly with Kang Sheng's wife through her own husband, who served with her on the Central Disciplinary Commission.

Red Guards and Communes

Throughout the revolution, the students had never been more than an auxiliary force. In the Cultural Revolution of 1966–8 (the broader definition extending it to 1976 was only made retrospectively) they became the vanguard force. Already concerned to create a new generation of 'revolutionary successors' which would steer China away from the revisionist trap into which the Soviet Union had fallen, Mao pinned his faith upon its youth. The Red Guards were loose groupings of college and secondary school students, formed initially to 'struggle' against teachers and cadres in their own institutions but soon encouraged to act as the catalyst of a wider movement. Red Guards could be as young as 12 or as old as 30, but the majority were in their teens. Red Guard representatives attended the Eleventh Plenum of the Central Committee in August 1966, which adopted a sixteen-point directive on the Cultural Revolution. A million Red Guards had already reached Beijing in time to welcome the sixteen points at Mao's first mass rally on 18 August. At least another million passed through the capital during the autumn. Red Guard activists from the provinces reported to the new Cultural Revolutionary Group appointed at the Plenum and were sent back to initiate new 'struggles' against local Party leaders. In most cases the targets compounded their presumed crime as 'capitalist-roaders' by seeking to muzzle or 'suppress' their youthful persecutors. 'All those who have tried to repress the student movement in China have ended up badly', Mao warned his colleagues.[16]

Red Guards, mostly from the secondary schools, led the movement to criticize the 'Four Olds' which involved house-to-house searches for books, money, documents, art treasures, and so on, which were considered decadent or counter-revolutionary. Red Guards from the colleges were dispatched to stir up rebellion against the Party bureaucracy among the urban workforce in the main cities and towns. Less systematically, Red Guards conducted propaganda for the Cultural Revolution as they passed through the rural areas, often hiking or hitching rides on their travels to 'exchange revolutionary experiences' throughout China—a mission which served many as the excuse for tourism. Early in 1967, a *Red Flag* editorial coined an extraordinary generalization in the students' favour:

All Cultural Revolution movements in contemporary Chinese history have begun with student movements and [have] led to the worker and peasant movements, to the integration of revolutionary intellectuals with the worker-peasant masses. This is an objective law . . . In 1967, China's great proletarian Cultural Revolution will continue to develop in line with this objective law.

This sequence of development was, according to a later statement by Mao, supposed to result in the emergence of the workers and peasants as the main force, after which the students would 'fall back into a subsidiary place'. In the event, a large number of urban workers became active but the movement had only limited impact upon the countryside. This was due in part to nervousness at the centre about the effect of the Cultural Revolution upon the economy. Red Guards were ordered not to 'exchange experiences' or 'engage in debates' with rural officials, while the peasants' own campaign against the 'Four Olds' should be carried out only 'in the slack season'. The countryside remained quiet, but discontented interest groups in the urban workforce—lower-paid employees and ex-peasants on limited contracts without job security, in particular—began to join the movement as 'Red Rebels'. The armed forces were explicitly exempted from Red Guard activity, and within a few months were called on by Mao to intervene to maintain essential communications and to police the factional struggles of the Red Guards and Rebels.

In the first months of the Cultural Revolution, when officials in one Chinese city and province after another were denounced and hounded out of office by young teenagers, it seemed to some observers that Mao's ultimate aim was to replace the Party itself. Mao had described Nie Yuanzi's Beida poster as 'the Manifesto of the Beijing People's Commune of the 1960s'. His remark was later interpreted (1 Feb. 1967) by *Red Flag* as a prediction that 'our state organs would take on completely new forms'. In the end Mao himself backed away from such a radical step, but the implied challenge to Party hegemony would not be forgotten.

The August 1966 sixteen-point Decision on the Cultural Revolution had called for the 'struggle and overthrow of those in authority taking the capitalist road', a formula usually reduced to the single word *dou*, 'struggle', and linked to *pi*, 'criticize' (bourgeois academics and ideology), and *gai*, 'transform' (the world of literature and education and wherever else necessary in the superstructure of culture and politics). But it was not clear how comprehensively the struggle was to be carried out. Was it just a question of removing a few 'capitalist-roaders', or would it require restructuring the party machine which supported them? The new Cultural Revolutionary Groups set up after August 1966 were defined as 'organs of power', but their jurisdiction was confined to the Cultural Revolution itself 'under the leadership of the Communist Party'. However, the sixteen-point Decision also specified that the Cultural Revolution would take 'a very, very long time', and that in this sense the new mass groups would be 'permanent and not temporary'. All the evidence pointed not just to a compromise reflecting the current balance of political forces (Liu Shaoqi, though demoted in status, still held his Party offices, and Zhou Enlai had worked to insert moderating phrases into the Decision) but to a sense of improvisation on Mao's part similar to his hesitancy in the early stages of the Great Leap Forward.

'You must pay attention to affairs of state and carry through the revolution to the end!', Mao had told one of the Red Guard rallies in Tiananmen Square. But which affairs of state? The sixteen points did contain a hint which chimed with the inchoate urge of the Red Guards to challenge all authority. The new Cultural Revolutionary Groups, it stated, should be

established by 'a system of general elections, like that of the Paris Commune
. . .'. Once elected, members could be criticized at any time and recalled if
they proved incompetent. Earlier in 1966 a long *Red Flag* article, probably
written by its editor Chen Boda, had suggested the relevance of the Paris
Commune to current events in China in the same terms. 'The masses were
the real masters in the Paris Commune', it argued. They supervised the
work of their elected officials, and ensured that they should be not the
masters but the servants of society.

When, in January 1967, groups of revolutionary activists—discontented
workers and dissident cadres as well as students—began to 'seize power'
from the Party bureaucracy, they appropriated the name of the Commune
and claimed to embody its principles. The most famous was the 'Shanghai
People's Commune', briefly proclaimed early in February. Others were
announced in Beijing, Taiyuan, and Harbin, but neither Shanghai nor these
were given national publicity. The new name implied a new organizational
form which for a moment seemed to threaten the very existence of the
Party. *Red Flag* again had hinted in this direction. Through the 'wisdom of
the masses', it said, 'a completely new organizational form of political power
better suited to the socialist economic base will be created'. The lesson of
the Paris Commune, as Marx had pointed out, was that the existing state
machinery must not only be taken over but thoroughly smashed. 'It is
absolutely impermissible to merely take over power while letting things
remain the same and operating according to old rules.'

Zhou Enlai was quick to observe, however, that the new 'communes' had
been set up in a fever of factional struggle, and without the mass participation on which the analogy with Paris in 1871 depended. The Shanghai
Commune, far from having been 'elected', had excluded one of the two
most important rebel groups in the city, which now took its grievance to
Beijing. Mao himself had to adjudicate on two questions: was the name
right, and should the new organization supplant the Party? Mao's answer to
the first question (which attracted most attention) was that a self-styled
'commune' which failed to live up to its name would ultimately undermine
the enthusiasm of the people of Shanghai and elsewhere. The commune's
advocates in the national leadership, Zhang Chunqiao and Yao Wenyuan,
returned to Shanghai with instructions that the Shanghai People's Commune
should become the Shanghai Revolutionary Committee. On the second
question, which had also been raised by the few surviving moderates
(particularly Tan Zhenlin) in the central leadership, Mao's answer was

unequivocal. Shanghai could not be governed by students and workers alone, Zhang told a rally in the city on his return from consulting Mao. To keep the city functioning needed the co-operation of senior army leaders and cadres. The number of top officials required, he said precisely, was six thousand. He conveyed orally Mao's comments, which characteristically ranged from a diplomatic quibble about the name to a firm affirmation of principle.

If the entire nation established People's Communes, should the name of the People's Republic of China be changed? If it is changed to the 'People's Commune of China' will we be recognized by everyone? The USSR may not recognize us while the British and French may recognize us. After the name is changed, what happens to our embassies in the various countries? Have you considered these and other questions? . . .

I believe that we need it because we need a hard core, a bronze matrix, to strengthen us on the road we still have to travel. You can call it what you please, Communist Party or Socialist Party, but we must have a Party. This must not be forgotten.[17]

Whither China?

By the autumn of 1967 the central authorities had made some progress in throttling back the Red Guard movement, although this would not be finally achieved until the late summer of 1968. The People's Liberation Army (PLA) had been licensed to intervene when public order broke down, and was beginning to do so with more confidence. The provincial 'revolutionary committees' which Mao preferred to the embryonic 'People's Communes' were based on a 'three-way alliance' between army, cadres, and 'revolutionary masses' in which, as time went on, the rebel forces played an increasingly junior role. In Beijing, after the shocking events of the summer when ultra-left leaders of the Cultural Revolution Group (CRG) encouraged attacks on the PLA—notably the 'Wuhan incident' in August—the most outspoken had been purged (including the sponsors of 'madman' Chen Lining). Jiang Qing herself had felt compelled to warn the Red Guards to leave the army alone.

The *Shengwulian* (Hunan Proletarian Committee) was an alliance of some twenty Hunanese groups, mostly student bodies from secondary schools but including at least one civil service organization and numbering two former PLA officers in its own leadership. Set up in October 1967, it published three documents in the winter which were rapidly denounced by the CRG in Beijing. Jiang Qing described it as 'a hotchpotch of rubbish from the old society' and much was made of the fact that the father of one of its student leaders was a former Secretary-General of the provincial committee. But as K. S. Karol has noted, the *Shengwulian* could claim that they were merely remaining faithful to the ideas of Mao and his team from the first phase of the Cultural Revolution. They even quoted a directive from Lin Biao stating that 'Hunan is the vanguard area of revolutionary struggle of the whole country.'

The *Shengwulian*'s famous essay 'Whither China?' began by evoking the spirit of the 'People's Commune of China', which Mao had 'brilliantly foreseen' at the start of 1967. It accepted reluctantly that Mao was right to oppose the establishment of the Shanghai Commune although this was something that 'the revolutionary people find hard to understand'—because what was being established was only a 'sham commune'. But it insisted that the committees must be regarded as only a 'transitional form' to prepare the way for the ultimate product of the Cultural Revolution: the genuine commune. The struggle had to continue within the Revolutionary Committees, which were dominated by the army and Party cadres and simply amounted to 'another kind of bourgeois rule of bourgeois bureaucrats'.

. . . the Cultural Revolution is not a revolution to dismiss officials from their office or a 'dragging out' movement, nor is it a purely Cultural Revolution, but it is 'a revolution in which one class overthrows another'. Seen from the facts of the storm of the January [1967] revolution, the class to be overthrown is none other than the *class of bureaucrats formed in China over the past 17 years.* . . . The programme of the first Great Proletarian Cultural Revolution was put forward in editorials in an embryonic, not very concrete state in the final stages of the storm of January. [It included] the decaying class that should be overthrown, the old state machinery that should be smashed, and even social problems on which people formerly had not dared to express a dissident view. (*my italics*)

If the Cultural Revolution was directed against 'capitalist-roaders', argued the *Shengwulian*, then one must ask how such people had emerged since 1949. The answer was that China had inherited a state machinery, particularly the army, police, and judiciary, almost unchanged from the past (here they found an apt quotation from Lenin). The majority of cadres who operated this apparatus, they claimed, had embarked upon the capitalist road unknowingly. But those who did so deliberately now formed a 'privileged stratum' which was the real target of the Cultural Revolution. The relations of production, to the extent that they were controlled by this privileged layer of cadres, had degenerated, and now lagged far behind the economic base which was capable of supporting a more genuine socialism. Only through the Cultural Revolution could a 'true beginning' be made in the socialist revolution.

The *Shengwulian* avoided the usual eulogies for the PLA, which was by now supposed to be the 'Great Wall' and bastion of the Cultural Revolution. It would be foolish to believe, it argued, that the PLA could be immune from the revival of bourgeois values in political life since 1949. Before Liberation the relationship between army and people was indeed like that between fish and water. But 'as soon as Chairman Mao issued the order for the armed forces to live in their barracks [to become a garrison rather than a revolutionary army] they became separated from the masses'. Why then had Mao ordered the PLA to 'support the Left' if it did not genuinely do so? The *Shengwulian* provided a subtle explanation. It was the Chairman's 'ingenious means' for extending the Cultural Revolution into the armed forces by involving it at second-hand.

The text for the *Shengwulian*'s brave new China was Mao's Directive of 7 May 1966, which was the first, and by far the most utopian, of his Cultural Revolutionary pronouncements. It was interpreted to mean that there should be no specialization or exclusivity in fields of work. Soldiers, to whom the message was primarily addressed, should learn to take part in politics, run factories, and engage in agriculture, as well as how to fight. Workers, peasants, and students should similarly diversify their activities. Of course the workers should still work, the peasants should still farm, and the students should still study. That was their 'primary task'. But by adopting secondary tasks outside their own field, they would break down the barriers between town and country and between intellectuals and workers. Everyone should be developed in 'an all-round way' to become 'a new communist person with proletarian political consciousness'. While Mao's colleagues attempted to ignore this embarrassing utopian vision, the Hunanese rebels said frankly that it was the only way forward. 'People in general rejected the sketch [of China's future] as an idealistic "communist Utopia" . . . Only some intellectual youths still keep reciting it . . . because they realize that only the new society sketched in the May Seventh Directive . . . is the society in which they may have liberation.' But, they claimed, the January 'seizure of power' had already shown that the idea was workable.

People suddenly found that without the bureaucrats they not only could go on living but could also live better and develop more quickly and with greater freedom. The bureaucrats had tried to intimidate the workers before the [January] revolution, saying: 'Without us, production will collapse and the whole of society will be in chaos' . . . But after the Ministry of Coal collapsed, production of coal went on as usual. The Ministry of Railways collapsed, but transportation was carried on as usual. . . . For the first time the workers felt that 'it was not the state that managed them, but they who managed the state'. For the first time they felt that they were producing for themselves.

This was far from the reality of packed trains running on abandoned time-tables, and factories where production slumped by half, which even the left leaders in Beijing had to agree justified the return of the cadres and inter-vention of the PLA. But the *Shengwulian* was accused not of naivety but of counter-revolution. By spelling out to a logical conclusion the ultra-left argument opportunistically used by the clique around Mao, they brought too visibly into the open its underlying challenge to Premier Zhou Enlai and the army leadership. In an episode which is unique for the Cultural Revolution, central leaders were compelled to argue their case against an alternative before a meeting of Hunanese delegates, even though they did so tendentiously. Kang Sheng claimed that the Hunan group had distorted their quotation from Lenin—and besides, it was an obscure one which no student could have known, which pointed to the *Shengwulian*'s programme being written by some member of Liu Shaoqi's counter-revolutionary black gang! But his real rage was directed against the alleged existence of a 'privil-eged stratum' which, said Kang, 'vilified the socialist revolution'. Jiang Qing's criticism of the group was briefer and more guarded, drawing a distinction between its 'backstage bosses' and the rank and file who had been 'hoodwinked'.[18]

This radical challenge from the grass roots was soon submerged in the wider tide of disorder which, a year later, led to the intervention of the People's Liberation Army on Mao's instructions to restore public services, reopen the schools, and send large numbers of students to the countryside. With life in China now restored to something approaching normality, the Cultural Revolution put on its best face to the outside world. But the *Shengwulian* stands in a classic line of revolutionary challenge which extends from Mao's own early pronouncements through the Beida protests of the Hundred Flowers to the post-Mao democracy movement.

5

Second Cultural Revolution
The abortive Great Debate

Just one month after Zhou Enlai had outlined the policy *of* the Four Modernizations at the 1975 National People's Congress (NPC), a great debate broke out among working-class students at the Shenyang College of Mechanical and Electrical Engineering over the relationship between technical skill and political morality.

Modernization, said one group of students, taking their cue from Zhou, required what Chairman Mao himself had called a 'huge contingent' of 'technical cadres' in order to build socialism. Why should those who sought to become proficient at their jobs be accused of 'just wanting to be a famous expert?' It was true that college students should not behave like 'intellectual aristocrats', but neither should they be deterred by criticism from making the best use of their training so as to become 'leaders of the working masses' after graduation. Otherwise how would China ever advance its national economy to the front ranks of the world?

The opposing view was also published as a wall-poster. Like the first, it came from a group of 'worker-peasant-soldier' students who were the product of the Revolution in Education, but took a more rigorously leftist line. They began with an assertive echo of Red Guard rhetoric: 'We should criticize revisionism and uphold Marxism . . . We think we should be nothing but ordinary workers, the more ordinary the better!' Those students who thought otherwise were merely repeating the old idea that 'he who excels in learning can be an official' and that 'the highest are the wise and the lowest are stupid'.

A proletarian intellectual is nothing but a member of the worker ranks. Moreover, to train such a vast contingent we do not primarily rely on the university. The forefront of the three great revolutionary movements is more important than ten, a hundred, or even one thousand universities. If the new-type socialist universities train nothing but plain, ordinary workers, then we can proudly say that they have completely destroyed the ladder for climbing to higher positions.

The two opposing views were published in the *Liaoning Daily* with an invitation to the reader to 'discuss and truly understand'. It was a rare example of real debate without editorial pre-judgement in the Chinese press. China did face genuine alternatives in the mid-1970s, and the Cultural Revolution had encouraged new forces in society capable of taking part in such a debate. But it had also generated factionalism and a warped political culture which debased most arguments into a distorted polemic. While the Liaoning students were arguing in public, secret discussions in the Party Politburo in Beijing were being conducted in a very different spirit which would lead to the final Deng Xiaoping–Gang of Four showdown a year later.[1]

The Maoist vision

There were two Cultural Revolutions. The first ended in July 1968 when Mao's reluctance to discipline the 'little generals' was finally overcome. Mao summoned the main Red Guard leaders in Beijing and reproached them for their lack of unity. A year's fighting was quite enough, and factionalism was creating 'tens of thousands of centres' throughout China.

Now, I am issuing a nationwide notice. If anyone continues to oppose and fight the Liberation Army, destroy means of transportation, kill people, or set fires, he is committing a crime. Those few who turn a deaf ear to persuasion and persist in their behaviour are bandits, or Guomindang elements, subject to capture. If they continue to resist, they will be annihilated.[2]

In Guangxi province, Lin Biao added, a thousand houses had been burnt down and no one was allowed to quench the flames—the same tactic used many years ago by the Guomindang generals whom he fought during the revolution. (So many people had been killed in Guangxi—many of them innocent victims of factional violence—that bodies floated down the Pearl River to emerge, bound and bloated, in Hong Kong harbour. The terrible story of how victorious factional fighters in Guangxi's Wuxuan County had ritually eaten parts of their enemies' bodies would not emerge till long after the Cultural Revolution.[3]) Mao still spoke with a touch of indulgence towards the Red Guards. Young people were entitled to make mistakes, and they reminded him of his own youth. But the people were tired of 'civil wars' between the factions. It was time now to send in the armed forces and the workers to restore order in the schools. These would be reopened under military supervision, accepting new students, while those Red Guards who should by now have graduated were to be sent to the countryside. Society, said Mao, was the biggest university.

In theory, power had now been 'seized' from the capitalist-roaders in the Party apparatus, and the new Revolutionary Committees, established at every level from factory or commune up to the province, had opened up management and government to popular participation. The bureaucrats had been chastened by criticism and by attendance at cadre schools in the countryside. Young people, the generation of revolutionary successors, were in the vanguard of social change, bridging the gap between town and village by going 'down to the countryside' to 'join the team and settle in a new household'. In reality a substantial transfer of authority had indeed taken place, and there was a genuine new spirit of involvement, but with certain important qualifications. First was the continuing struggle in the highest ranks of the leadership between the ultra-left and centre-left; which made ideology a battleground rather than a field for new ideas. This struggle was also diffused at lower levels, where policies were distorted into dogmas and political success usually depended upon their unquestioning implementation. Second was the dominance of the People's Liberation Army (PLA), which controlled more than one-third of the new Central Committee chosen at the Ninth Party Congress in 1969. Members of Revolutionary Committees, for example, visibly deferred to the army representative sitting democratically in their midst. Third was the continuing victimization of many of those detained in the first stage of the Cultural Revolution, often merely on the basis of past family or work connections or because they had been targets of the 1957 anti-rightist campaign.

Nevertheless, China now entered a second phase of Cultural Revolution in which an attempt was made to translate the Maoist egalitarian vision of the mid-1960s into an approximate social reality. Visitors to China saw an idealized but not wholly untruthful version of this. No tour was complete without a conversation with college students drawn from the ranks of 'worker-peasant-soldiers', another with students who had been 'sent down' to the countryside, a visit to a school-farm for city cadres (May Seventh Cadre School), a performance of a 'revolutionary opera', an inspection of a rural clinic run by 'barefoot doctors', and a session with a Revolutionary Committee in commune or factory. These were the *xinsheng shiwu*, the 'new (socialist) achievements', of the Cultural Revolution, and those taking part were the *shehuizhuyi de xinren*, the 'new socialist people'. Although the collective structure of the People's Communes antedated the Cultural Revolution, its practical approach to organizing peasant labour through the year had been integrated with a coherent theory on how to move to a higher socialist level in the medium to long term. Many visitors were greatly impressed, finding evidence of what the British sociologist Peter Worsley described after his own visit as an 'alternative reality' which posed 'a moral challenge . . . both to capitalism and to existing forms of Communist culture [in Eastern Europe]'. K. S. Karol, author of the most serious Western attempt to grapple with the ideology of the Cultural Revolution, observed that 'Mao's words struck home to them [the Chinese students], as to their counterparts in Berlin, Rome, and Paris.' After my own first visit in 1971, I reported in the *Guardian* that I had observed 'a collective way of life . . . which provides the moral imperatives for the youth of China'.[4]

The possibility that this second Cultural Revolution offered any sort of desirable social goal or effective weapon against bureaucracy has been denied repeatedly by the post-Mao leadership. The 1981 Communist Party resolution summing up Chinese history since 1949 insisted that the Cultural Revolution 'did not in fact constitute a revolution or social progress in any sense, nor could it possibly have done so. It was we and not the enemy at all who were thrown into disorder by the "Cultural Revolution" . . . It decidedly could not come up with any constructive programme, but could only bring grave disorder, damage, and retrogression in its train.' Examples of principled behaviour and self-sacrifice are either caricatured as a ritual response to political requirements of the time, or attributed to the efforts of good people to mitigate the worst evils. In this view, Mao's scathing comment on the public ethics of the Soviet Union under Stalin—'there was supposed to be "selfless labour", but no one did an hour's more work and everyone thought about himself first'—could be paraphrased to apply to his own China. Common sense suggests that this is an excessive denial. Although enthusiasm faded, and in retrospect is often labelled by those personally involved as misconceived, it was a genuine factor in the great social movements of the time which cannot be accounted for solely by political coercion. One Red Guard would recall that,

When I went to university in 1973, we former Red Guards met to exchange our experiences. We agreed that our stay with the people in the country had taught us the value of things—and of life itself.

Looking back dispassionately, whatever motivated Mao to launch the Cultural Revolution, some of the ideas which emerged from it are still valuable. The 'barefoot doctor' and 'barefoot teacher' system is certainly good for a country like China . . . Basic things like how to read, write, and calculate can be taught very cheaply if they are organized by the local people themselves.

At the beginning of the Cultural Revolution I feel the ordinary people were exhilarated by their new right to criticize and even to attack their bosses. The suppressed humiliation that one suffers at the hands of a faceless bureaucracy builds up a resentment that is like the surging tide blocked by a dam.[5]

Socialist new man might not be actually tilling the fields, but he could be perceived far off on the horizon. The peasant leader of the model Dazhai brigade, Chen Yonggui, an honest man who would later become totally out of his depth in national politics (he became a vice-premier and was denounced after the fall of the Gang of Four), summed up what seemed a reasonable ideal: 'A man's ability may be great or small, but if he works heart and soul for the public, he is respected and ensured a secure life even if he has limited labour power.' The Great Leap goal of narrowing the 'three great differences' (between industry and agriculture, town and country, and manual and mental labour) was reasserted. Both at the material and spiritual level, many from outside China found much to admire. 'Visitors to China consistently report', wrote an agricultural specialist in *Scientific American* (June 1975), 'that the population appears to be healthy and adequately nourished.' The economist John Gurley observed correctly that China's pavements and streets were not covered with 'multitudes of sleeping, begging, hungry, and illiterate human beings'—one of the earliest achievements of communist rule after 1949—but went on to draw a sweeping conclusion:

Maoists believe that while a principal aim of nations should be to raise the level of material welfare of the population, this should be done only within the context of the development of human beings, encouraging them to realize fully their manifold creative powers. And it should be done only on an egalitarian basis—that is, on the basis that development is not worth much unless everyone rises together; no one is to be left behind, either economically or culturally . . . Development as a trickle-down process is therefore rejected by Maoists.[6]

Worrying signs of factional feuding in the Chinese leadership were relegated to a subordinate place by those looking to China for solutions to more general Third World problems. It was assumed that the 'production in first place' mentality ascribed to Liu Shaoqi had been liquidated for all time, and that, especially after the 1975 National People's Congress (NPC), a broad consensus had been forged under Zhou Enlai. 'What should not be in doubt', wrote one commentator, 'is the shared commitment [in the Chinese leadership] to completing the task of the "transition to socialism", in spite of these controversies over the means and the place of implementation, nor should this be blotted out by the echoes of factional struggle too often magnified beyond their proper volume by Western China-Watching techniques.' (I was the author of this optimistic judgement.)

Revolution in education

The Revolution in Education, which between 1968 and 1976 sent over twelve million students to the countryside, and brought some of them back to attend college along with a smaller number of genuinely rural students, was the most visible 'new achievement'. Mao had already sharply criticized the educational system in 1964–5. His remarks echoed themes already discussed during the Great Leap Forward, and were meant to provoke discussion rather than to prescribe alternatives. Examinations, he said, were a method of 'surprise attack' on the students which should be changed completely—he suggested publishing examination questions in advance so students could learn through preparation. Too many teachers 'rambled on and on', he said, and students were entitled to doze off when they did so. The syllabuses were lifeless, the time spent studying was too long, and students were divorced from real life. 'We shouldn't read too many books,' Mao told his startled colleagues (who nevertheless agreed hastily). 'We should read Marxist books, but not too many of them either. It will be enough to read a dozen or so.' After all, Gorky only had two years of primary education, and Franklin 'was originally a newspaper seller, yet he discovered electricity'.[7] The Red Guards, not surprisingly, would welcome Mao's ideas. In September 1966 the Beijing No. 1 Girls' Middle School wrote a letter urging Mao to abolish college entrance exams:

Quite a number of students have been indoctrinated with such gravely reactionary ideas of the exploiting classes as that 'book learning stands above all else', of 'achieving fame', 'becoming experts', 'making one's own way', 'taking the road of becoming bourgeois specialists', and so on. The present examination system encourages these ideas . . .

We think that at a time when their world outlook is being formed, young people of 17 or 18 years old . . . should first of all get 'ideological diplomas' from the working class and the poor and lower-middle peasants. The Party will select the best . . . and send them on to higher schools.

In the May Seventh (1966) Directive which revived the notion of 'all-round people' first put forward by Chen Boda in 1958 (see above, p. 75), Mao told students that 'they should in addition to their studies learn other things, that is, industrial work, farming, and military affairs'. This did not constitute an alternative educational theory (and no one else dared to construct one except some foreign sympathizers who did so on China's behalf), yet it did suggest a very different spirit from the mixture of Confucian and Soviet pedagogy which the Chinese system had inherited.

When the schools and colleges reopened in the early 1970s, they possessed new features which to Western educationalists were recognizably 'progressive'. Schoolchildren took part in regular manual work—up to two months a year at secondary level (this had been done on a smaller scale before the Cultural Revolution). Local workers and residents served on school management committees, and taught useful skills in class. Tuition was still fairly formal, but there were few or no examinations. The 'key schools' were no longer supposed to practise selective admission of the most able or privileged. College education was completely transformed, with all curricula reduced to a maximum length of three years. All applicants were required to have three qualifications: (a) two to three years' practical experience in factory, countryside, or armed forces; (b) the recommendation of their fellow-workers; (c) at least three years of secondary education (rather than the full five previously required). Students who could claim a 'worker-peasant-soldier' (gongnongbing) background were preferred. Practical work was stressed during university courses. Architecture students would work on building sites; language students would serve as waiters in hotels for foreigners; art students spent time on the factory floor before painting industrial themes. The underlying approach was known as 'open door schooling', which also involved a large number of short and part-time courses run by colleges for the community. Another directive by Mao (22 July 1968) had urged the setting-up of vocational colleges at the place of work. 'Students should be selected from among workers and peasants with practical experience, and they should return to production after a few years' study.' By 1973 there were twenty-three factory-run 'universities' in Shanghai, and Beijing's prestigious Qinghua University had twenty part-time lecturers from local factories. Universities also ran correspondence courses for peasants, and established 'branch schools' in the countryside.

The problem with the Revolution in Education lay not in its philosophy but in the highly charged political atmosphere which surrounded it. Mao had instructed that 'teaching material should have local character. Some material on the locality and the villages should be included.' But all textbooks were tightly controlled by the provincial or national authorities, and scrutinized so closely for 'incorrect' material that no one ventured to innovate. Recommendation 'by the masses' for a college place usually meant selection by the Party committee—sometimes of the offspring of influential cadres, at other times to get rid of trouble-makers. Teachers were reluctant to criticize students for fear of being criticized themselves. (A 12-year-old girl named Huang Shuai in Beijing became nationally famous for denouncing her teacher.) Many of the best university teachers were still condemned to menial tasks while their places were taken by the ambitious and the ill-qualified. 'Open door schooling' was often organized merely to satisfy the requirement for a fixed number of days spent away from college, with little educational value. It was not surprising that education became the new battleground in the mid-1970s between the leftists and the modernizers, or that, when they gained victory after Mao's death, the latter should condemn the whole period as 'ten wasted years'.

The ultra-left fostered its own model of 'going against the tide' in the dubious case of Zhang Tiesheng, the student who filed a 'blank exam paper' with a letter addressed to the authorities on the reverse. Zhang was sitting a college entrance test in 1973 after five years in the Liaoning countryside. Unable to complete it (critics later pointed out that he had not actually left it 'blank'), he protested against the new requirement for a written exam:

To tell the truth, I have no respect for the bookworms who for many years have been taking it easy and have done nothing useful. I dislike them intensely. During the busy summer hoeing time, I just could not abandon my production task and hide myself in a small room to study. That would have been very selfish . . . I would have been condemned by my own revolutionary conscience.

I have one consolation. I have not slowed the work of the collective because of the examination . . . The few hours of the examination may disqualify me from college and I have nothing further to say.

But he had, spoiling the effect by going on to claim that given a couple of days' study he could have passed the test. He was then successful in a second 'supplementary test', arranged specially for him by the authorities. His letter was published in the provincial newspaper and then nationally, and Zhang was rewarded with a place in college. He later published an embroidered account of the famous exam: he had dozed off in the lunchtime break and had to climb into the examination room through the window. He could more or less have answered the questions, but felt that they were not a proper test of real ability.[8]

Revolution in health

The Revolution in Public Health, another 'newly born achievement' which attracted favourable attention abroad, showed similar strengths and weaknesses. It too was based on a pre-Cultural Revolution directive from Mao (26 June 1965) criticizing the Ministry of Health for its bureaucratic ways, and stating that the centre of gravity for medical work should shift to the rural areas. ('The Ministry of Health', Mao said, 'is not a Ministry for the people, so why not change its name to . . . the Ministry of Urban Gentlemen's Health?') Training periods were shortened to three years for doctors and between six months and a year for 'barefoot doctors' (paramedics). Many urban doctors were sent to improve rural health services, and research was directed away from complex areas to 'the prevention and improved treatment of common diseases . . . the masses' greatest needs'. New rural clinics were opened, and others which had been closed since the Great Leap were reopened. The most visible reform was the nationwide introduction of a rural co-operative medical scheme by 1968, organized at the brigade or commune level. A similar scheme during the Great Leap had failed because peasant incomes were too low to subsidize it effectively. Although the co-operative system was open to abuse by local cadres who claimed preferential treatment, its positive role has not been seriously challenged by post-Mao reformers. But it became a casualty of the reaction against collective organization and a return to individual peasant 'responsibility' for the land in the early 1980s. It was not until two decades later, when the SARS epidemic in 2003 threatened for a time to spread unchecked into the countryside, that the extent of the decline of rural health provision was widely deplored.

Health also became a political battlefield. In 1976 *Spring Shoots*, a feature film in praise of barefoot doctors, was widely promoted by the ultra-left propaganda apparatus as a work which 'reflects the maturing of barefoot doctors and new socialist sprouts in the thick of the struggle between the proletariat and the bourgeoisie'. It told the story of Chun-miao, a young woman peasant who seeks to become a barefoot doctor after seeing a baby wrongly treated by a local witch-doctor and then allowed to die by the commune hospital. Eventually she is allowed to study at the hospital, but her efforts to learn are 'obstructed by the bourgeoisie'. 'Using an injection needle is not the same as wielding a hoe', she is told. 'Filled with indignation', she returns to the village, gathers herbs, and makes the round with a medical kit. Eventually a plot to frame her by administering a toxic injection to a peasant for whom she is caring (a poor peasant naturally) is exposed. The villains are denounced, and the hospital returns to the hands of the people.

A year later the same film was being condemned in anti-Gang of Four propaganda as a big poisonous weed which slandered the leadership of the Communist Party (responsible for running the hospital) and, worse still, 'advocates spontaneous mass movements' for medical reform! Between these two extremes there was little room for serious discussion of the uses and limitations of barefoot doctors. (A new play, *Loyal Hearts*, staged in 1978, gave a very different picture of the Revolution in Health. It told the story of how an old doctor was accused of being a 'bourgeois specialist' and prevented from conducting research into heart disease. 'I simply wanted to do some medical research in order to cure more patients!', he cries. 'Is this a crime?')[9] In 1980 the Minister of Public Health Qian Xinzhong said that 'under the slogan of putting the stress on the rural areas, medical and health work in cities, factories, and mines was weakened'. Certainly there was a shift of resources to the countryside at the expense of the urban system, although some basic-level urban services were extended in compensation.[10]

Rural revolution

From outside it was the collective structure of the People's Communes which most often impressed those with experience of rural dislocation and urban immigration elsewhere in the Third World, or of the errors of Soviet collectivization in the 1930s. By the early 1970s, a coherent theory seemed to have emerged on how this post-Great Leap structure would in time evolve towards a higher level of socialism. China appeared to have struck a rational balance between individual and collective interest within a socialist framework which linked the further socialization of production and distribution to material as well as political factors. Accounts were kept and the proceeds of work were distributed mostly at the basic 'team' (village) level. But larger enterprises which would benefit the community—irrigation dams, roads, rural industry, secondary schools, and so on were handled by the higher-level commune. The intermediate-level brigade would frequently run smaller enterprises, primary schools, and often a co-operative medical scheme. The individual peasant in the team could still increase his or her income by working harder and earning more work-points, which would be converted into cash in the annual 'share-out'. But the value of these was aggregated at the village level, so that the industrious to some extent supported those who were less strong or able. (The system also benefited the more lazy, as post-Mao critics complained but few remarked at the time.) The lesson of the Great Leap Forward had apparently been learnt. There would be no 'leaping ahead' to a higher stage of socialist collectivization regardless of local circumstances. Progress to a higher stage—transferring the accounting level from teams to the brigade and eventually to the commune—was to wait until sufficient material progress had been made for all those participating to benefit more or less equally from pooling their resources. Precise figures were set. Transfer of land-ownership back to the commune from the villages would only be allowed when

(a) the economy of the commune as a whole has developed so far that the cash income per inhabitant exceeds 400–500 *yuan* . . .

(b) the commune-owned sector has attained absolute preponderance [more than 50 per cent] within the economy of the commune as a whole.

(c) the income of the poorest teams has caught up with that of the more prosperous; and

(d) mechanization has reached at least the half-way point.[11]

The transition from collective to state ownership was even further away. But in the meantime each team contributed 'cheap' labour, especially in the slack season, for the construction of collective projects which would provide the material basis for this gradual progression. The strategy of incremental advance towards the point where the collective unit could be expanded was explained in Mao's own province of Hunan as

To actively develop the commune and brigade enterprises, expand the accumulation of the commune and brigade, purchase large farm machinery which the production teams have no means to purchase themselves, build farmland and water conservancy projects which they also cannot manage by themselves, and help the poorer production teams to develop production . . . Speaking in the long term, ownership in the People's Communes always advances from ownership by the small collective to ownership by the big collective and then to ownership by the whole people.[12]

The hidden weaknesses of the system and the existence of large areas where rural poverty remained extreme, while not easily visible, prompted even those most committed to 'advancing the transition' to acknowledge that it could not be done 'ahead of time'. Zhang Chunqiao in his 1975 polemic (see below) on the need to limit 'bourgeois rights' had insisted that 'the wind of "communization" . . . shall never be allowed to rise again', and that changes would only occur 'over a fairly long time'. However, some local cadres still sought to demonstrate their zeal by promoting ill-advised schemes to 'raise the accounting level' from team to brigade.

Revolution in leadership

Another 'achievement' of the early 1970s was the Revolutionary Committee which replaced local government organs up to the provincial level and also provided a collective substitute for the administration or management in factories, schools, and all other standard units into which China was divided. At the government level, the Committee was a device to harmonize the different interest groups which emerged during the first Cultural Revolution, typically, the 'rebel' radicals, the Party cadres, and the armed forces. Painfully, between January 1967 and September 1968 the twenty-nine provinces, autonomous regions, and major cities set up their Committees (the earlier ones had a more radical complexion than those at the end, which were dominated by the army). In the enterprises the magic three-thirds formula was varied: workers, cadres, and technicians in the factory; teachers, parents, and students in the school. Sometimes it was expressed in terms of 'old' (cadres), 'middle-aged' (technicians), and 'young' (workers). Meaningless in some cases, in others the formula did reduce conflict and incorporate new voices into the political system, but before long the post-1971 search for unity rehabilitated many cadres and reduced the radical influence.

In 1974 a new round of wall-posters appeared on the walls of Beijing for the first time since the Red Guard movement. Their authors had evidently taken heart from the Tenth Party Congress (1973) which wrote into the Party Constitution a new clause saying that it was 'absolutely impermissible to suppress criticism and retaliate' against those who exercised their right to complain to the authorities. They were also encouraged by the new Party Vice-Chairman, Wang Hongwen, presented as the proletarian ideal of new China, who told the Congress that 'we must . . . constantly use the weapons of arousing the masses to air their views freely, write big-character posters, and hold great debates . . .'. Yet the 1974 posters had a spontaneous character, although their authors took advantage of the licence granted by Wang to 'go against the tide' and criticize authority. In Beijing six writers describing themselves as 'worker rebels' put up a poster of complaint in June 1984:

We worker rebels joined the Beijing Revolutionary Committee during the great Cultural Revolution in a Great Alliance with the peasants, students, and Red Guards, but no one took any notice of us! The authorities said 'The Rebels can fight but they should not sit down.' They repressed the Red Guards and told the Rebels to go back to work. The result is that out of 24 workers on the Committee only one remains, which is just four per cent of the total. Many of the Rebels have been dubbed as counter-revolutionary elements. They have been arrested, struggled with, reassigned, dismissed, and suspended.[13]

Other posters revealed a call for more industrial democracy by factory workers who took seriously the 'Two Participations' (cadres taking part in work and workers taking part in management—another 'new achievement'). There were claims that protesting workers had been laid off, that posters were banned upon factory premises, and that factory revolutionary committees failed to meet. The official press published reports of posters which criticized factory managers for attempting to reintroduce bonuses and for stifling 'the revolutionary enthusiasm of the masses', but there were also less orthodox, unreported expressions of workers' dissent, including strikes (which were to be legalized in the new 1975 state constitution). Matters came to a head in the summer of 1975 in Hangzhou, where industrial unrest spread to twenty-five factories and required army intervention to settle. It is said that Wang Hongwen, who in theory championed the workers' right to strike, was first sent by Deng Xiaoping to handle the situation and totally failed. The strike was settled by improvements in collective welfare for the workers and by arranging for cadres to 'participate in labour' as they were supposed to.[14] But Hangzhou's real significance was the emergence of an assertive workforce, partly radicalized by the Cultural Revolution, whose demands were unpalatable to all leadership factions in Beijing. Even the behaviour of the Shanghai workers who denounced the restoration of quotas (under the slogan 'Let's be masters of the wharf, not the slaves of tonnage'), though acceptable for propaganda purposes to the ultra-left, implied a rejection of 'unreasonable' Party control. While condemning managerial 'economism', the workers' argument was ultimately based on sound materialist grounds: the work would be achieved more successfully and under better working conditions if they were not obliged to pursue rigid targets. (One shift of dockers, for example, could more usefully prepare the ground for a second shift to unload cargo than attack the task itself by merely unloading the most accessible items.)

The final struggle

In January 1975, at the long-delayed Fourth National People's Congress (NPC), Zhou Enlai made his last public appearance outside hospital to deliver the crucial 'Report on the work of the government' which set the policy guidelines for the whole country. Zhou revived a target date originally set by Mao himself for substantial economic development by the end of the century—the 'Year 2000', by which time China should have become a strong socialist industrial country capable of making 'a bigger contribution to mankind' (Mao, November 1956). Zhou now presented a two-stage economic plan. The first, which in theory had been operating since 1965, would build a 'relatively comprehensive' industrial and economic system by 1980. The second, which would run from 1980 to 2000, was to achieve 'the comprehensive modernization in agriculture, industry, defence, and science and technology'. Thus the Four Modernizations appeared on the political agenda. Zhou sought to validate them by reminding his audience that he had mentioned them, with Mao's approval, at the last Congress in 1964.

The NPC convened in an apparent spirit of compromise. It elected a strong team of Vice-Premiers spanning the political spectrum. After Deng Xiaoping and Zhang Chunqiao came former finance minister Li Xiannian. The 'new left' of the Cultural Revolution had three places, including Chen Yonggui, the peasant leader of the model Dazhai Brigade. They were matched by three ministers with experience in economic planning and construction, including Yu Qiuli who had almost single-handedly written

China's interim one-year plans since the Cultural Revolution began. Control of the armed forces was balanced between Deng Xiaoping as chief of staff and Zhang Chunqiao as head of the political department. The appointment of this new team with an emphasis on economic expertise also seemed to indicate a political consensus for the new strategy. Deng, in charge of the team, now effectively ran Zhou's state apparatus as the Premier returned to spend the last year of his life in hospital.

But behind the scenes a bitter factional struggle had already broken out in which Mao played an ambiguous role. It came after months of indirect sniping at Zhou Enlai and Deng Xiaoping by the ultra-left. They had taken control of a propaganda campaign originally authorized by Mao, to 'Criticize Lin Biao and Confucius', publishing barely disguised attacks on Zhou Enlai as the Duke of Zhou (founder of the Zhou dynasty and traditionally the source of the Way which Confucius developed). At the heart of the new dispute were legitimate questions of economic strategy, particularly concerning how far China should seek foreign imports of new technology and how they should be paid for. The reopening of relations with the US in 1971 had led to a shopping spree in which thirty complete industrial plants were purchased from the West in 1973–4 alone, worth some US $2,000 million. A second round concentrating on the energy sector was now proposed. But this debate was intertwined with a struggle for the post-Zhou and post-Mao succession, which falsified any attempt at serious argument. The struggle had begun with the 'Fengqing' affair and would not end until Mao's death nearly two years later. Its intense and intricate nature is revealed by the record of the first few weeks:

4 October 1974. Mao proposes that Deng should be elected First Vice-Premier of the State Council at the NPC.

17 October. At a meeting of the Politburo, Deng has a row with Jiang Qing over the Chinese-built freighter 'Fengqing'. The ship, though hailed in the media as the first 10,000 ton ship built in China, has a poor performance which for Deng indicates the futility of a narrow policy of 'self-reliance'. Deng walks out of the meeting, and the Politburo is unable to reconvene for more than a month.

18 October. Jiang Qing sends Wang Hongwen to Changsha where Mao is resting, to sow doubt in his mind about the relationship between Zhou and Deng. He is to insinuate that 'although the Premier is hospitalized, he is busy summoning people for talks far into the night', and that 'the atmosphere in Beijing is now very much like that of the Lushan meeting [in July 1959]'. Wang is rebuffed by Mao, and told (according to the later version) not to 'gang up' with Jiang Qing.

On the same day, Mao's two interpreters, Wang Hairong (his niece) and Tang Wensheng, due to take some foreign guests to meet him in Changsha, are summoned to the Diaoyutai Guesthouse. Jiang Qing asks them to make a report to Mao about the 'Fengqing' incident. Zhang Chunqiao tells them that some 'leading members of the State Council [are] worshipping everything foreign and spending too much on imports, thus causing state deficits'. Wang and Tang rush to tell Premier Zhou what they have been asked to do. Zhou explains that Deng Xiaoping has been baited many times at Politburo meetings, and has restrained himself till now.

20 October. After Mao has seen the foreign guests, Wang and Tang pass on the story (as interpreted by Zhou, they later claim, not by Jiang Qing). Mao is very angry, dismissing the freighter row as a trifle which has already been settled. He sends them back to Beijing with an 'instruction': The Premier should remain in charge. Matters relating to the National People's Congress (NPC) and new appointments should be 'handled jointly' by Zhou and Wang Hongwen. Deng should be appointed First Vice-Premier, a Vice-Chairman of the Party, and Vice-Chairman of the Party Military Committee.[15]

But Mao would change his mind again, failing to attend the Congress or even send it an opening message. The *People's Daily* on 9 February quoted a new 'instruction' from him warning that 'lack of clarity' on the need to 'exercise dictatorship over the bourgeoisie' would 'lead to revisionism'. The editorial clearly labelled Deng Xiaoping's group as 'sham Marxists' and reproached the mainstream Maoists—leaders such as Chen Yonggui—with having 'muddled ideas of one kind or another . . .'. This was soon followed by two polemical articles by Zhang Chunqiao and Yao Wenyuan which plunged the country into a new campaign to 'study the theory of the dictatorship of the proletariat'.[16]

The flawed debate

The articles by Yao and Zhang, backed up in the official press, presented an ambiguous mixture of serious theoretical argument and vicious polemic. Their starting-point, already endorsed by Mao and capable of being supported by carefully chosen quotes from Marx and Lenin, was the persistence of inequality under socialism and of the conditions in which a 'new bourgeoisie' could re-form. Mao provided the authority with an 'instruction' which reflected that, although China's system of ownership had changed, it still possessed an 'unequal' wage-system and a commodity economy which was not so different from that under capitalism. It would be quite easy, he reflected moodily, 'for people like Lin Biao to push the capitalist system, if they came to power'.

A group of theoretical workers in Shanghai, under Zhang Chunqiao's guidance, had been preparing since 1971 a new textbook on the political economy of socialism. Their work (no doubt nudged in the desired direction by Zhang) strongly emphasized the 'incomplete' aspects of socialist society which provided the material basis for the possibility of the emergence of a new bourgeoisie and the restoration of capitalism. Echoing Mao, they argued that 'many Cultural Revolutions' would be required to prevent this happening, until the surviving capitalist factors in the 'relations of production' (ownership, distribution, and management) had all been eliminated. Only when this had been done would the material basis for a new 'privileged class' have been eliminated.[17]

The political cutting edge of this theory of 'capitalist restoration' (which had originated in Mao's view that such a restoration had already occurred in the Soviet Union) lay in the assertion by Yao and Zhang that a new bourgeois class could be formed *within the ranks of the Communist Party itself*, and indeed that in some areas this 'new bourgeoisie' was already in place. The ideological form of such a restoration, it was argued, would be a new 'theory of productive forces'. Thus the target was pinpointed as Zhou and Deng, the champions of the Four Modernizations. The argument also underlined the necessity of maintaining forward progress in the development of new 'socialist achievements' and in the struggle to substitute the new for the old. The Cultural Revolution, it implied, must be resumed. One ultra-left polemicist wrote:

Socialist new things may look somewhat weak and not deep-rooted at the start, but they are full of revolutionary vigour. Compared to the old things which seem strong and deep-rooted but reek of decay, they have a fine future for development . . . The development of new things always proceeds from superficial to deep, from weak to strong, and from a low to a higher level. A big revolutionary movement, like the turbulent Yangtze rushing down from the gorges on the upper reaches to swell at the mouth, must pass through a process involving a beginning, a climax, and a deepening stage.[18]

This call for a new revolutionary tide—Yao liked to say that 'the tide of history is just like a river'—was given a precise political target by Zhang. One-half of his article was a rational discussion of the 'incomplete' nature of socialist ownership in China. He pointed out that state ownership in industry accounted for nearly all the fixed assets but only 63 per cent of the industrial population, while agriculture was almost entirely still in collective hands, and hence that the issue of ownership had 'not yet been entirely settled'. The persistence of the 'capitalist factors' discussed above meant necessarily that 'new bourgeois elements would be engendered'. Then abruptly shifting style and mood, Zhang attacked his real target:

There are undeniably some comrades among us who have joined the Communist Party organizationally but not ideologically. In their world outlook they have not yet overstepped the bounds of small production and of the bourgeoisie. They do approve of the dictatorship of the proletariat at a certain stage and within a certain sphere and are pleased with certain victories of the proletariat, because these will bring them some gains; once they have secured their gains, they feel it's time to settle down and feather their cosy nests. As for exercising all-round dictatorship over the bourgeoisie, as for going on after the first step on the 10,000 *li* march, sorry, let others do the job; here is my stop and I must get off the bus. We would like to offer a piece of advice to these comrades: it's dangerous to stop half-way! The bourgeoisie is beckoning to you. Catch up with the ranks and continue to advance!

Deng regarded these documents correctly as a declaration of war, and decided to take on his enemies while Mao was still alive and all around him hesitated. In the summer of 1975 Deng launched a counter-attack on the ultra-left. He called them 'sham Marxist political swindlers' and announced his intention of purging them from the Party. 'These anti-Marxist class enemies', it was said in the first important document (the General Programme of Work) which Deng inspired in his role as deputy for Zhou Enlai, 'have stepped into the shoes of Lin Biao. They take over our revolutionary slogans all the time, distort them, twist them, and appropriate them for their own use, mix up black and white, confound right and wrong.' Judging correctly that the ultra-left would overreach itself and that accounts would be settled after Mao's death, Deng challenged them on their own ground, orchestrating a critique of leftist policies in education, led by the Minister of Education Zhou Rongxin. Other documents inspired by Deng in 1975–6 dealt with problems of industrial development and science and technology, where he argued that China had fallen dangerously behind. He rephrased his provocative view that the colour of the cat did not matter so long as it could catch the mice. The best scientists, he said, should be 'red and expert', but those who were 'white and expert' could also serve China. They were a much greater asset than 'those who just lie idle, cause factional fighting, and hold up everything'. With a touch of Mao's scatological style, Deng denounced the Gang and their followers as the sort of people who would 'sit on the lavatory and not do a shit'.[19]

The argument on foreign trade and economic strategy also continued. An anti-Jiang Qing cartoon published after the Gang's arrest would show her shouting 'Foreign slave! Compradore' at an unseen Deng Xiaoping, while wearing a wig made in France and false teeth made in Japan. Total two-way trade had already increased significantly from some US $3.9 billion in 1969 to US $14 billion in 1975. Trade deficits were incurred in 1974–5 for the first time, and China had begun to purchase complete plant from the West on deferred terms, although still refusing to accept foreign loans. Deng proposed to modernize the Chinese coal and oil industry through the import of new technology, to be paid back out of future production. More generally, he argued that for China to 'catch up' with the advanced world, it must study foreign technology with an open mind and import it where required. Technology was international, argued Deng. 'Dismantle any imported product and you will find that many of its parts are from yet other countries.' Raw materials should also be imported if the alternative was idle production lines. Oil customers should be sought in Europe as well as Japan in return for 'fine technical equipment'. The ultra-left seized on the target presented by Deng, but countered it in chauvinistic terms:

We absolutely cannot place our hopes for realizing the Four Modernizations on imports. If we do not rely mainly on our own efforts but, as Deng Xiaoping advocated, rely solely on importing foreign techniques, copying foreign designs and technological processes and patterning our equipment on foreign models, we will forever trail behind foreigners and our country's development of technology and even its entire national economy will fall under the control of foreign monopoly capital . . . China would be reduced step by step to a raw materials supplying base for imperialism and social-imperialism, a market for their commodities, and an outlet for their investments.[20]

The educational debate was resumed in an atmosphere of tragicomedy. Zhang Tiesheng, the student with the 'blank paper', now toured the country as a spokesman for the ultra-left attacking Minister Zhou Rongxin. Zhou complained that 'culture' and even 'socialist conscience' had become forbidden words. He did not object to students being selected from the working class, but asked why after graduation they had to go back to being 'simple workers' instead of using their talents as technicians and cadres. Zhang Tiesheng challenged Zhou to a debate, which was widely believed to have precipitated a heart attack from which Zhou died soon afterwards. After the Gang's fall Zhang was denounced in the press as 'not worth a horse's fart' (he had trained as a veterinary student), and was later jailed as a counter-revolutionary. A young man who found himself totally out of his depth, Zhang Tiesheng illustrates how the potential material for serious discussion, based on the ideals of the Cultural Revolution, was turned so easily into farce by its warped political culture.

Confrontation

At noon on 5 April 1976, with Mao Zedong just five months from death, China's supreme leaders—several of them barely on speaking terms— gathered in the Great Hall of the People to watch an amazing event outside. On the previous day thousands of Beijing citizens had come to Tiananmen Square with wreaths to mourn the recent death of Premier Zhou Enlai. (The Gang of Four had tried, unsuccessfully, to ban the sale of crêpe paper in the mourning colour of white.) Slogans, letters, poems, and cartoons had been held aloft, pasted to the marble sides of the Martyrs' Memorial, or chalked on the polished stone pavement. One or two were written in blood and read out by their authors. A banner saying 'We mourn the Premier' was launched, suspended from a bunch of balloons. During the night, all the wreaths were removed from the square by pro-Gang militia. The demonstrators returned on the morning of the 5th, and furious quarrels broke out with militia and policemen on the steps of the Great Hall. Soon after noon, the first car was set on fire. Later on, a police station was also set alight. The square was eventually cleared by force as darkness fell.

All of this was watched by the leadership from inside the Hall, through binoculars which aides had hastily provided to help them read the slogans and follow the action on the other side of the square. No one had any doubt that by demonstrating *for* the late Premier, the crowd was also demonstrating *against* the ultra-left leadership. Zhang Chunqiao laid down his binoculars, turned to Deng Xiaoping, and accused him of having organized the demonstration. Zhang 'scolded Deng face to face', according to the account given four years later at the trial of the Gang of Four, and called him 'an ugly traitor'. Within days, Mao had been persuaded to dismiss Deng from all his Party offices, and Zhang, the number two in the ultra-left leadership, wrote triumphantly to his son that the struggle for the succession had been decided. But he was wrong. Deng made a diplomatic retreat to the south to wait out the summer, while the *People's Daily*, firmly under the control of the ultra-left, raged against the 'ghosts and monsters, demons and clowns who dance to the music from Deng Xiaoping's flute'. Rumour and speculation—denounced by the paper as 'counter-revolutionary'—began to spread while Mao lived out his last enfeebled months. There was popular talk of portents and ill omens: these seemed borne out when the coal-mining city of Tangshan was devastated by an earthquake on 27 July. More than two hundred thousand perished and the interim regime under Hua Guofeng, now confirmed as premier, proved incapable of providing adequate aid. The Red, Red Sun himself died just over a month later on 7 September: within another month the Gang of Four had been arrested and in the black-bordered magazines which mourned the Chairman's death, they were clumsily airbrushed out of the photographs of his funeral.

Economics in Command
The modernization of China

'It is not a question of whether we achieve the Four Modernizations', said the cadre at the banquet table in the headquarters of Shengli (Victory) Oilfield. 'It is only a question of how soon we achieve the targets ahead of time.' Shengli is planted on the eastern coast in Shandong province, on low-lying, poor, and alkaline land. In the village next door to the oilfield headquarters, the peasants could be seen defecating into open cesspits, whipped by the cold wind blowing across the salt marshes from the Yellow River.

The oil field cadre was not concerned with the local people—they were the responsibility of the county government. Shengli's workers had all come from outside, mobilized into a General Battle Headquarters under the Ministry of Petroleum. At first they lived in mud hovels with straw stacked a foot high on the roofs like those of the peasants. Now they had cinemas, schools, and new apartment blocks.

The time was September 1978 and oil was China's Magic Weapon. With the profits from expanding oil production, said the cadre, China would fund the foreign imports for Chairman Hua Guofeng's Four Modernizations of Agriculture, Industry, Science and Technology, and National Defence. In northern Hebei province, in the South China Sea, oil had been found so sweet and so sulphur-free that the Japanese would gorge themselves on it.

The Four Modernizations was a Magnificent Plan, Chairman Hua had said, to build China by the Year 2000 into a Powerful Socialist Country so that its economy would rank as among the

Most Advanced in the World. The current Ten-Year Plan had started two years late, but it did not matter.

The state plans to build or complete [by 1985] 120 large-scale projects, including ten iron and steel complexes, nine non-ferrous metal complexes, eight coal mines, ten oil and gas fields, thirty power stations, six new trunk railways, and five key harbours. [This] . . . will provide China with fourteen fairly strong and fairly rationally located industrial bases and will be decisive in changing the backward state of our basic industries.

Outside the Shengli headquarters a roadside poster promoted the Four Modernizations. Against the background of the figure '2000', pierced by a speeding rocket, stood a worker, peasant, and soldier, looking resolutely ahead over a landscape of oil derricks, factory complexes, and satellite dishes. The peasants' carts, piled high with winter fodder, shambled past the hoarding, their drivers wrapped in sacking against the cold.

(Visit to Shengli Oilfield, Nov. 1978)

The economic plateau

By the 1970s China had reached an economic plateau at which the Maoist policy of 'hard struggle and self-reliance', though admired by many abroad as a superior model of development for the Third World, offered diminishing returns to the Chinese people. A healthier, better educated, better organized population lived, still mostly in rural areas, on land which had been considerably improved through the massive application of labour-intensive inputs. Grain production had at least kept pace with the rapid increase in population, except during the Great Leap Forward, and higher yields were achieved on the same or even smaller sown areas. Industrial development had tripled steel production, laid the foundation for a significant petroleum industry, created a machine-building industry virtually from scratch, and provided the base for China to become a nuclear power. Light industry provided a reasonable flow of consumer goods by comparison with, for example, the Soviet Union, although still a long way below potential demand. In spite of political disruptions, China held together as a coherent economic entity with nationwide communications and functioning mechanisms for shifting surpluses to areas of need. The first World Bank report on China concluded that Chinese development had been impressive: GNP per capita had grown at between 2 and 2.5 per cent per annum during 1957–77 in spite of a 2 per cent per annum population growth rate. This compared with an average growth rate of only 1.6 per cent for other low-income countries. Net output of industry grew at an annual average of 10.2 per cent during 1957–79, well above the average for other low-income countries of 5.4 per cent. The World Bank report 'regard[ed] China's most remarkable achievement over three decades as making its low-income groups far better off in terms of basic needs compared with their counterparts in most other poor countries'.

Yet for a variety of reasons China could no longer continue on this path. A high psychological price had been paid by which self-reliance led to self-destructive isolation during the Cultural Revolution. This further reduced the motivation, difficult to sustain at best of times, for the Chinese population to work harder indefinitely for the sake of far-off rewards. The abandonment of the policy of 'containment' by the United States offered China choices in economic strategy which had not been available before and were immediately seized. In 1971–3 China signed contracts for US $1.8 billion worth of imports of machinery and equipment. It was also becoming apparent that the Maoist model was not so different from the Soviet model of centralized planning with excessive emphasis upon heavy industry, which it had set out to avoid. China suffered from most of the defects of the Soviet and other planned socialist economies. Incomes rose much more slowly than GNP; hardly at all in the rural areas. Far too high a proportion of the national income was 'accumulated' by the state for investment rather than passed back to the producer to stimulate 'consumption'. (The rate was an average of 33 per cent in the first half of the 1970s.) Industrial growth was based on huge investment spurred by the high rate of accumulation, but output per unit of fixed capital actually declined. In spite of the policy of putting agriculture first, the peasants continued to be starved on investment funds and were poorly rewarded for their produce. Urban incomes were twice as high as those in the countryside, where inequalities between rich and poor areas persisted. The system of centralized 'command planning' encouraged wasteful use and duplication of resources in industry. The domination of planning by the Party also discouraged innovation and experiment which might lead those responsible to be criticized. The decentralization of industry to the interior of the country for defence reasons also duplicated scarce resources. Meanwhile, shortages in consumer goods, with privileged access to goods in short supply by Party and government cadres, further reduced popular commitment to what was sometimes referred to as 'socialism which we cannot eat'.[1]

The reforms take off

Previous attempts at reform of the systems of planning and production had been contained within a framework of socialist thinking which always put 'politics first'. Material incentives, autonomy for enterprises, the encouragement of competition, pricing goods according to the real cost of production, and similar proposals were judged on political as well as economic grounds. The decade of reform which began in the late 1970s saw a steady loosening of these constraints, as socialism was first redefined and later more or less put to one side. The scene by 1989, with agriculture effectively privatized and the profit motive now accepted as the dominant force throughout the economy, was unimaginable at the start of the decade. 'Having mounted the saddle', Trotsky had written of the unknown art of organizing a socialist economy, 'the rider is obliged to guide the horse in peril of breaking his neck.' In China the horse was soon galloping in a very different direction.

At first, when new priorities were asserted after Mao's death, it was done in a hyperbolic style which owed much to the recent past. The rhetoric of round-number targets and millenarian goals was deployed by cadres who effortlessly switched slogans from those of the Cultural Revolution. The 'magnificent plan' of the Four Modernizations, inherited from the late Zhou Enlai by Hua Guofeng (appointed Party chairman after Mao's death at the Eleventh Party Congress in August 1977), who now loudly proclaimed them as if they were his own, legitimized the shift to economic objectives by claiming continuity with Mao's own concern to 'catch up and surpass' advanced world levels of production and technology 'at an early date'. Hua's grandiose plans, requiring continued high levels of accumulation and investment at the expense of consumption and living standards, helped to make the initial turn from Politics to Economics in Command more acceptable, but soon proved unrealistic.[2]

The economic 'readjustment' of 1979–80 (later extended to 1982–3), which strengthened the hand of Deng Xiaoping's reformers, scaled down Hua's targets and sought to remedy the imbalances in the Chinese economy, boosting consumption instead of accumulation, raising farm prices at the expense of industry, and focusing on infrastructural needs—transport, energy, and communications—while reining back the grandiose goals of

heavy industry (particularly where they involved expensive imports of foreign technology). It also began to tackle the over-concentration of authority
in economic management and recognized a growing problem of urban
unemployment. But it was anchored by the admission—unthinkable only
two or three years before—that the Chinese people were still mostly poorly
fed and badly housed, and unimpressed with a socialism that could not
remedy either condition. Deng Xiaoping's veteran colleague and critic of
the Great Leap Forward, Chen Yun, later to be a critic of Deng's reforms too
as they began to break orthodox boundaries, warned of the consequences of
continued popular hardship in a memorable speech. There are four main
reasons, he said in the spring of 1979, why people criticized the Hua Guofeng
leadership in spite of its achievements in liquidating the Gang of Four:

(1) They understand things that were not understood before. For example, they
     point out that workers abroad have a higher standard of living than workers
     here . . .

(2) They are not willing to swallow the same old line. For example, the slogan that
     the situation is good—and yet you need a ration coupon to eat. You have to
     stand in line to buy commodities. In this situation you can mouth slogans all day
     without filling your stomach.

(3) They want to be reapers of the harvest, not offerings to adorn a tomb. They
     want to live well in this present life. Since Communism is a kind of heaven, they
     are willing to leave it for the next generation to enjoy.

(4) They are impatient and tired of waiting. They feel they have been waiting thirty
     years and now have to wait another thirty years . . . They say: You cadres have
     already been rewarded for your suffering. Why must we the people go on
     suffering without end?[3]

The route to Communism did not lie through enforced accumulation of
state funds to invest in industry and public works while material conditions
failed to improve. The Hua leadership was criticized for allowing the
national income percentage of accumulation to rise from 30.9 in 1976 to
36.5 in 1978, a rate exceeded only during the Great Leap. Such a rate, said
the critics, occurred at a time when the Chinese population had increased
by more than two hundred million in the past fifteen years, while living
standards had not improved, average incomes had hardly risen, and problems in welfare, housing, education, and health had in many areas actually
worsened. As Deng was to explain:

During the 'Cultural Revolution' there was a view that poor Communism was preferable to rich capitalism. After I resumed office in the central leadership in 1974 and 1975, I criticized that view. Because I refuted that view, I was brought down again. . . . The main task of socialism is to develop the productive forces, steadily improve the life of the people, and keep increasing the material wealth of the society. Therefore, there can be no Communism with pauperism, or socialism with pauperism. So to get rich is no sin. (2 Sept. 1986)

As the reforms developed and deepened, theory struggled to catch up with practice and to explain it in politically acceptable terms. The Hua Guofeng leadership had reasserted economic against political priorities but still maintained that Chinese socialism was well advanced and capable of attaining high targets. After Hua it was conceded that China had progressed very little distance along the transition to socialism. This now legitimized a widening range of incentives and the encouragement of market forces. The planned economy remained supreme in theory but increasingly the reforms led into areas which challenged its domination and undermined the parallel supremacy of state ownership. The wider targets of reform may be summarized as follows:

(*a*) the need for enterprise autonomy involving a system of profit retention. This would only stimulate production effectively if decision-making power was devolved to the enterprise management and not to the local government or Party hitherto responsible for the enterprise. Real autonomy would also require provisions for hiring and firing labour, abolishing the 'iron rice bowl' or unconditional guarantee of jobs to those already in employment, and a bankruptcy law as the ultimate sanction for inefficiency.

(*b*) the need for price reform which would eliminate hidden subsidies to both producer and consumer, and ensure that resources and products were not over-ordered or over-produced or stockpiled and allowed to go to waste. This would involve the shedding by the state of responsibility for fixing prices for all except a very small number of essential goods and services.

(*c*) the need for a market not just in goods and services but in labour (the selling of skills and job mobility), housing and land (to replenish the ageing stock of urban housing and discourage wasteful use of 'free' land by enterprises), and capital (enabling enterprises and entrepreneurs to raise funds for expansion either by more readily available loans or from stocks or bonds).

Deng Xiaoping sought to channel these new ideas into an acceptable package labelled 'Socialism with Chinese characteristics'. But by 1984 he had begun to part company from Chen Yun and other conservatives for whom reform meant returning to the ideas—mostly their ideas—of the mid-1950s, which they had labelled the 'economic laws of socialism'. Most younger reformers no longer accepted such laws, and believed that China was now engaged on an exploration of new territory. Not far below the surface lurked the thought that if 'skipping the capitalist stage of development' had weakened China's ability to enter into socialism, perhaps some of the features of that stage should be restored.

The rapid progression of economic theory to keep pace with the escalation of reform is well illustrated by the writing of the leading economist Xue Muqiao. Xue was a liberal associated with the Chen Yun group who since the middle 1950s had, whenever possible, argued against the high level of accumulation and in favour of relaxing the planning structure, but he also (like most of his colleagues) clung to some elements of Maoist orthodoxy. Xue was only able to resume work on his research into socialist economics after the Cultural Revolution, bringing out a standard textbook in 1979. His first edition stated as 'economic laws of socialism' a set of propositions which Mao himself would have accepted in the early 1960s. The aim was 'to secure the maximum satisfaction of the constantly rising material and cultural requirements of the whole of society', by the 'planned, proportionate development of the national economy'. Collective and state forms of ownership still existed side by side, together with 'some remnants of private ownership', but would eventually merge into a higher form. But two years later Xue published an 'addendum' to cover the new reforms already under way: his book, he said, had left much to be desired in clarifying the 'Left' mistakes of economic policy within the Party. Xue now criticized the tendency of 'blindly going after a higher level of public ownership' and the domination of state planning. It was time to reconsider whether moving from smaller to larger collective units in the countryside was invariably the best form of progress. Xue also wrote more positively of 'the existence of a small number of other forms of ownership, for example, private ownership'. He attached more importance too to the role of the market, with which state planning should be 'kept in line'. Price controls should be loosened, and the state-owned monopoly of commerce should be supplemented by 'large numbers of collective retail stores and some private ones'.

Five years later, Xue's ideas had progressed further, though he still lagged behind his more adventurous colleagues. He now wrote that China had 'blundered' after 1949 in trying to substitute 'planned production and distribution' for the market, and in imposing restrictions on the 'commodity–money relationship'. A planned and centralized economic system belonged to Communism, not socialism. Xue criticized Marx for taking an 'abstract' view of socialist society and predicting the complete public ownership of the means of production. He envisaged instead a system of 'free competition between the state, collective, and private sectors' under the guidance of broadly written—'macro-economic'—state plans. The state sector was still dominant, wrote Xue, so why should one fear private enterprise? Finally, after the 1987 Party Congress, Xue argued openly that certain 'capitalist factors' would continue to exist in China in 'co-operation' with socialism, just as in the world as a whole there was collaboration as well as competition between the socialist and capitalist countries. Capitalism need not become 'extinct' during the initial stage of socialism—which the Congress had agreed would last for a hundred years.[4]

Bonuses in command

'More work more pay' was the straightforward Chinese way of referring to the Marxist principle of 'From each according to his ability, to each according to his work.' No one ever denied that reward for labour could not be wholly equal during the socialist transition. Only once Communism had been achieved would the conditions for 'distribution according to need' be satisfied, when (a) there would be more than enough to satisfy everyone, and (b) people would have sufficient 'communist spirit' to accept an egalitarian ethic. But from the time of the Great Leap onwards, the conventional wisdom was that wage differentials should be narrowed and increasing use should be made of moral rather than material incentives to stimulate labour productivity. During the Cultural Revolution bonuses at work were progressively abolished. Piecework rates were also condemned, although some factories quietly kept them in operation. All workers were paid a monthly wage according to the national eight-grade scale. Only the lower rates were increased during the 1960s, and promotion was by age rather than ability. The result, said many Chinese after the Cultural Revolution, was a situation of 'more work less pay'. Even worse, the conscientious worker subsidized the lazy worker who enjoyed the luxury of 'less work more pay'. Similar complaints were heard in the countryside, at least from the younger and more able, or those with larger families possessing more work-power who could now benefit from higher reward for individual effort. This

writer recorded dozens of scornful jingles about the past in autumn 1978 as
the bonus movement gathered pace:

'Work or skive, we all got five', one is told contemptuously by a commune leader
with reference to the work-point system where allegedly everyone had been credited with the same total regardless of achievement. 'Work, slack, or game, it was all
just the same', was the corresponding jingle at a grain warehouse in Beijing which
during the Cultural Revolution adopted a time rate system and abolished bonuses
with disastrous results, it is claimed, on productivity. Phrases like these, which sound
particularly effective in monosyllabic Chinese, are not just incidental to the argument . . . 'No reward for the workers: no punishment for the shirkers.' It often
seems as if the very neatness of the phrase is supposed to convince one of the
soundness of the argument.[5]

Meanwhile wages in real terms had declined in purchasing power in the
past two decades, rising by only 10 per cent while inflation for the urban
worker had increased by over 16 per cent. Bonuses and piecework rates
were restored cautiously at first. The rule was that only heavy manual
workers should be paid by results rather than by the day, and that bonuses
should not exceed 10–12 per cent of standard wages. In many places
bonuses were only awarded after 'discussion by the masses', rather than
automatically in response to above-average performance. The new policy
was to 'combine material rewards with moral encouragement', which took
the form of public praise for advanced workers, the award of banners and
flags to 'advanced units', recording 'merits' in personal dossiers, and award-
ing the title of advanced worker. However, the limits were soon relaxed.
Many factories adopted a mixture of time and piece-rates, and a fully
fledged system of bonuses linked to the retention of a proportion of above-
the-plan profits became a concealed supplement to wages. By 1980 the
bonus boom had become alarming as Deng Xiaoping told a Central
Committee meeting on 16 January:

Some [workers and factories] have gone so far as to ignore the interests of the
country as a whole and to flout discipline. For example, because we were somewhat
negligent in our work last year, bonuses were issued indiscriminately to the tune of
over five billion yuan. While many such bonuses were distributed legitimately, a
considerable proportion of the total, amounting to a sizeable sum, was not. Bonuses
were issued even by some units which failed to fulfil their quotas of production and
profit. Indiscriminate price rises for some commodities were often directly related
to the pursuit of bonuses by certain enterprises. In many places, workers' real
income was doubled as a result of excessive bonuses.

After many years of depressed wages, the pent-up demand was bound to lead to inflationary rises. This was only encouraged by the official explanation (which later had to be denied) that China needed to emulate the developed world by moving from 'low wages and low consumption' to 'high wages and high consumption'. The problem, it was soon realized, was that as long as factories were not responsible for their profits and losses, bonuses could become concealed pay rises at the expense of the state. The existing wage scale was also far too complicated to administer efficiently. The eight-grade scale had led to 'bunching', with most workers clustered in the medium grades regardless of their job or aptitude. Each branch of industry had its own rates of pay, based not on performance but on its presumed value to the nation, with heavy industry the most highly rewarded. Reforms in the early 1980s made bonuses in theory dependent upon profits, while enterprises were required to pay taxes to the state. But by 1985 many factories were paying bonuses equivalent to one-third of annual wages. The problem was exacerbated by distortions in the pricing system: factories which produced goods which were overvalued came into large windfall sums through the profit retention scheme, arousing considerable envy among workers whose products were undervalued. The habit of equal distribution of extra rewards which had been part of the old system also helped to undermine the economic rationality of the new system. 'Many enterprises issue bonuses equally, thus turning them into disguised extra wages', wrote Liu Guoguang in 1987, attributing this to 'the long historical background and broad social basis of egalitarianism in China'. Egalitarianism had long since become a term of abuse. The Gang of Four were censured within two years of their fall for trying to 'limit' the necessary inequalities of the distribution system, thus causing 'great ideological confusion and economic loss'—and as they were conspirators whose only ambition was to seize power in the ensuing chaos, this had been their purpose, it was argued, all along![6]

Demoting the plan

Higher wages and bonuses would not lead to greater efficiency, it was already realized by the Chinese reformers, unless accompanied by substantial changes in economic management and in the running of industry and commerce. This required an assault upon what up until then were regarded as the two prime indicators of progress towards socialism—the domination of the plan and state ownership—opening the door for the growth of a

substantial market sector and the expansion of collective and private ownership. After thirty years of communist rule, the planning network had
enmeshed more than 90 per cent of the economy. This was equally true
whether the plan was supervised from the 'centre' (Beijing) or by the local
authorities. In these three decades, planning had shifted several times between
the centre and the provinces, devolving in theory at times (as in the Great
Leap) to even lower levels. But the planners in every case were administrative cadres working in Party or government offices, not the factory or
enterprise managers. There was more decentralization in Mao's last years,
but with 'politics in command' even less attention was paid to such criteria
as real costs of production, the need to secure a return on investment,
the fixing of proper prices, and other 'market' factors. Local cadres were
often more tempted than central planners to downgrade the satisfaction of
ordinary consumer demands, investing instead in prestigious 'capital
construction' for industry and public works.

Critics of planning orthodoxy had to proceed 'bashfully', as Liu Guoguang
later recalled. The 1981 resolution on Party history defined Chinese post-
Mao economic strategy in cautious terms: 'We must carry out the planned
economy on the basis of a system of public ownership, while at the same
time developing the subsidiary role of market adjustments.'[7] This amounted
to a return to the mid-1950s and the policy associated now as then with
Chen Yun. In March 1979 Chen stressed that, though the market was
indispensable, it was 'supplementary and secondary in nature'. The conservative reformers warned that 'we cannot waver in the policy of taking the
planned economy as the key, nor can we abandon directive planning, cen-
tralization, and unification of administrative methods'. If the plan and the
market were put on an equal footing (argued *Red Flag*, no. 8, 1982), this
would lead to a return to capitalism. The plan should still dominate the
heights of economic production—iron, steel, grain, cement, fertilizer, and so
on—which would be both produced and sold by the state. The market
should be confined to the circulation of 'local products' and other less
essential items. Chen argued in his memorable 'birdcage' analogy that the
planning framework should not be loosened too far:

While reviving the economy, we must guard against the tendency to diverge from
the state plan. Revitalization should be under the guidance of the plan; it should not
depart from the plan. This can be compared with the relationship between a bird
and its cage. A bird cannot be held tightly in one's hand because that would kill it; it
must be allowed to fly. But it can only fly within the cage; without the cage it will

escape. If the bird represents economic revitalization, then the cage represents state planning.[8]

But a more formidable critique was developing against the plan, with implications for political as well as economic reform, and influenced by experiences in Eastern Europe which were beginning to be studied seriously. Critics argued that the planning process had led to the fixing of grandiose targets and excessive accumulation of funds at the expense of living standards. By setting targets in terms of quantitative output and value it had encouraged stockpiling of raw materials and the production of poor-quality goods to meet the norm. Because the state was responsible for profit and loss, there was no incentive to innovate or to improve product quality. The complexity of a vast society also meant that no planning mechanism could accurately carry out the thousands of statistical operations necessary to measure consumption and demand. Examples were numerous: planners in one city had arranged for production of 1.4 million pocket-knives which would take thirty years to sell. Factories imported coke from hundreds of miles away instead of buying it from local mines which belonged to a different ministry. Locating raw materials and spare parts was so difficult that on any one day up to three million people were travelling around China on purchasing missions.

By the late 1980s, economic theory had progressed from regarding the plan as primary and the market as secondary to the unification of the two concepts. The goal was a 'planned commodity economy' in which the 'law of value' operated throughout the system, and there was an 'organic unity of planning and the market'. This also meant that those products which were produced and disposed of on the basis of the plan were no longer regarded as immune from market forces. Liu Guoguang wrote, 'It had long been held that in a socialist economy only consumer goods are commodities. Commodities were limited to those items obtained without ration coupons, and only these commodities were actually regulated by the market.' But now the 'means of production'—industrial products, technology, finance, land, and labour itself—were all to be regarded as commodities which could be priced, bought, and sold. The plan no longer had a special 'socialist' character. Planning and the market mechanism were merely 'methods' by which production and consumption could be regulated, and they were both used in capitalist as well as socialist societies, argued another leading reformer, Gao Shangquan.[9]

As the 'market' lost its 'subsidiary' relationship to the plan, so collective and private enterprise began to assume a more equal relationship with the state-owned sector. The number of workers employed in the collective sector grew by 32 per cent between 1978 and 1986, against 23 per cent growth in the state sector. The collective units were becoming larger and more productive, and their total share of industrial output rose in the same period from 19 to 29 per cent. No longer regarded as a necessary legacy of 'bourgeois right'—as Zhang Chunqiao had argued in his famous 1975 polemic—they were now seen as an often more productive alternative to the comparable state-owned enterprise. In the retail and service trade, the increase in privately owned small shops and trades was even more striking. The number of private owners or employees grew from 4 per cent in 1978 to just under 50 per cent in 1986, accounting for more than one-sixth of total business. Everyday urban life had been transformed by the return of private restaurants, cobblers, bicycle repair shops, small food and clothes shops, and pedlars. By the end of this period, it was agreed not only that the private sector could coexist with the state sector, but that it provided healthy competition and could create new jobs more cheaply than if funded by the state. Some economists wrote of a 'multi-ownership system' in which private and public enterprise learnt from each other—for example, state shops were forced to provide better customer service to compete with the private sector, while private businesses copied the state sector's provision of labour insurance for their employees. Attempts were made to define an acceptable proportion of state to collective to private enterprise in the retail industry—the ratio of 5:3:2 was suggested.

The new entrepreneurs

By the mid-1980s, economic thinking had reached the point where for the first time a distinction could be made between 'ownership' and 'management', borrowing from the capitalist system where the two are usually separated. The great error of the past, said the Central Committee in October 1984, had been to equate the concept of 'ownership by the whole people' with 'management by the state institutions'. Reform in the countryside had already handed over management of the land to the peasant while reserving the title of the land to the collective. Why should a government department—a ministry or provincial bureau—run a factory as well as own it? Real ownership 'by the whole people' meant letting them manage affairs at their own workplaces (or at least find a capable managerial team to do so for them), the 1984 resolution argued.

The well-spring of vitality of the enterprise lies in the initiative, wisdom, and creativeness of its workers by hand and brain. These can only be brought into play when the status of the working people as masters of their own enterprise is guaranteed by its rules and regulations and when their labour is closely linked with their own material benefits. This has been vividly and convincingly proved by our experience in rural reform. In restructuring the urban economy, it is imperative to handle correctly the relationship of the workers and staff to their enterprise so that they are its real masters and can work as such at their jobs.

The most important and controversial reform to flow from this decision was the attempt to give the factory director full responsibility for management, while the Party and state, whether represented by the factory committee or by local government organs, ceased to 'interfere'. In theory this would leave their hands free to concentrate on larger questions of economic policies, principles, and plans. In practice the reform could easily offend vested interests in the bureaucracy.

This 'separation of ownership from management power' was called a breakthrough in traditional economic theory. Adapting the responsibility system from agriculture, it was proposed that managers should sign contracts with the state with their incomes pegged to the profitability of their enterprise. They would no longer 'eat in the state canteen'. The new policy required several provisos. Managers must reinvest part of their profits rather than distribute them entirely as income. It was also necessary 'to avoid indiscriminate price increases, shoddy building, scrimping on materials, or any other illicit means of increasing income'. The managers sometimes found that, in spite of the new policy, underlying relationships of power had hardly changed. Some complained that they had to accept over-staffing and incompetent performance while taking the blame for its economic consequences. It was quite usual to find whole families at work in the same factory—work allocation in the past was often based on family connections—who formed powerful 'clans'. Managers resented their responsibility for social welfare, traditionally based upon the place of work. 'When you're a factory manager', said one, 'you have to take care of everything: what the workers eat, where they live, their medical care, birth, ageing, sickness, and death. . . . How much energy can you have left for production and business?'

But management reform in spite of these difficulties was regarded as essential for the more than 800 large and medium enterprises which account for over 40 per cent of total industrial production. The first priority of the Seventh Five-Year Plan (1985–9), said Premier Zhao Ziyang, was 'to make socialist producers and managers wholly and truly independent, self-managing, and solely responsible for their own profits and losses'. The reform was carried further for smaller factories and many shops which could now be leased outright to their managers, thus reducing what the *Economic Daily* called 'the "government-run" feeling that businesses of this kind often have' (26 June 1987). Critics still claimed that this was opening the door to capitalism. A woman manager in Benxi in the north-east became the subject of national debate in 1987, after leasing a total of eight food stores in the space of two years. She employed 1,000 workers and soon dominated food sales in the town, paying herself an income equivalent to twenty times the average worker's wages. The arguments were deployed for and against:

Against: Guan Guangmei may work hard, but who does not? The manager of any business or factory is as busy every day, doing his best for his enterprises, his workers, and the state. But their salaries are only two or three times that of their workers. Why should she earn so much?

For: It should be remembered that she took over the business on contract, with six guarantors . . . and assumes full financial liability. If her profit falls below the level stipulated in the lease agreement she has to pay the difference herself, so she takes a high risk. Anyone who cannot accept the fact of her high income should tender for the business himself and make his fortune! (*Economic Daily*, 16 June 1987)

Mrs Guan was an 'entrepreneur', a term previously unknown in Chinese socialist economics but now increasingly valued. Directors and managers before, said the *People's Daily*, had been 'simply government officials with no freedom to make management decisions independently'. Now they had the opportunity to become entrepreneurs 'through competition, taking risks and demonstrating ability'. Studies were made of the role of the entrepreneurial manager in the West, from his nineteenth-century origins when ownership first became separated from management to today. The entrepreneurial manager played the key role, it was said, both in small risk-taking enterprises which were in the vanguard of scientific research, and in the multinationals which were 'the most advanced form of production'. Modern entrepreneurs were 'a group of brilliant people', and a country with foresight should 'go all out to develop the enterprise economy' (*People's Daily*, 30 May 1985).

   By 1985–6 the reform of ownership was hovering on the brink of restoration of shareholding and the stock-market—potent political symbols of economic collapse 'before the Liberation', and easily represented by contemporary critics as 'restoring capitalism'. Experiments were launched in Shenyang and Shanghai, and leaders in Beijing gave a warm welcome to the chairman of the New York Stock Exchange. The rationale was that industrial autonomy from the state as ultimate owner would only work if industry was able to raise the bulk of its own funds for investment and improvement. Bank loans and retention of profits would not necessarily suffice. If markets were now allowed in commodities, technology, and labour, why should there not be a 'socialist financial market?' The first experiments involved mostly small companies whose shares were bought for dividend income rather than speculation. Many shareholders—over 90 per cent in Shanghai in the first year—were employees of the company concerned for whom dividends became a concealed form of extra bonus. With such 'dividends' ranging between 30 and 100 per cent of share value, there were schemes to fix maximum levels and to tax the payments. There were also more ambitious plans. 'What is needed', said the *Workers' Daily* (16 Oct. 1986), 'is for a large number of well-established, influential state enterprises to enter a large-scale top-level share market. This market should also include stocks and shares issued by State banks.'

The problem of prices

The most immediate point of contact with the economic reforms for most Chinese was not management or share-owning but prices. As elsewhere in the state socialist world, while the reformers regarded price reform as 'the key to the reform of the entire economic structure' (Central Committee Decision, October 1984), the public regarded it more often as a threat to living standards. They were prepared to accept higher wages but not higher prices, complained the reformers: a 1986 survey showed that 56 per cent of the population of working age believed that 'preserving stable, unchanging prices is what gives socialism its superiority'. The percentage was largest among the poorly educated, workers, the elderly, and others with low incomes (*Guangming Daily*, 12 March 1987).

The most puzzling phenomenon is that though many people have benefited from price reform, they still think it is better to return to the old days when neither prices nor wages rose. This poses a new task to reformers: how to educate people to be better psychologically prepared for a more changeable and unstable society. (*China Daily*, 7 Sept. 1987)

The purpose of price reform was twofold: to cut down on state subsidies and (more important but less visibly) to stimulate competitive efficiency among manufacturers. The increase in urban wages and in state purchase prices for rural products in the late 1970s had led to a consumption boom which sharply increased the state's burden of subsidies. The cost of keeping down market prices rose 50 per cent from 1980 to 1981. Subsidies of all kinds (including housing and transport) occupied nearly 30 per cent of state budget expenditure. The news of impending price increases led to panic buying not only of daily necessities such as cooking oil and toilet paper but of quality consumer goods, such as TVs and videos, which should not have been affected. Most urban dwellers were given compensatory subsidies to ease the transition, but these could not match the price increases or keep up with the resulting inflation.

The reformers were in a familiar dilemma: 'As soon as they relax, there is chaos,' went a popular comment on the situation, 'and as soon as there is chaos they draw back.' In theoretical terms it could fairly be argued by Xue Muqiao that problems were to be expected in a transitional period while the old and new systems, regulated and free-market prices, coexisted. But popular trust in the long-term future was hard to generate: the reality of inflation was compounded by visible evidence of corruption and profiteering. In a message to the first issue of *China Consumer News*, Xue Muqiao recounted a familiar tale:

In one small town, I found that Da Qianmen cigarettes were unavailable in the shops but were offered outside by street sellers at ten cents above the fixed price, on condition that one packet of otherwise unsaleable cigarettes should be bought at the same time. I asked if the sellers all had permits and was assured that they had. I then asked why the [relevant] bureau was not dealing with the matter. The whispered reply—after a few moments of hesitation—was that the vendors were all relatives of cadres in the Bureau and the state-run shops. They were not only not prevented from this practice, but were even informed whenever a new shipment of the cigarettes arrived. The shops could sell off their entire stock immediately at the retail price, increasing turnover and profits so that they even won prizes. (*People's Daily*, 10 Oct. 1985)

In August 1987 a drive against speculators was launched in Beijing, spreading rapidly throughout the country, with the 'Mr Fixers' who siphoned state goods to the market via the backdoor as prime targets. Price ceilings were also reimposed on some produce. The result was a fall in prices—and in supplies. Many farmers feared that they would be labelled as speculators, while the lower prices offered little reward. Cucumbers, eggplants, tomatoes, and chillies disappeared overnight from the Beijing markets. The price ceilings had to be scrapped within a month.

Land and housing was another sensitive area affected by price reform. In the villages, where the peasants had mostly owned their own houses throughout the political changes of the 1960s; the agricultural boom caused a rash of new building which aroused the envy of town dwellers. Municipal housing authorities now looked for schemes to raise more funds. Town dwellers might live in poor accommodation, they argued, but they paid next to nothing and improvements must be geared to outright sales or higher rents. In 1987 the State Council's housing research office called for the sale of all new housing and market-price rents for the older stock. As incomes rose, average rents had fallen from the already low figure of 2.6 per cent of family income in 1964 to just over 1 per cent twenty years later. A Tianjin newspaper described some of the problems:

Who wants to buy when you can get a home virtually free from the state and there is the fear of losing a private home in another political campaign? For a long time, people have developed an attitude they don't want to change: Under socialism, you do not spend money on buying a home. On people's shopping lists are a colour television, a refrigerator, a set of furniture—but not a home.[10]

The well-off city of Yantai in Shandong province served as the model for a new scheme in which rents were raised sharply and those least able to pay were given temporary subsidies. But cadres who had benefited most under the old system—since they were allocated more living space than others at the subsidized rates—lobbied to exempt their own dwellings from the reforms. Another scheme for land sales (technically speaking, the sale of 'the right to use' land) to industry was pioneered in the Special Economic Zone of Shenzhen adjoining the Hong Kong border.[11]

The real battle over prices took place not in the market or housing bureau but in industry, where most goods previously allocated by the state at fixed prices were now bought and sold under looser or no controls. The 1984 decision had been described as establishing 'a new system which can reflect more sensitively the supply and demand of the market, changes in labour productivity, and which can satisfy better the needs of economic development' (Outlook, 3 Feb. 1986). A dual system of prices developed for raw materials, which might be supplied at a controlled price for production falling within the state plan but were otherwise allowed to find their market level. The new entrepreneurial managers were supposed to make rational decisions on investment and output, based upon real costs of production and materials. They should respond to higher prices of raw materials and wages not by turning to the state for subsidies, but by 'reducing costs through technological innovation and selling goods at competitive prices' (*China Daily*, 15 Oct. 1987). Here, too, the 'transition' proved painful. In practice the state still underwrote most industrial and manufacturing operations, although increasingly at local rather than national level. Instead of competition among enterprises, there was competition among local authorities for control of raw materials and markets. 'Enterprises don't take responsibility for increased costs of production', said the economist Dong Fureng (*Washington Post*, 12 March 1987). 'They just ask for an increase in the price of the products they sell.' Planners now favoured more sophisticated forms of price liberalization. These included 'floating' prices with upper and lower limits fixed by the state, and 'authorized' prices where the producer submitted a cost-plus-profit price for approval. Paradoxically, such a system required more subtle state intervention at a time when the role of the state was supposed to be weakened and was already less effective.

The triumph of 'reform'

At the Thirteenth Party Congress in October 1987, the various strands of economic reform of the 1980s were drawn together to form a strong new 'line' of what was still claimed to be a socialist strategy. Reform was not just a mechanism for making socialism work. It was what socialism was about at this early stage in its history. This 'primary stage of China's socialism', which would last until the middle of the twenty-first century, was dominated by the transformation of China from

an agricultural country, where farming is based on manual labour and where people engaged in agriculture constitute the majority of the population . . . into a modern industrial country where non-agricultural workers constitute the majority. . . . The fundamental task of a socialist society is to expand the productive forces. During this primary stage we must shake off poverty and backwardness, and it is therefore especially necessary for us to put the expansion of the productive forces at the centre of all our work. Helping to expand the productive forces should become the point of departure in our consideration of all problems. (Zhao Ziyang, *Report to Congress*)

The new approaches to ownership and planning worked out in the past few years were now elaborated in more systematic theory. Zhao was praised in the media for having for the first time given a clear definition of the 'private sector': a sector which involves wage labour and is a useful supplement to the public sector. This sector should be encouraged to expand, along with various forms of co-operative ownership and management. Industrial output value of the private sector only accounted for a mere 0.6 per cent of the national total, and this was not enough (*Xinhua News Agency*, 29 Oct. 1987). The economists were urged by Zhao to explore further in an area where, he admitted, not much was yet known about its contradictions and laws. Discussion was also encouraged on the nature of the private sector, although the Xinhua agency report explained somewhat naively that this was 'rarely covered by the media to avoid confusion in people's ideology'.

The preferred phrase for state planning was now state 'regulation', using indirect means which were based upon the real value of production and proper reward for good management. In a new formula, it was said that 'the state regulates the market, and the market guides enterprises'. Less than 50 per cent of industrial output was now subject to state planning, said Zhao, and before long this would be much further reduced. Zhao also elaborated upon the various ways in which management could be separated from formal state ownership: entering into contracts between enterprises and/or managers and the state, giving them a financial stake in success to encourage 'entrepreneurship', involving workers and staff in management, selling shares in enterprises, and so on. As one government official told foreign bankers at a conference just after the congress, ways must be found to 'build up a mechanism by which [management] responsibility, power, and profits are closely knit' (*China Daily* on Business Leaders Symposium, 10 Nov. 1987).

For the first time since the break with the Soviet Union, the Chinese again saw themselves as part of an international phenomenon: that of the socialist countries which were in differing degrees breaking away from 'leftist centralized planning' and embarking upon a 'new economic policy'. China, they said, had started with a double handicap. It had to tackle not only the familiar problems of all socialist countries—bureaucracy, low efficiency, and dogmatism—but also those of all developing countries, such as lack of skilled administrators, low educational level, rapidly growing population, and shortage of funds and materials. Yet, argued the economic reformers to whom Zhao Ziyang's report gave a new and brighter green light, this double handicap was a unique challenge. If poor and backward China could succeed, would this not be an even more glorious proof of 'the superiority of socialism' over capitalism than the reformation of the other socialist countries which had started from a higher level of development? (*Beijing Review*, 16 Nov. 1987). Statements of this kind, carrying a powerful echo of Mao's belief in the virtue of being 'poor and blank', indicated a continuing need to present new policies in an optimistic millenarian framework not so very different from the one offered by the Hua Guofeng leadership when it relaunched the 'Four Modernizations'.

More often the word 'socialism' was ignored altogether, particularly in discussions of the relationship between China and the world economy (see Chapter 11, below). In the countryside, where changes in economic policy offended fewer bureaucratic interests and could proceed with less direct supervision from central Party authorities, the post-Mao reforms had already come close to demolishing the entire structure of what were previously regarded as the 'socialist relations of production'.

7

Peasant China Transformed
The rise of rural enterprise

The old village houses are built in rows with packed mud walls, tamped mud floor, and a thick thatched roof now dripping in the spring rain. Small children peer out of front doors, buffalo and oxen huddle close to the back doors. A few chickens scurry in the liquid mud. We pick our way carefully to the higher ground, where there is the beginnings of a new housing estate. Mr Yang, the richest man in the village, has built a two storey stone-walled house with a tiled roof and balcony. Mr Yang makes so much money from 'sideline production'—selling pigs, tobacco, and vegetables over and above his grain quota—that the villagers call him 'Mr Five Dollars Everytime He Opens the Door'. There is a couplet outside his door, written on red paper and pasted on both sides in the traditional style for Chinese New Year:

> Better live among men than in paradise dream,
> Better farm my own patch than work in a Team.

Mr Yang is the head of a Ten Thousand Yuan household in one of the villages of Fengyang county, Anhui province. Once notorious for its beggars who roamed as far as the streets of Shanghai, Fengyang has benefited from the new Agricultural Responsibility System. This allocates the land to individual families and allows them to work it as they choose, after paying taxes and fulfilling a quota of grain to the state. Mr Yang has just returned from a congratulatory conference for Advanced Peasants at the provincial capital, where he was also given a free bicycle. We splosh through the mud to another stone house, with a wall around for privacy, which Mr Yang has built for his eldest daughter and new husband. The couplet outside it reads:

> My new tiled house is bright and clean,
> Here comes the cart with our sewing machine!

Inside there is an amazing sight. Eight young women and eight sewing machines are crammed into one room, receiving instruction from Mr Yang's daughter. The idea is to establish a small work-shop for making clothes. Sewing machines are eagerly sought after by peasants just beginning to acquire the money to become more conscious of clothes. Officials in the county town are discussing how to import dressmaking and hair-cutting expertise from the big city. It is 1982: the People's Commune of Kaocheng in Fengyang county is being abolished 'experimentally'. Every other province has been instructed to set up a similar experiment, and the whole of China will follow within little more than a year.

(From a visit in Febuary 1982)

The fading of the communes

China's second rural revolution began cautiously within three years of Mao's death, but by 1983 had demolished the essential structure of the People's Communes and had largely reversed the philosophy of collective labour and reward on which they were based. At first, attempts were made to reconcile the new 'Agricultural Responsibility System' and its associated reforms with the spirit of the past; later that spirit was sweepingly rejected. Both were political overstatements. The truth was that the People's Communes in their modified form after the disasters of the Great Leap did provide a basis for rural development which was slow but consistent with the socialist goals of the time. The post-1980 system, which at first returned to the more cautious co-operative policies of the mid-1950s but soon led to the effective privatization of the land, encouraged much faster rural growth, but its negative effect upon social cohesion was beginning to be assessed by the late 1980s. Whether the communes, if properly managed, could have provided a smoother path, was now an unrealistic question. In rural as in industrial policy, the state and its cadres had proved unable to provide the sophisticated leadership required for a unified system of management. The

Great Leap and Cultural Revolution bias against free markets and sideline production meant that at best most peasants had enough to eat but were always short of money. In some areas, as the Chinese sociologist Fei Xiaotong has observed, the situation had begun to improve by the early 1970s with the development of commune and rural-run industry. But it was too late. Most Chinese peasants were no longer willing to be mobilized for 'hard struggle' without more immediate returns, and had been alienated by dogmatic policies restricting initiative and flouting rural common sense. Fei writes of a relatively well-to-do area in the Yangtze valley which he had studied since the 1930s:

Peasant incentives for economic production were drastically reduced by the combined effects of several policies: first, the policy of promoting grain production at the expense of sideline occupations and rural industries; second, the increased power of higher level cadres unacquainted with local conditions, leading to arbitrary bureaucratic command from the top; and third, the leftist emphasis on the doctrine of absolute egalitarianism. As a consequence, the rate of increase in grain production declined from the 8.25 per cent figure of 1966 to 3.95 per cent by 1976. Even these small increases were cancelled out by increases in the population. The average income in 1976 thus lingered around 114 yuan, with no increase from the 1966 level.[1]

China in the 1980s was still a cereal-based culture where 'eating food' was synonymous with 'eating grain', and where it was a mark of real dedication to duty to 'let one's bowl of rice grow cold'. No matter what improvements had been made in health, education, and the provision of consumer goods, progress still had to be measured by the yardstick of grain output. The average annual increase from 1952 to 1957 was 3.5 per cent, and during the next two decades fell to only 2 per cent (46.8 per cent overall). Even these gains were nullified by the increase in population. The Chinese nation grew from 646 million in 1957 to 958 million in 1978, a rise of over 48 per cent, which meant that grain consumption remained unchanged over the long term. Other necessities showed a similar pattern. Consumption of cloth rose by 76 per cent in the first period, but actually declined by 8 per cent in the next two decades, even though output increased by 32 per cent. This slow progress must be set in the context of improving life expectation (from 57 years in 1957 to 68 in 1978) and a decline in infant mortality from 139 per 1,000 in 1954 to 20 per 1,000 in 1980. Yet even this figure cannot be recorded without also observing that the Great Leap Forward led, according to the best calculations, to more than 19 million 'excess deaths'—

that is, those who died outright of starvation or ahead of expectation as a result of severely reduced diet. (Higher figures often quoted of 30 or even 40 million are misleading, because they include—sometimes without explanation—an estimate of the reduction of births which was also caused by food shortage.)[2]

In some parts of China life had hardly improved overall since Liberation. A survey in 1977 showed that the level of production in 200 out of some 2,000 counties was not far from that of the early 1950s. Most were located in the backward north-west and south-west. At the other end of the scale, the most advanced production brigades, with an average per capita income in 1979 of over 300 yuan (£60) occupied less than 2.5 per cent of the total number of brigades. Over half of these were located on the outskirts of cities, and one-quarter were located on the periphery of Shanghai alone. Over these detailed statistics hung the largest one of all; agriculture had to sustain four-fifths of the Chinese population, and yet since 1949 it had created only one-third of the total value of industrial and agricultural output. A labour force of 400 million people, plus the aged and the young, were crowded on to a limited area of arable land (10.4 per cent of the total national territory) which had actually declined in the past decade.

In 1979–80 the traveller in China began to encounter two sights which had been rarities for over a decade. The rural fair was no longer infrequent and tightly controlled by local authorities, zealous to 'cut off the capitalist tails' of any peasants too keen to make a profit. Chinese officials were no longer embarrassed if the foreigner witnessed the scene. (The Italian film-maker Antonioni had been denounced in 1973 for filming a rare roadside market. He also filmed, the *People's Daily* complained, 'a tiresome succession of laboured shots of small plots, lonely old people, exhausted draught animals, and dilapidated houses'.) Most localities now reverted to the regular market dates based upon the old rural ten-day week (markets would be held on, say, the 3rd, 13th, and 23rd of each month). The other sight was the urban free market where peasants sold their produce—eggs, chickens, peanuts, and vegetables—grown mostly on private plots. It provided welcome variety to the diet of urban dwellers and was sufficiently profitable for peasants to travel up to 50 miles from the countryside, sleeping overnight on their carts before the market opened in the early morning.

Restoration of the rural and urban markets, coupled with expansion of the size of private plots which thus generated the surpluses for sale, was one of the main decisions taken by the Central Committee's Third Plenum in

December 1978 which opened up the new course of reform under Deng Xiaoping's leadership. The Plenum also announced that the state would increase the grain purchase price by 20 per cent, with an additional 50 per cent for grain purchased above the quota, and would raise prices for another sixteen staple items. There would be a shift away from the 'one-sided emphasis on grain production' which had been fostered during the Cultural Revolution when peasants were expected to 'Take Grain as the Key Link', and diversification into cash crops and 'sideline' products would be encouraged. New regulations also prohibited local officials from commandeering peasant labour and funds without proper payment, and provided for democratic management of the communes and for public accounting. All these reforms went no further than to correct some of the excesses brought about by the Cultural Revolution and to restore the more flexible policies of the early 1960s. Official belief in the superiority of the 'Large and Public' organization of agricultural production was still widespread. As recently as November 1977, it had been decided to prepare about 10 per cent of the nation's production brigades for 'unified accounting' (that is, to abolish the financial autonomy of the smaller production teams and handle the accounts at the brigade level). The Plenum countered this tendency by reasserting that the 'system of three levels of ownership with the production team as the basic accounting unit . . . should remain unchanged'.

Within four years the new rural revolution would effectively lower the 'level' of accounting for most productive activity to the household, would divide up the land on a long-term basis, and would remove most administrative powers of the commune, brigade, and team. None of this was even hinted at in the Plenum's decision. 'In a series of changes which gathered pace after 1978', wrote the British economist Peter Nolan, 'the rural institutional structure was transformed in as profound a fashion as occurred in the mid-fifties in the "Socialist High Tide". The difference is that this time the Party was *responding to* rather than *leading* the peasant masses.'[3] This voluntarist interpretation of what occurred is essentially true. The new 'rural responsibility system' was at first introduced in a limited form, and was only intended to apply to a minority of areas. Instead, its more radical version spread to 90 per cent of the peasant population. Yet it seems likely that for a small number of leaders and their advisers this was the original intention all along, and their initial silence was necessary to avoid conservative criticism.

In 1979 the Central Committee circulated a document on the 'responsibility system' which emphasized that 'different forms of management should be allowed to coexist in the light of local conditions'. The word 'management' was technically correct. All the 'means of production'—land, and at this stage all machinery, tools, and animals—still belonged to the collective team which continued to 'manage' agricultural production by assigning work to team members. The difference was that production tasks now began to be assigned to smaller groups of peasants, and that their reward was based largely upon performance of those tasks. As one of the early accounts explained:

The general practice is to reduce the size of the labour groups in the production team, which is currently the basic accounting unit in the countryside and which is in charge of twenty to thirty households. A group formed voluntarily by several peasant households or individual peasants' households, or single peasants regularly makes a contract to undertake a certain production task with the production team. According to the terms of the contract, the contractor has certain rights and responsibilities. He is paid for his actual work and will be awarded for overfulfilling production targets and will compensate for reduced production, so as to ensure more pay for more work.

In its least radical form, the contract was made with a group of households for a precisely defined quota of a particular crop, with all the necessary tools, fertilizer, and so on supplied by the collective. This was called 'fixing output quotas based on the group' (*bao chan dao zu*). The other extreme was not just to make the contract with a single household (*bao chan dao hu*), but to extend its scope. The household only needed to supply a relatively small proportion of produce to the collective, which could be regarded as a form of tax. It was still supposed to grow only those crops specified in the contract, but it bought or hired all the necessary inputs for itself, and made its own arrangements for selling the surplus produce. This system was called 'fixing work based on the household' (*bao gan dao hu*).

At first these measures were in theory applied on a sliding scale, with the most radical forms of assigning production responsibility reserved for those areas which were judged to be least advanced. In spring and summer of 1980 Party leaders toured rural China to investigate the changes. In October a Central Committee directive acknowledged that 'all forms of responsibility system can be adopted including the household contract'. But the assignment of *work* to the household (*bao gan dao hu*) was judged to be only suitable 'in the poor and backward areas' which accounted for less than 20 per cent of rural China, and was not needed 'where the development of production is normal'. At the end of 1981 the Central Committee was still insisting that 'allotting work to individual labourers, households, or production groups . . . is suitable only in places where scattered operations or management are most needed'. Orthodoxy was preserved by insisting on the 'superiority' of collective management at a higher level wherever the conditions were already 'ripe'.

By 1983 this assumption had been abandoned. Household contracts had replaced team contracts among 97 per cent of the rural population, and nine out of ten adopted the most radical form of full contracted responsibility (*bao gan*). This was not all: peasants were now able to buy their own 'means of production'—tractors, and so on—directly from the manufacturer. They could also buy or hire them from the collective. The prohibition on the hire of labour had also been lifted. A 1982 regulation cautiously allowed peasants to hire 'five labourers and two apprentices', but even this restriction was later relaxed. A revolution in rural government was also under way. The People's Communes lost their administrative powers and became units of economic management alone. They were replaced by 'township' governments, reverting to the situation before the People's Communes, in a process completed by March 1985.[4]

The Fengyang experiment

Two provinces had taken the lead from 1979 onwards, going far beyond the cautious approval from Beijing for their experiments in rural reform. They were chosen for their extremes: populous and fertile Sichuan was guided by its first Party Secretary Zhao Ziyang—shortly to move to the centre as Premier; Anhui, where large pockets of poverty had persisted into the 1970s, was run by another ally of Deng Xiaoping, Wan Li (later Vice-Premier). Their successes gave rise to a peasant jingle: 'If you want some *liang* (grain) ask for Ziyang; if you want to have *mi* (rice) look for Wan Li.'

One of the first models to emerge publicly was Fengyang county in central Anhui, an area of traditional hardship which had generated a much older rhyme:

> Who has not heard of Fengyang's fame,
> From where the first Ming emperor came?
> His folk took all the land, and then
> Fengyang had famine, nine years in ten.

In the year before Liberation, half the population of Fengyang went outside the county begging or looking for work. Local statistics showed a rapid improvement after land reform, with grain production rising from 99 million to 260 million *jin* (catty or half-kilo) in 1955. But the People's Communes caused complete confusion, local peasants would recall (when visited by this writer in 1982).[5] At first the peasants were not allowed to keep a single catty of grain at home, and free food for everyone was handed out from the apparently overflowing public granary. The grain soon ran out, and before long people were eating dog to survive. In the years 1959–61, out of a population of 380,000, more than 60,000 died 'in an irregular manner'— the usual euphemism for starvation. Local officials issued travel permits to let peasants go outside the county to beg for food (as late as 1978, Fengyang beggars still knocked on doors in Shanghai). Grain output recovered slowly, reaching a high of 360 million *jin* in 1977 but falling back to 295 million *jin* in the drought year of 1978. Looking back, Fengyang people conceded that collective labour for construction work did lead to improved fertility: three reservoirs were constructed to irrigate two-thirds of the land. But they described the collective organization of production as inefficient and wasteful. 'We went out to work like a lazy dragon [in a long shuffling dragon's "tail"] but we came back from work like a gust of wind!' While they were in the fields, the peasants recalled, 'we did our jobs all raggle-taggle, just as if we were working for a foreign boss' (slowing down the moment the cadres were not looking).

The system of reward for work was also severely criticized: How could local cadres organize anything between 60 and 120 peasants to work efficiently, record the results, and then assign work-points which distinguished adequately between those who made more and less effort? One exasperated team cadre recounted the difficulties:

I have tried the system of assigning work-points to quotas. I spent a lot of energy making different rules for how many work-points there should be if one does this kind or that kind of work and if one performs a certain amount of work. In the case of ploughing, for instance, the rules for work-points differed depending on whether one used a strong or weak buffalo, or one of average strength. Even for the same kind of buffalo, there were also different kinds of land, and for the same type of land, the case was also different if it had rained or if the soil was dry . . . With so many rules, it was almost endless. If they were printed into a book, it would be quite a thick edition. They were so elaborate the peasants were not interested at all.[6]

Difficulties of this kind had been cited occasionally during the Cultural Revolution as further reason for adopting the 'Dazhai system' of work-points. (At the model Dazhai Brigade in Shanxi province, the only task distinction was between heavy and light work. Work-points were 'self-assessed' and recorded no more frequently than every three days—sometimes only every five or ten, visitors were told in 1971.) Even if this really happened, everyone admitted that it required 'a high level of political consciousness' which had not yet been achieved in most parts of the countryside. In Fengyang and many other places, realistic assessment of work-points caused too much strife, so cadres were tempted to narrow the differentials. The hard worker might get ten points but the lazy would still get seven or eight. Favouritism was also shown towards relatives and friends, and cadres were suspected of exploiting their control of resources. (In one commune the peasants stood around while a grain-processing plant burnt down, saying 'Good! Our cadres' wine-cups have turned to ashes!') The high number of bonus work-points allocated to full-time cadres who did no productive work was also criticized. A production team leader earned 7,000 points worth 700 yuan at a time when the average annual cash income was only 70 yuan.

By the Chinese New Year in 1982 the new responsibility system had been installed throughout Anhui province in its most radical *bao gan* form, with the land parcelled out to individual households. Allocation was made according to the size of a household or the number of adult 'labour power' or a combination of both. It was usually divided into several patches providing a mixture of more and less fertile land located nearer to or further from the village. Title remained with the collective team and a 'readjustment' was promised within five years to account for changes in family size. Every household possessed its *hetong shu* or 'contract book', sitting on the mantel-piece in a shiny red plastic cover. It recorded the area of allocated land, expected yield, sown acreage and prescribed quotas of the main crop, as well as deductions including payment to collective welfare and accumulation funds. Average disposable income had risen from 70 yuan in 1978 to 197 yuan in 1981. (One-third of the increase was attributed to the rise in state purchase prices, the rest to the reforms.) Five per cent of the rural house-holds were estimated to be still in difficulty because of age or sickness, and received welfare aid.

The first trial 'separation of powers' anywhere in China was also put into effect in Kaocheng Commune within Fengyang county. In a vivid phrase, the previous system combining administrative, economic, and political power was described as 'one man wearing three pairs of trousers'. The commune was now turned into a marketing and production company to manage the various collective rural factories and other enterprises. Administration was in the hands of a reconstituted *xiang* ('township') government. The intermediate-level 'brigades' had been abolished. The village 'teams' survived to administer the responsibility system, although with reduced powers. The Party branch was now supposed to stick to education and propaganda, leaving policy to the *xiang* government and production to the peasant. People spoke frankly about the basic problem: under the new system, explained one supporter, 'the bureaucracy from which we have suffered so much may still exist. But if it is separated from production, then it cannot harm the peasants so much.' The cadres themselves admitted they had been reluctant at first to see their political power reduced, but they were now free from 'aggravation' and had more time to 'make money'. In Fengyang and elsewhere it was noticeable that many cadres belonged to the most successful entrepreneurial families. (According to a 1984 survey in Shanxi province, 43 per cent of affluent peasants were either current or former cadres.)[7]

The privatization of land

The abolition of the People's Communes as the basic administrative unit in the countryside was part of a second surge of reform which meant that the Chinese peasant now owned his land in practice and controlled the major means of production, legally owning some of them as well. The purpose was not simply to liberate peasant initiative but to stimulate market forces in the countryside and pave the way for a commercialized agriculture. The original 'responsibility system', even when extended beyond the poorest minority for which it was at first intended, had still stressed the role of the collective in allocating land and equipment and of the state in setting quotas. Both principles were sensationally undermined in successive years by the Party Central Committee's 'Document No. 1' on agriculture, by custom the first directive to appear every New Year. Document No. 1 for 1984, it was explained, was drawn up in the face of 'remnants of Leftist influence' with the explicit aim of 'doing everything to make the peasants rich'. To this end it stipulated (*a*) that peasants should be allowed to hold contracted land for a period of at least fifteen years; and (*b*) that contracted land might be transferred from one household to another. The longer lease of contracted land was intended to encourage peasant lessees to invest more labour and capital to develop its productivity rather than to milk the soil dry of fertility for the sake of short-term gains (and for fear that the land might be taken away from the lessee again after five years or less). But it also reinforced the assumption that the land was now individually owned, even though title still belonged in theory to the 'team'. The term was further extended for hilly land, which in 1983 began to be parcelled out to peasant households on a 'from generation to generation' basis. They could not be expected, it was said, to plant timber on the hillsides unless they could be sure that their descendants would enjoy its benefit.

The provision for transfer of land holdings was intended to encourage the concentration of land in the hands of those most able to farm it efficiently, while other peasants would give up cultivation altogether and work in the expanding sector of rural industry and commerce. The transaction was supposed to be handled by the collective, but money would still change hands. Transfer would be accompanied by the payment of 'proper compensation' on the basis of the original land price 'appraised according to its grade'.

A year later the Central Committee issued another directive which was described as 'setting free the rural economy'. The new policy shifted the emphasis from state planning to market demand, in particular by abolishing all purchasing quotas except for grain and cotton. Prices of other agricultural goods were also to be allowed to float on the free market. An increasing number of peasant producers were now becoming 'specialized households', concentrating their effort upon the marketing of a particular crop or product. Some were 'contracted' to produce for the collective, producing cash crops or livestock which previously would have been directly managed by the team or brigade. Specialized households grew fruit trees, flowers, and medicinal herbs; cultivated tea and raised pigs, chicken, and fish; leased agricultural machinery from the collective to process farm produce. An increasing number were known as 'self-managing'. They had no contractual obligation to the collective except to pay taxes, and they purchased their own equipment and other means of production. By the end of 1983, there were nearly 25 million specialized households in China, accounting for 13.6 per cent of all rural households.[8]

By the mid-1980s, the dividing line between specialized households which were still loosely within the collective sector and private businesses outside it was becoming blurred. The 1985 document now encouraged the sale of state-owned vehicles and boats which were lying idle to the specialized households. Allowing peasants to own such means of production had been official policy since mid-1983 after a much-publicized case where local officials in Hunan province confiscated trucks and tractors bought privately, on the grounds that it was 'encouraging capitalism'. Such owner-ship was now described as forming part of 'the private sector of the national economy which is supplementary to the socialist economy'. As this sector expanded, the restrictions on it were relaxed. Reformers now accepted the 'capitalist' label placed on it by critics, admitting that 'when hiring of labour exceeds a certain limit, they become capitalist enterprises'. By the end of 1985 over four-and-a-quarter million rural households came within this sector, owning their own tractors, trucks, and machines. Private and collective ownership now coexisted side by side. The reformers argued that such enterprises would still remain smaller in scale than during the 1950s, when the socialist state was easily able to keep national capitalism 'under control'. Yet the growth of the private sector threatened to undermine the con-ventional wisdom that new collective forms of production, more genuine and popular than those of the People's Communes, would emerge in time spontaneously out of the responsibility system. 'The development of the collective economy', Deng Xiaoping had said in 1980, 'continues to be our general objective.'[9] Local officials in Fujian province in 1983 went further:

Deng Xiaoping has made it clear that the new forms of organization contained in the responsibility system are only satisfactory for the present time. As for the future, we still have to investigate how it can be developed. We have only just made a beginning—it is not clear where we shall go next—but we do know that we cannot return to the old system. We also know that we have to create a new spirit of enthusiasm and a new form of collective.[10]

The Twelfth Party Congress in 1982 had pointed the way: in the not too distant future, it predicted, many forms of peasant co-operatives would appear as 'the main economic formation' in the countryside. It was believed that these new forms would arise organically out of small-scale peasant specialized production, as peasants came to appreciate the advantages of genuine co-operation instead of the enforced collectivization of the past. Such co-operatives did emerge, often replacing operations previously run by the collective (such as orchards and piggeries) and allowing peasant families to invest money as well as—or instead of—their labour, thus creating 'shares'. (This led to charges of capitalism which were answered with the argument that the money invested had accumulated from the peasants' own labour and was not 'capital' from 'capitalists who rely upon exploitation'.) Yet it was increasingly recognized that peasant entrepreneurship could

equally well head into the private field, and must be regulated by government control rather than self-regulated by co-operative management. 'China
has a long history of agricultural family operation', noted one agricultural
journal in 1984, 'which has displayed a surprisingly stubborn vitality.'[11]

The rise of rural industry

By the late 1980s a second rural revolution was under way which went far
beyond land cultivation and the reorganization of agricultural production.
The Great Leap Forward into rural-based industrialization had at last taken
off, a quarter of a century after its over-ambitious beginnings in 1958. By
1985, wrote one observer, 'independent rural enterprises employed seventy
million people, 19 per cent of the rural labour force, and generated 19 per cent
of China's total industrial output by value. They were responsible for 29 per
cent of the country's coal output, half its garment production, 53 per cent of
all building materials supplies and earned US $4 billion in exports.' (In 1976
rural industry had only produced 8 per cent of a much smaller gross total of
national industrial output.) Some factories were well equipped with modern machines, including technology bought from abroad. Others used
labour-intensive methods to recycle used materials such as old plastic bags
and broken glass. Output thus ranged 'from complete sets of equipment to
shirt buttons'.

The growth of rural industry had a direct effect on the rise in income
levels in the countryside; in the interior provinces where it was less visible,
standards of living were also lower. More than a half of all rural industries
(usually referred to as 'township enterprises') were located in the eastern
half of the country, from Guangdong in the south to Liaoning in the north.
Over 30 per cent of the rural workforce in these areas had moved away from
crop cultivation. Less than 3 per cent of China's rural industry was found in
the underdeveloped north-west, where 85 per cent still worked on the land.
Apart from generating more income locally and nationally, rural industry
provided employment for China's surplus labour. (The extent of such
underemployment had been concealed previously by the all-inclusive provision of work, regardless of efficiency, through the People's Communes.)
Figures for 1983 now showed that out of the total rural labour force of
350 million only 140 million were needed for agriculture, while another
90 million worked in rural industry and other non-agricultural activities.
This left a theoretical labour surplus of over 100 million—in fact these

people were nearly all 'underemployed' in agriculture. Projections showed that this labour pool would be increased by a further 100 million by the end of the century.[12]

One of the foremost champions of rural commercialization and industrialization was the well-known Chinese sociologist Fei Xiaotong (quoted at the start of this chapter). It was the only solution, Fei argued, to China's population problem, which as a result of the post-Liberation baby boom had led to an increasing shortage of real jobs in the countryside from the mid-1960s onwards. China's future lay in the development of township enterprises and the growth of small towns, supported by local industry and commerce, with a population of between 20,000 and 50,000 each. In this way China would be able to transfer half of its agricultural labour force to industries and tertiary trades, without the creation of urbanization on the scale familiar elsewhere in the Third World. The small towns would act as population 'reservoirs', helping to prevent a heavy concentration of people in the big cities. But this role could only begin to be played after the Cultural Revolution, when the economic reforms allowed China's small towns to resume the marketing functions of which they had been largely deprived since the late 1950s. For the past twenty years, collective and individual commerce had been limited and severely criticized while the state's domination of purchasing and marketing meant that only those few small towns which were also administrative centres continued to serve the surrounding rural areas. A revival of this organic commercial relationship between the small town and the rural community around it was only possible after the revival of peasant sideline production and rural industry in the early 1980s. The peasants, wrote Fei, 'figured out new and ingenious ways to make money in addition to farming their small contracted plots. Freed from constraints, the rural labourers developed a flourishing industrial base in the small towns across the country-side.' Industrialization in China could now follow an entirely different path from that in the West, where historically modern industry had grown at the expense of the countryside, with farmers driven to bankruptcy and forced to swarm into the cities to become the tools of capitalism:

In contrast, industrialization in socialist China is following an utterly different road. On the basis of a prospering agriculture, the peasants, filled with enthusiasm, run collectively owned township industries. These industries, by assisting, consolidating, and promoting the agricultural economy, bring about the simultaneous development of agriculture, sideline occupations, and industry. The co-ordinated development of all three sectors of the economy has led to a thriving and prospering

countryside. This road of industrialization was not planned in advance by theoreticians. Rather, it has been created by the peasants on the basis of their experience in
real life. Over the years, millions of peasants have left the land, but not their village,
to enter township industrial enterprises.[13]

The costs of reform

In less than a decade the second rural revolution had visibly transformed
the face of much of China, but proceeded at a pace which outstripped
theory and created new problems of its own. These provided ammunition to
more conservative critics whose concern was first given voice by the senior
Politburo Standing Committee member Chen Yun at a special Party conference in September 1985. Grain production, after rising by 33 per cent
between 1978 and 1984, had fallen back by 7 per cent in 1985. Although
bad weather was partly to blame, the abolition of grain quotas in the same
year had encouraged a shift to more profitable cash crops by entrepreneurial
peasants and a reduction in the size of grain acreage. Chen Yun warned that
grain must still be the basis for a healthy rural economy. Feeding and clothing a billion people constituted one of China's major political as well
as economic challenges, and grain shortages would lead to social disaster.
Controls on grain production were reimposed, but a rise in the price of seed
and fertilizers meant that although production picked up again, farmers
made little money and often expended more effort on poor land. The
answer could have been to allow grain prices to rise proportionately—but
the Chinese leadership feared that this would add to concern about inflation
and create a 'Polish problem' of urban unrest. Grain imports were increased
in 1986 for the first time in five years.

Chen Yun's criticisms also prompted more open acknowledgement that a
significant minority of peasants were still seriously disadvantaged. 'There are
regions with around one hundred million people whose problems of keeping
warm and not having enough to eat have yet to be solved', commented
Liaowang (no. 45, 1985), the reformers' popular magazine. More precise
figures were later provided by the *Farmers' Daily* (8 May 1986): 356 counties,
14 per cent of the total, had average incomes of less than 200 yuan in 1985.
Their population totalled nearly 124 million, or 14 per cent of the rural
population. Nearly one-third of this group had an average income of less
than 150 yuan. (These figures compared with an average rural income
nationally of 339 yuan, which included 400 counties—one-fifth of the

total—where the figure was in excess of 500 yuan.) Most of the poorer areas had shown at least some improvement since the late 1970s, but a few had made no progress at all. Videos were privately circulated within the Party showing areas where life had not significantly improved since Liberation.

For the majority of peasants whose lives improved, the first priority was to eat more and better food, the second to build a new and better house. While cadres pointed with pride to new building as evidence of successful reform, rural planners voiced increasing concern at the loss of arable land. The housing boom also indirectly caused land deterioration. A village near Fuzhou visited by this author in November 1983 had recently levelled a tangerine orchard while it expanded its local industry, including workshops to produce saws, wooden furniture, plastic rope, and bricks. Tangerine trees grow best on raised mounds of earth: this rich soil from the destroyed orchard provided the raw material for the bricks. A letter in the provincial *Fujian Daily* (25 Nov.) indicated that the problem was widespread. 'The evil trend of digging up the fields to make bricks', said the headline, 'must be stopped.' The writer complained that throughout his county the peasants were helping themselves to good earth for brick-making, in some places baring the soil till they reached bedrock. When reproached, they would reply that 'Now the land has been contracted out to us peasants you can mind your own business. What's the harm anyhow in taking a bit of earth to make bricks?' But more perceptive peasants, according to the letter-writer, understood the problem very well: 'This is killing the chicken to get the eggs,' they lamented. 'If it does not stop, we shall be smashing the ricebowl of our children and grandchildren.'[14]

House-building also diverted newly created surpluses away from product-ive investment which the reforms were supposed to stimulate (although rural investment still increased sharply in the 1980s). In 1986 per capita expenditure on building new houses averaged 51 yuan. Spending for pro-ductive purposes in the same year was less than 17 yuan per capita, 10 per cent less than in 1985. Many peasants had gone into debt to build new houses with extravagant features such as porches and balconies. Peasants also tended to regard investment in housing (privately owned in the countryside throughout the political campaigns of the past, including even the Cultural Revolution) as the safest form of family legacy. Not all of the loss went to private housing: it also supplied land for new roads, public buildings, rural factories, and recreation grounds. Figures issued in 1985 showed that in the previous year the amount of arable land had decreased by over 1.25 million hectares—an area equivalent to the total of such land in Fujian province. The survey revealed that some land was actually taken back into illegal private ownership, claimed by its original owners as 'ancestral fields' or 'ancestral hills'. (The scale of this problem in the 1980s would continue to grow until the situation at the turn of the century when across China an area the size of an average county was being taken out of production every year. In 2003, China lost 2.5 million hectares of arable land out of its national total of 123 millions.)

There was also growing concern that the reversion to household farming had weakened the ability of the collective to maintain and improve vital irrigation and drainage facilities. The village or township still had the power to mobilize peasant labour when required. (In Shanxi province, famous for its village opera, there was a saying that 'the collective provides the stage and the peasants sing the opera'.) But the task was becoming much harder. China possessed some 68,000 reservoirs and 700,000 kilometres of river dykes, mostly built during the Great Leap or in the Cultural Revolution, and often to low standards. A 1986 survey reported that many had not been properly maintained and were now in 'a dangerous state'. Investment in irrigation and drainage had also decreased—the figure for 1985 was the lowest for twenty-five years—although some argued that it had been much too high and misdirected in the past. (The price to be paid was brought home in the devastating floods of 1998 which were made much worse by the failure to maintain traditional flood basins and the collapse of poorly maintained dykes and levees.)

By 1986–7 the new problems generated by the rural reforms were openly discussed. The journal *Rural Economic Questions* (no. 2, 1986) wrote of a loss of momentum in rural economic reform and the growth of 'a new kind of hesitancy':

The new labour system has on the one hand stimulated economic development and on the other has created challenges for population control . . . With the family as a basic economic unit, more children means more work hands. In some places in particular, over the past one or two years there have been large drops in grain and cotton production. As a result, non-agricultural trades have felt the pinch and private individual businesses have withered. . . .

   In the flurry of encouraging rural development, the problems of collapsing irriga-tion systems, pests, soil destruction and erosion, and the excessively small scale of farm units have dimly come into view. If rural China underwent a 'quiet revolution' in the 1980s, it is now in a 'silent crisis'.[15]

In broad economic terms, the reformers now concluded that the problem in the countryside was not simply that of institutional reform, which had now been largely completed. The peasant still suffered from the classic 'scissors' of low prices for its produce and high prices for the essential inputs. Because of inflation, a system of indexing to establish price parity between industrial product and farm produce prices was required. The peasant needed more incentive to stay on the land and particularly to grow grain. He also needed assured sources of fertilizer and fuel at guaranteed prices. The experts also argued that agriculture was still under-capitalized. In 1987 agriculture accounted for only 5 per cent of state expenditure against an average of 11 per cent in the previous five Five-Year Plans. The state should invest more in the countryside, and persuade peasants to invest more themselves (in agriculture, for local money was being poured into commerce and industry). It was also generally agreed that farm units were far too small, and there was a growing shortage of rural technicians (previously funded by the collective). Early in 1987 a joint investigation by research bodies set up by the State Council and the Communist Party recommended: (a) raising prices to guarantee farmers 'a fair return for their work'; (b) spreading technologies that could give 'high yield for low investment'; (c) curbing use of land for non-agricultural purposes (a building tax was to be levied on the conversion of cultivated land); (d) encouraging large-scale farming by the merger of individual farms; (e) bringing rural workers into the towns to cope with the expected growing labour surplus; and (f) increasing the number of farming technicians by two hundred thousand. In addition, peasants were now assured that the period for which land was contracted to them would be fifty—not fifteen—years, and that children might inherit their rights.

The rural argument

Were twenty years of the People's Communes a disaster for China, or was it overall a necessary stage which laid the basis for the higher yield but possibly also higher risk policies of the 1980s? The official view became increasingly critical not only of the Great Leap Forward but also of the whole ethos of collectivization. In 1980 Deng Xiaoping had cautiously agreed that there was 'some ground' for the view that 'the pace of socialist transformation [in the countryside] had been too rapid'. The result might have been better, he continued, if the transition to higher forms of co-operative organization had 'advanced step by step' (31 May 1980). By 1985 his verdict had become wholly negative: Mao Zedong, he said, had made the grave mistake of neglecting the development of the productive forces, and the People's Communes had been established 'in defiance of the laws governing socio-economic development'.

Our experience in the twenty years from 1958 to 1978 teaches us that poverty is not socialism, that socialism means eliminating poverty. Unless you are developing the productive forces and raising living standards, you cannot say that you are building socialism. (15 Apr. 1985)

It is evident (although rarely acknowledged today in China) that the special-ized farming and rural industry of the 1980s derived some benefit from the earlier collective efforts of the rural workforce when it was organized into communes, brigades, and teams. An orchard near Fuzhou, visited in 1983, had been planted in 1977 and was just beginning to show a profit which was shared under the new responsibility system. How had the land, previously barren, been cleared in the first place, and when? The answer was that the work had begun in 1972 with the use of volunteer labour to open up the land and plant it with mulberries as a first crop. Yet the suggestion that voluntary labour under the People's Communes had played a positive role was greeted with embarrassed laughter. A more thoughtful response was to admit that current achievements were based upon labour-intensive 'capital construction' investment in land improvement of the 1960s and 1970s, but to argue that under the previous system the investment could never have been fully realized. By emphasizing single-crop (particularly grain) cultivation and by discouraging markets and rural commerce, the advocates of 'Big and Public' production and distribution of agricultural produce made it impossible for the countryside to escape from a low level of self-sufficiency. (Paradoxically, given the lack of a thriving commodity economy in the countryside, a policy concentrating upon grain production did at least guarantee a minimum standard of living—except during the near-starvation which followed the Great Leap.)

Agricultural planners at the national level were more willing to recognize that the earliest efforts to stimulate rural industry during the Great Leap Forward had prepared the way, and that many enterprises were the successors to local 'brigade industries'. While the ambitious 'backyard steel furnaces' and other attempts at rapid industrialization collapsed, more modest indus-trial advances such as farm machinery repair workshops, brick kilns, and simple food-processing plants survived. But policy during the Cultural

Revolution was ambivalent towards local industry: on the one hand it was encouraged as a sign of progress towards 'self-sufficiency'; on the other the low level of rural productivity and the discouragement of rural commerce deprived local industry both of funds for expansion and of markets for its goods.

Despite all its defects, the People's Communes strategy could hardly be regarded as the neglect of agriculture, and comparisons between Mao and Stalin in this context later heard from disillusioned Chinese economists were incorrect. Yet Mao's repeated exhortations to decentralize economic decision-making and to shift priorities from industry to agriculture were largely cancelled out by the imposition of inflexible policies from above and the discouragement of the peasant market economy, without which the countryside could never compete against the economic weight of the industrial sector. The irony is that the politics of centralized command and the disapproval of bourgeois-labelled rural commerce also stemmed from Mao. The question remains whether after Mao's death the collective structure could have been made viable by selective reform, or whether it had to be virtually abolished. As has been shown, the original intention had been to adopt the responsibility system only in areas of need, while reviving rural markets and encouraging diversification of crops and the growth of rural industry. But the headlong spread of the responsibility system led the whole of China, within the space of four years, into almost universal private land-use. There was no opportunity to discover whether the reforms in marketing and production could have been effectively linked to a continuation of full-scale collectivization. William Hinton would argue that it was unlikely that if the collectives 'had been given the same autonomy in production and the same freedom to develop markets that private producers now enjoy' they would have lagged behind.[16]

This may be true, but only in the context of the survival of shared collective values which were already severely eroded. The second rural revolution could not be constrained, partly because of the 'all-or-nothing' tendency in the implementation of party policy, but chiefly because most peasants—given a glimpse of something different—quickly tired of a system which had long ago lost the gloss of the first revolution. For the first time since 1949, the Chinese peasant now had the opportunity to enrich himself without being censured. Deng Xiaoping advocated 'getting rich first' on the grounds that 'once a person has become rich, the others will soon follow his example'. Worries about polarization of income were rejected by the evidence that while relative inequalities might increase, in absolute terms the poorer peasants were also better off than before. The *People's Daily* rejected 'the old concepts of egalitarianism' (9 July 1987):

In the past, we feared prosperity in varying degrees while striving for common prosperity. This resulted in common poverty. Today, we have implemented the policy of allowing some people to become rich before others, and the trend towards common prosperity has appeared . . .

Had we practised egalitarianism as we did in the past, failed to award the diligent and punish the lazy, treated those who do their work properly in the same way as those who do not, we would have only encouraged people to choose the easiest job, to hold back their efforts in work, and to be satisfied with low efficiency. Many localities would probably still be worried about food and clothing.

But increased opportunities also meant increased risks, even among the 'ten-thousand-yuan households' which had reached this annual income by specializing in farming, crafts, or trade. A 1987 study of 104 such households in a county in Hubei province showed that half of them had 'stopped production, went bankrupt or were in poor condition'.[17] More generally, the gains of rural reform in the 1980s, although considerable in most areas, were not maintained in the following decade. By the beginning of the new century, when agricultural production was again stagnating in large areas and the gap between rich and poor farmers (and between town and country-side) had widened more than at any time since Liberation, it became apparent that the abolition of so-called 'egalitarianism'—more often in reality a sense of community which had now been seriously eroded—was far from cost-free.

8

The Growth of Dissent
Poets and democracy

The train had slowed down on the Gansu corridor line to the far north-west, pausing at a station so small that there was no platform. Outside there were more people begging for food. 'If they are not landlord elements,' explained a passenger, 'then they must be idlers. Let them starve!' But the 16-year-old Wei Jingsheng, on his way to Exchange Revolutionary Experiences in Xinjiang, felt sorry for a woman wearing rags beneath his window, and leant out to give her some cakes he had bought in Lanzhou. What he then saw would set him on his career as China's most famous dissident.

I twisted my head back and left my hand hanging in mid-air. For what I had just seen was quite beyond imagination and up till then unbeliev-able. That woman with her hair over her shoulders was a girl of about seventeen or eighteen. Apart from the hair, there was nothing at all to cover her body which could be called clothing. Her whole body was just covered with ashes and mud which from a distance might look like clothes. Since she was among a crowd of little naked beggars, one might miss it altogether.

'There's a lot of them like this around here . . .' explained the passenger, chuckling. 'Some are quite pretty, and if you give them some food then without it costing anything you can . . .'.

Wei spent the rest of the journey pondering how such things could be allowed under socialism. In Xinjiang he met students, 'sent down' to the countryside, demobilized soldiers, 'rightists' who had been exiled there for years, all with stories to tell about being cheated or victimized by the Party. He learnt a great deal more serving in the army for four years, then working quietly as an electrician in Beijing. His first wall-poster 'Democracy: The Fifth Modernization', attracted a small group of readers at Democracy Wall in December 1978. Their 'unofficial magazine' *Exploration* was the most outspoken, criticizing even Deng Xiaoping. In October 1979 Wei defended himself against charges of betraying secrets and counter-revolution. 'The fate of Marxism', he told the court, 'is like many religions in history: after the second and third generations its revolutionary essence is abstracted and its theoretical ideals are used to deceive the people.' Wei was sentenced to fifteen years in jail.

(From Wei's account of his Red Guard experiences in 1966)[1]

The Red Guard legacy

The Cultural Revolution took an entire generation of young students or slightly older 'educated youth' and gave them an unintended education into how the Chinese political system worked. They learned through experience, one ex-Red Guard recalled, that 'the new authorities were a hundred times harsher than the old, that "eleven years [1966–76] are not as good as seventeen [1949–66]", and that the revival of feudalism is a much more real danger in China than the rebirth of capitalism'. (The Cultural Revolution leaders had argued that the first seventeen years had been mostly wasted until they discovered the correct revolutionary path.) New perspectives were opened up by allowing large numbers of young people to travel freely around the country to 'exchange experiences' and by their subsequent immersion in factional fighting. 'One might say that the first two weeks of March [1967] marked my political coming of age,' recalled a Red Guard from Canton. 'It was the first time that I ever really sat down and independently questioned politics in China.' Personal suffering also prompted unfamiliar questions. 'Why should two good people like my parents be forced to divorce each other?' asked the Hunanese student Liang Heng after enduring a long interrogation. 'Why did the peasants fear the cadres so terribly if they were representatives of our great Communist Party?' More profound politicization followed the 'sending down' to the countryside of twelve million young Chinese. The reality of hard rural life and the experience at first hand of oppressive and ignorant cadres led to disillusion with the Party and often with Mao himself, mixed in retrospect with a certain pride at having survived. A poem written (in English) in 1984 by a language student at Xiamen University conveys something of the reality of being a 'worker, peasant or soldier'.[2]

Poem: The Past

I dreamed my yesterday last night,
It made me toss about in bed.
The past I've undergone in the border areas
Was fully ten years long.
Could you imagine that
My family was sent into exile,
From the capital city to the centre
Of Taklamakan Desert?!

A boy soldier only fifteen had to risk
His life in numerous dangers.
He left bloodstains in anti-atom tunnels in the depths
Of Tianshan Mountains.
He dripped sweat in large crop fields in the hinterlands
Of the Gobi Desert.
He indulged in fantasy that he might contract a serious disease
And was sent to hospital to take a rest.
Oh, what a poor thing!

I rejoice that the past at last has passed,
Our country and people have been reliberated.
I prize my yesterday,
It tested and taught me a lot.
People say that 'When the bitter is finished,
Then comes the sweet'.
I believe that to prevent
The reappearance of yesterday's nightmare,
Forever we must keep sober and work hard.

Dissenting arguments were expressed sometimes obliquely through the medium of the 'great democracy'—wall-posters and manifestos—of the Cultural Revolution itself, but more often were circulated clandestinely. To write anything at all was regarded as dangerous. The poet Bei Dao recalls how he took advantage of his employment as a photographer, recording progress on a building site, to lock himself in a hut which he designated as a darkroom to work on his first novel, *Waves*. Later he borrowed a room in the suburbs but was spotted writing by the local neighbourhood committee through the window, fled, and never dared return. The Tiananmen demonstrations of 1976 (the 'April Fifth Movement') brought together many young activists for the first time, who formed friendships and began to discuss politics in private. Those who survived persecution or in some cases escaped execution formed the core two-and-a-half years later of the Democracy Movement.

Poets who do not believe

Poems which had been written in private notebooks and passed from hand to hand in the early years of the Cultural Revolution were read out in Tiananmen Square in April 1976, chalked on the pavement, and inscribed over mourning wreaths to Zhou Enlai. The authors of the most famous verses were pursued wrathfully by the ultra-left authorities. The immediate post-Mao leadership under Hua Guofeng not only failed to rehabilitate those who had suffered after Tiananmen but allowed the arrest of many more activists. Prison established new links between individual protesters who had previously been isolated, while underground literary journals began to circulate outside. Many of the poems had been copied and secretly preserved—in 'flowerpots, hollowed-out candles, the linings of coal stoves, or [by] burying them in the countryside'. The issue of whether or not to 'reverse the verdict' on Tiananmen was taken up by Deng Xiaoping's economic reformers as a way of discrediting the centre-left Maoists led by Hua who had acquiesced at the time. Sixteen teachers at the Second Foreign Languages Institute in Beijing pasted up on the college wall a collection of poems on the first anniversary of Zhou's death. Later they published, unofficially but evidently with covert official support, several volumes totalling more than 1,500 poems and prose pieces written in April 1976. Finally, on 15 November 1978, the original verdict was 'reversed' by the Beijing Party Committee, which declared it to be 'a completely revolutionary event'. On the day of the announcement, a bus from the No. 2 Foreign Languages Institute parked in Tiananmen Square to sell the unofficial poetry books. Hua Guofeng hastily yielded ground and wrote an inscription for an authorized edition of one of the volumes—to the anger of its original compilers. Hua had been Minister of Public Security at the time of the Tiananmen demonstration and was therefore responsible for its suppression.[3]

The poetry of this period was heroically defiant, asserting the ultimate triumph of revolutionary values which, many young participants in the Cultural Revolution still believed, had been subverted by a coalition of

left- and right-wing 'feudal bureaucrats'. They condemned the feudalism of
the first emperor of China, with whom Mao in his final years liked to
compare himself:

> The premier's spirit lives for ever,
> Children and grandchildren will lift the Red Flag.
> China is no longer the China of the past;
> The people are not completely stupid.
> The feudal society of Qin Shihuang is gone never to return
> And we believe in Marxism-Leninism.
> Those Outstanding Scholars who have emasculated Marxism-Leninism
> Can go to hell!

A four-line poem with a total of twenty Chinese characters by Wang Lishan,
a young factory worker from Shaanxi province, was judged by the ultra-left
leaders to be the most 'counter-revolutionary of all'. To add to their fury,
its text was quoted in full by the official account—supposedly hostile to the
demonstrators—of the Tiananmen incident. (Yao Wenyuan, in charge of
the ultra-left's propaganda, suspected this inclusion was itself a 'counter-
revolutionary' act.)

> In my grief I hear demons shriek;
> I weep while wolves and jackals laugh.
> Though tears I shed to mourn a hero,
> With head raised high, I unsheathe my sword.[4]

Wang was pursued in a national police hunt but evaded arrest. In December 1978 he joined the Communist Party, thus symbolizing the reversal of
verdicts on Tiananmen. Soon after he published a challenging article in the
unofficial Democracy Movement journal *Beijing Spring* (no. 5), which must
have pushed Party tolerance to its limits: Wang argued that in the revised
Constitution then under discussion, the clause on freedom of speech should
include the freedom to make counter-revolutionary statements, including
those which were 'against the Party'. His own experience showed that what
was counter-revolutionary at one time could be applauded at another. He
also argued that the Party was not the state but a private body whose
discipline should only extend to its own membership.[5]

The defiant optimism of this transitional period was shared by other less
evidently political poets. 'Trust the future!' by Guo Lusheng had been written in 1970–1 and became widely known as it circulated illegally among
Chinese youth. Guo was one of the very first Red Guards, belonging to the

United Action group which was condemned at the time as 'conservative' but had itself attacked Lin Biao, at that time Chairman Mao's 'chosen successor', as a conspirator against the Cultural Revolution. *Beijing Spring* now published a sequel to 'Trust the future', with the title 'Trust in life' (the first and last verses are reproduced here).

> When I was imprisoned in the black cage
> I could still endure the pain after punishment
> By struggling to my feet, biting my finger
> And writing in blood on the wall: Trust in life . . .
>
> .   .   .   .
>
> As long as the earth continues to revolve,
> So long as history advances,
> So long as my successors do not come to an end
> Then I will—trust the future, trust in life.[6]

An early poem by Bei Dao, 'The Answer', written in 1972 but revised at the time of Tiananmen, was reprinted from the first issue of the unofficial journal *Today*, which he jointly edited, and published in the official *Poetry Journal*.

> I come into this world
> Bringing only paper, rope, a shadow,
> To proclaim before the judgement
> The voices of the judged.
>
> Let me tell you, world,
> *I do not believe!*
> If a thousand challengers lie beneath your feet,
> Count me as number one thousand and one.
>
> I don't believe the sky is blue;
> I don't believe in the sound of thunder;
> I don't believe that dreams are false;
> I don't believe that death has no revenge.[7]

Publication of this poem marked the start of what became known by its critics as the 'poetry of shadows', upsetting older poets by its loose structure, unusual imagery, and lack of a clearly positive message. Poetry groups were formed to discuss and recite shadows poetry and a national conference was organized in April 1980, while numerous examples were published in provincial and local poetry journals. Bei Dao himself was attacked by the distinguished elder poet Ai Qing, who had in his youth urged Chinese poets to follow the revolutionary rhythms of Whitman and Mayakovsky. Ai mocked a 'poem' of one word supposedly published by Bei Dao for being shorter than its two-word title. (In fact this was a misunderstanding: the 'poem' was only a stanza, with subtitle, from his 'Notes from the City of the Sun'.) Ai had been the target of a bitter campaign during the 1957 'anti-rightist' movement and remained silent for twenty-one years, spending much of the time in labour camps. Like other rehabilitated intellectuals who now sought to regain confidence in the system which allowed them a second chance, Ai was disturbed by the subversive implications of the new 'obscure' poetry. He celebrated his return to writing with a more positive affirmation:

> Red fire,
> Red blood,
> Red the wild lilies,
> Red the azalea blooms, a red flood,
> Red the pomegranate in May,
> Red is the sun at the birth of day.
>
> But most beautiful of them all,
>   the red flags on forward march![8]

Martyrs of the Cultural Revolution

The Party also rehabilitated posthumously some of the dissenting voices of the Cultural Revolution who had paid for defiance with their lives. But its nervousness is illustrated by the contrasting treatment of the three most famous 'martyrs' of this period, Yu Luoke, Zhang Zhixin, and Wang Shenyou.

'So the Chinese ping-pong team has won thanks to keeping Mao's Thoughts in Command,' wrote China's earliest young dissident in his diary in May 1966. 'But people are asking, didn't the basketball team also study the Chairman's Works . . . and how come they were beaten by the Russians?' Yu Luoke, then aged 24, had already written an article criticizing the ultra-left propagandist Yao Wenyuan, part of which was published in a Shanghai newspaper—but as 'negative material' inviting criticism by the 'revolution-ary masses'. Later, in the first year of the Cultural Revolution, Yu wrote an essay, soon to become famous, 'On Class Background', in which he demol-ished the so-called 'blood lineage theory' (*xuetonglun*) that only the sons and daughters of revolutionaries could be good revolutionaries. Bands of Red Guards with the correct class pedigree were searching out and murdering whole families who came from the 'five black categories' of class enemies. They chanted a jingle: 'Heroes breed heroic sons; baddies all hatch rotten ones.' The Red Guard magazine in which Yu's essay appeared became a valued item on the unofficial market for swapping Cultural Revolutionary materials, worth many prized Mao badges. Yu argued at length that the influence of the family was outweighed by that of society, and that to condemn future generations to wear the same black political label was the product of feudalism and not socialism. Soon put under secret police surveillance, Yu was arrested in January 1968 and executed in March 1970. He had been offered a chance to recant but, so the story goes, contemptuously rejected it, telling his jailers instead: 'I've thought things over. My toothpaste has run out. Could you ask my family to send me another tube?'

Post-Mao leaders of the Chinese Communist Party adopted a cautious approach towards those who, unlike most of them, boldly challenged the ultra-leftists (and sometimes Mao himself) during the Cultural Revolution. Yu was formally rehabilitated in 1980 but was rarely mentioned in the official press. Unofficially he had become the foremost folk-hero of Cultural Revolutionary dissent, the subject of many poems and eulogies by activists of the Democracy Wall period. His reputation also spread through his sister Yu Luojin, whose autobiographical novel *A Winter's Tale*, dedicated to him, circled obsessively around her guilt at having failed to conceal his diary from the authorities—desperate for a hiding place, she left it in a public lavatory where it was discovered and used in evidence against him. Luojin herself became a controversial figure in 1981 by denouncing conventional sexual morality—she fell out of love with her second husband and was granted a divorce. In 1986 she left China and sought political asylum in West Germany.[9]

The authorities felt easier with the story of another dissenter, Zhang Zhixin, a young Party member in Liaoning province who was executed after having her throat cut so that she could not profess continued loyalty to the Party with her last breath. Zhang had defied the provincial leadership, headed during the Cultural Revolution by Mao's nephew and 'Gang of Four' supporter Mao Yuanxin, refusing to accept that the previous leadership consisted of 'capitalist-roaders'. Similarly she defended the reputation of Peng Dehuai and Liu Shaoqi at the national level and criticized Lin Biao's ultra-leftism. She was sentenced to indefinite imprisonment in August 1970. In 1975 the new ultra-left campaign to 'exercise all-round dictatorship against the bourgeoisie' led to a call by Mao Yuanxin for exemplary death sentences on those deemed to have deserted the revolutionary cause for the bourgeois camp. 'Every day she lives longer she becomes more counter-revolutionary. Let's kill her and have done with it', Mao Yuanxin is alleged to have said. Her windpipe was severed without anaesthetic at six o'clock one evening. The next morning, with her throat heavily bandaged, she was paraded before the other prison inmates for a formal sentencing, then taken to the execution ground and shot.

In March 1979 the case of Zhang Zhixin was finally reversed. Her tale offered safer ground for post-Mao beatification than that of the principled Red Guard Yu Luoke. The particularly horrible circumstances of her death, combined with her firm support for the (in retrospect) 'correct' leadership of the Party, provided an apt morality tale for the late 1970s when the Cultural Revolution was being officially blamed solely on a small handful of 'anti-Party' criminals. Two songs which she had written in prison (she came from a music teacher's family) called 'Whose Crime?' and 'Seeing the New Year In' were published. Even so, the fact that her dissenting views began with criticism of Mao himself, for having gone too far to the 'left' from the Great Leap onwards, did not feature in the official hagiography. Zhang Zhixin's defiant essay, 'My Views Remain Unchanged', said of Mao that after the Great Leap 'his scientific attitude grew weak, his sense of modesty diminished, and his democratic style of work also weakened'. The ultra-left's argument that new bourgeois elements could 'emerge' under socialism also originated with Mao. The Party's uneasiness even while rehabilitating her is reflected in a speech by Ren Zhongyi, successor to Mao Yuanxin in Liaoning province, which sought to explain why no one protested at her death at the time:

First, when the Gang of Four were on the rampage doing all they could within the Party to stifle the atmosphere of 'seeking truth from facts', it was impossible for the case of Zhang Zhixin to be brought up in detail and freely discussed at meetings. Secondly, because of the evil influence of the Gang of Four's ultra-left ideas, some of our comrades failed to recognize the correctness of Zhang's views and did not consider her innocent. Thirdly, lack of political courage in face of the despotic rule of [Mao Yuanxin] in Liaoning led some people to remain silent before the abuses and depredations of the Gang and their henchmen; a few persons even followed the Gang servilely.

It was left to the unofficial magazines to publish her argument in full, and to complain that many of those involved in the case (including the prison doctor who cut her vocal chords) still remained at large. The doctor was alleged to have cut the windpipes of more than sixty prisoners before their execution—Zhang was the forty-third.[10]

Wang Shenyou, a third pioneer dissenting voice from mainstream Maoism, had still not been officially rehabilitated ten years after his death. What made his case particularly unmentionable was the date of his execution, 21 April 1977, *after* the overthrow of the Gang of Four. The son of a working-class cadre family, Wang discovered Marxism for himself during the Cultural Revolution, but believed that it had been corrupted into a rigid dogma, compounded in China's case by the non-proletarian composition of the Communist Party. In an article seeking to rehabilitate Wang, the Shanghai dissident Fu Shenqi wrote:

He felt that the dogmas that Mao proposed in his old age were simply a cover for feudalism. Since China lacked a mature working class, the Communist Party developed as a peasant party led by revolutionary intellectuals, and the revolution it carried out was not proletarian-socialist but peasant, with a strong feudal tinge. After the revolution Chinese society therefore gradually evolved into a new form of oriental despotism. Once Wang said, 'Mao is just a peasant with a military cap'.[11]

Wang also supported the post-Stalinization reforms in the Soviet Union as a sign that 'scientific socialism' was gaining ground. Wang was arrested immediately after Mao's death, when Shanghai was still under ultra-left control, but was sentenced after the change of regime. 'It would be disloyal to Chairman Mao not to kill this person', the Shanghai authorities are supposed to have said. In 1986 the crusading journalist Liu Binyan cited Wang's case as an example of the still unmentionable 'hidden corners' of recent history. Wang was 'a much better thinker than Zhang Zhixin', a 'real hero deserving our admiration'. Liu said that there were as many as eighty similar cases of such people who struggled against the Gang of Four and were executed by their successors. Naming those high officials who had signed Wang's death warrant, he asked why no writer had yet tackled the story. (Two months later Liu himself was expelled from the Communist Party, accused of 'making trouble' by his investigations: see below, pp. 201–03.)

The search for genuine Marxism

One of the most remarkable features of the Cultural Revolution was the speed with which young rebels graduated from mechanical repetition of the dogmatic slogans of the Mao-cult to a search for 'genuine Marxism-Leninism', especially after disillusion set in with the Lin Biao affair and the 'educated youth' were consigned to the countryside. 'This search for a yardstick against which Mao could be measured', noted Anita Chan in her survey of ex–Red Guards, 'brought most of my interviewees to read Marxist classics for the first time.' The ex–Red Guard Liu Guokai later described the effect of the 1968 'Whither China' critique by the *Shengwulian* group (see above, pp. 73–76) upon an emerging political consciousness:

The Cultural Revolution widened people's horizons. They learnt so many things hitherto unknown to them. They began to think and analyse. After the onslaughts of the Cultural Revolution, the existing regime lost its former holy lustre. Cadres were unmasked and lost their former prestige, which was built upon deceit, whitewash, and administrative order . . .

The outcry of 'Whither China' struck a responsive chord in the hearts of many people. It made people think, and had a profound and far-reaching influence. Although such ultra-left thinking made only a brief appearance in society, the ideas were spread far and wide . . . Those who read it told others about it in secret. Quite a few students and educated young workers accepted ideas in the article and developed them further. They lost interest in factional struggles and turned their attention to the bigger issues of the existing system.[12]

In Guangdong a group of young ex–Red Guards studied the Marxist classics so well that Jiang Qing, while condemning the result of their work, conceded that 'the right-wing seems to study Marx and Lenin better than the left!' In the more relaxed political atmosphere of the south, the group displayed its first draft of 'On socialist democracy and legality' in September 1973, written under the collective pseudonym Li Yizhe, with a revised version in November 1974 timed to coincide with the eve of the long-delayed Fourth National People's Congress (NPC). Condemned as a 'reactionary document', the essay became the target of a compulsory criticism campaign. In Guangzhou alone, 7,600 'Criticize Li Yizhe' groups were formed within four months. Worse followed *after* the fall of the Gang of Four, when the authors were perversely accused of being followers of the Gang and sent to labour camps. Writers on the 1978 Democracy Wall in Beijing called for their release, which was achieved in February 1979, but the most active member of the group thereafter, Wang Xizhe, was rearrested two years later.

The Li Yizhe document argued that many of the characteristics of the political system established by Lin Biao persisted after his death. The main danger to the socialist system was a 'feudal social-fascist dictatorship' which appeared ultra-left on the surface but in reality belonged to the extreme right. No intelligent reader would fail to grasp that Li Yizhe's description of the Lin Biao 'system' still largely applied; indeed, the document openly argued that it was a fundamental part of the political practice of the Communist Party. 'China went straight into socialism from being a semi-feudal, semi-colonial society,' they wrote. 'The evil habit of feudal autocratic tyranny is buried deep in the minds of the masses and of nearly all members of the Communist Party.' Their targets were easily identifiable as stock-in-trade dogmas of current ultra-leftism:

• the theory that 'a "genius" appears once every several hundred or thousand years, that a "genius" deserves unbounded adulation and absolute loyalty . . . and that anyone who opposes a "genius" should be overthrown'. (The 'genius theory of history', commented Li Yizhe acidly, 'simply abolishes eight hundred million brains'.)

• the emergence of a 'highly privileged stratum' in the leadership, which constituted a 'new form of bourgeois ownership [whose essence] is the private takeover of public property when the means of production are socially owned'. (The ultra-left leadership, who themselves privately enjoyed many 'socially owned' privileges, later appropriated this argument to criticize Deng Xiaoping for allegedly representing the 'new bourgeoisie' in the Party.)

• the wholesale condemnation of loyal Party cadres, nominally blamed on Lin Biao but (as everyone knew) the result of much more widespread ultra-left intrigue. 'Why should the thousands of unjust verdicts at national and local levels not be set right? . . . Should such comrades as Deng Xiaoping and Zhao Ziyang never be readmitted to the Central Committee?'

• the undermining of enthusiasm for work by 'the craze for common ownership which did so much damage to the basic interests of the workers and peasant masses'. This was a particularly daring criticism which anticipated the post-Mao abolition of the People's Communes.

• the favourable comparisons made between the first Chinese emperor Qin Shihuang and Mao which helped to legitimize the semi-feudal system now in operation. If one said that feudalism had been progressive in its time, asked Li Yizhe, should one not say the same about bourgeois democracy? 'As we are such merciless critics of the bourgeoisie from Cromwell to Robespierre . . . why do we find the landlord regime of Qin Shihuang so splendid?'

The Li Yizhe group still believed, as did many young Chinese in the mid-1970s, in the forms of mass democracy which had been popularized early in the Cultural Revolution. They welcomed a circular by Mao in 1974 which approved of the display of handwritten posters. They approved the idea of young revolutionaries 'going against the tide' which was promoted by Wang Hongwen at the 1973 Tenth Party Congress. Yet they commented that such exhortations were meaningless as long as 'fetters, manacles, bars, and bullets still awaited those who spoke out fearlessly without the backing of important people at the Party's centre'. Li Yizhe also mocked the famous 'blank exam paper' which was supposed to have 'boldly challenged the revisionist line in education' (see above, pp. 84–85):

In August [1973] someone called Zhang Tiesheng emerged to 'go against the tide'. But the result was not that his head was cut off, nor that he was sent to jail; nor, apparently, did he have a wife to divorce him. Instead he soared right up to the top. It is said that he retired to some palace of learning to invent the profound mystery of 'going against the tide'. But as for many of the revolutionaries who really fought against the Lin Biao system, many were beheaded and are still headless, many were sent to jail and are still inside, while those who lost their jobs are still jobless.[13]

Copies of the Li Yizhe manifesto circulated clandestinely among groups of educated youth, just as the 'Whither China' document had done previously, and both documents in turn provided a theoretical basis on which other Marxist—and to some extent neo-Maoist—enquirers would build. Perhaps the most remarkable of these was Chen Erjin. Chen, who worked as a teacher and statistician in a coal mine for most of the Cultural Revolution, is known to us only through the text of his essay 'On Proletarian-Democratic Revolution', written in the early 1970s but published in an unofficial Beijing magazine during the 1979 Democracy Movement. (Later active in the National Association for Democratic Journals formed by dissidents after the suppression of Democracy Wall, Chen was sentenced in 1982 to ten years' imprisonment for counter-revolution and specifically for 'trying to organize a political party'.) Chen, in the words of his English commentator Robin Munro, produced a synthesis of key aspects of both anti-bureaucratic Cultural Revolutionary theory and the post-Mao movement for democratization: 'On the one hand, revolutionary transformation, class struggle, erosion of the division of labour, direct mass action, and the building of genuine organs of workers' power; on the other, constitutional integration, stability and social harmony, economic rationality; individual freedom, and institutionalized democracy and legality.'

Chen described the emergence of an embryonic new ruling class in post-revolutionary China which was based on the possession not of capital, as under capitalism, but of power. The Party asserted a unified dominance over the twin powers of political leadership and economic control. Further adapting Marxism, Chen argued that classes in this new society were determined not, as in the past, by the 'division of labour' in the process of production, but by the 'divison of labour' in the exercise of power. China now found itself at the crossroads between further degeneration into a 'social-fascist dictatorship by the new ruling class', and the emergence of a true 'proletarian-democratic' system. This would be based on a system of people's conferences possessing real legislative power—here Chen's stress on the separation of powers anticipated official Party policy of the mid-1980s. Chen went further still by arguing for a two-party system in which a second party, also communist, would have a membership and run candidates in free elections against the existing Party. This would provide a 'rational form' for the conduct of internal Party argument which had hitherto been conducted out of the public eye and by conspiratorial 'inner-Party struggle'. Chen's scheme also included detailed proposals for grass-roots democracy in the factory, countryside, and even in the armed forces. Officers up to regimental level would be elected by the rank and file, although higher appointments were prudently reserved for the Minister of Defence! All of this, Chen insisted, was not 'pie in the sky' but arose inevitably from the growing resistance of the Chinese people themselves to being oppressed by the Party's monopolization of privilege, which amounted to a new form of private ownership:

Privilege-ownership involves the stripping from the working people as a whole of all human rights, as the bureaucrat class strives with might and main to reduce these to such 'rights' as are commonly enjoyed only by beasts of burden. Such a reduction of rights is utterly intolerable! Gradually, steadily, there is arising within the proletariat and working people as a whole, the most powerful call-to-arms of our time: Give us back democracy! Give us back freedom! Give us back equality! Give us back human rights! We want to live as human beings—we *will not* be beasts of burden![14]

Democracy Movement and new dissent

The rehabilitation of the 1976 Tiananmen demonstration in November 1978 gave the green light to a revival of *dazibao* (big-character) posters on the streets of Beijing, which soon escalated into the Democracy Movement. This served a specific political purpose for Deng Xiaoping. It targeted the mainstream Maoist leadership around Hua Guofeng, denouncing them both for complicity in past injustices and for current privileges, and generated a genuine expression of public opinion which helped Deng to isolate this group (though not yet Hua himself) at the important Third Plenum in December 1978 where Deng's reform policy was launched. Thus Mao's former bodyguard Wang Dongxing, whose unit played a critical role in the arrest of the Gang of Four, was now denounced for building a palace (at an alleged and doubtless exaggerated cost of one hundred million pounds!) in the Zhongnanhai government area. Yet the posters originated as an outpouring on paper of a wide range of grievances, often brought to Beijing by petitioners with complaints to the central authorities, which gave the Democracy Movement a broader basis, linking for the first time a specific political argument with the demand for social justice. A central theme was that the past could not be blamed just on a handful of wicked leaders: 'Every government unit', said one of the earliest posters, 'still has secret lairs where the minions of the Gang of Four still hide. Unless we dig them out, then their poison will rise again and infect the masses.' New toleration for a degree of exposure to foreign ideas, and the presence of foreign journalists and students, also encouraged a more eclectic range of political thought. One journal, in discussing constitutional reform, quoted in turn from the American Constitution and that of North Korea. Another sent a message of support to 'our Dear Brothers, the Workers of Poland' on behalf of 'the young generation of the working class in China'.

Poems and short stories emerged from underground, while young artists, many of whom were seeing their first reproductions of Impressionism, Expressionism, and other modern forms in the liberalized art magazines, experimented with new styles. One group of mostly non-professional artists named themselves the Single Spark (which, Mao once said, can Start a Prairie Fire). Their first show was broken up by the police, but in 1980 they were allowed to exhibit in the Beijing Art Gallery where their works included powerful woodcuts and other graphics stemming directly from the political art tradition of the 1930s. In 'Breath', a woodcut by Ma Desheng, a

Chinese peasant was shown driving his wooden plough across the chest of a
sleeping man. Ma explained his intention:

Whenever I go to the countryside, I see how the peasant pursues his heavy and
primitive work, so far behind the city in his material and cultural life, yet carrying
on silently without a word of complaint. Yet it is quite the reverse back in the city,
where some cadres talk about the poverty of our country and how we must tighten
our belts, but build great mansions for themselves while other people have no
houses.

The very first abstracts made a daring public appearance. The young sculp-
tor Wang Keping posted a set of gently mocking questions and answers at
the entrance to the exhibition:

Q. What is this sculpture about? I can't tell what it's meant to be.
A. It is itself. It doesn't have to be like something else in order to be worthwhile.
Q. I can't understand this picture. All I can see are some colours leaping about.
A. You have understood it correctly.[15]

Pasting posters on the walls led to the publication of a score of unofficial
magazines, including one or two that were believed to have the backing of
reform-minded cadres. The young men and women, mostly workers with
high school or college education and a Red Guard background, could be
contacted through addresses or post box numbers. They soon made contact
with other dissenters around the country, and some talked with foreign
journalists (just as Deng himself had done in order to send a positive message
in December 1978 to Democracy Wall, when the posters were beginning to
attack his leftist opponents). Though Deng's tolerance was short-lived, those
who were arrested no longer simply disappeared without trace. They could,
to a limited extent, assert some rights under the newly emerging system.
Many of the arrests led to new protests, generating a complex set of case
histories known abroad as well as at home. The social issues to which ideological dissent was now linked soon included the inhumanity of the same
prison system under which many dissenters would suffer.

The first to be arrested was Fu Yuehua, a 37-year-old unemployed
woman who had petitioned the authorities, accusing a Party cadre of having
raped her, and came to know many other petitioners who suffered injustice.
Up to 10,000 flocked to Beijing that winter—mostly people from ordinary
working families whose complaints against authority dated back many years.
Fu was charged with 'disrupting public order' after helping to organize two

demonstrations of peasants who carried banners calling for democracy and
an end to 'hunger and persecution'. Eventually she was also charged with
libel for the rape allegation: this rebounded embarrassingly for the authorities when at a second trial Fu revealed 'certain new questions'. According
to one story, a jurist from outside Beijing, invited to join the handpicked
audience at the trial, had recognized the alleged rapist who complained
against the 'libel' as a man of bad reputation. In another version, Fu had
revealed intimate details of his anatomy before the court. After a two-month
adjournment, Fu was sentenced to two years' imprisonment on the original
charge. The charge of libel was dropped, although the judge still dismissed
her claim of rape. 'The rulers have their swords—the people only have their
mouths!' protested Fu's supporters.[16]

Wei Jingsheng, China's most famous dissident of this period, who was
sentenced to fifteen years' imprisonment on Deng Xiaoping's personal
intervention, had been an outspoken agitator on Fu's behalf. His magazine
Exploration championed the cause of the *shangfang* (literally, those who 'visit
upwards' to appeal to the authorities), and published an account of Wei's
visit to the police station responsible for Fu's arrest. An article by Wei
exposing conditions in the main prison for political prisoners just outside
Beijing, 'The Twentieth Century Bastille', was widely circulated in the
dissident press. Wei was sentenced in October 1979 for passing 'military
secrets' to a foreign journalist and for producing 'counter-revolutionary'
writings. The first charge related to his incautious revelation of details about
the Chinese action in Vietnam (which had been published in the internal
bulletin *Reference News*). The second arose from an article directly criticizing
Deng Xiaoping which precipitated his arrest.

Wei was a natural polemicist in a tradition which consciously referred
back to the early years of the Republic. 'Those who fear that democracy
will lead to disorder', he wrote in his first wall-poster ('Democracy: The
Fifth Modernization'), 'are the same as those who said at the time of the
1911 revolution that if China has no emperor there will be lawlessness.' A
sequel to the first essay echoes the challenging rhetoric of Mao's early
polemics:

Can the Four Modernizations be achieved in a society governed by overlords
and worked by professional and amateur slaves? Impossible! The situation in our
country presents a tragic reality: not so long ago we were even forbidden to mention the Four Modernizations. The fact that we can talk about them now is put
forward as a great dispensation, a favour granted us by those on high. Aren't you

overwhelmed with gratitude? If you fail to shed tears of emotion, beware. Someone is likely to take down your number. Not all professional slaves are in uniform.

Wei was arrested within days of publishing an article calling on people to ensure that 'Deng Xiaoping does not degenerate into a dictator'. In response to Deng's recent speech (16 Mar. 1979) which set strict limits on the Democracy Movement, Wei called for a 'genuine general election' as the only way to save the leadership from its chronic afflictions—personal ambition and megalomania. More political rhetoric than programme, Wei's arguments nevertheless touched on a nerve still sensitive eight years later during the 1987 student movement, when Deng would condemn as 'bourgeois liberals' those who called for his release. Deng's colleagues were less sure: Chen Yun refused to get involved, commenting that 'others arrested him [Wei] and others must dispose of him'. Several calls for Wei's release were made in the months leading up to the Beijing massacre. (Though in ill health from years of imprisonment, during which he lost most of his teeth, Wei's defiant spirit was unbroken. After being released in 1993, he continued to write critical articles and to communicate with other dissidents and foreigners. He was rearrested the following year and finally expelled to the US in 1997.)[17]

The unofficial journal *April 5th Tribune* (no. 9) had taken issue with Wei's last article, arguing that to call Deng a dictator was to follow the Gang of Four's habit of 'capping' people with labels. It would take time to recover from problems whose roots lay deep in a defective system, the editors wrote. The upper levels of government were 'sincere' in wishing to reform it; opposition came from bureaucrats at the 'lower and middle levels'. Yet the journal's co-editor Liu Qing, a machinist and ex-student from Nanjing, obtained a transcript of Wei's trial and attempted to sell it at Democracy Wall. Though Liu escaped arrest in the confusion, he went straight to the police station where his friends were detained and defended his action: Wei's trial was supposed to be public, and the *People's Daily* had talked about it to the whole world. 'What divine law are we breaking? What is there about it that's illegal?' Arrested himself that night, Liu was assigned without trial to three years' 're-education through labour'. On completion of this period he was secretly sentenced to seven years' imprisonment, apparently having provoked the authorities with a nearly 200-page letter (*Notes from Prison*) which was smuggled abroad. Liu described in calm, scientific detail the regime of the re-education camp, most of whose inmates have not been sentenced by a court but are consigned by an administrative police order. A fellow-prisoner at his first jail in Beijing summarized the system humorously for him:

You haven't done anything? Fine. You haven't broken a single law? Even better. Then we won't sentence you; we'll just send you to a camp for reform through labour . . . Even if you haven't done anything wrong, you're capable of it, because you're the type that easily turns to crime . . . Please believe me, this is for your own safety and your own good. That's why I am swallowing you up. You won't feel better until you're in my stomach, because there nothing can happen to you.[18]

At the end of 1979 Democracy Wall was moved from the main avenue of Beijing to a small park in the western district where poster-writers had to formally register their names in a prefabricated building specially erected for the purpose. Deng Xiaoping now proposed cancellation of the right to display posters—one of the 'four great freedoms' (speaking out freely, airing views fully, holding great debates, and writing big-character posters) first coined by Mao in 1957 and later included in the Constitution. It was withdrawn at the National People's Congress (NPC) in September 1980 (one delegate dared to spoil his ballot in protest), and the displaced Democracy Wall was closed down.

The surviving dissidents had enjoyed a breathing space during 1980 although kept under close surveillance. An informal provincial network developed between the various unofficial journals which survived, leading to the formation of the National Association of the People's Press in August 1980. In April 1981 more than twenty of these activists were arrested across the country, many of them charged with organizing or participating in 'counter-revolutionary groups'. Liu Qing's co-editor, Xu Wenli, was sentenced to fifteen years' imprisonment on the evidence of a provocateur. Xu's account of his arrest and trial, also smuggled out of prison, is a moving document of courage by a young man who loved his wife and child but could not keep silent. During eight months of interrogation, he kept his spirits up by winning (or imagining) small psychological victories over his questioners. By this time there was some form of legality—Xu praises his defence lawyer—but the verdict was still a foregone conclusion:

I fixed my gaze directly upon [Judge] Ding Fengchun, and the more I looked at him the more panicky he became, until his voice—for he had been affecting a northern accent—went right out of tune; finally, he became utterly discomfited, and as he uttered his last hysterical shout of 'Take below the counter-revolutionary element Xu Wenli', I turned around even before he had finished speaking, let them handcuff me, slightly raised my head, assumed a rather amused expression, and— without looking to either side—walked calmly out of the courtroom; leaving total silence behind for the benefit of Ding Fengchun, who was by then probably in danger of falling out of his judge's throne. I thought to myself: I've recovered my dignity!

Xu and those arrested with him still belonged to the generation which was formed politically during the Cultural Revolution, although neo-Marxist influence from abroad was beginning to filter through (Xu argued in favour of polycentrism and quoted Eurocommunist arguments for a multiparty system). Xu's generation still believed in the power of selfless action: in his 'Self-defence' he quoted the last words of the Copernican Giordano Bruno before being burnt at the stake for denying the myth of the Deluge. The document ends appropriately with Xu's invocation of the first dissenting martyrs of the Cultural Revolution: Yu Luoke, Zhang Zhixin, and Wang Shenyou. 'In comparison with these great figures, these household names,' he wrote, 'I am merely a minor "counter-revolutionary element"— uninformed, and of little learning or scholarship.' But he hoped that his would be the last generation which needed to join their struggle. It was certainly the last to engage in a struggle still grounded ideologically in Marxist thinking and with the declared intention of defending and improving socialism in China.[19]

From dissent to protest

The mass arrests of 1980–1 combined with the enormous material changes now under way to break the link between the Cultural Revolutionary dissent and contemporary protest. Young people in the late 1980s were criticized by the 1970s activists for being unconcerned with 'social issues' and overpreoccupied with personal lifestyle, especially sex and material comfort. They in turn criticized the older activists for being too 'political' and failing to jettison 'all that Cultural Revolutionary stuff'. The new generation had not been inactive: the student demonstrations for democracy in December 1986 in Shanghai were the largest since the Tiananmen demonstration ten years before, and provided conservative leaders in the Party with the pretext for forcing the resignation of the reformist Secretary-General, Hu Yaobang. Yet the character of protest had changed. Student discontent was less focused and easier for the authorities to contain temporarily, but at the same time more likely to seize opportunistically upon a new issue and break out again. Its political statements, no longer rigorously argued in neo-Maoist terms, often sounded closer to those of the young Republic in rejecting traditional doctrine (then 'Confucian', now 'Marxist') and in looking to foreign example for reform. The messages on posters and in manifestos were shorter and more emotional, reminiscent of 4 May 1919.

A campaign in 1980 for participation in local elections marked the transition from ideological argument to single-issue action. The new election law (June 1979) had sought to demonstrate a new spirit of democracy by insisting that contests for local People's Congresses should not be unopposed, and providing that any member of the electorate could stand on the nomination of only three voters. With the closure of Democracy Wall, student activists tested the limits of this new tolerance, particularly in the traditional seat of protest at Beijing University and at the Hunan Teachers' Training College in Changsha, resonant with Mao's memory. The Beijing contest was notable for the lively debates in which seventeen candidates (for two seats) took part, accompanied by election posters, still allowed within institutions though by now banned on the streets. The candidate with the highest number of votes, Hu Ping, had as editor of an unofficial journal in Chengdu at the start of the Cultural Revolution published Yu Luoke's famous article refuting the 'blood lineage theory'. (Five years later Hu would be in exile in the United States, editing the dissident magazine *China Spring*.) Hu was not allowed to take his seat, and the University also refused a run-off to fill the second seat as required by the election law. In Hunan the authorities intervened at an earlier stage, provoking a students' hunger strike which was only settled after mediation from Beijing. One candidate, Liang Heng, had married an American student (after a direct appeal to Deng Xiaoping), through whom the election row became known outside China. A new election was supposed to be held but this never took place. The other leading popular candidate, Tao Sen, was expelled from college a year later and sentenced to three years' labour education. Released early, Tao Sen headed in the opposite direction from Hu Ping, deciding that China's future lay with the economic reforms, and set up a private company to market the works of China's most famous painter (and native of Hunan) Qi Baishi.[20]

The generation of the Cultural Revolution was increasingly dispersed, and the next round of elections in 1984 was uncontested by democracy activists. When student protest reappeared a year later, it had more in common with the single-issue campaigns familiar in the West. In June 1985 more than three hundred former Beijing students, 'sent down' to Shaanxi province during the Cultural Revolution and still unable to return, staged a sit-down demonstration outside the Beijing city hall. (Similar demonstrations in Xinjiang province, where large numbers of Shanghai students had been 'sent down', had taken place in 1980–1.) In September 1985 Beijing students marched to Tiananmen Square to commemorate the Japanese invasion of China, protesting at Japan's new economic 'aggression'. Their slogans included 'Down with Japanese militarism', 'Down with Nakasone', and 'Boycott Japanese goods'. The anti-foreign overtone of these demonstrations was embarrassing to Deng Xiaoping, and there were suspicions that conservative opponents had encouraged it. In fact, some aspects of modernization, particularly the re-equipment of the Chinese police with new technology (including electric batons), were widely unpopular among young people, who complained that the police were 'worse than ever before'. One poster linked the two themes of police oppression and Japanese commerce (which was alleged to have flooded the Chinese market with inferior goods). 'What has all our sacrifice of blood given us?', it asked. 'Police and refrigerators.' Other demonstrations planned for 9 December, the fiftieth anniversary of the 1935 anti-Japanese protest, were deflected after lengthy meetings between students and senior reformist Party leaders. The students' own economic situation, with grants unable to keep pace with inflation, had increased their unhappiness, and one of the proposed slogans for 9 December was 'We have to eat'. The price of books had risen sharply, and students could see young people of their own age earning large sums in street markets and through inflated factory bonuses. Officials made a point of showing their concern, eating in student canteens and inspecting the heating facilities in their dormitories. At the same time police surveillance was stepped up, and activists were warned 'not to start a new Cultural Revolution'. Any protest meetings in Tiananmen Square would be regarded as a challenge to the Communist Party and subject to punishment.[21]

A new issue now surfaced in the north-west minority region of Xinjiang. More than a thousand students in the capital of Urumqi demonstrated on 12 December 1985 against nuclear tests in the region, and against family planning policies which they claimed had depressed the birth rate of the Uighur minority. A second demonstration by Uighur students in Beijing compelled a vice-mayor to make an unprecedented explanation to foreign journalists: 'It is necessary for our country to conduct a small number of nuclear tests,' he said. 'This is supported by the people of the whole country. These tests were carried out with effective safety measures. Data compiled in the past has shown that these tests brought no ill effects to the inhabitants and surroundings.'

During 1986 the Party reformers, with encouragement from Secretary-General Hu Yaobang's group and (more equivocally) from Deng Xiaoping, pressed their arguments further. Just as in 1979–80, when the Party's Third Plenum reawakened perennial hopes as to Deng's liberalizing intentions, Chinese youth now responded. The student demonstrations of winter 1986/7 were on a larger scale, but more diffuse and less coherent politically than the Democracy Movement, snowballing in the space of less than a month from the relatively isolated provincial capital of Hefei via Shanghai and Tianjin to Beijing. Hefei students in early December 1986 returned to the election issue, complaining that they had no say in the selection of candidates for the local People's Congress. Later, large demonstrations broke out in Shanghai, often turning into rallies which professed support for Deng Xiaoping and the official reform movement but called for speedier demo-cratic change and for greater press freedom. Educational authorities at the time said it was 'understandable' that students should voice their opinions, and there was speculation of behind-the-scenes encouragement, this time from the Party reformers. (A few slogans calling for the overthrow of the Communist Party, however, were probably provoked by conservatives who wished to discredit the movement.) The students' manifestos were passion-ate rather than closely argued: 'Maybe the police will come and break us up,' shouted one leader (in fact the police mostly refrained from intervention), 'but the Chinese people will not be slaves!' They also reflected the same sense of shame at China's backwardness that had informed so many demonstrations of the 1920s:

Between the past and the future lies the present. We cannot rewrite history, but we can change the present and create the future. Faced with the reality of poverty and dictatorship, we can endure it. But we cannot allow our descendants to grow up in the stranglehold of lack of freedom, democracy, and people's rights. We cannot let them stand beside the offspring of foreign countries and feel like poor and ashamed ghosts. Citizens, please understand! Bureaucracy, the policy of looking down on the people, lack of democracy and powerlessness, these are the sources of our backwardness.[22]

Spreading to Beijing, the student demonstrations of 1986 became a direct challenge to the Party's authority, both by their scale and by their mere presence in the political capital and traditional starting-point for national movements. Conservative forces played on the Party's fears that China might see a revival of 'disorderly' behaviour of the Cultural Revolutionary type, and warned that other issues, such as the students who were still 'sent down', might be raised again. They soon won Deng Xiaoping's support for a crackdown, and the demonstrations turned into a series of confrontations with municipal and police authority. The traditional rhetoric of Beijing University blossomed briefly. One poster echoed an argument used by Hu Ping in the 1980 election campaign:

The Chinese people already have two thousand years of history behind them. Two thousand years! Archimedes said 'Give me a place to stand on and I can lift the world.' Now there is a place to stand on. It is one billion people. Students of Beijing University, why don't you spring into action!

Their optimism was short-lived. New regulations were published banning unauthorized demonstrations, student leaders were arrested, and the rank and file warned that their job prospects would suffer if the action continued. Parents and relatives were mobilized to summon the students home for the Chinese New Year—with rail vouchers thoughtfully provided by the authorities. For the second time in less than a decade, Deng Xiaoping was seen by many to have betrayed his own supporters, although others still believed that he had been either misled or forced to concede ground tactically to the conservatives. The struggle subsided for a while into a mood of confused dejection, well illustrated by one of the last posters from Beijing University. Signed anonymously by 'A Very Frightened Person who Loves Life', it lamented:

I thought our superiors were working hard, that they were trying to bring about a better life for the people. I had no idea that in their eyes the people counted for nothing—nothing at all. Their first priority is to protect the status quo. They want to hold on to what they've got—and then get more. They use smiles to get it. Their attitude is 'Democracy is something we can give you out of our own generosity' . . . They carry out their 'reforms'. But if you want to participate and if those reforms develop to the point where their interests are in danger, what do they give you? I'm afraid. I'm not afraid. I'm still afraid. It's really tragic.[23]

This despairing mood was compounded by the dismissal of Hu Yaobang in February 1987, and the conservative backlash which followed within the leadership around Deng Xiaoping. No one on either side—students or leaders—anticipated what would happen two years later.

9

The Party under Pressure
Reform and reaction

The reform of the Chinese Communist Party was a slow and painful process, which began only haltingly after Mao's death and is still far from complete three decades later. For the first two years, a vast oil painting hung in the Beijing railway station above the escalators in the marble foyer. It showed Hua Guofeng, by now Party Chairman (and Premier, and also Chairman of the Military Commission) receiving his mandate from Mao.

The scene was set in Mao's study; the date was supposed to be 30 April 1976, just weeks after the Tiananmen demonstration. Mao's face was passive, as if barely able to control the effects of Parkinson's Disease from which he now suffered severely. Hua was beaming with warm deference, against the background of traditionally bound Chinese books. Every railway passenger knew that at this meeting Chairman Mao, no longer able to speak intelligibly, had allegedly handed a sheet of paper to Hua, bearing the phrase: *'Ni ban shi, wo fang xin'*—'With you in charge, I feel at ease.' The same picture was reproduced on propaganda posters available for a few cents in every bookshop in this first post-Mao period. Other posters bore slogans including:

Chairman Mao trusted Chairman Hua completely; the people and army warmly endorse him too! (*a picture of vast crowd marching in celebration with portraits of Mao and Hua*).

Chairman Hua, the people of China love you! (*a picture of representatives of all China's nationalities holding banners*).

Chairman Hua leads us in drawing a new map for the future! (*Hua and workers amidst blocks of stone on a hillside*).

Sincerely support our brave outstanding leader Chairman Hua! (*portrait of Hua surrounded by smiling Uighurs and Kazakhs*).

The picture disappeared from Beijing railway station after the December 1978 Third Plenum, but it took over two more years before Hua was finally replaced by the reform-minded Hu Yaobang—and the posters were removed from sale. There were several theories about Hua's 'mandate' from Mao. Perhaps Mao was merely expressing approval of Hua's conduct of the 1976 campaign against Deng Xiaoping (in which case Mao was wrong). Or else the note was simply a forgery. Was not Mao too ill to write the characters so clearly? If it was not a forgery, then it lacked his signature and so was not a proper mandate. Even if it had been signed, was that the right way for a modern Communist Party to settle the succession?[1]

The post-Mao transition

At a crucial moment in 1975, the 40-year-old Wang Hongwen, China's youngest Party leader and Mao's chosen model of a 'revolutionary successor', had taunted Deng Xiaoping with his age. 'Let's wait and see how things stand in ten years' time,' he threatened. Deng was sufficiently worried to discuss the matter with some of his old companions. 'I was then already 71,' he later recalled. 'In terms of life expectancy we were no match for the Gang.'[2] In the ensuing struggle, age triumphed over youth, with the restoration to power of the generation which had been pushed aside in the Cultural Revolution, and the re-establishment of the ideas which they had advocated in the 1950s. The magnitude of this turn-around can hardly be exaggerated. It required not just a change of personnel at the top, but the reshaping of both Party rank and file and its body of cadres who themselves had been substantially reshaped in the previous ten years. This in turn necessitated the rejection of a complete set of theoretical positions adopted during the Cultural Revolution, and the search for a comprehensive substitute. Both in terms of power and principle, Deng in the decade 1977–87 masterminded an arduous campaign involving the demolition of the old apparatus—a task which was fairly complete by the Twelfth Party Congress in 1982—and its replacement by the beginnings of something labelled (from 1986 onwards) 'political structural reform', which was much more contentious.

The coalition leadership established at the 1975 National People's Congress (NPC) had been destroyed by its own internal contradictions and by Mao's erratic judgement in accepting the exclusion of Deng Xiaoping after the Tiananmen demonstration. It fissured within a month of Mao's death. The mainstream Maoists led by Hua Guofeng sought the help of the armed forces under Ye Jianying to remove the ultra-left from its control of the Party propaganda apparatus. At their trial four years later, three of the Gang (but not Jiang Qing) were accused of having planned an 'armed rebellion' in Shanghai. The actual evidence shows that the ultra-left had attempted to build up the Shanghai militia as a defence against any move against them ('What worries me most', Wang Hongwen had said, 'is that the army is not in our hands'), but that their followers surrendered without a shot being fired. The coup which they planned was based not on military strength but the attempted manipulation of the Party apparatus. The heart of the charge against them was not the methods which they used but their effect, which would have resulted (in the view of the old guard which now regained power) in the 'destruction of the socialist state'.

The final act which precipitated their arrest was the republication (in the *Guangming Daily*) of one of Mao's last instructions which had allegedly been tampered with. When Mao transmitted his ambiguous 'mandate' (see above sketch) to Hua Guofeng after the Tiananmen affair, he also conveyed two other instructions. One of these, which Hua promptly read out to the Politburo (although oddly he did not read out his own 'mandate'), conveyed the message 'Act according to past principles.' The Gang of Four misquoted this to read 'Act according to the principles laid down.' The significance of the difference between the two versions is obscure but it had immense political symbolism. It could perhaps have prepared the way for the production of a forged 'testament', allegedly 'laid down' by Mao, appointing Jiang Qing as his successor. Or the 'tampering' with it may merely have provided Hua and his supporters with the necessary pretext for joint action against the ultra-left.

It was the anti-Gang coalition which now summoned a secret Politburo meeting and moved into position the special forces led by Mao's bodyguard, Wang Dongxing, to arrest all four Gang members in the night of 6/7 October. When Jiang Qing was arrested, the story goes, her personal attendants spat upon her, demonstrating the hatred in which she was held and perhaps also a healthy instinct for self-preservation. An awkward period now followed in which the mainstream Maoists led by Hua were obliged to reincorporate Deng Xiaoping's forces while seeking to keep intact as much as possible of the Cultural Revolutionary past. Some Chinese journals published in October inserted correction slips to say that Deng was no longer a 'capitalist-roader' although he had still 'made mistakes'. On May Day 1977 Hua said that China would cling to Mao's 'correct line' and 'continue the revolution'. At the Party Congress two months later he announced that the smashing of the Gang of Four had marked 'the triumphant conclusion of our first Great Proletarian Cultural Revolution'—indicating that there would be more. But his emphasis upon the need to 'grasp the key link of class struggle' was balanced by a new call to 'bring about great order across the land'. Ye Jianying (who had guaranteed military support for the anti-Gang coup) tipped the balance more sharply: centralism was more essential than democracy, and Party discipline must be restored. A new group of five was established with Chairman Hua and the four Party chairmen (again including Deng) as the Standing Committee of the Politburo. In his closing speech to the congress, Deng called for the goal of making China 'a great, powerful, modern socialist country by the end of the century'.

History now briefly repeated itself as farce, with a cult of Hua being developed along lines which comically aped that of Mao. His portrait appeared everywhere beside that of the late Chairman. His hair was grown longer and in a swept-back style to match Mao's more poetic look. His simple calligraphy was appended to books and monuments. Factory workers were exhorted to greater efforts by rhyming jingles: 'The heights to which he does aspire | are what the masses all desire.' Tales were told endlessly of his simplicity and homely style. A 1978 New Year poster showed him making dumplings with peasants at the earthquake site of Tangshan.[3]

Hua's behaviour demonstrates the persistence of a political culture which had become so enveloping that he and his supporters could not see its danger to their own cause. Hua also blundered theoretically, producing a formula not so far removed from the 'fabricated' one which had precipitated the Gang of Four's downfall. This was the famous Two Whatevers: 'We will resolutely uphold whatever policy decisions Chairman Mao made, and unswervingly follow whatever instructions Chairman Mao gave.' This statement was intended to deflect efforts to 'reverse the verdict' on the anti-Deng campaign of the previous year and on the Tiananmen incident. It was countered by Deng and other veteran leaders, particularly Chen Yun, with the call to 'Seek Truth from Facts' (a phrase once used by Mao which implied that policies should be based on reality and not on dogma). At stake was not just a factional quarrel but two opposing views on the relation of theory to practice. The Two Whatevers, Deng argued, took statements by Mao out of context and ignored the fact that he himself had said that some of them were wrong. Truth could only be tested by practice; otherwise thinking would turn rigid and everything would be done disastrously by the book:

The more Party members and other people there are who use their heads and think things through, the more our cause will benefit. To make revolution and build socialism we need large numbers of pathbreakers who dare to think, explore new ways, and generate new ideas. Otherwise we won't be able to rid our country of poverty and backwardness or to catch up with—still less surpass—the advanced countries. We hope every Party committee and every Party branch will encourage and support people both inside and outside the Party to dare to think, explore new paths, and put forward new ideas, and that they will urge the masses to emancipate their minds and use their heads. (13 December 1978)

The pragmatic emphasis of this approach disturbed those who wished to cling to certainties. As late as September 1982 (after Hua had lost power) he queried the argument that practice is the only test of truth. Communist society had not yet been tested in practice, nor could it be, Hua objected. Yet its ultimate realization was not only a necessity but also a truth, thus proving that not all truths had to be tested. (The argument was countered by the ideologue Hu Qiaomu, who replied that the communist *movement* had already been tested in practice by sixty years of Chinese experience and a century and a half in the whole world.)[4]

Deng's ascendancy was first established at the Third Plenum in December 1978, which endorsed Seeking Truth from Facts and criticized the Two Whatevers. It also reversed the verdict on the Tiananmen demonstration, leading to the dismissal of senior officials who had suppressed it at the time. It would take another two and a half years to bring to an end Hua Guofeng's transitional leadership and return a verdict not only on the Gang of Four (who were sentenced in January 1981) but on Mao and the Cultural Revolution. This was achieved at the Sixth Plenum in June 1981, when Hua was finally replaced as Chairman of the Party, and the 'Resolution on Party History (1949–1981)' was adopted. Hua was criticized for allowing the personality cult to continue around him, for his 'Left' economic policies, and for failing to correct past injustices such as the Tiananmen Incident. Deng also claimed that Hua was still being supported by 'the remnants of the Gang of Four and others who have ulterior motives'. Certainly the length of time required to remove Hua indicated the strength of feeling among many Party leaders that Deng's reforms would threaten their own bureaucratic grip on power. At the Twelfth Congress a year later, Hua made a partial self-criticism but claimed he was the victim of slander, including accusations that he had leaked the news of a 'state secret', namely the theft of a television set from his home, and that he was somehow implicated in the suicide of a nurse who had been assigned to his personal staff.[5] Hua remained an important symbol as late as 1987, when to general surprise he was re-elected to the Central Committee at the Thirteenth Party Congress (and was not finally removed for another fifteen years).

Reaching a verdict

'Don't think there can be no more chaos in China', warned Deng Xiaoping in July 1979. 'Those who belong to the factional systems of Lin Biao and the Gang of Four are deaf to the Party's directives and would like nothing better than nationwide confusion.' One-half of the Party membership (35 million in 1980) had joined since 1966; one-third since 1973. Many still believed that while the leadership now stressed material progress, the pendulum would shift again to a renewal of Cultural Revolution. One young cadre encountered in Shandong province offered a typical rationalization: 'At the moment we are stressing one thing [i.e. materialism]. In the future we shall stress another.' The new resolution on Party history was only approved after two and a half years of argument which muffled the force of its condemnation. The senior leaders, Chen Yun and Deng himself, were anxious to ensure that the resolution did not pass too 'negative' a verdict upon Mao and the Party. It was a document, Deng stressed, which must 'unify thinking and unite our comrades', and he criticized an early version for being too 'depressing'. Two questions were primary: Did Mao's achievements outweigh his mistakes, and did the Party's achievements in the period up to the Cultural Revolution also outweigh its mistakes? To produce negative answers would be 'to discredit the Party and the state'.

The resolution identified three causes behind the Cultural Revolution. First was Mao's 'tragedy'. As he grew older, he no longer made 'a correct analysis' of the situation but 'confused right and wrong and the people with the enemy'. Nor could he bear to accept criticism from far-sighted leaders such as Deng Xiaoping. His 'errors' were taken advantage of by Lin Biao and the Gang of Four, who 'committed many crimes behind his back, bringing disaster to the country and the people'. The resolution still sought to salvage as much as possible of Mao's reputation, arguing that even during the Cultural Revolution he had at times criticized the Gang of Four and had safeguarded China's security by formulating correct principles in foreign policy. The second reason, which made possible Mao's 'tragedy', was the tradition of 'feudal autocracy' in China to which the Party largely succumbed. This was compounded by the influence of 'certain grievous deviations . . . in the history of the international communist movement'—a code-phrase for Stalinism. 'Conditions were present', the resolution cautiously suggested, for the development of arbitrary personal rule which made it hard for the collective leadership to prevent the Cultural Revolution. Third and more convincingly, the resolution argued that the Party's birth and maturation over decades of 'war and fierce class struggle' had made it ill-equipped to deal with the more subtle contradictions of a peaceful society. Its tendency to exaggerate the continued role of 'class struggle' was exacerbated by the split with the Soviet Union. China's legitimate struggle against Soviet 'big-nation chauvinism' abroad led to an internal campaign against 'revisionism'. Normal differences within the Party leadership were presented as a 'struggle between two lines'.

The resolution concluded (as instructed by Deng) that '[Mao's] merits are primary and his errors secondary', even if he had committed 'gross mistakes' in his later years. It distinguished between these mistakes and Mao Zedong Thought, a synthesis of Mao's own ideas and the Party's collective wisdom over the years, which it described as 'Marxism-Leninism applied and developed in China'. Failure to preserve the main elements of Mao Zedong Thought, Deng had argued during the drafting, would undermine all those activists who had struggled in Mao's name to transform the country after 1949.

Deng's second key question—the responsibility of the Party as a whole and leaders of his generation in particular—produced the ritual admission that 'the Central Committee of the Party should be held partly responsible'. There was not a word about the specific responsibility of any leaders, even though Deng had originally instructed that the resolution should contain a 'fair evaluation of the merits and demerits of some leading comrades'. A section claiming that the Party's work in the decade leading up to the Cultural Revolution was 'generally good' had been inserted on Deng's insistence. After all, he argued, 'didn't the rest of us go along with him?' The limits of criticism were set by Deng in a crucial speech just before the resolution was approved:

Why are we now stressing that assessments must be balanced? Because certain recent remarks about some of Mao Zedong's mistakes have gone too far. These excesses should be corrected so that, generally speaking, the assessment will conform to reality and *enhance the image of the country and the Party as a whole* [my emphasis]. Part of the responsibility for some past mistakes should be borne collectively, though the chief responsibility, of course, lay with Chairman Mao. We hold that systems and institutions are the decisive factor, and we all know what they were in those days. At the time, we used to credit everything to one person. It is true that there were certain things which we failed to oppose and for which we should be held partly responsible. Of course, in the circumstances, it was really difficult to express any opposition. (22 June 1981)

The need to preserve the Party's authority also made it necessary to insist that it had continued to exist during the Cultural Revolution and that the Politburo and Central Committee had continued to be legitimate organs. Even the October 1968 Plenum which had condemned Liu Shaoqi as a traitor and expelled him from the Party was judged to be constitutional. (Only a bare majority of the Central Committee took part, outnumbered by members of revolutionary committees and army representatives, including one who was not even a Party member.) 'To deny their legitimacy', said Deng, 'would pull the rug out from under us' by conceding that the Party had lost control. Instead, it must be argued that it was only thanks to the Party remaining in existence, and to its use of Mao Zedong Thought, that the Gang of Four were finally defeated![6]

This insistence upon legitimacy worked against the Party when the Gang of Four went on trial. When the indictment was read to Jiang Qing, she asked the court how it regarded the Party Congresses held during the Cultural Revolution. She too was carrying out the instructions of Chairman Mao, she argued defiantly. The difference was that she had remained loyal to the Chairman and to the millions of revolutionary Red Guards. The official media went to some lengths to justify the trial by distinguishing between the 'mistakes' made by the Party and particularly by Mao, and the 'crimes' committed by the Gang of Four and by the Lin Biao group with whom they were tried. The main charges against the Gang were that (*a*) they had attempted to overthrow the socialist state, (*b*) they had planned armed rebellion, and (*c*) they had caused people to be killed and tortured. The first two 'crimes', though regarded officially as the most serious, were not supported fully by the evidence. On the first charge, it could equally be argued that the Gang were seeking to defend their conception of a socialist state against the subversion of their rivals. The evidence of 'armed rebellion' was based upon plans made in Shanghai to arm the militia after Mao's death, which, as we have seen, came to nothing. But evidence supporting the third charge was abundant. Cases of victimization and torture often leading to suicide and death were common knowledge. The most damning piece of evidence was a tape-recording of the brutal questioning of Zhang Zhongyi, a 67-year-old professor who had the misfortune to have had a colleague who was friendly with Liu Shaoqi's wife, Wang Guangmei, before Liberation. His evidence was required to support the charge that she had been a Guomindang agent. Zhang was interrogated as he lay dying from liver cancer. His feeble attempts to parry the questioning had been recorded and were played in court:

Q. What espionage activities was Wang Guangmei engaged in?
A. I hope to get this question clear.
Q. This is your chance. Do you want to take the question along into the coffin with you?
A. No. I am not clear at all about this question . . . I cannot cook up a story, either.
Q. You are making yourself a nuisance. You are resisting to the end.
A. I've never thought about that.
Q. Why don't you confess? Do you want to put yourself against the people to the very end? Who is Wang Guangmei?
A. She is a Communist.
[Professor Zhang at one point did describe Wang as a 'secret agent', but added that he had learnt about this from a 'government communique'.][7]

Jiang Qing and Zhang Chunqiao (who, suffering from terminal cancer, remained as defiantly silent during the trial as Jiang Qing was defiantly vocal) were sentenced to death but with a two-year stay of execution. Jiang had already dared her captors to have her executed before a mass rally in Tiananmen Square. Two years later, the sentences were commuted to life imprisonment even though there is no evidence that she had shown the required 'signs of repentance'. Yao Wenyuan received a twenty-year prison sentence but Wang Hongwen, whose rapid 'helicopter' promotion in 1973 enraged the veteran cadres, was sentenced to life. Mao's former theoretical adviser Chen Boda, in prison since 1971, was sentenced to eighteen years' jail. (All except Yao Wenyuan would die in detention by the end of the decade or soon afterwards.) Five senior military officers, also imprisoned since the Lin Biao affair in 1971, received similar sentences. With the trial concluded, many expected a thoroughgoing purge of Gang supporters at lower levels of the Party. But this proved politically delicate, while in the meantime new problems of Party discipline had arisen.

The Party's cancer

By the end of the 1970s, the Chinese Communist Party had reached its lowest point so far in morale and public esteem. Economic reform would be of little value unless the Party could also be reformed. The agenda for rectification was set by Deng Xiaoping in an important speech to the Politburo (18 Aug. 1980). It covered 'bureaucracy, over-concentration of power, patriarchal methods, life tenure in leading posts, and privileges of various kinds'. In Mao's classic metaphor, the Party depended upon popular approbation just as the fish requires water to survive. In a later speech Deng gave the phrase a new gloss, quoting the proverb that 'water can keep a boat afloat, but it can also sink it' (12 Nov. 1981). If there was no improvement in Party discipline within a couple of years, he said, it could become an insurable disease. The Party had 39 million members and 2 million grass-roots organizations. One could not stand idly by while the cancer spread until whole sections were 'paralysed or even completely rotted'.[8]

The official catalogue of Party failings could not have been worse if it had been invented by China's enemies. (In fact Western comment, by now universally favourable to the open-door reforms, tended to minimize the extent of China's internal disarray or to regard it as a necessary price to pay for developing a market economy.) On the Party's July 1982 anniversary, its propaganda head Wang Renzhong produced the following list of manifestations of 'individualist thought':

1. 'An ardent quest for individual ease, comfort, reputation, and position.'
2. Putting 'personal benefit' before service to Party and people.
3. Arrogance and self-righteousness, 'refusing to submit' to Party directives.
4. 'Striving for power, position, reputation, and pay', and sulking when these could not be obtained.
5. Using one's office for private advantage, choosing the best housing, placing one's children in the best jobs, and so on.
6. Nepotism, forming small groups and cliques.
7. Preferring the interests of one's own unit to those of the community.
8. Protecting one's friends and being reluctant to go after 'bad people'.

   9. Looking for money in everything, and taking bribes.
  10. Infatuation with a capitalist lifestyle, falling into 'corruption and decadence'.

Perhaps even worse, there were many who took the view that 'selfishness is human nature' and made no effort to struggle against these deviations from communist morality. At the other extreme, there were those, especially former supporters of the Cultural Revolution, who wrote off the Party, saying that 'it has already degenerated . . . and a new dynasty has been established in its place'. Even honest Party officials were often unwilling to investigate internal misdeeds (especially when committed by their friends), or did so reluctantly, as if 'trying to catch a sparrow with their eyes closed'. This particular phrase had been Mao's, and there was no shortage of pithy sayings to dramatize the Party's crisis. Too many Party members, said Wang, were like 'pleasure-seekers who want to enjoy the cool shade but are unwilling to plant trees'.[9]

   How had the Party got into such a mess? As the austere Chen Yun (head of the Party's new Discipline Commission) remarked, 'Ice which is three inches thick was not formed in a day.' Part of the explanation lay in the fertile ground provided by the Cultural Revolution for authoritarian attitudes which were loosely labelled as 'feudal'. In the absence of normal political rules, it was the strongest individuals who usually survived, only paying lip-service to Party discipline. 'At what time in the past', complained Deng Xiaoping in November 1979, 'did a Party committee secretary—a secretary of a county or commune Party committee, say—have as much power as he has today? Never!' Discipline had declined even in the armed forces, where officers sometimes simply refused to take up new appointments, obliging Deng to say that 'when a cadre is reassigned, he must change his residence' (June 1978). The acquisition of privilege also became more blatantly feudal, and so did its loss:

During the 'Cultural Revolution', when someone got to the top, even his dogs and chickens got there too; likewise, when someone got into trouble, even his distant relatives were dragged down with him. This situation became very serious. Even now, the abominable practice of appointing people through favouritism and factionalism continues unchecked in some regions, departments, and units. There are quite a few instances where cadres abuse their power so as to enable their friends and relations to move to the cities or to obtain jobs or promotions. (Deng, 18 Aug. 1980)

The loosening effect of the new reforms quickly added another layer of indiscipline and corruption. It was no longer just a question of the traditional need to entertain officials (especially when they were paying visits of inspection to subordinate units) with banquets, cigarettes, wines, and rare local produce. A report from the Discipline Inspection Commission in 1981 said that the Party's standing had been seriously damaged by speculation, profiteering, and the misuse of state funds which caused 'hundreds of millions of yuan to flow into the hands of small collectives and individuals through hundreds of thousands of loopholes'. Such bribery was often conducted as much for the benefit of the factory or enterprise as for the individual (although he would share through bonuses in the resulting profits). Contracts were now regularly negotiated on the basis of what were called 'under-the-table relations' in which gifts or cash rebates were expected. As central planning began to loosen, local officials now had the new freedom to do business directly. The restoration to favour of the archetypal 'national bourgeois' businessman, who now enjoyed the use of private cars and luxury accommodation, also offered a tempting example. So did the opportunity to secure goods such as cameras, TV sets, and calculators from visits abroad or from foreign businessmen. One small drama group on tour to Japan was said to have returned with sixty-nine colour TVs and 138 watches.

By the mid-1980s corruption had grown considerably, and was now said to involve a number of 'veteran cadres and Party members' either directly or through their families. The *People's Daily* felt obliged to warn (11 Mar. 1985) that one reason why the Guomindang fell in 1949 was that 'officials were engaged in business and used their special powers to make large fortunes'. *Party Branch Life* (no. 5, 1985) carefully distinguished between 'old and new malpractices'. The former were the familiar types of activity over housing, jobs, college places for children, and changing the residence status for relatives from rural to urban areas. The latter involved economic activities carried out in the name of reform, and led to unjustified price increases, wasteful production of goods, and huge bonuses.

Some Party members . . . believe that 'reform means contracts and contracts means fishing for money', and they see reform purely as the reallocation of profit. In order to make money, they use any means they can to evade taxes, make false reports of profits, seize any opportunity to sell anything, raise prices at random, and engage in other illegal activities which undermine the foundations of society, harm consumers, and will lead to disorder and anarchy.

Party misbehaviour was tackled by the Central Discipline Inspection Commission, which carried out a three-tier 'rectification' of the membership between the 1982 and 1987 Party Congresses. It reported to the 1987 congress that more than 650,000 members had been disciplined, including over 150,000 who had been expelled. But it was evident from an earlier report by its president, the veteran leader Bo Yibo (in May 1987), that these figures were only achieved by counting in a large number of Party members who had supported the Gang of Four and had been 'ferreted out' in 1982–3 before the rectification began. The 1987 report admitted that the problem of 'unhealthy practices' was still acute and had seriously damaged popular trust in the Party.

Much was made of a small number of cases where high-ranking Party officials had been disciplined or expelled. The highest were the Minister of Forestry Yang Zhong, held responsible for the incompetent handling of a disastrous forest fire earlier in 1987 in the north-east, and a Central Committee member and director of Chinese civil aviation, Shen Du, who had mishandled funds. A few provincial officials were also exposed, as well as the unfortunate writer Zhou Erfu, who had watched pornographic films on a visit to Japan (this was described as 'seriously contravening discipline in foreign affairs'). Several other notorious cases, though not mentioned in the report, concerned the children of senior cadres who had been exposed and in at least two cases executed for rape. (This followed an instruction by Deng Xiaoping that an example should be made of such 'glaring cases'.)

But whatever would be claimed at the 1987 Party Congress, the lack of results had prompted the setting up of a new Party task force in the hands of the reformers in January 1986, after a meeting of 8,000 government and state cadres. This amounted to a challenge to the Discipline Inspection Commission, which claimed exclusive rights. The more conservative Commission also offended by arguing that economic reform was the main source of corruption. The reformers replied that, in the words of Hu Qili, 'we should not give up eating for fear of choking'. They also sought to shift the emphasis of rectification towards the more traditional 'feudal tendencies', especially in high places. When a year later the conservatives took the offensive in the anti-bourgeois liberalization campaign, backstreet gossip in Beijing claimed that it was because they had been touched too closely by recent attempts to rout out the 'little tigers'—their own sons and daughters. Corruption at this level faced the conservatives with a dilemma: they realized that it should be exposed to protect the reputation of the Party, but feared that exposure of its full extent would provide more ammunition for those who held the Party in increasingly open contempt. The veteran army leader Nie Rongzhen, in an open letter published in the army newspaper (25 Apr. 1987), instructed the Political Department of the armed forces to promote 'family education' among its senior cadres:

A small number of children of senior cadres have indeed done evil and perpetrated outrages by relying on their powerful family connections, or have lined their pockets or obtained official positions through the influence of their parents. Such things will certainly cause popular indignation and disgust. As a popular saying goes: 'A piece of rotten meat may ruin the whole pot of soup.' We should handle these cases impartially: those who are not promoted or appointed through regular organizational procedures should be demoted and dismissed; those who have committed crimes should be arrested and executed according to the law . . .

On the other hand, it is also necessary resolutely to expose the sinister plots of a small number of people who viciously slander cadres' children in an attempt to evoke a grievance from the masses and stir up trouble in society.

Towards political reform

If modernization was the magic weapon of the first decade after Mao, then 'political reform' became the new weapon of the late 1980s without which economic reform would not succeed. It was approached cautiously by those in the Party who saw it as a threat to their own status and the Party's prestige, but enthusiastically by those who wanted to reduce the Party's dominating role. (Deng Xiaoping's own position was somewhere in between.)

The failure of the rectification process to tackle seriously Party abuse breathed new life into the demand for political reform early in 1986. The need for it had been diagnosed several years before. The main problems in the Party and state leadership, Deng Xiaoping had said in August 1980, could only be overcome through reforms which would make people 'trust our leadership, our Party, and socialism'. Party reformers were already arguing in favour of the election of cadres, a proper system of supervision and removal, improvements in the legal system so that the Party would not be above the law, and the separation of the Party and state apparatus. Feng Wenbin, deputy director of the Central Party School, asked outright in the *People's Daily*: 'Why does the political system of our socialist country have so many defects?' His answer was a combination of 'feudal autocracy' (the relationship between the leader and his subordinates, Feng commented, had become like that 'between the cat and the rat'), excessive emphasis upon 'class struggle', and 'over-centralization'.

Six years later Deng returned to the theme, explaining that in 1980 nothing concrete had been done to put it on to the agenda. The press was dominated now by reformist arguments: Party malpractices, said the *People's Daily* (5 May 1986), could only be cured through political democracy including 'the right to criticize and supervise'. The greatest obstacle to economic reform, judged the *Workers' Daily* (30 May 1986), lay in 'serious abuses in the political system, feudal vestiges . . . the patriarchal system'. In July 1986 the Central Committee's Party School for cadres held an unprecedented seminar, which included academic reformers from outside the Party propaganda and theoretical establishment. One young scholar even suggested a multiparty system.[10]

It could fairly be said that since 1976 some progress had been made in overhauling the political machine. The achievements were listed by the Party propaganda head, Zhu Houze, and other speakers. They included:

- a return to more normal political life with the arrest or dismissal of Gang of Four supporters;
- the re-establishment of central control over wayward provinces;
- strengthening of state control over the armed forces; greater autonomy for trade unions, professional groups, and the small 'democratic parties';
- the beginnings of a legal system, with codified laws and regular courts under a judiciary with a degree of autonomy;
- abolition in principle of life tenure for Party and government cadres;
- direct elections at the county level and below for people's congress delegates;
- restoration of the rural townships, separating out Party, government, and economic authority in the countryside, which had previously been combined on the 'one man wearing three pairs of trousers' principle.

Conservatives were happy with reforms which returned to the more 'normal' practices of the mid-1950s, but reformers argued that China had to move on. If socialism has not yet reached its highest stage, said the *Guangming Daily* (7 June 1986), then neither has democracy. Besides, even today there are places 'where even formal democracy does not exist, the will of the people cannot be expressed, and the views of the leader are not transmitted downwards'. Political reform, the Party seminar was told, should follow the development of the economy, according to the law that the 'superstructure' should conform to changes in the 'economic base'. The new reforms required the services of talented managers who were held back by the current cadre system. The Party secretariat leader Wang Zhaoguo, himself talent-spotted a few years before by Deng Xiaoping as a successful factory manager at the Second Automobile Factory in Harbin, told the seminar that cadres from now on should become 'Marxist theorists, excellent political leaders, and socialist entrepreneurs'.

Deng's support was vital for the reformers. A quotation in which he had talked of 'comprehensive economic restructuring' as also affecting the political field gave them the authority to proceed. The journal *Social Sciences in China* (Mar. 1986) admitted that some people thought that 'political restructuring' should be postponed to the 1990s. But others quoted Engels: when state power moves in the opposite direction to economic development, it can do great damage and cause enormous waste of energy and material. In a crucial passage, the journal extended the frontier of political reform to the verge of creating a classless society:

The socialist state should mark the transition from a state based on class to one based on society, and from primarily direct control to primarily indirect control, and become a democratized and socialized state.

Deng soon gave a more direct testimonial to political reform: 'In the final analysis,' he said, 'all our other reforms depend on the success of the political reform, because it is human beings who will—or will not—carry them out' (28 June 1986). But Deng also set limits which should have warned the academic reformers that they were in danger of going too far. The separation of Party and government had already been forecast in his August 1980 speech. His other main requirements were for the devolution of some powers to local authorities, and the streamlining of administration. But he added soon afterwards (13 Sept. 1986) that the present structure of leadership had some advantages: 'For example, it enables us to make quick decisions, while if we place too much emphasis upon checks and balances, problems may arise.' More explicitly, he stipulated on 12 June 1987, after the campaign against bourgeois liberalism, that 'we should neither copy western democracy nor introduce the system of a balance of three powers'.

Deng's position flowed from his desire to fashion not a weaker but a stronger Party which would be capable of modernizing China where it had previously failed. The Cultural Revolution had come about because the Party in 1966 failed to use its theoretical majority to vote down Mao's plans and press ahead instead with the Four Modernizations. Nor had it been able to prevent the alienation of public opinion which resulted from the Cultural Revolutionary excesses. Deng sought a responsible and responsive Party, but not a Party which allowed a dilution of its leading role. No one should be interested, said the *China Daily* (17 July 1987), in 'a separate purely political effort to reform the political structure'.

The conservative reaction

A Chinese cadre with many years of experience abroad laments in conversation the declining morale among youth which he discovered on returning home in 1985. For example: his nephew had turned up from the countryside, seeking his advice. Where could he buy a foreign-made refrigerator? The cadre advised him to hang around outside the shop where Chinese workers who have earned money abroad can purchase such goods—which are then resold on the street at a profit. The nephew took his advice. But instead of just purchasing one for his own use, he bought four, took them all home, and sold them to rich peasants! How could such things have been imagined only a few years ago?

Another cadre worries about his eldest son. Instead of working hard for college, he watches foreign videos on subjects which could not be shown publicly. He belongs to the Youth League, but says quite openly that it is only for the purpose of getting recommended to a good job. Worse still, he has been reading Jean-Paul Sartre and other favourite authors of those who espouse 'bourgeois liberalism'. The cadre explains the Party position on Sartre: he made a very good stand in the Spanish Civil War. But the Party cannot accept his existentialism: it does not reflect socialist reality.

Party support for what is generally labelled the 'conservative' reaction to reform and change, expressed notably in the campaigns against spiritual pollution (1983) and bourgeois liberalism (1987), was fuelled by an instinctive disquiet among large numbers of lower- or middle-level cadres at the way things were going. A generation brought up to be wary of 'the sugar-coated bullets of the bourgeoisie' against which Mao had warned after Liberation, found that its own children enjoyed the taste. Such cadres had often acquiesced or benefited from the small-scale privileges which came their way 'through the backdoor' during the years of hardship. Now they baulked at the enormous profits made by the new 'suitcase businesses', paper companies set up by the families of senior cadres taking advantage of their official connections. Ideologically, the conservatives still saw nothing wrong in asking people to show a proper 'communist spirit' and to practise the 'hard struggle' style of Lei Feng, the model soldier of the 1960s.

The five years between the Twelfth and Thirteenth Party Congresses (1982–7) was a period of uneven transition in which Chinese society changed more rapidly than at any time since 1949 (although still sluggishly compared to its transformation in the 1990s).

The most senior conservative leaders had themselves been targets of the Cultural Revolution (Peng Zhen) or advocates of reform in the 1950s (Chen Yun). Their strongest political weapon was that while they were still in office, the rejuvenation of the leadership regarded as essential by the reformers could only proceed lamely. A dominant political theme during these five years was the step-by-step easing out of the 'old bosses' into the newly set up Central Advisory Commission. It was also a period of uneven transition in the style of political argument. The reformers deployed their views at conferences and seminars, sometimes with foreign participation, or in new journals like the *World Economic Herald* (which had a contents page in English). The conservatives relied on more traditional organs such as the Party monthly *Red Flag* (whose circulation had slumped and was now hard to find on sale, even at post offices which were supposed to stock it). Their arguments had a leftist tinge, often resorting to selective quotes and to accusations of lack of patriotism which carried an ugly echo of past rhetoric. Their theoretical chief Deng Liqun had been Liu Shaoqi's secretary, but several among his team of ideological hacks had ultra-left connections with the Cultural Revolution. Personal prejudice and ambition played a part in the reaction. The veterans resented the assurance of a clique of younger leaders around Hu Yaobang (most of whom had worked with him when he ran the Youth League). They complained that Hu had not properly consulted them—just as Mao once complained that Deng Xiaoping ignored him. Deng Liqun had resisted the Gang of Four campaign against Deng Xiaoping in 1976, and wished to be rewarded with Hu's post of General Secretary. But these factional motives were intertwined with serious ideological objections. The conservatives still asserted the validity of the central core of post-1949 doctrine: the necessity of Party leadership, the primacy of the state in the economy, and the dominance of a socialist spirit. The reformers did not openly dissent, but diluted these principles in practice, and tolerated or encouraged reform-minded economists and social scientists to go much further. Hu Yaobang's famous statement in December 1984 that Marxism could not solve 'all of China's problems' was in principle not much different from Mao's sinification of Marxism in the 1940s, but it was viewed correctly by the conservatives as a green light for ideological revision.

The People's Liberation Army (PLA) adopted a left-of-conservative position. Although the target of the Gang of Four in 1975–6 (and, under Marshal Ye Jianying, the guarantor of the anti-Gang coup after Mao's death), it had been politically moulded by a decade of Lin Biao's 'politics in command'—the Little Red Book was originally compiled as an army manual. During the Cultural Revolution army units had worked hard to carry out Mao's instruction to 'support the left', seeking to keep essential communications going and to encourage the less extreme rebel groups. Many now failed to see why all their efforts should be written off as 'negative'. In essence, the PLA resented the loss of its shining vanguard role and a fall in prestige which meant that military service was no longer so socially desirable. (The new economic policies now offered career opportunities which at one time were only available through the PLA.) Nor was the PLA sufficiently compensated by new military technology. Defence spending was cut—to 10 per cent of the budget by 1987—and defence was the least prominent of the Four Modernizations. Throughout the 1982–7 period Deng Xiaoping found it necessary to retain control of the chairmanship of the Party's Military Commission and (from 1983) of the new State Military Commission which had been intended to provide a separate source of civilian authority over the PLA. Finally, soldiers were still fighting and dying on the Vietnamese border after the ill-advised war launched by Deng in 1979, where they were exhorted to remain living examples of self-sacrifice and the Lei Feng spirit. Why should they continue to do so if the rest of society turned its back on socialist hard struggle?

The ambiguous feelings of many Chinese leaders towards reform were summed up most influentially in the person of Deng Xiaoping himself. Every bout of conservative reaction had been licensed by Deng, although he withdrew the licence when it had served his purpose. Some reformers claimed he was acting for reasons of tactical necessity, but he drew a firm and consistent line which was not to be crossed. This had been defined first at the height of the Democracy Movement when in March 1979 he proclaimed the Four Principles:

1. Red Army veteran, Nanniwan, Shaanxi province, 1980. The soldiers of Nanniwan were renowned for "hard struggle" in the revolution and grew their own food.

2. Peasant activists, Dazhai Brigade, Shanxi province, c. 1968. Dazhai under its leader Chen Yonggui (fifth from right, front row) was the national model for agriculture.

3. Mao Zedong and Lin Biao reviewing Red Guards, Tiananmen Square, 1966. Lin died in an aircrash in 1971 after allegedly launching a failed coup d'etat

4. Beijing citizens mobilised by "ultra-left" leaders, 8 April 1976, on an official march to counter a genuine demonstration mourning the death of Premier Zhou Enlai.

5. Portrait of Zhang Zhixin, victim of Cultural Revolution, placed unofficially in Tiananmen Square, March 1980. Zhang's throat was cut to prevent her protesting her innocence.

6. Traffic in Tianjin, the third largest city, 1980: China would remain a nation of bicycles for another decade. The home-made sidecar is for carrying a child.

7. Pro-democracy students march on May Day 1989, watched by crowds. They carry slogans ridiculing Premier Li Peng and calling for an end to corruption.

8. Deng Xiaoping, aged 75, visiting Mount Huangshan, July 1979. As part of his new reforms, Deng called for the expansion of Chinese tourism.

9. School children queue to enter the temple of Yue Fu, Henan province, 1991, as the religious revival spreads in China. The large character denotes "filial piety".

10. Volunteers in a public safety campaign, Guang'an, Sichuan province, 1995. They are handing out material on the safe use of electrical appliances.

11. A modestly well-off taxidriver and family, Taiyuan, Shanxi province, 1999. He has bought his taxi with a loan from relatives and owns his own house.

12. On the telephone, Fuzhou, 1998. Public phones are no longer hard to find and China has become the world's largest producer of cell-phones.

13. A poor village school teacher, Poyang Lake, Jiangxi province, 2002. His blackboard has been in use for thirty years.

14. Jiang Zemin and Hu Jintao, National People's Congress, 14 March 2004. Though Hu had already become head of Party and State, Jiang continued to wield influence.

1. We must keep to the socialist road.
2. We must uphold the dictatorship of the proletariat.
3. We must uphold the leadership of the Communist Party.
4. We must uphold Marxism-Leninism and Mao Zedong Thought.

It was Deng who had insisted on the punishment of the dissident Wei Jingsheng. Seven years later he still argued defensively that it was justified, linking Wei with those now calling for 'bourgeois liberalism'. In October 1983 Deng endorsed the criticism of 'spiritual pollution' already raised tentatively by Deng Liqun. People working in the ideological field, he said, 'must not spread spiritual pollution . . . They have engaged in discussions of the value of the human being, humanism, and alienation, and have only been interested in criticizing socialism, not capitalism.' Many at the time believed that Deng was forced to sanction the campaign after private pressure from his veteran colleagues, who had pointedly asked him to 'pay attention to the nation's state of health'. But Deng's speech of 12 October 1983 showed the same hurt bafflement shared by many senior cadres. Why is it, he asked, that China had allowed 'harmful elements of bourgeois culture to be introduced without impediment', including the import of material which was regarded even in the West as 'pernicious junk'? Deng also criticized the reform-minded intellectuals—at this stage still only venturing their views with circumspection—for objecting to conservative censure. Real Marxists should be allowed to step forward and speak up against wrong ideas without people complaining that the big stick of the Cultural Revolution was being wielded again. The same resentment at what conservatives regarded as modish reformism which cried foul when it was criticized would be voiced in the 1987 campaign against bourgeois liberalism.

The campaign against spiritual pollution betrayed the obsession of old men and jealous cadres with the trivia of daily life and a nostalgia for earlier simplicity. The reformist Party secretariat was soon able to compile a dossier of absurdities: women had been told not to let their hair descend below the shoulders; soldiers had been ordered to hand over photographs of their girlfriends; the Beijing Party Committee posted a notice banning long hair and high-heeled shoes; young people had their sunglasses confiscated in the street. More seriously, some newly rich peasants committed suicide because their bank accounts were frozen; cadres and soldiers from the countryside were forbidden to seek spouses in the towns; and foreign investors were postponing signature of contracts. At a critical Politburo meeting, Premier

Zhao Ziyang produced a letter from Japan asking for a postponement of loan negotiations, and threatened to resign.[11] In the resulting compromise, a limit was set on the campaign, notably excluding the rural population as well as interference with clothing and hairstyles. The Chinese working class regarded the campaign with amused contempt—'I think I'll buy a tube of spiritual pollution', said fashion-minded girls as they purchased lipstick and make-up. Teachers and intellectuals, who had destroyed lecture notes and manuscripts or paintings in the first days of panic, felt less confident. The ultra-left ideologues waited for another chance to ally with Party conservatism.

The Party style

Only the first of the three targets set at the 1982 Party Congress—to 'bring about an all-round upsurge' of the economy—had been achieved. Progress towards the other two goals, to fundamentally improve 'standards of social conduct' and 'the working style of the Party', was slower and in the view of many non-Party people almost non-existent. It was supposed to be helped by the selection of more responsive and younger leaders. By the late 1980s cadres at the most senior level often showed a degree of informality and initiative which was refreshingly new. At local levels, the new economic policies also favoured younger people with entrepreneurial talents. The main problem lay at the intermediate level, the thick 'filling' in the bureaucratic sandwich which was most resistant to change. 'It is not the new policies I find difficult,' said the Mayor of Shanghai in 1984; 'it is finding good people to carry them out.'

The transformation of *dangfeng*—the Party's style of work—was slow and still heavily influenced by past political culture. It is doubtful whether any of the younger generation of leaders now in their late forties or fifties could have reached their present office without the sponsorship of senior leaders. Potential successors from existing cadre families would start with an advantage, and those with real talent who lacked family connections usually needed to catch the personal attention of leaders from the 'higher level' in order to make their way.

When in January 1987 Premier Zhao Ziyang took over as acting Party Secretary-General from the disgraced Hu Yaobang, two names were immediately mentioned as likely successors to his own post of premiership. These were the two Lis, Vice-Premier Li Peng and Mayor of Tianjin Li

Ruihuan, men of widely contrasting background who nevertheless had both been 'fostered'.

Li Ruihuan, born in 1934, was a self-educated carpenter who caught the Party leadership's eye in 1959 when he was working on construction of the Great Hall of the People in Beijing. In keeping with the Great Leap spirit of technological short-cuts, he proposed to eliminate the need for detail mock-ups by master craftsmen. As a result, the time taken to lay the flooring in the Great Hall was cut from an estimated one month to sixteen days. Later he wrote an article in the *China Youth* magazine using carpentry technique to demonstrate the truth of Mao's dialectical argument that 'One Divides into Two'. Li achieved further merit after Mao's death as deputy manager of the construction of the Mao Zedong Mausoleum, another rush job which was finished in six months. He came to the attention of the reforming Vice-Premier Wan Li, and was sent to Tianjin where he solved the problem of temporary housing for victims of the 1976 Tangshan earthquake within a year. He was promoted to become Mayor in 1981, replacing Hu Qili (a protégé of Hu Yaobang who moved to the Party secretariat in Beijing). He rapidly acquired a national reputation for tackling Tianjin's rundown urban environment. A scheme to arrange for workers to swap flats so that long hours of commuting to their jobs could be saved was particularly admired. Li became known as the 'darling' of the national leadership. Although he was not the eventual choice for Premier, he joined the Politburo in 1988.[12]

Li Peng, born in 1928, the son of the 'revolutionary martyr' Li Shuoxun, was informally adopted by Zhou Enlai at the age of 11. He spent the war years in Yanan, and was sent to the Soviet Union in 1948, graduating with honours six years later from the Institute of Dynamics. Protected by Zhou during the Cultural Revolution, Li became responsible for energy policy in the late 1970s, tackling this crucial area of the economic superstructure with enthusiasm. He joined the Party Politburo and Secretariat in 1985, having visited both the Soviet Union (for the Chernenko funeral) and the US, where he studied nuclear and other energy projects, in the same year. Li became Premier in 1988, but was not a popular choice. His careful avoidance of difficult political issues pleased the Party's conservatives but was judged colourless and disappointing by public opinion. Although fairly able, his rapid promotion was not so dissimilar from the 'helicopter' elevations for which the Cultural Revolution leaders had been criticized—and public opinion would soon take a much harsher view of him.[13]

The mythology of self-sacrifice on the part of Party leaders survived in the 1980s but was greeted with growing cynicism outside. At the top they were still conventionally described as working late into the night with little regard for their personal comfort, in the tradition of the late Premier Zhou Enlai. At lower levels, they still sought merit by going on tours of inspection to 'listen to the opinions' of the masses, braving bad weather, missing meals, and rolling up their sleeves to join in hard work. In 1986 Hu Qili, then head of the Party secretariat, described the selflessness of the leadership (and in particular of his patron, Secretary-General Hu Yaobang) in these terms:

The central leaders working on the front line handle a host of things every day as regards domestic and international affairs, but they still keep in contact with the broad masses of the people through different channels. Our leaders do not have spare time and a day off is, of course, out of the question. Moreover, in order to read documents and letters from the people, they often have to work late into the night . . . Every year, the central leaders try and find time to go down to factories and the countryside in order to make investigations and studies. There are more than 2,200 counties through the country. Secretary-General Hu Yaobang has been to at least 1,500.[14]

Total Party membership in 1988 was 47.75 million. There was still a steady flow of applicants to join. Two million were accepted in 1987 out of eight million applicants, according to the Party's Organization Department. Yet the assumption that one only joined the Party in order to secure personal advantage was widespread, and the reformist leaders recognized the gap which had to be bridged. Political reform, said the *People's Daily* (1 July 1987), was

a gigantic social systems engineering project, which involves straightening out the relationships between the Party and the government, power and judicial organs, mass organizations, enterprises, and institutions, and between central, local, and grass-roots organizations; it concerns hundreds of millions of people. This is an arduous and protracted task.

It would be brought to a juddering halt by the bloody confrontation between reform and reaction, with the student democracy movement as catalyst, in 1989, and the years of caution which followed. More than a decade later, the momentum for political reform had still not been restored.

10

The Scholars Speak Out
Humanism or Bourgeois Liberalism?

In November 1985, a year before he became known as 'China's Sakharov', the astrophysicist Fang Lizhi had given a speech to students at the Department of Wireless Electronics at Beijing University (Beida). Fang argued that Chinese intellectuals should be concerned with society as a whole, and should be encouraged by the Communist Party to do so. Instead the leadership had tried to solve the current crisis in education by simply inviting a few notable professors to 'come and have a meal'. Intellectuals in China, Fang complained, had for too long been marginalized from political life. 'Take care of pulling the cart,' said the authorities, and 'never mind anything else.' How different this was from the West where, in spite of the hollowness of much of its society, many intellectuals had a real sense of social responsibility which was lacking in China.

Perhaps Fang's speech would have been overlooked, but he broke the rule strictly observed by more cautious reform-minded scholars in China of the 1980s: He named names. If there was a crisis of ideals as the present leadership lamented, he said, then it started at the top—and he offered a 'practical example':

Recently an academic seminar on acceleration equipment was held in the US, with both Taiwan and the mainland participating. I naturally assumed that experts and specialists in this field would go. However . . . many of those who went were not even physicists and had nothing to do with acceleration equipment. Is this how we abide by our rules and regulations? Among those who went was the vice-mayor of Beijing, Zhang Baifa [applause]. I don't know what he was doing there! [loud laughter]. If you're talking about lack of discipline and breaking rules, here is a flagrant example! . . . (*China Spring*, Feb. 1987)

The next day, Fang received a message from the Academy of Sciences, parent body of his own college, ordering him to apologize to the Beijing Party Committee. He refused to do so and thereby gave offence to one of the senior Academy officials, Gu Yu, the wife of the conservative ideologue Hu Qiaomu (once Mao's secretary). He soon had to apply to her office for his passport to leave the country for another conference in the US. It was withheld until he 'recognized his mistake'. In Anhui province where he worked, the top-ranking Party leader came personally with the same request: Everyone else did what the 'high-ups' asked. Why couldn't he? Eventually, Fang spent half a day talking with Hu Qili, one of the leading Politburo reformers. At last he got his passport, but he would soon be in trouble again.[1]

The scholars' licence

Chinese scholars have traditionally played a validating role for those in power, whether rewriting history to prove the iniquities of a fallen dynasty or demonstrating the Confucian propriety of the new emperor's edicts. The obligation to validate may be accompanied by a degree of licence to enquire beyond the established frontiers. During the Cultural Revolution, such liberty was available only to the committed or opportunistic. (The most famous was the Liang Xiao—a homonym for 'Two Schools' because it was drawn from Beida and Qinghua universities—Big Criticism Group organized by Jiang Qing in 1973 to renew the attack on 'bourgeois ideology'. It was housed in a lakeside guest-house with private rooms and access to foodstuffs in short supply elsewhere. A similar writing group in Shanghai, serving Zhang Chunqiao and Yao Wenyuan's polemical needs, was lodged comfortably in the Ding Xiang Guesthouse—the former residence of the young concubine of imperial official Li Hongzhang.) For the rest, as one scholar later recalled, 'when someone above says you are right, then you are right. Otherwise, you are wrong.' The story of intellectual activity in the 1980s was largely that of the struggle by a growing number of reform-minded intellectuals to broaden this licence, particularly in the sensitive fields of political and social science. A few of them would go beyond the bounds, denying (to the disapproval of some of their more cautious colleagues) that a licence was needed at all, and falling foul of the campaign against bourgeois liberalism in winter 1986. Party Secretary-General Hu Yaobang, who had greatly widened the scope of permissible intellectual enquiry in the previous two years, was forced to resign. Within another two years, the licence had been renewed under the new Party leader Zhao Ziyang, although with important provisos—and was abruptly withdrawn in 1989.

Intellectuals had been regarded with mixed feelings by the Party after it took power in 1949. Distinguished artists and scholars were personally honoured by Mao, whose own scholarly pretensions were far from modest, but many Party cadres were suspicious of those with a better and often foreign education. Mao himself periodically accused intellectuals of taking too tender a view of past Chinese history. The origins of the Cultural Revolution would later be traced back to these earlier interventions, starting with his denunciation in 1951 of a film, *The Life of Wu Hsun*, which presented an overly favourable view of a poor peasant in the mid-nineteenth century who became a wealthy philanthropist. 'Our writers', he said, 'do not bother to study Chinese history and learn who were the enemies oppressing the Chinese people.' By the mid-1950s the intellectuals appeared to have won the leadership's confidence. Bracketed until then as part of the bourgeoisie, their social status was reclassified during the Hundred Flowers campaign by Zhou Enlai. 'The overwhelming majority of the intellectuals', he said, 'have become government workers in the service of socialism and are already part of the working class.' Living conditions at Beijing University were improved, recalls Yue Daiyun, then a young teacher. 'Everybody was excited in 1956; we thought the fight had finished and that we could concentrate finally on building our country.'[2] But Mao took a more critical view as the wave of scholarly criticism broke over the Party during the campaign. Most intellectuals, he concluded, had not yet managed to shed their 'bourgeois world outlook . . . and unite with the workers and peasants'.

As many as 200,000 intellectuals were labelled as 'rightists' in the reaction to the Hundred Flowers, prevented from teaching or writing, and sent to work for long periods in the countryside. Conditions for many improved again in the early 1960s, but they remained easy targets for denunciation in the Cultural Revolution. Paradoxically the old 'rightists' often suffered less, physically, than the newly identified 'black elements' in the Party, but the physical and psychological toll was still enormous. (Out of a group of ten Chinese students in Britain who returned home after Liberation, two committed suicide during the Cultural Revolution, and one had his back broken by the Red Guards.)

From 1978 onwards China's intellectuals gained new confidence from the Party's new policies of reform. Sometimes they even received an apology for past mistreatment. In spring 1983 Lu Dingyi, once head of the Communist Party's Propaganda Department, sent a self-criticism to Hu Yaobang on 'the question of knowledge and intellectuals'. (It was Lu who in May 1956 had launched the Hundred Flowers.) Lu wrote that, although a graduate himself, he had 'failed to take note of the particular importance of knowledge and intellectuals during the period of socialist construction'. An army without culture was a dull-witted army, he continued. The Party leadership and its poorly educated cadres shared the weakness of ignorance, which led 'those without knowledge to look down upon those with knowledge'. Intellectuals had been subjected to oppression 'and were even listed as the "target of dictatorship" during the Cultural Revolution'.[3]

In spite of such admissions, the intellectuals' position was still vulnerable. They could reasonably complain that they were the first to suffer when the political wind blew from the conservative quarter and the last to benefit from its easing. They felt the chill in 1980, after the army writer Bai Hua was criticized for his film-script *Bitter Love*. The film's hero was an intellectual who returned home to help China and was victimized. 'You love the motherland, but does the motherland love you?', it asked. It portrayed Mao too openly as an idol 'blackened by the smoke of burning joss-sticks and candles of faithful believers'. The literary and art worlds were among the first targets in the 1983 campaign against 'spiritual pollution', accused of promoting modernism, abstract humanitarianism, pessimism, egoism, and sexual liberation. A depressing feature of every conservative backlash was the willingness of more than one radical figure from the past to side with the critics. In 1983 this included the feminist Ding Ling, who had been purged from 1958 to 1978, spending five of those years in prison and three more raising chickens and pigs in a Shanxi village. Perhaps disturbed by the bolder ideas of younger writers, she now wrote censoriously:

If light music is played in the theatres, everyone applauds, but when they hear serious music, no one does. It has even got to the point that when someone sings 'Without the Communist Party there would be no New China', people laugh. Another peculiar thing is that, because some foreign scholars praise certain works, our people say they are good. Young people like liberalism too much.[4]

Yet overall the intellectuals' licence to enquire and explore continued to broaden. In part this was a response to market pressures: writers and film-makers were now supposed to be entrepreneurial and provide saleable books or films, reducing the need for state subsidy. The interest of the outside world in Chinese intellectual activity also provided some security. Political and social scientists were more directly involved in providing the intellectual back-up for the Party reformers while depending on their patronage. This relationship of mutual dependence would directly provoke the next conservative backlash, the 1987 campaign against bourgeois liberalism.

Opening the debate

Chinese scholars—'theoretical workers' in Marxism and economics—established an informal alliance with the reform wing of the Party leadership to prepare the ideological ground for change. Over ten years they shifted official thinking from the repetition of the dogmas of the Cultural Revolution to the acceptance of market socialism and the separation of Party and state powers. The scholars were not tame ideologues and sometimes moved ahead of their political backers, almost disastrously in 1986–7 when several heads were sacrificed to the conservatives, but although always cautious about public expression of their ideas, they gained a degree of intellectual autonomy unthinkable a decade before. As the *People's Daily* observed (21 July 1986):

Encouraging the people to speak their minds is not easy, because once in our country there prevailed a political atmosphere of not allowing them to say what they really think and also of being unwilling to listen to their innermost thoughts and feelings . . . In those days, to speak one's mind was to invite an unexpected calamity; without feigning politeness and compliance, it was hardly possible to live a peaceful life. But those who were willing to kiss the feet of some people would be in their good graces . . . Such a situation was completely abnormal . . . To encourage people to speak their minds, we must first and foremost adhere to the principle of freedom of speech as stipulated in the Constitution and we should not infringe on the right of the people to state their views.

In May 1977 a small group of scholars were brought together by Hu Yaobang to discuss the proposition that 'Practice is the only criterion of truth'. This apparently innocuous statement, which echoed Mao's earlier teachings ('No right to speak without investigation'), was in fact a direct theoretical challenge to the mainstream Maoist view that socialist truth was self-evident and

enshrined in Mao Zedong's policies and directives (the 'Two Whatevers').
Politically it meant an offensive by Hu on Deng Xiaoping's behalf against
the leadership known as the 'Small Gang of Four' under Hua Guofeng
(Beijing Mayor Wu De, Mao's former bodyguard Wang Dongxing, Beijing
regional commander Chen Xilian, and Politburo member Ji Dengkui). By
February 1978 the power struggle had begun to shift in Deng's favour. Li
Xin, the conservative historian who had drafted the 'Two Whatevers', failed
to enter the Politburo and the Small Gang of Four began to lose influence.
In May 1978 the proposition that 'Practice is the only criterion for truth'
was published in an article in the *Guangming Daily*, then known as the
intellectuals' newspaper. This opened the way for public discussion and was
shortly followed by speeches in which both Deng and Hu attacked the 'Two
Whatevers'. The significance of this theoretical argument was later stressed
in official Party histories on the grounds that it provided a 'good preparation' for the Third Plenum in December 1978 which approved Deng's
new course of reform. The *Guangming Daily* article argued that even when a
theory had been tested in practice, it must be tested again, and altered if
necessary, as circumstances changed. Its appeal for a scientific approach was
central to the reformers' attack upon dogma:

In theory or in practical work, the Gang of Four set many 'forbidden zones' which
fettered people's minds. We must dare to investigate these 'forbidden zones' and
dare to correct them because in fact there are no forbidden zones in real science.
Wherever there is a 'forbidden zone' which transcends practice and styles itself as
absolute, there is no science of real Marxism-Leninism-Mao Zedong Thought;
there is only obscurantism, idealism, and cultural despotism . . .

Immediately after the Third Plenum the discussion group was enlarged to
form the nucleus of a running internal 'Seminar on the ideological principles of theoretical work' which became seen as another landmark in Party
history. But on this occasion the reformist scholars discovered the point at
which Deng Xiaoping would draw the line, and divisions began to appear
within their ranks. In the phrase much used to indicate the rejection of
dogma, those who attended had 'liberated minds' and put forward proposals
which would not be aired publicly for several more years. These included
the abolition of lifelong tenure for Party and government leaders, the concept that socialism should be divided into different stages, and the proposal
that more than one candidate should stand in elections.

After more than two months of discussion, Deng Xiaoping returned from
the United States and (at the same time as the first arrests were made on

Democracy Wall) set a firm limit on the scholars' debate. China's long-term task, he said, was to modernize, and politics was now above all about modernization. But it could only be achieved on the basis of the 'Four Principles' which Deng now enunciated for the first time: 'To keep to the Socialist Road, to uphold the Dictatorship of the Proletariat, the Leadership of the Communist Party, Marxism-Leninism and Mao Zedong Thought.' At this point the more orthodox theoreticians led by Deng Liqun detached themselves from the reformers, seeing the Four Principles as a weapon against too radical change. The more outspoken reformers regarded the Four Principles as contrary to the spirit of testing theory in practice, but the formula could not be directly opposed, particularly after it was incorporated into the Constitution.[5]

Extending the frontiers

Reformist scholars provided much of the intellectual groundwork for the 1981 Party Resolution, although the leadership and particularly Deng had the last word. The Resolution included the crucial sentence that 'China's socialist system remains at its initial stage', a formulation originated by neo-Marxist Professor Su Shaozhi, which would legitimize further enquiries. Before and after the Resolution, the frontiers of debate were steadily extended against conservative opposition.

Class struggle

The December 1978 Plenum had marked the initial victory of the reformers by saying that the Party could now 'shift the focus of work' from class struggle to economic construction. But the 1981 Resolution still said that 'class struggle will continue to exist within certain limits for a long time to come and may even grow acute under certain conditions'. This provided a reserve weapon for leftist critics to employ when they had the opportunity. In December 1981 the Party reformer Liao Gailong spoke on 'the problem of class struggle in socialist society', returning to Mao's view during the Hundred Flowers period (1956–7) that this had been 'basically resolved' in China. Su Shaozhi had already gone further, suggesting that the term was either out of date or to the extent that it was still used meant something different. Mao's formulation in 1957 had allowed that 'class struggle within the ranks of the people' could, if handled properly, remain 'non-antagonistic' and susceptible to being resolved peacefully. Su said that it would be more sensible to rename this as 'ideological remoulding' to avoid the term being abused by those who, like Lin Biao, had wished to widen the struggle. The real effect of this argument was to empty the term 'class struggle' of its previous connotations while preserving it as a concession to the Party purists. Su similarly sought to redefine the 'dictatorship of the proletariat', which had been used to justify the deprivation of many people's most basic rights during the Cultural Revolution and was still insisted upon by official post-Mao dogma. Yes, it still existed under socialism, Su conceded, but as a means of exercising political leadership rather than ruling by force.[6]

Alienation

The 1981 Resolution on Party History had accounted for the Cultural Revolution largely in terms of a historic failure 'to handle the relationship between the Party and its leader correctly'. Wang Ruoshui, deputy editor-in-chief of the *People's Daily*, wrote that the problem was not just the relationship between the Party and its leader, but that between the Party, the leader, and the people. 'Not only did the Party and state find it hard to prevent the initiation of the Cultural Revolution, but also the people did not have the strength to prevent that disaster'—nor indeed, he added, had they necessarily wanted to. The relationship between the leader and the masses was a form of alienation in which the people who had made the revolution and from whom the Party and its leader emerged transferred the power which they had won to those in authority. He compared the near-deification of Mao with man's attribution of his own wisdom and nature to God. It was the people, not Mao, who were the life-giving 'sun', and the people, not the Party, who should be compared to the 'mother'. The problem was not merely how to avoid the return of plotters like the Gang of Four, but how to prevent 'public servants of society transferring themselves to masters of society':

Once a Party which was formerly under oppression comes into power, its position is changed. There is the danger that it will cut itself off from the masses and become alienated; there is the possibility for it to become alienated. When a Party, which formerly served the people and was a tool and servant of the people, is divorced from the people and becomes an aristocratic overlord, it no longer belongs to the working class but has become an alienated force . . .

This problem exists at all levels of our leadership and has not yet been solved. The Party Central Committee has taken notice of it. Promoting democracy, perfecting the legal system, laying down the rules governing life in the Party, and abolishing the system of life-long appointment of cadres—we may say these are all measures for preventing alienation. ('On Alienation', May 1981)[7]

Democracy

The concept of democracy as the 'fifth modernization', first put forward by the Democracy Wall dissident leader Wei Jingsheng, was applied concretely by the neo-Marxist scholars to the drive for economic rationality and efficiency. It could be argued that the Chinese economy had made its best progress when there was a relatively more democratic atmosphere (the mid-1950s, early 1960s, and post-1978). 'Without democracy', Su Shaozhi had written in a paper for an international conference in Yugoslavia (Sept. 1980), 'there are no Four Modernizations . . . The masses of the working people are the masters of the country and of the enterprises. It is therefore important to ensure that the people truly have the power to manage the affairs of the state and of the enterprises. It is an important factor for preventing the evils of bureaucracy.'

Party traditionalists had always reacted to calls for democracy with the warning that this could lead to a collapse of the Party's leadership. This argument was countered by the director of the Fujian Academy of Sciences Li Honglin, who wrote in March 1982 that the opposite of democracy is not 'authority' but 'autocracy', and that the real opposition is between 'the authority of democracy and the authority of autocracy'. He also rejected the claim that too much talk about democracy led to social disorder, arguing that on the contrary it was the lack of publicity in favour of democracy which fostered the survival of the kind of 'feudal autocracy' that had led to the 'anarchy' of the Cultural Revolution.[8]

Early in 1983, the scholars' enquiry reached a new high point at a conference called to celebrate the anniversary of Marx's death. Su Shaozhi argued that Marxism was often accused of being out of date but had only itself to blame for treating new questions in a dogmatic manner. He called for a fresh analysis of advanced capitalist society and a scientific study of the errors committed by Stalin and Mao Zedong, while looking again at the ideas of Rosa Luxemburg and Bukharin. The veteran Party ideologue Zhou Yang, known in the past as a conformist who was willing to denounce his colleagues, now spoke positively on the concept of alienation in analysing socialist society. His speech created a sensation, but the conference was instantly adjourned for two days to give the conservatives time to organize criticism of Zhou. Led by Hu Qiaomu, another veteran ideologue whose thought had not moved with the times, they would prevail upon Deng Xiaoping to endorse the autumn campaign against spiritual pollution, closely identified with the concept of alienation.

The failure of this short-lived period of reaction underlined the essential weakness of the conservative-left critique—its lack of a coherent intellectual alternative other than to warn that the *political* effects of reformist argument might be dangerous. Even Hu Qiaomu did not deny that the concept of 'Marxist humanism' was valid, but he warned that even 'well-intentioned' discussion of it would encourage anarchist and individualist tendencies of thought. With remarkable speed the reform argument was resumed, encouraged once again by Hu Yaobang, who warned sharply against 'residual leftist poison' which had penetrated the Party very deeply. In December 1984 Hu dramatically extended further the terms of the scholars' licence in a manner which attracted international attention:

[Marx's] works were written more than a hundred years ago. Some were his tentative ideas at that time, and things have changed greatly since then. Some of his tentative ideas were not necessarily very appropriate. Many things have happened which Marx and Engels did not experience, and which even Lenin did not experience, so they had no contact with them. We cannot expect the writings of Marx and Lenin at that time to provide solutions to our current problems. (7 Dec.)

In the storm (fanned by the foreign press) which followed, the *People's Daily* quickly published a correction: the last sentence should read 'We cannot expect the writings of Marx and Lenin at that time to provide solutions to *all* our current problems.' It was explained unofficially that the commentary had been based on notes taken at a briefing by Hu Yaobang, and that the qualifying adjective had been omitted. Even with this proviso, the way was now cleared to discard openly some elements of traditional doctrine: 'We must study Marxism in close connection with realities,' explained the Party journal *Red Flag* (no. 3, 1985), '. . . and distinguish clearly what is still applicable from what is not.'

The Great Debate

In 1986 Deng Xiaoping, by now convinced that economic reform would not succeed without the reformation of the political structures which still dominated the economy, granted a new licence, although in somewhat limited terms. The initial quote on which the reformers relied merely said that 'During this time [the Seventh Five-Year Plan] comprehensive economic restructuring will affect every field: politics, education, science.' Deng spoke more clearly later on, but always presenting political reform in a wholly utilitarian context:

As economic reform progresses, we deeply feel the necessity for changes in the political structure. The absence of such changes will hamper the development of productive forces and the success of the Four Modernizations.[9]

The summer of 1986 saw the most lively and varied intellectual movement that China had known since the Hundred Flowers. Suddenly there was a rash of seminars, often with innocuous-sounding titles: 'The Chinese Import of Culture' or 'Historical Aspects of Western Democracy'. The subject matter was far from historical. In July 1986, at an important seminar on theoretical work which was fully reported in the Party journal *Red Flag*, social scientists called for a new democratic spirit of scientific enquiry. 'Without a spirit of democracy', said Su Shaozhi, 'there will be no spirit of science':

Theoretical workers must have real courage and boldness of vision, and must ponder questions independently rather than mechanically following the instructions of higher authorities and books. They must not be afraid of being regarded as advocators of 'unorthodox opinions'. Many such opinions were later proved correct through scientific experiments. Our theoretical workers must have such courage in the course of promoting our socialist spiritual civilization.

Su demonstrated his own boldness by talking of the persistence of 'feudalist autocracy' among the leadership and its corrosive influence on the economic reforms. For example, the development of widespread commerce (the 'commodity economy') was being undermined by the phenomenon of the children of senior cadres 'engaging in commercial activities'. He also cited opposition to 'bourgeois democracy' in the past as an example of dogmatism. Had it not been advocated during the French Revolution, and was it not valid to discuss the issues of universal suffrage and checks and balances of power? 'The real situation at present is very complicated,' said You Lin, another participant in the 1986 seminar. 'There is neither pure capitalist society nor pure socialist society in this world. The situation is especially complicated when socialism is in its primary stage.'

Other speakers criticized the lack of a tradition of free intellectual discussion. China should follow Lenin's example, argued Lin Jizhou, and allow policies to be debated in the press before being decided by the Party Congress.

If our theoretical workers cannot make daring explorations and cannot air their views freely, it will be harmful to our socialist construction. The abnormal phenomenon of regarding all articles published by newspapers and magazines as a reflection of the will of the central authorities should be changed.[10]

Many scholars called for an end to 'old idols' and the development of a real scientific spirit. Gao Fang criticized the view that veteran Party cadres necessarily understood Marxism. On the contrary, they had been affected by many 'non-Marxist or semi-Marxist theories'. A scientific spirit meant three things, said Jin Guantao: first, the principle on which modern science had developed ever since the Renaissance, that 'practice is the criterion of truth'; second, an attitude of 'conditioned scepticism', in support of which he quoted T. H. Huxley; and third, the creation of a friendly and tolerant atmosphere in academic circles, where people would no longer be criticized over 'a single source or a single sentence'. The events of the next few months showed that this atmosphere was still some way off. As the argument for political reform came closer to a call for real internal Party democracy (even though no one in the debates yet mentioned pluralism), it began to be echoed in the official press to the alarm of the conservatives. Li Honglin demanded democracy 'even if it grates on the ears of the leaders'.[11] His article in the pace-setting Shanghai *World Economic Herald* was quickly followed by a *People's Daily* commentary with the title, 'There can be no socialist modernization without socialist democracy':

The people are the masters of a socialist state, and their initiative can only be brought into play and turned ultimately into material force if they indeed play their role as masters of the house in political, economic, and all social life . . . Socialist democracy also confers on the masses the right to criticize and supervise, thus ensuring the flourishing vitality of the cause of socialist modernization . . . Malpractices such as abusing power for private purposes, and persistent ailments such as bureaucracy must, in the final analysis, be solved through relying on political democratization. The most elementary thing here is to allow the masses to speak out and to listen to their views. (2 June 1986)

Three who went too far

Dissenting scholars in China who go too far have traditionally expected punishment. In imperial days it used to be banishment or even decapitation. In the milder atmosphere of Deng's China it meant expulsion from the Communist Party. The student demonstrations of winter 1986/7 gave the conservatives the pretext they needed to attack the reform-minded scholars with, for the time being, Deng's approval. Three leading critics were singled out by Deng himself. In the Chinese idiom he 'marked their names' as surely as the emperor had once circled the names of those meriting punishment with his vermilion pen. Each of them had already made many enemies, and had shown a deliberate impatience with the slow pace of democratic reform.

Fang Lizhi

Born in 1936, Fang had drawn attention to himself as a Beijing University physics student in 1956 by interrupting a Youth League meeting to suggest that it should discuss 'what kind of person is education supposed to develop?' He was later named as a rightist and expelled for the first time from the Party. During the Cultural Revolution, he took up the study of astrophysics while doing labour in the countryside. Returning to the Chinese College of Science and Technology in Anhui, he soon became internationally known, but did not confine himself to cosmology. In speeches and interviews on Chinese university campuses, he stressed his two favourite themes: the role of the intellectual as an independent force for social reform, and the need to consider democracy 'as a right and not a gift from above'. In both respects he regarded the West as much more advanced. When appointed vice-president of the college, he had pledged to make 'freedom of thought' one of the principles of university education. His handling of administration and finance, where he encouraged internal staff elections and open budgeting, was praised in a series of articles in the *People's Daily* only weeks before his second dismissal from the Party.

Fang's stress on proper recognition of the intellectual's contribution to society led him to propose not just that class labels traditionally applied to the intellectual were outdated but also, much more heretically, that the intellectual constituted a new and more dynamic class than the traditional working class.

Marx classified people into different groups according to the means of production they owned. In my view, this was tenable in the last century and the beginning of this. However, in modern society, the development of science and technology, knowledge, and information, including high-tech and soft science, has become an important force propelling society forward, and is bound to involve a change in the concept of who leads in the political and economic fields. *Intellectuals, who own and create information and knowledge, are the most dynamic component of the productive forces, and this is what determines their social status* (my italics). (*Beijing Review*, 5 Dec. 1986)

Fang also spoke of the need to substitute a sense of 'intellectual consciousness' for the old concept of 'class consciousness'. It was hardly surprising that he should be accused of 'exalting the role of intellectuals while sowing discord between them and the Party', and of 'instigating trouble by saying that Chinese intellectuals . . . ought to constitute an independent force'.[12] There was indeed an elitist tinge to Fang's ideas which the professional theorists disliked, although it appealed to a new, less political generation of students.

Wang Ruowang

Wang belonged to an earlier tradition of outspoken scholarship. He joined the Communist Youth League in Shanghai in 1933, was thrown into prison by the Nationalist government, and moved in 1937 to Yanan where he joined the Communist Party. He wrote one of the first biographical articles on Mao, and edited cultural journals in the liberated areas. In Shanghai after the war, he was criticized even before the anti-right campaign as an editor of the *Literary Monthly*.[13] The campaign labelled him a 'right-wing element' for his articles attacking dogmatism and expelled him from the Party, but his membership was restored in 1962. Imprisoned for four years in the Cultural Revolution, he emerged swearing to devote the rest of his life 'to struggle with those false Marxists who accuse people unjustly and inhumanly of crimes'. Wang had long possessed a reputation for fearless criticism. When the rural co-operative movement was stepped up in 1955 and led to a vogue for collectivizing everything, Wang wrote a sharp critique for which he was later accused of 'rejecting the Party's leadership'.

It seems that when the trend was towards the collective feeding of livestock in the co-operatives, various theatrical groups and publications in Shanghai were also in the process of being collectivized . . . One could hardly escape being branded as a conservative if one failed to support the movement. None the less, the facts have shown that when both cattle and men were collectivized, the cattle became scrawny, the arts became scrawny, the theatrical troupes and publishing houses became scrawny. This . . . does not reveal the superiority of socialism; on the contrary, it reveals our blindness. (Literary Gazette, no. 21, 1957)

By 1985 Wang's increasingly libertarian views had already led to renewed calls for his expulsion from the Party. He also caused offence by circulating an open letter calling for a national conference to commemorate the thirtieth anniversary of the 1957 Hundred Flowers movement. An article 'Zest for life', written for the popular magazine *Youth Generation* (no. 4, 1986), reflects his eclectic approach: he recommended a sense of optimism, humour, and a willingness to express one's innermost feelings as characteristics which were far superior to the traditional virtues of Chinese sobriety and reticence. He cited with approval President Reagan's ability to joke about an operation, and asked why people should always ascribe credit for their achievements to 'the Party and the government', quoting instead the Argentinian footballer Maradona who had acknowledged the support of his family and girlfriend![14] Wang showed his own zest for life by writing his autobiography under the provisional title 'I Feel Good about Myself'. Criticized for behaving like 'a trolleybus without a line', he retorted that Mao Zedong's trolleybus, by keeping to its line, had led China straight into Shanghai's Huangpu River.

Wang caused maximum offence late in 1986 by publicly taking issue with some remarks by Deng Xiaoping about the need for economic reforms to avoid the polarization of incomes. Wang's argument—that relative differentials between rich and poor were a necessary part of economic development—was not so different from the official justification for allowing some entrepreneurs to 'get rich first', but his real offence was to criticize Deng by name. 'Can the common people carry on a public discussion with the leaders of our country?', he asked in his article, published provocatively in the Shenzhen Special Economic Zone (*The Worker*, 5 Nov. 1986). He was expelled from the Party for errors including 'distortion and denial of its leading role' but continued to speak out fearlessly.[15]

Liu Binyan

'Wherever he writes something, chaos ensues', complained Party bureaucrats in Shaanxi province after the investigative journalist Liu Binyan had exposed corruption in the province. When he was expelled from the Party in January 1987, there were threats of libel action from the administrations which he had offended. Using the device of *baogao wenxue* (reportage literature), Liu had begun his writing career with articles on bureaucratic bungling at a bridge construction site and in a local newspaper, which earned him a 'rightist' label in 1957. He was only rehabilitated as a journalist in 1979, having spent over twenty years either in the countryside or as a proofreader or translator. Writing for the *People's Daily*, he quickly made his reputation with 'Between Men and Monsters', the story of a county Party secretary in Heilongjiang province who made a fortune by taking bribes. The official concerned was later sentenced to death for embezzlement. His next major work, 'A Second Kind of Loyalty', praised the supreme loyalty of those who dare criticize the Party when it does wrong. In 1985 he was elected vice-chairman of the Chinese Writers' Association, declining nomination for chairman, which he would easily have won.

Liu gave particular offence by consistently focusing his attack upon the 'left' in the Party, which he blamed for twenty years of misrule. From the 1950s onwards, he observed, the Chinese train had 'raced towards the Cultural Revolution' uncontrollably, and even today 'the main danger still comes from the left'.[16] After his second expulsion from the Party in January 1987, the *People's Daily* accused him of painting a picture of 'utter darkness' in which the Party was 'corrupt from top to bottom'. Liu was also accused of 'vilifying the broad masses of intellectuals' by saying that many of them took the safe way out, and joined the 'going-with-the-wind faction'. Liu certainly upset many colleagues by refusing to exempt them from responsibility for what he regarded as intellectual timidity. People in their thirties, he observed, 'generally hate politics, are uninterested in Marxism-Leninism, and disillusioned about China's future'. But he urged them to write about the political struggle: after all, it was extremely dramatic, 'which should be an advantage for artistic creation!'[17]

Liu regarded the post-Mao claim that ultra-leftism could be blamed on a 'small handful' of careerists around Mao Zedong as a shameful alibi. Its roots lay deep in China's 'great ocean of small scale farmers', and were overlaid even today by a strong tinge of anarchism which easily degenerated into oppression of a wholly unpolitical and gangsterist nature. The brutality which he had witnessed in the land reform campaign before 1949, when minor landlords were cruelly tortured, even when this had been explicitly forbidden by the leadership, had its counterpart in Heilongjiang during the Cultural Revolution:

A platform inspector, Liu Shulan, was brutally attacked because she would not let the friends of a leading official board a train without a ticket. Several times, to make fun of her diseased womb, Zhao Yufeng [the local Party boss] forced her to take down her trousers at meetings. When it became serious she went into the hospital, womb and anus swollen together; they sent people to the hospital to drag her back on a truck, without trousers, for more struggle.[18]

The conservative reaction

The reaction was bound to come. Party scholars who had been 'formed' as a new generation of 'ideological workers' in the 1950s felt themselves to be ridiculed by a coalition of old and new rightists who unaccountably enjoyed both the support of foreign friends and domestic Party reformers. Backed by the Party conservatives, they found their voice again with a real sense of grievance when Hu Yaobang was forced to step down in January 1987. The world of Marxist theory, they complained, had been turned upside down. Those who dared to criticize Marxism were regarded as having 'liberated their thought' and were well received, those comrades who persisted in their correct opinions were suppressed. 'Marxists should be full of courage and have the confidence to speak out.'

Everyone sees clearly that for some time the ideological trend of bourgeois liberalization has spread unchecked, and a few people have been busy writing articles and delivering reports that negate the Four Basic Principles and advocate Total Westernization, while not allowing others to say No. Some papers, journals, and platforms controlled by them have refused to give the slightest space to Marxists, and even the Central Committee's opinion that 'Marxists should stand out and speak' has been mocked. Comrades who adhere to the Party's stand have been isolated and subjected to joint attacks . . . they have been labelled as 'ultra-leftists,' 'ossified' and 'purgers'. (Xinhua, 28 Jan. 1987)

Simple truths were reasserted with an unashamed chauvinism. 'Socialism is good!', proclaimed the people of Henan province, according to a commentary on their radio station. 'It is socialism that has made China, a poverty-stricken and backward country that allowed itself to be bullied and trampled on . . ., stand proudly among the nations of the world' (Shenyang radio, 2 Feb. 1987). The social evils of Western society were highlighted by the Beijing Daily: 'drugs, alcohol abuse, violent murder, suicide, divorce, prostitution, homosexuality, and AIDS'. The conservative Guangming Daily asserted in a barely disguised critique of the Open Door policy that 'even if the

Chinese people intend to study and learn from the Western system, the result can only be to become a semi-feudal and semi-colonial society and the object of imperialist designs' (5 Feb.). 'Do not forget the spirit of hard work and plain living; persist in building China frugally,' wrote Bo Yibo, one of the veteran conservative patrons, in an inscription for the new Tianjin Development Zone. The glossy face of Western-style consumerism was condemned: 'All over the country,' said the *People's Daily*, 'people with money in their pockets are spending it on building high-class hotels, shopping malls, theme parks, sports grounds, commemoration halls, "centres" for this and that, repairing temples and travel and entertainment at public expense' (22 Jan.).[19]

The weakness of traditional theory was its failure to transcend old-fashioned leftist arguments and produce coherent alternatives. A conference of conservative ideologues was convened in April 1987 at Zhuozhou, Hebei province. It was hoped that this would lead to production of several hundred articles by well-known theorists for publication in the next three years. (Contributors, gossip had it, would be paid 90 yuan per thousand characters or nearly ten times the usual rate.) Yao Xueyin, author of a famous trilogy on the Taiping Revolution, returned to print to urge Chinese writers not to abandon China's 'brilliant tradition of revolutionary literature'. The Maoist poet He Jingzhi argued for the suppression of 'unhealthy works'. Yet the conference produced only a handful of passable articles, and one episode which delighted progressive scholars: a professor of Chinese from the leftist province of Hunan had denounced the translation of a book which he referred to as *Lady Thatcher's Lover*. 'Besides corrupting the morals of our youth,' he declaimed, 'would not this spoil our relations with Britain?' The right-wing offensive demonstrated once again how factionalism and chauvinism undermined the conservative critique. It gave Premier Zhao Ziyang much-needed ammunition: only four or five of the articles passed muster, he said. Some echoed the Cultural Revolution and most failed to convince. The futility of it reminded him of a Cantonese saying: 'Water has been poured over the duck, but its feathers are still dry.'[20]

Reform had also weakened the intimidatory effect of yet another conservative campaign. Deng Xiaoping himself lamented that only a few intellectuals could be found to speak up against 'bourgeois liberalization'. They included the novelist Wang Meng, now Minister of Culture, who judged it prudent to give his lukewarm approval to the campaign rather than run the risk of replacement by a leftist. Distressingly, the elderly sociologist Fei

Xiaotong, who thirty years before had called courageously for a real spring thaw at the time of the Hundred Flowers, now spoke in favour of the winter clampdown. Many scholars, summoned to meetings to denounce the three heretics, pleaded illness or came only to sit in silence. Yet another device was to link criticism of bourgeois liberalization with an attack upon 'feudalism'—the mentality of those who were running the conservative campaign. Among cadres and students, the reading out of selective quotations from Fang Lizhi and Liu Binyan often had the opposite effect from that intended. Extracts from Liu condemning ultra-leftism as 'against humanity and despising man', and from Fang insisting that it was 'better to study socialism than to Love Socialism' were greeted with appreciative laughter.

Another weakness of the conservatives was that they kept company with activists of the Cultural Revolution. The editor of the *Beijing Daily*, which denounced the student demonstrations, deputy Party Secretary Xu Weicheng, had been active in the Gang of Four's 'Two Schools' Writing Group. When the conservatives sought to make him the Party's new propaganda head, the widows of four Party leaders persecuted in the Cultural Revolution wrote to Deng Xiaoping denouncing him. Xu caused alarm in the first weeks of the anti-bourgeois liberalization campaign by compiling blacklists, but within the year he had been demoted to work far away from Beijing in Guizhou province.

Compromise

At 8 a.m. on 1 August 1987, while the Party leadership was meeting by the seaside at Beidaihe to resolve the argument between conservatives and reformers, the playwright Wu Zuguang heard someone coming laboriously up three flights of stairs to his Beijing apartment. It was the Politburo ideologue, 75-year-old Hu Qiaomu, bringing a verbal message from the Central Disciplinary Commission urging Wu to resign from the Party. The charges ranged from Wu's alleged 'rightist' activities in 1957 to a recent speech arguing against play censorship. Touched, Wu said, by Hu's personal attention, and not wishing to embarrass the Party, he agreed to resign quietly (but a full account of the visit and of Wu's subsequent letter to the Disciplinary Commission was leaked shortly afterwards in the Hong Kong press). Wu then circulated to his friends a proposal to compile a collection of essays on the pleasures of drinking. Four other prominent intellectuals, including

Su Shaozhi and Wang Ruoshui, also received visits that day in what became known as the 'Incident of the Five Gentlemen'.[21]

Fellow intellectuals were briefly alarmed, but the incident was soon seen as a last token gesture to the conservatives, necessary in order to save face for Deng Liqun and the leftist ideologues who had compiled much longer lists of suspect scholars after the spring offensive against Fang, Wang, and Liu, and who would shortly be isolated at the Thirteenth Party Congress. Far from winning a post on the Politburo (he had even hoped at one stage to become Party Secretary-General), Deng did not even remain in the Central Committee. The weight of official condemnation of 'ossified thinking' fell heavily on his shoulders. Su Shaozhi and others on the original list reappeared after the Congress, quoted extensively on the theory of reform. Nevertheless, their statements reflected the price which had to be paid for the curtailment of the leftist campaign. Once again Chinese intellectuals were required not to cross a line drawn by others. The first neo-Marxist scholar to reappear, Yan Jiaqi, author (with his wife) of the frowned-upon history of the Cultural Revolution, set the limit:

Yan Jiaqi stressed that the next five to ten years would be a crucial period of China's political structural reform. He said: Building democratic politics to a higher degree than in other developed countries will be a long-term process . . . At present, any social unrest might lead to the rise of ultra-'leftist' ideology. People must bear in mind the historical lesson as regards this issue. *Political structural reform must be carried out step by step, in an orderly way, under the leadership of the Party* [my italics]. (*China News Service*, 29 Oct. 1987)

The same phrase (adapted from Zhao's report to the Congress) was repeated by Ma Hong, head of the Chinese Academy of Sciences, where Su and so many of the reformers worked. 'The method of a political movement and of "great democracy" will not be adopted', said Ma, stressing that the 'ultimate purpose of political reform is to promote the development of the social productive forces' (*Guangming Daily*, 29 Oct.). The novelist Wang Meng continued to play his delicate bridging role, warning the scholars not to expect too much from reform nor be depressed at the need for cautious advance. Many men of letters, he said, had 'gone ahead of their times' in calling for reform. Yet when they met with setbacks or 'complex situations', they easily became downcast and sighed in despair. They should realize that the situation was rich with hope as well as with 'troublesome issues'. Wang also expressed the view of many of his older generation of intellectuals that some reformers were publicity-seekers: he spoke of people who were 'cheer-leaders' rather than practical reformers, and who copied Western styles and 'indulged in narcissism' (*People's Daily*, 17 Nov.). Wang's argument carried some weight among many intellectuals who feared that they would be the first to suffer if too forceful a demand for reform led to another clampdown: for them the lesson of the 'anti-rightist' persecution of recent decades was still too fresh.

11

The Door Opens Wide
China and the world economy

The new hotel opposite the foreigners' apartment blocks in north-east Beijing was ready to celebrate its opening. It was near the Sheraton Great Wall, but it was a joint venture not with the Americans but with an extremely patriotic—and wealthy—Chinese, Mr Y. K. Pao from Hong Kong. The hotel was named after his father—the Zhaolong Hotel—and Mr Deng Xiaoping himself had agreed both to open it and, in a further 'generous gesture', to pen the calligraphy for its neon sign. One day in October 1985, the main road outside was cordoned off several hours before the event. The stalls selling clothing and fruit on the other side were thoroughly searched and closed for the day. Finally a convoy of Mercedes swept through the gates. They contained Mr Deng, Vice-Premiers Wan Li and Xi Zhongxun, the deputy head of the Military Affairs Commission Yang Shangkun, the minister in charge of China's 'Open Door' policy Mr Gu Mu—and Mr Pao.

Mr Deng entered the foyer to the applause of the hotel staff, lined up smartly in their uniforms (and many of them the sons or daughters of officials who had secured these desirable jobs for their offspring 'through the back door'). He glanced appreciatively at the hotel fountain and hanging chandelier, and then unveiled a plaque which recorded the patriotic intentions of Mr Pao:

. . . in a dedicated effort to help promote the tourist industry of his mother country, he proposed to the Central Leadership his preparedness to contribute US $10 million to build a hotel in filial memory of his father . . .

Tourism to China had increased by more than 20 per cent in the years 1982–5. One and a half million foreign nationals would visit in 1986, of whom half a million came from Japan and nearly 300,000 from the US. (The total figure for tourism was much higher—over 21 million: the remainder were overseas Chinese who would not usually stay in the Zhaolong or Sheraton Great Wall.) Foreign currency income was in excess of one and a half billion US dollars.

The foreign businessman no longer brought his own bottle of Scotch to China or spent long evenings reading *China Pictorial* by low wattage bulbs. There were now joint venture hotels in all the main cities, with late-night coffee shops, in-house videos, and air conditioning. The cisterns flushed and the staff were taught to say 'Good Morning, Sir (or Madam)'. The flask of hot water and packets of green tea had been replaced by a drinks cabinet.

The new patriotism

China's new opening to the West in the 1980s would have been instantly denounced by the ultra-left ten years before as capitulationism or 'national betrayal'. (Only a few remnant Maoist sympathizers outside China now used such terms.) Certainly it contained elements of what Mao once condemned as the tendency to believe that 'foreign farts smell sweeter' or, more decorously, that 'the moon shines brighter in the West'. But to limit an analysis of the Open Door policy to the importation into China of the Holiday Inn culture of international tourism, the establishment of Colonel Saunders' Kentucky Fried Chicken in Tiananmen Square, and the pursuit of imported videos and computer technology, is to miss the policy's main thrust. This was concerned with the central theme of Chinese nationalism for a hundred years: how to Revive the Country and make it Strong. Woven into the Open Door was a strong thread of 'patriotic' sentiment, often expressed in language which could have been used by Sun Yat-sen. It shaded into a more sophisticated form of international realpolitik in which China's role as a potential superpower (although still formally denied in the formula that 'China will never be a superpower') was quietly taken for granted. A less chauvinistic form of nationalism was expressed by younger intellectuals, especially those who had studied abroad, who viewed China as interdependent with the rest of the world, participating in a global economy and culture. The Party leadership accepted such participation in economic terms but baulked at cultural universality. For the 'socialist system', although less well defined than in the past, was now subsumed into a definition of Chinese nationhood—'socialism with Chinese characteristics'—which must be defended. Complicated by these more and less modern strands of thought, the Open Door by the late 1980s had nevertheless become the concept most capable of unifying the country. After the Thirteenth Party Congress it was inseparable from the concept of reform, almost wholly replacing the earlier mobilizing concepts of Revolution and Socialism. Through the 1984 agreement with Britain on Hong Kong, the Open Door policy also sought to restore the integrity of the Chinese nation, regaining the first territory to be lost to Western 'semi-colonialism' and offering a model for the eventual reintegration of Taiwan.

The Chinese word for patriotism, 'love-countryism', is explicit, as is the word for native land, 'land-of-our-ancestors', whose long civilization, say all the school textbooks, dates back nearly four millennia. The chronology is extended further by a succession of legendary rulers, popularly spoken of as if they were historical figures. The very first ancestor was the Yellow Emperor, who ascended to heaven from a small town which still bears his name in present-day Shaanxi province, in the year 2697 BC. When Deng Xiaoping in 1984 appealed to the rulers of Taiwan to follow Hong Kong's example and return to the ancestral land, his exact words were an invitation to rejoin the descendants of the Yellow Emperor.[1] Chairman Hu Yaobang had made a similar appeal to the President of Taiwan;

'A tree may grow ten thousand feet high, but its leaves fall back to its roots.' Does Mr Chiang Ching-kuo not love his native land? Doesn't he want to have Mr Chiang Kai-shek's remains moved back and buried in the cemetery of the Chiang family in Fenghua? . . . Foreign aid is important, but what is most important, most reliable and most powerful is the great patriotic unity of the 1,000 million people of our own country.[2]

When Mao Zedong wrote in 1939 jointly with some of his colleagues a textbook to educate Communist Party members on the significance and strategy of the Chinese revolution, he began by describing Chinese history as extending back a full five thousand years (later corrected to 'nearly 4,000 years'). Sun Yat-sen had lamented the tragedy that, in spite of its long history, China occupied the lowest position in international affairs. 'The rest of mankind', said Sun in discussing the principle of nationalism, 'is the carving

knife and the serving dish, while we are the fish and the meat . . .'.[3] Paying
tribute to Sun in 1956, Mao echoed his regrets. With its vast population and
territory, he said, 'China . . . ought to make a greater contribution to humanity. But for a long time in the past its contribution was far too small. For this
we are regretful.' Deng Xiaoping also regretted that progress since 1949 had
been too slow, even though (and partly because) he and his colleagues had
been so anxious not to waste time. China would have to work hard for
another fifty or sixty years, he said (30 Apr. 1987), to demonstrate 'the superiority of socialism over capitalism'. The proof would come when China had
reached a figure of US $4,000 billion GNP and occupied a position 'among
the advanced countries of the world'. Patriotism was compatible not only
with socialism but with the concept of 'proletarian internationalism' which
China had once reproached the Soviet Union for abandoning. An official of
the All-China Federation of Trade Unions explained:

Patriotism is unfortunately not possible for workers under capitalism, but under
socialism one can be both patriotic and internationalist. After all, to love one's own
country and to build socialism in it is what the proletariat of the whole world want.
So for the Chinese worker today, the most practical task is to build one's own
country. Only then can we make our contribution to the world, otherwise we have
no strength and can do nothing.[4]

But Deng Xiaoping's thoroughly traditional desire to Revive the Nation
was transformed by his refusal to do so behind closed doors, or to accept the
equally traditional Maoist explanation for China's weakness. China had
suffered in the past, Deng told the Party's Advisory Commission in October
1984, from the withdrawal of the Qing dynasty into isolationism. 'As a
result, China fell into poverty and ignorance.' Chinese historians elaborated
on the theme: the emperor Qian Long, wrote a professor from Beijing
University, was wrong to reject the British envoy Lord Macartney's mission
in 1793. By refusing to open up China's ports to trade, and limiting foreign
commerce to Guangzhou (Canton), the Manchus 'confined the economic
and cultural exchanges between China and foreign countries to a very
narrow scale. . . . In short, during this time China underwent a change from
progress to backwardness.'[5] This was a total reversal of the standard view
that the Manchus, while acting in part out of straightforward fear that their
own domination would be threatened by the Westerners, also displayed
what the Party historian Hu Sheng had called 'a natural reaction to the
lawless conduct of the marauding European merchants'. Deng Xiaoping

also dismissed fears that the European merchants of the 1980s would be marauders. Some veteran comrades, he told the Advisory Commission (largely composed of such veterans), feared that 'undesirable things may happen' if the door was opened. They should not be afraid: the negative consequences could be contained. It was the country and the people who would benefit most from opening up to foreign investment and participation in joint ventures, not the capitalists. It was on this argument that Deng effectively staked his political reputation in the last years of his life.

Rethinking self-reliance

The Open Door policy in the late nineteenth century had been inflicted upon China by the Great Powers to provide equal access to China's markets and to ensure (unsuccessfully in reality) that no one power gained special privileges from which the others were excluded. It was aptly described by President Wilson as 'not the Open Door to the rights of China but the Open Door to the goods of America'. Both sorts of doors had closed after 1949, when China was largely excluded from significant trade with the West under pressure of a US embargo, and obliged to enter an unequal relationship with the Soviet Union which broke down within ten years. China's new Open Door policy in the late 1970s was initiated by the post-Mao leadership, as a reaction against two decades during which the door had been closed, and as an assertion of China's right to participate in the international market. Post-Mao reformers now looked back, arguing that Mao had gone too far in making a virtue of self-reliant necessity. It had been elevated into 'closed-doorism', a refusal to countenance anything beyond minimum contact with the outside world, which had strong overtones of the chauvinism of the feudal empire. A country such as China should still be self-reliant in the sense that its progress ultimately depended upon its own economic resources and moral/political commitment, but it should not exclude the outside world and attempt to go it alone. The Party journal *Red Flag* (16 Apr. 1982) argued for steering a middle path:

In our history, there were two kinds of people. One kind of people worshipped and had blind faith in foreign things and was subservient to foreigners. As a result these people humiliated the nation and forfeited its sovereignty. Whether it was the Empress Dowager Cixi, Yuan Shikai [first president of the Republic, who capitulated to Japan's '21 demands' in 1915] or Chiang Kai-shek, they were without exception cast aside by the people. The other kind of people upheld closing the country to international exchange . . . [such as] the diehards at the end of the Qing dynasty who regarded China as the 'heavenly kingdom' and treated all foreign countries as 'uncivilized nations' . . .

These two tendencies are still to some extent reflected in the minds of some of our Party members and cadres. This may perhaps be regarded as a kind of historical legacy. Some people feel ashamed before foreigners and that everything is good in other countries and bad in ours. Others are very apprehensive about opening up to the outside world and are of the opinion that there will be no peace and security if we do so . . .

But the new Open Door involved basic questions not only of policy but of theory towards the outside world which challenged accepted truths on the relationship of socialism to capitalism. Deng Xiaoping's advisers now credited the capitalist system with vitality and the ability to adjust for a long period to come, during which it would 'coexist' with socialism. The old view that 'imperialism will soon die out and socialism will soon win a total victory', said Huan Xiang (vice-president of the Academy of Social Sciences), was 'at odds with reality'. So was Mao's doctrine that world war was inevitable and that socialism would survive it, which had so shocked Khrushchev at the 1957 Moscow Conference and helped create the 1960s image of China as a 'bellicose' nation. (It took time to discard an argument which had led the entire Chinese urban population in the early 1970s to dig air-raid shelters to 'prepare against war'. Hu Yaobang in November 1980 was the first to say that an imperialist war could be 'postponed or even prevented'.)

How China, and indeed all socialist countries, should relate to the world market was also radically rethought. In the early 1950s China had accepted the Soviet 'two bloc' view that there were two separate markets, capitalist and socialist, and that the latter was the stronger. A decade later Soviet attempts to enforce an 'international division of labour' in the socialist market were regarded as a form of covert imperialism and the bloc was rejected. 'The correct method', wrote Mao, was for every country to strive for 'regeneration' as independently as possible.[6] Chinese economists argued that foreign trade and economic relations must play only a subsidiary role. 'The people of every country', wrote one advocate of self-reliance, 'have for hundreds and thousands of years depended on their own hard toil.' In the early 1980s Chinese thought now adopted a 'one world' view of the international economy which had been rejected ever since Liberation (although during the revolution Mao had sought to tempt visiting Americans with a vision of Sino-American economic co-operation). Not only was there a single economic world system, said Huan Xiang, but 'both capitalism and imperialism occupy a dominant position' in such a 'unified market'. The first issue of the new journal *Social Sciences in China* (Mar. 1980) carried a pioneering article on the international division of labour. China could only avoid a 'lopsided economy', it argued, if it removed both internal and external obstacles to its development and 'established foreign economic relations based on equality and mutual benefit'. The fact that it was a socialist country, capable of 'highly social large-scale production', made it even more necessary to join the world market. To confine economic activity to national boundaries would, in a Marxist sense, become 'a fetter upon the productive process' (just as private enterprise under capitalism became a fetter on production).

Younger Chinese economists and sociologists showed less interest in whether or not China was a socialist country, basing their analysis rather on the relationship between the developing nations (among whom they counted China) and the developed world.

The developing countries, when they began to take their first steps, were faced with advanced industrial nations which were well beyond the pre-industrialization stages and were absolutely pre-eminent in technology and wealth . . . Confronted with a fully developed world market, it is impossible for a country which cuts itself off and relies on the spontaneous role of its home market to catch up, let alone surpass the economically advanced countries. (*Beijing Review*, 2–8 Nov. 1987)

There was a degree of ambivalence in this classification of China as a 'developing country'. It was at the same time the largest and most populous of the developing group, and the strategy proclaimed in the mid–1980s was that it should have attained or neared the level of the world's most developed nations by the middle of the twenty-first century. Sometimes different categories were used: Huan Xiang spoke of the 'great trilateral relationship' between China, the USSR, and the USA, which was linked to two sets of four-cornered relationships (China, USSR, USA, and Japan in Asia, and USA, USSR, and Western and Eastern Europe on the European continent). For a long period to come, he said, it was the great trilateral relationship which would 'truly determine' the international scene. But however the analysis was framed, China was definitely cast in a global economic role far removed from its 1960s role as a self-sufficient exemplar for the revolutionary people of Africa, Asia, and Latin America.[7]

Reshaping foreign trade

'There are still some comrades', wrote the economist Ji Chongwei in the *People's Daily* (6 Nov. 1981), 'who insist that the fewer exports the better and the fewer imports the better.' Until recently there had been little choice. For more than twenty years China had maintained a low level of balanced trade, unable even if it had so desired to enter the Western market for technology and investment on any significant scale. This policy of restraint began to come under pressure in the early 1970s as US–Chinese relations improved, but a careful line was drawn. 'China will never try to attract foreign capital or exploit domestic or foreign natural resources in conjunction with other countries', said the Minister of Foreign Trade Li Qiang in June 1974.

She [China] will never go in for joint-management with foreign countries, still less grovel for foreign loans as does that superpower [the Soviet Union]. China welcomes technical interchange with other countries and imports essential equipment on a planned and selective basis according to the needs of socialist construction. Methods of payment are arranged through negotiation by the two business parties in the light of common international trade practice.

At first after Mao's death these principles were reaffirmed. The increased imports of foreign technology were laboriously rationalized with the argument that by the process of adaptation to Chinese conditions they became a Chinese-developed technology. But Chinese financial experts quietly complained that valuable foreign currency was being wasted by a refusal to take advantage of normal commercial credits. Chinese oil surpluses were also reaching their peak, available for financing export growth, and justifying the Deng Xiaoping plan for mortgaging Chinese fossil fuels resources against imports of new technology which had ignited the great 1975 controversy. Before long Minister Li Qiang reversed his position entirely, announcing that 'by and large we now accept all the common practices known to world trade'. It was argued that China's historic share of the world market—about 1 per cent—was far too low and should be quadrupled by the end of the century. A theoretical balance between exports and imports was still asserted, but with the important qualification that it should be calculated over a longer period than one year.

Not surprisingly the shift of policy led to a splurge of buying complete turn-key plants and new technology which caused three successive trade deficits in 1978–80. In the flush of modernization, factory directors competed to order new plant from abroad, which in some cases ended up deteriorating in its packing cases. Though the buying spree stemmed from Deng's policies, he was able neatly to offload responsibility on to Hua Guofeng. In the 'readjustment' of 1979–80, a moratorium was declared on new contracts and more than two-and-a-half billion dollars' worth of contracts with Japanese firms were temporarily suspended. Traders with China, long accustomed to regard a handshake as sufficient guarantee, now discovered that increased volume led to increased uncertainty. It also became more difficult to establish where the ultimate power of decision-making lay. A new tension arose in the mid–1980s between the desire to increase local initiative in promoting foreign trade, which implied decentralization, and fears that the process would get out of hand, which prompted new moves to concentrate power at the centre. Over the single year 1984–5, policy shifted three times. In March 1984 the Ministry of Foreign Economic Relations and Trade announced plans to tighten control, re-establishing the authority of the six great foreign trade corporations which had begun to lose ground to local export promotion, fixing prices and quotas, and increasing commodities subject to export licence. In September the policy was reversed as part of the new package of 'urban reform' promoted by Zhao Ziyang. Accountability was to be devolved to the actual importers and exporters, operating through a total of more than 900 specialized foreign trade companies. In reality most staff in these local bodies lacked the experience to hold their own with foreign negotiators, or were easily subverted by bribes and kickbacks, while the lack of central control allowed an unrestrained import boom. Within months control was reimposed following a disastrous fall in China's foreign exchange reserves. Once again many contracts were cancelled or deferred, causing further loss to China's traditional business reputation.

Control of foreign trade, whether at the centre or locally, could still be regarded as control by the socialist state. More difficult problems were raised by inviting foreign capital to participate in *production* by investing in the new joint venture companies. The reformers relied on Lenin, painting an exaggerated picture of the scope of foreign concessions allowed in the Soviet Union under his New Economic Policy. (*Red Flag* said there had been more than two hundred such concessions, but as Alec Nove has written, the policy 'came to very little', accounting for only 0.6 per cent of industrial output by 1928.)[8] Chinese writers also blamed Stalin for concentrating on 'building socialism in one country surrounded by the capitalist world', and for failing to elevate the question of 'opening to the outside world' to the level of theory. The new joint ventures in China were now defined as a form of 'state capitalism' which was analogous to the jointly owned state–private industries allowed in China in the early 1950s.

Joint venture controls were indeed sufficiently strict to provoke many complaints from foreign businesses accustomed to easier terms in other Third World countries. By 1987, out of a total of 9,000 joint ventures licensed to operate, less than 3,500 were actually operating—one-third of these still at a loss. More than half of them functioned in the four Special Economic Zones (Shenzhen, Zhuhai, Shantou in Guangdong province, and Xiamen in Fujian). Complaints included excessive taxation and charges for labour, of which the greater part did not benefit the individual worker, and lack of access to the domestic market or payment in non-convertible Chinese currency where access was allowed. In November 1987 new regulations allowed some joint ventures to sell their goods within China as import substitutes and to be paid in foreign exchange. Admitting that China fell short of foreign capitalists' aspirations, the State Councillor chiefly responsible, Gu Mu, asked them 'to take a dynamic perspective with regard to investment in China—a long-term point of view which puts greater stress on the future of China's investment environment'.[9] By 1986 China had made use of over US $20 billion in foreign credits to import technology, although substantial potential credits for another US $7 billion remained unused. More than US $17 billion in investment contracts had been approved, although less than one-third had been taken up. China had also issued what one Western news agency called 'the first international bond under Communism'. Fifty million dollars' worth of bonds were snapped up, underwritten in an echo of 'semi-colonial' history by a ten-bank international consortium. The 'current West European euphoria for everything Chinese', said the experts, 'had helped brush away any reservations among investors'.[10]

Regional development

By far the greatest part of investment and participation in joint ventures came from 'patriotic' business in Hong Kong. Mainland disapproval of Hong Kong capitalism surfaced occasionally during the Sino-British negotiations (1982–4) but was soon submerged by an appreciation of Hong Kong's usefulness, not just as an existing source of foreign exchange (it continued to furnish about one-third of China's earnings) but as an open window to the world. Leading Hong Kong businesspeople whose families had 'fled' the mainland after 1949 and loudly advertised their fears of a 'communist takeover' during the negotiations were quickly reconciled. (But some quietly made alternative arrangements for the future, while younger Hong Kong professionals expressed open doubts about the agreement and many decided to leave.) In the post–1984 internal argument over democratization of the Hong Kong government, the business community sided with the Beijing view (shared also by the British government) that serious democratic reform—in particular, direct elections to the Legislative Council, which became the central issue—should be undertaken only 'step by step', if at all. Many of them were welcome guests in the Chinese capital, as Deng Xiaoping had promised when he first met a Hong Kong industrial and commercial delegation (22–3 June 1984):

It must be required that patriots form the main body of administrators, that is, of the future government of Hong Kong . . . Who are patriots? The qualifications for a patriot are respect for the Chinese nation, sincere support for the motherland's resumption of sovereignty over Hong Kong, and a desire not to impair Hong Kong's prosperity and stability. Those who meet these requirements are patriots, whether they believe in capitalism or feudalism or even slavery.

Hong Kong now began to play an important role in a new theory of economic development by regional stages. Ever since the First Five-Year Plan (1953–7) Chinese planners had viewed their country in terms of three separate regions, divided roughly into north–south segments from the 'western' through the 'central' to the 'eastern' or 'coastal' section. For most of the time the view prevailed that the more advanced eastern region should lead the way, although efforts were made to shift the balance towards the interior, particularly during the Great Leap and in the early 1970s. The Open Door policy strengthened the argument for sequential development from East to West. Not only was Hong Kong to be increasingly associated with the coastal region, but other sub-regional units emerged which would take the lead. The Open Door policy, said Zhao Ziyang in his 1987 Party Report, should be extended 'progressively from the Special Economic Zones and coastal cities, then to coastal economic regions, and finally to interior areas'.

In the Seventh Five-Year Plan (1986–90), the east was expected to focus on modernizing old industry and the development of high technology and 'quality consumer goods'. Its four Special Economic Zones and fourteen

Open Port Cities would become China's main base for foreign trade. The central region would serve as China's energy reservoir, stepping up development of electricity, oil, and coal and the production of minerals and building materials. The west would devote its main energy to expanding agriculture, forestry, animal husbandry, and transport. Exposure to foreign economic activity was strictly graded. Conditions in most of the western region, explained the economist Xue Muqiao, 'have not yet matured for the import of foreign funds'.[11]

The Special Economic Zones (SEZs) were originally assigned a special role as 'windows on the world'. The economist Ji Chongwei said that to some extent they would act as 'filters between China's socialist system and the capitalist world, allowing market mechanisms and the law of value to operate under the guidance of socialist planned economy, and taking in positive things and sifting out negative aspects of Western culture'.[12] According to the Deng Xiaoping doctrine of 'One Country Two Systems', the SEZs would thus serve as a controlled conduit between the capitalist economy of Hong Kong (including Macao and eventually, it was hoped, Taiwan) and the socialist economy of the rest of China. Deng insisted that while capitalism in Hong Kong would be guaranteed until the middle of the next century, the same must be true for socialism on the mainland. But by the late 1980s, the pressure for economic change had diffused more widely in the eastern region, leading potentially to a much larger 'window' on the world. In the north, Tianjin emerged to dominate what became known as the 'golden necklace' of fifteen cities and prefectures around the Bohai Basin of North China. Three 'golden triangles' of development were identified, in the Yangtze River delta centred on Shanghai, southern Fujian centred on the Xiamen SEZ, and the Pearl River delta centred on Guangzhou. Neat dividing lines were discarded as the new leaders spoke of development spreading from the coastal areas to the interior 'in a gradual wave-after-wave manner' (Gu Mu).[13] The goal, said Zhao Ziyang, was 'to change from closing various parts of the country from the world to opening them'. A new bout of sub-regional door-opening began immediately after the Thirteenth Party Congress had reaffirmed the reform policy, in an unashamedly competitive mood. The island of Hainan was told to prepare for provincial and special zone status, and its Party secretary Xu Shijie boasted that he had been given the green light by Zhao Ziyang:

Hainan is to implement 'a policy which is more "special" than the present special zones' . . . He [Zhao] also said that Hainan would be given more independent powers and more preferential treatment, greater examining and approving powers, a more extended and less restricted scale of basic construction than in other regions, freer entry and exit policies for foreigners, and a more relaxed foreign exchange administration . . . Ah [exclaimed Xu], with such effective measures Hainan definitely will become the country's biggest special zone![14]

As a gesture of encouragement for the new coastal entrepreneurs, the man held most responsible for the great Hainan scandal in 1985 was now rehabilitated. Under Party Secretary Lei Yu, the island had imported 79,000 foreign cars and trucks in the space of one year for illegal resale at inflated prices to other provinces and cities in the interior. (Other profitable imports were 347,000 TV sets, and 45,000 motorcycles.) The resale racket brought in vast sums of foreign currency from the purchasers, and allowed pay-offs to local officials of up to one million yuan (£200,000). In January 1988 Lei Yu was appointed a vice-mayor of Guangzhou, with the citation that he was 'receptive to new things . . . familiar with economic affairs . . . and enjoys considerable prestige among cadres and people'.

Party leaders in Guangdong (who until now had been responsible for Hainan) had their own reasons for optimism, with the expansion of the Guangdong Open Zone to include the Pearl River 'golden triangle'. The party secretary Lin Ruo confessed that the anti-bourgeois liberalization campaign earlier in 1987 had caused alarm: 'Should there be a mere rustle of leaves in the wind, it would make people abroad uneasy.' Now that the Party was committed to speeding up reform and the Open Door, Guangdong was in a position to benefit more than most. Lin forecast that the province would show a 'two-digit' rate of increase in economic output, and that by the end of the century, it should attain the current level of Asia's 'four little dragons' (Hong Kong, Taiwan, Singapore, and South Korea). A former Party secretary, Xi Zhongxun (an old friend of Deng Xiaoping), sitting at Lin's side chipped in: 'We should be a little faster!' The example of Asia's 'economic miracles' had been much discussed in the early 1980s, when it was concluded that their circumstances and experiences were very different from those of China and should not be taken as a model. Yet by the late 1980s the coastal districts of the eastern region were increasingly tempted by their success, and could argue that while China as a whole could not be compared with these relatively small, self-contained, and export-oriented states, their zones had more in common. They too offered a labour surplus capable of learning new technologies for low wages, good communications with South-East Asia, and a positive investment environment under a centralized system of government which minimized the chances of labour unrest. If Hong Kong capitalism had feared that it would be subverted by mainland socialism, it now appeared more likely that Chinese socialism would be subverted in the spearhead sectors of the eastern region.

Across the border from Hong Kong, in the Pearl River delta, more than a million out of a total population of 23 million were already servicing Hong Kong industry by 1988. Lorries with dual Chinese and Hong Kong number plates headed north and south between Shenzhen and Guangzhou (a superhighway was also under construction) carrying in cloth, leather, plastics, and electrical parts, and taking out garments, shoes, toys, and assembled electrical goods and electronics. Deep in the countryside factories sprang up employing local peasant labour at a quarter of the rate paid in Hong Kong and half of that in the Shenzhen Special Economic Zone. Migrants from the interior sat in village squares, hoping to pick up casual work for even lower wages. In the town of Dongguan, a centre of this new industry, 1,800 new cable circuits were installed in 1987 to provide direct telephone links with Hong Kong. (Guangzhou City was spending five times as much as Shanghai on telecommunications.) Hong Kong's own economy was increasingly dominated by mainland investment—at least 30 per cent according to most estimates—and the territory also provided a free management school with several thousand mainland visitors at any one time learning new skills.[15]

Towards an open society?

'The present world is an open one', Deng told a group of Japanese businessmen in June 1984. 'China's past backwardness was due to its closed-door policy . . . the experience of the past thirty years or more proves that a closed-door policy would hinder construction and inhibit development.' China was still self-reliant in the sense that a country of such a large size must provide most of its own inputs for development, but Deng looked forward to increased economic interaction with the outside world, with a considerable increase in foreign trade over the next fifty or seventy years. 'If anything, we will only open up still more. Our people would not allow anything else.'

Neo-Marxist scholars attempted to translate this limited and expedient view of the Open Door policy into an operating principle which would open the ideological as well as the economic doors. There was a dangerous flaw in Deng's argument: The Open Door was bound to increase China's prosperity, he said, and therefore the Chinese people would insist that it remained open. But what if the policy produced a negative result in these narrow economic terms when, for example, China found itself adversely affected by foreign competition or a reverse in the international terms of trade? Would not some people insist that the door be shut again?

The Open Door had to be linked to socialism by much more than its presumed economic benefits. An important essay by Li Honglin, published in the *People's Daily* (15 Oct. 1984) with the provocative subtitle 'Socialism should be an open society', tackled this question squarely. Li argued that there was a basic trend not just in economic life but in all social existence to develop 'from ignorance to the nation, and from the nation to the world'. Feudalism relied on and sought to perpetuate a self-contained economy; capitalism broke down the national barriers. It would be nonsensical to suggest that socialism, a more advanced system than capitalism, should seek to restore those barriers. Socialism should start from the high level already reached by capitalism, and not feel obliged to begin all over again.

Facts have proved that in the past we did not have a clear idea of what Marxism and socialism were . . . Opening to the outside world gives us an opportunity to know about new situations, new problems, new materials, and new ideas in the world. This will inevitably speed up the course of 'purification' and development. Is this not a more favourable condition for upholding the Marxist scientific truth? . . .

Communist society will not flourish in a courtyard behind locked doors. Opening the country to the outside world is not an expedient measure but a fundamental principle for building a socialist society, as well as the only road to a communist society. Let us spare no effort in discarding all outmoded viewpoints which have suppressed us for many years, free ourselves from the parochial concept of small-scale production, and open the doors and windows wide to the world!

It was a valiant appeal but a few years later would itself seem strangely outmoded after China had emerged from the destructive hiatus of the Beijing massacre and its aftermath. To anticipate the conclusion to this story, when the doors and window were flung open again from the early 1990s onwards, no one bothered to square the policy with the long-range interest of socialism, far less Communism: it would be justified almost entirely in terms of the material interest of the Chinese people and of the global interests of the Chinese state.

12

Tiananmen Square, 1989
Turning-point for China

At 10 p.m. on 3 June 1989, the students around the Martyrs' Memorial in Tiananmen Square took a solemn oath: 'We swear to protect the cause of Chinese democracy. We are not afraid to die. We do not wish to continue living in a troubled country. We are here to protect Tiananmen to the death. Down with Li Peng's military government!' The crowd of students, workers, and citizens of Beijing included families with small children, young men and their smartly dressed girlfriends riding pillion on their cycles, even a few invalids in their wheelchairs. It ebbed and flowed east and west along Changanjie, the Avenue of Everlasting Peace which separates the north of the Square from the Forbidden City. To the south-west, a company of soldiers was immobilized by the masses behind the Great Hall of the People. On the previous night, an influx of unarmed troops into the capital had been triumphantly thwarted by its citizens. During the day there were scuffles and tear-gassing near the Square. Two weeks after martial law was declared, would the authorities finally admit defeat? No one in the Square knew that hundreds of tanks, armoured personnel carriers, and troop trucks were already on the move, and that the killings had begun.

The army's offensive was signalled at midnight by two armoured personnel carriers which smashed their way through hastily improvised barricades to the east and west. Unable to believe worse could follow, the crowds swore defiance: 'Heartless fascists! Those who have money have power! The people will not give in!' Troop trucks edged towards the Square from the west. There was the sound of explosions. 'Don't panic, it's only tear-gas', some students called out. Official loudspeakers repeated their message: 'The government of Beijing is the people's government. Obey its instructions. Leave the square.' Soldiers on foot advanced under cover of the trucks. More shooting. The first casualties, young men and women with bloody wounds, were hoisted by their limbs into pedicabs and rushed to hospital. By 3 a.m. the army had secured the Square, sealing it with tanks and troops. Around the Martyrs' Memorial plinth there was an agonized debate as the soldiers closed in. Finally, the students marched with banners still flying out of the south-east corner which the army had left open. No one could be sure what happened to those who stayed behind. Outside the Square, they took their chances with the rest of the Beijingers. Crossing Changanjie to the west, eleven students were crushed by tanks. Next day some brave citizens still approached the army lines, to protest or hoping to enquire about the fate of missing relatives. Six or seven times they were driven back by deadly fire. The policy was one of deliberate intimidation. Army convoys raced east and west during the next few days, belching exhaust, shooting at the slightest gesture of defiance or just randomly. The last truck of an incoming convoy on the 7th idly shot up a crowd of early morning spectators outside the International Hotel. The victims included a boy with schoolbooks strapped to his bicycle and a traveller from the north-east, just arrived at the railway station. In the Square, smiling officers told a group of handpicked Chinese journalists that no one had been killed. But the TV cameras picked up bloodstains on the pavement and bullet holes on the Memorial.

The mounting uncertainties about China's future course at all levels of society, which have been charted in the last four chapters, accelerated the movement towards disaster in and around Tiananmen Square on 3–7 June 1989, when hundreds of ordinary citizens were shot dead by the People's Liberation Army (PLA) in the Beijing massacre. Two overlapping crises lessened any chance of a positive and peaceful response by the Party leadership to a new, more coherent and unified, demand for democratic reform. Political reform had stagnated since the 1987 conservative counter-offensive and a new struggle was under way for the successor to Deng Xiaoping. Economic reform had been checked by rising inflation and by shortages both of investment funds and of energy and other essential supplies—giving the con-servatives further ammunition against Zhao Ziyang. The new united front of students and scholars put the Party bureaucracy on the defensive as never before: when it was joined by large numbers of workers and ordinary citizens of Beijing, the authorities would resort to desperate measures. Zhao was already extremely vulnerable, accused (like Hu Yaobang before him) of neg-lecting the Party elders and Deng himself. Only days before the Democracy Movement came to life, the ambitious Premier Li Peng hardly troubled to conceal his differences with Zhao. 'On the whole we co-operate very well,' was the lukewarm phrase he chose, 'but of course we are not entirely of the same views' (Tokyo, 14 Apr.). In the same week, the central authorities put out a denial that a 'regent group' of elders comprising Deng Xiaoping, Chen Yun, Yang Shangkun, Bo Yibo, and Wang Zhen was supplanting the Politburo headed by Zhao. These were the old men who weeks later would have their revenge on the young people of China (*FE*, no. 0435, 15 Apr.). The worsening situation in Tibet was a prelude to the bloodshed in Beijing. Martial law was introduced in Lhasa in March after Chinese forces had shot and killed unarmed demonstrators for the second time in three months.[1]

The government was seeking to narrow the limits of dissent at the very time when the Democracy Movement was being relaunched. A new theory on the need for states at China's level of development to adopt a 'neo-authoritarian' form of government had been approved by Deng Xiaoping. He believed that 'the modernization process in a backward country needs strong-man politics with authority rather than Western-style democracy as a driving force' (*FE*, no. 0431, 11 Apr.). The official press quoted Deng on the need for 'stability' and revival of the 'spirit of hard struggle'. It talked of the absolute necessity to 'uphold the authority' of the central government. This was not only an attempt to recentralize economic decision-making in order to cool the overheated economy, but an explicit warning against the forces of 'social disturbance and chaos' (*People's Daily* editorial, 5 Apr.). Zhao Ziyang continued to speak a different language, urging the Party to become more 'attractive' to the non-Party masses, and to gear its work to 'the needs of building socialist democracy' (*People's Daily*, 17 Mar.). His supporters argued in favour of turning trade unions at the grass roots into 'democratic mass organizations'. This was a very different view from the conservative approach which likened the relationship between trade unions and managements to that between 'two nostrils of the same nose' (*FE*, no. 0408, 14 Mar.). Zhao also pressed ahead with the controversial 'gold coast' policy, insisting on the correctness of allowing China's seaboard areas to 'get rich ahead of others'. But he was vulnerable to criticism on the persistence of corruption and speculation in these areas, and the rise of social phenomena such as pornography and prostitution. The looser controls and greater wealth of provinces such as Guangdong and Fujian encouraged an alarming influx of migrant workers from the interior. More than two-and-a-half million job-seekers flooded into Guangdong after the 1989 Chinese New Year. Railway stations in neighbouring provinces were jammed with labourers waiting for trains.

In March 1989 Deng Xiaoping had already identified the growing assertiveness of Chinese intellectuals as the biggest threat to 'stability', and told colleagues of his absolute determination to tame them. 'We must not be afraid of foreign opinion, far less must we allow any foreigners to lead us by the nose. We have our sovereign rights; we have our own criteria.' China must use whatever methods were needed, he concluded, to 'stabilize the country' (*Zheng Ming magazine*, Apr. 1989). Zhao Ziyang also regarded this assertiveness as a threat but from a very different perspective, fearing (only too correctly) that it would provide the combined forces of the conservatives and ultra-left with a lethal weapon against him. He told President Bush, who visited China in February 1989, that the present leadership—i.e. his own—represented a political centre between two extremes. One extreme view was that the reforms had gone wrong and that China should return to its old path. The other blamed the difficulties in reform upon the lack of political change and called for the introduction of Western-style multiparty politics. This second view, he warned, would 'provide a pretext to those who would turn back the reforms, and [would] stir up public disorder'. (*Far Eastern Economic Review*, 9 Mar. 1989). Zhao was a natural centrist struggling to retain his grip when the centre would no longer hold.

Revival of dissent

The scholars regained their voice in the winter of 1988–9, not because the atmosphere was more encouraging but because in the sterile air of the Party's paralysis they feared that worse was to come. Professor Su Shaozhi, who had avoided public argument since he was removed from his post as head of the institute of Marxism-Leninism-Mao Zedong Thought, returned from abroad to attend a Party symposium convened to celebrate the tenth anniversary of the famous Wu Xu seminar on ideology—the first blossoming of 'liberated thought' (see p. 192, above). Outraged by the subtle forms of intellectual repression which underlay the proceedings, Su spoke out against 'ideological prejudices, bureaucratism, sectarianism, Zhdanovism [Zhdanov was Stalin's cultural policeman in the 1940s], and cultural autocracy'. Su defended colleagues of his who were only allowed on sufferance to attend the symposium, labelled 'scholars who have been criticized and dealt with'. He referred in barely veiled terms to Deng Xiaoping's sponsorship of the previous campaigns against 'spiritual pollution' and bourgeois liberalism, and warned that Marxism in China was now in crisis.

Although many sweeping promises have been made, a lot of forbidden zones still remain in our academic and theoretical studies. Recently it has been ruled that writers must refrain from writing about the Cultural Revolution, that publishing houses must refrain from publishing articles and literary works on the Cultural Revolution, that reportage regarding some leaders must be submitted for examination before being published, and that writers and scholars must refrain from commenting on certain questions about the CCP's history, about the history of the international communist movement, and concerning international relations. (FE, no. 0367, 21 Dec. 1988)

The strands of disparate dissent over the past ten years now began to mesh together. Early in January, the outspoken natural scientist Professor Fang Lizhi (dismissed by Deng Xiaoping two years before: see Chapter 10, above) wrote to Deng appealing for the release of Wei Jingsheng and the other political prisoners of the 1979 Democracy Movement. Fang's petition was signed by a wide array of thirty-three intellectuals. They included the young poet Bei Dao, who later organized a second letter calling for an amnesty, signed by over one hundred intellectuals; Professor Su; the playwright Wu Zuguang (criticized at the same time as Su); the independent-minded woman writer Zhang Jie; the journalist Wang Ruoshui, who had been a prime target of the 1983 'spiritual pollution' campaign; and Chen Jun, a young entrepreneur with an American wife who ran a bar in Beijing. A year before, Fang had already expressed openly what many of them believed privately: the Party's 'relaxation' was only on the surface. The Party elders, he warned prophetically, might have retired, 'but their secretaries and their aides now are in positions of power. These old guys just get on the phone and say, "Do this" ' (Washington Post, 12 Feb. 1988). Now he warned that the repression could soon resume—'We always swing from thaws to freezes'— and called on 'famous people to make a stand' (Associated Press, 2 Feb. 1989). Socialism of the Lenin-Stalin-Mao variety, he wrote in the New York Review *of Books*, had been thoroughly discredited by the past forty years of Chinese history. Dictatorship bred corruption, which could not now be eradicated without allowing 'a more effective role for public opinion and a more independent judiciary. This means, in effect, more democracy' (2 Feb.). Fang's petition was then signed by Chinese citizens abroad, including the investigative journalist Liu Binyan (see pp. 201–03, above), who was now in virtual exile, as well as by scholars in Taiwan. The Chinese Justice Ministry was stung into replying, 'It is against China's legal principles . . . to stir up public opinion . . . by soliciting signatures.' The scholars were undeterred: in a new petition they renewed their demand for political reform, although taking care to avoid advocacy of a multiparty system. Yan Jiaqi described such a system as 'detached from the reality of China'. Even the more outspoken Fang Lizhi only favoured the establishment of 'pressure groups'.

The Party elders were outraged by the facility with which dissenting scholars were able to employ tactics of 'bourgeois liberal' protest. They knew that attempts to suppress the protest would attract negative publicity abroad. But with the same determination which would lead to the Beijing massacre, Deng Xiaoping personally authorized the police to prevent Fang from attending a banquet for President Bush to which he had been invited by the US Embassy in Beijing. Deng was unperturbed by the reactionary image which this conveyed to the outside world. In the words of the young journalist Dai Qing (who would be arrested after the massacre): 'Their methods are neolithic. Our government has changed so much for the better, it was pitiful for them to do this now. They slapped themselves in the face. They did this foolishness right in front of the Americans' (Associated Press, 27 Feb.). Face was much less important a consideration to the Deng leadership than maintaining the Four Principles and the primacy of the Communist Party. Younger Party leaders with ambitions to rise could now identify the explosive mix of intellectual rigidity and authoritarian outrage from which, if they made the right noises of approval, they would profit. The Party journal *Qiushi* [Seeking the Facts], which had replaced the doctrinaire *Red Flag*, carried an article warning pointedly against such people in high places 'who scheme against others'. A follow-up article argued prophetically that China was threatened by a return of the opportunistic behaviour displayed by Yao Wenyuan and other ultra-leftists during the Cultural Revolution.

We must not underestimate the presence of these people and their power. No one can guarantee that today we do not have people who are sharpening their swords and biding their time in the dark. When they calculate their time has come, they will come out, brandishing their swords and axes and working in concert with their allies. Their action may inevitably lead to small or large 'bloody incidents', throwing the people into bewilderment and disrupting the excellent situation of stability and unity. . . . [We must] create an environment where things are conducted above-board, where there is strong openness and where the 'schemers' are eliminated. Only in this way can we guarantee that the historical tragedy will not repeat itself. (Li Keyin in *Qiushi*, no. 3, 1989)

The Fourth Plenum of the Central Committee, scheduled for March before the annual National People's Congress (NPC), had been postponed without explanation. The NPC stuck to a strictly economic agenda, without the lively debates which had been an encouraging feature of the previous year. The Hong Kong press published 'inside reports' of harsh remarks made by the Party elders about Zhao Ziyang. He was ultra-right, he oppressed genuine Marxists, he should make a self-criticism, he should step down . . . If Deng Xiaoping had died first instead of Hu Yaobang the outcome might have been different. But Hu's death provoked a new student mobilization in circumstances where the at best lukewarm forces of the Zhao group favouring political reform were already on the defensive.

The students return

The students seized on the opportunity offered by Hu Yaobang's death to return to Tiananmen Square. Only five hundred—mostly from the Chinese University of Political Science and Law—demonstrated on 17 April, two days after his death. Five days later, half a million packed the square for the funeral ceremony. There had already been two skirmishes with police half a mile west at the Xinhuamen gate outside the Zhongnanhai where the leadership works and resides. On the funeral day there were two riots in the provincial capitals of Changsha and Xian, caused apparently by unemployed youth and rural migrants (although there was a suspicion of official provocation). Most students in Beijing were now on strike, writing and reading the wall-posters which blossomed inside every college. The atmosphere remained calm until 26 April when the *People's Daily* published an editorial, inspired by Deng Xiaoping, which described the events as a 'planned conspiracy and turmoil', allegedly provoked by 'an extremely small number of people' in order to 'once and for all negate the leadership of the CCP and the socialist system'. There was an ugly echo of the 'class struggle' politics of the Cultural Revolution in this judgement, which led to the joke that the imprisoned Jiang Qing had indignantly asked her jailers why she was still in captivity when Yao Wenyuan was being allowed to write again! The provocative editorial brought half a million demonstrators on to the streets, sweeping aside police cordons who were apparently instructed not to resist by force. Astutely insisting that they supported the Communist Party, the students demanded a 'genuine dialogue' between their own unofficial representatives—not the tame student unions—and the government, but neither side could agree on the terms. Respected intellectuals pleaded with the government to give ground. Zhao Ziyang (absent on a visit to North Korea when the editorial was published) returned, and the crisis eased. Another mass demonstration for the 4 May anniversary passed peacefully, with police cordons again giving way. Zhao's speech did not mention, 'turmoil' nor refer to 'bourgeois liberalization', and he assured governors of the Asian Development Bank (ADB) (meeting in the Great Hall of the People next to the Square) that the demonstrations would 'gradually calm down'. Most students agreed to return to classes. Even Premier Li Peng, when he met the ADB governors, said reassuringly that the students' and government's positions were 'basically identical'. Many students did return to campus while their organizations prepared to shift the focus away from mass activities towards long-term political education. Yet the struggle had acquired a critical momentum on both sides—within the leadership which was now even further divided, and among the students where a vocal minority believed that the opportunity for change would be lost if the public protest slackened.

With some discreet advice from the radical scholars, the students displayed from the start an articulate grasp of China's central contradictions which had been lacking in their conduct of the 1987 demonstrations. Their ideas had matured during two years of low-key repression, and irrespective of Hu Yaobang's death some demands would have been voiced on 4 May. A sharper political edge was rapidly acquired as the students found themselves in more direct confrontation with the authorities than they could have anticipated. But Deng and the conservative/ultra-left forces now grouped around him could have had no difficulty in recognizing at an early stage the potential challenge to their authority: On 21 April the Beijing University Students' Preparatory Committee demanded that the government:

1. make a fresh evaluation of the merits and demerits of Hu Yaobang, and approve his support for expanding democratic freedom.

2. punish those who have beaten students and masses, and oblige those responsible to pay compensation.

3. publish soon a [freedom of] information law, allow the people to publish newspapers, and acknowledge freedom of the press.

4. require the state leadership to declare openly before the people the situation regarding their personal and family possessions and income, check official corruption, and publish detailed information [regarding it].

5. require those officials responsible for the errors in educational policy to make a full self-criticism and find out who is responsible; demand a large increase in expenditure on education and improve the treatment of teachers.

6. re-evaluate the 'anti-bourgeois liberalism' campaign and completely rehabilitate those who were victimized.

7. allow accurate reporting of this democratic and patriotic movement.

The students used scorn and satire as much as political argument, appealing both to the egalitarianism officially fostered in the Maoist decades and still strong among the urban working class, and to widespread contempt for official corruption and nepotism. Marching from Beijing University to Tiananmen Square on 4 May, the students shouted the most subversive slogan of all: 'Long live the people!' The people of Beijing responded by cheerfully allowing their work to be disrupted and their buses to be immobilized by the mass demonstrations, by applauding from shop doors, office entrances, and factory gates, by buying lollipops by the dozen for the marchers, by contributing ten-yuan notes to the students' collecting boxes, by relishing the pointed questions asked in mimeographed leaflets (technically illegal like the marches) which were thrown in the air or pasted to bus shelters. One set of questions put out by the Beijing Workers' Federation—one of many new organizations which challenged the authority of official student or trade unions—began by asking how much Deng Pufang (Deng's son) had spent on gambling at the Hong Kong race course and where he had obtained the money. The next question enquired about the source of the golf fees paid by Zhao Ziyang's wife. (Zhao at this stage was not regarded as significantly more liberal than the rest of the Party leadership, and his private opposition to Deng's hard line was not yet known.) The list ended with a sarcastic request for the Party's definition of the following words: Party, Revolution, and Reaction. The students' denunciation of official corruption and speculation in foreign consumer goods was vivid and various. A poem on display at Shanghai's Fudan University, parodying the popular song 'I give you all my love', attracted large crowds:

We give our land to the east [Japanese concessions on Hainan Island]
We give our coal to the west [coal was exported in spite of shortages at home]
Ah, our native home, alas! alas!
We give colour TVs to the son of Deng [said to have profited from an import deal]
And saloon cars to the son of Ye [Governor of Guangdong, son of the late Ye Jianying]
We give them everything!
Our young women . . .
We give the emperor power over them
Our young men . . .
We give the officials the advantage over them
We give them everything!

A cartoon at Beijing University showed a mandarin with opium pipe and a tray of fine dishes beneath the ironic inscription 'Democracy on High'. A pair of antithetical lines read:

He will gladly tolerate democracy throughout the land. He will cheerfully smile because the people have been fooled.

The power struggle intensifies

While the students considered their next move, the leadership was stalemated. Zhao Ziyang, back from his visit to North Korea, urged that the inflammatory *People's Daily* editorial condemning the 'turmoil' should be repudiated. He would later be accused of having approved the text when it was telexed to him in Pyongyang, but it seems more likely that he had been presented with a fait accompli. Zhao's moderate words on 4 May soothed the situation in the Square but implied the existence of divisions within the leadership. Later he would also be accused of betraying Party unity by this revelation. Not surprisingly, no real dialogue emerged between the students and the leadership. The authorities offered various forms of semiofficial 'dialogue' but refused direct talks with the unofficial student leaders. Meanwhile student posters and leaflets increasingly turned to consider broader questions: the influence of feudalism on Chinese political culture, the relative merits of one-party and multiparty rule, the social basis for corruption, the need for freedom of the press and information. . . . The growing breadth of enquiry may be gauged from the following selection of wall-poster headings:

Evils of Stalinist political system
What does the factional struggle explain?
Can there be pluralism in a one-party state?
Oppose dictatorship and tyranny, Beijing belongs to the people
Who has caused 'turmoil' for the past 40 years?
Long-term tactics for the democracy movement
The Geneva Declaration of Human Rights
On our country's current grain shortage
What is law? What is truth?
Why can't we publish this article?

This last issue had been dramatized by the Shanghai authorities' action in removing the editor, Qin Benli, of the progressive *World Economic Herald*, and censoring an issue which published a symposium on Hu Yaobang's death. Beijing journalists marched on 4 May (anniversary of the 1919 May Fourth students' movement, see p. 65, above) behind banners with such slogans as 'Don't force me to spread rumours, news must report the truth', and 'Our pens cannot write what we want to write. Our mouths cannot speak what we want to speak'. The Party's propaganda department was beginning to lose its grip: on the 9th a petition signed by more than one thousand journalists called for talks with the department to protest at the muzzling of press reports on the Democracy Movement. Some students returned to the streets to support the journalists' petition. While the government remained in total paralysis as the date approached for President Gorbachev's arrival (15 May), the students again took the initiative. Hundreds of them returned to Tiananmen Square to begin a hunger strike on the 13th, lying motionless under makeshift awnings and tents on the vast hot expanse of paved stone. As well as demanding government dialogue with their representatives, they also insisted that the student movement should be 'positively appraised'. Zhao Ziyang on the very same day had argued in the Politburo Standing Committee for repudiation of the negative appraisal contained in the *People's Daily*'s 26 April editorial. Whether or not this was coincidence, it could easily be presented to Deng as another action by Zhao which undermined 'Party unity'—and repudiated his own judgement. On the 15th Zhao proposed to visit the Square, but was prevented from doing so by the Party secretariat on the grounds that this would 'violate inner-Party discipline'. With Zhao admittedly in a minority on the Standing Committee, his enemies could now turn Deng decisively against Zhao in the same way that the Gang of Four had poisoned Mao's mind against Deng in the final year of the Cultural Revolution.

The Party elders also believed—or professed to believe—that the student movement was replicating the chaos of the Cultural Revolution. President Yang Shangkun later described in shocked tones how the students at Beida had repudiated the official students' union and had occupied the campus broadcasting office. Sensitive to the charge, students at the People's University published a chart detailing the differences between the two movements. The present movement was a 'people's awakening', the Cultural Revolution had been a 'severe disturbance'; one arose spontaneously from the students, the other had been ordained by Mao and no one else; they were fighting feudalism and bureaucracy; the Red Guards had raised the cult of personality to new heights.

China was now on the brink of calamity. In the week 15–22 May, Gorbachev's momentous visit to Beijing was totally overshadowed by the Democracy Movement, which wrecked the official schedule and humiliated the Chinese leadership by forcing it to cancel the official welcoming ceremony in Tiananmen Square. Two crucial votes in the five-member Politburo Standing Committee went against Zhao Ziyang after Deng, his resolve stiffened by other Party elders, had intervened. Zhao withdrew from power while his rival Li Peng proclaimed martial law. When the army moved into the suburbs, students and citizens of Beijing lay before their vehicles, set up makeshift barricades, and kept the tanks and troop carriers at bay. Yang Shangkun, in a speech justifying the imposition of martial law to the Party's Military Commission, gave a vivid account of the crucial meeting with Deng, apparently convened on the 16th or 17th after the Politburo Standing Committee had failed to agree, while Party elders led by Chen Yun and Li Xiannian urged that a final decision should be reached. Yang's version (compiled below from his speeches of 22 and 24 May) underlines both the decisive role of the elders and their unshakeable conviction that for the Party's authority to be undermined would be the ultimate disaster.

Deng Xiaoping put the question: If we give way [to the students], to what point should we give way? I then said that this was the last stone in the dam. If we took it out, everything would collapse. Deng then said: I know you people have been arguing, but we are not talking about that, we are only talking about this question: To give way or not to give way. . . . (22 May)

To give way would mean yielding something to [the students]. Not to give way would be to insist on carrying through the policy laid down in the 26 April editorial. This was the first time for many years that our elders in their eighties had sat together to discuss affairs of the Party centre. Deng, Chen Yun, Peng Zhen, Madame Deng [Zhou Enlai's widow], and Wang Zhen all agreed that there was no way to retreat. If we did we would fall from power. The Chinese People's Republic would lose power. Capitalism would be restored. Just as the American [John Foster] Dulles had hoped, after several generations our socialism would turn into liberalism. Chen Yun made a very important comment. He said that if we allowed the People's Republic which had been achieved through decades of war, and all the achievements secured by the sacrifice of countless thousands of heroes, to be destroyed overnight, this was the same as negating the Communist Party. (24 May)

On the 19th Zhao at last visited the hunger strikers in the Square, apologizing for not having come sooner. Li Peng followed him there, furious at this further breach of unity. Zhao then sent in a sick note to absent himself from the afternoon meeting at which Li announced that the army would be mobilized to occupy the Square. Zhao was too late both within and outside the Party headquarters. Well-intentioned but irresolute, he had already offered to resign and thus could do nothing to help the Democracy Movement with which his political future was now intertwined. No one else in the leadership spoke out: it was the students of China and the people of Beijing versus the army and the new Li Peng regime.

The citizens resist

It was two weeks from the imposition of martial law until the troops finally occupied Tiananmen Square, during which time the illusion grew that they would never actually do so. Some of the stories alleging disaffection within the armed forces were fanned by rumour and by deliberate student propaganda. But President Yang Shangkun himself admitted the authenticity of a protest letter signed by former Minister of Defence (until 1988) Zhang Aiping and six other retired generals, demanding that the troops be withdrawn. In his 24 May speech Yang spoke frankly of internal doubts:

Is our thinking unified in the army? It will depend upon you doing your work [of persuasion] well. I think there is no problem with the comrades of the big military regions, but are there not people with problems from the army level downwards?

Yang also revealed that critics in the armed forces had objected to the martial law order being signed by Deng alone (in his capacity as Chairman of the Party's Military Affairs Committee)—on the grounds that it should have been countersigned by Zhao Ziyang, who was Deputy Chairman.

These hesitations may explain the half-hearted way in which army units lumbered in from the suburbs of Beijing, quickly immobilized by students and citizens who placed themselves peacefully in the way. Statements from the army warned that it would 'firmly carry out its orders', but appeared to nullify the threat by pledging that nothing would be done to harm 'the fish-and-water relationship' between army and people. Military experts were puzzled by the whole operation, which almost appeared to have been designed not to succeed. The truth is probably that no one at this stage was prepared to order the troops to use force if they were opposed—though the brave citizens who held them at bay could not have known this at the start.

The *shimin*—city people—were the real heroes of that first weekend, sturdy and plain-speaking men and women from the *hutong* lanes of Beijing who gathered at street corners around hastily erected barricades. 'We'll never let them in', they said during the tense hours of Sunday 21 May, keeping a night-long vigil. 'Only the old people and children are asleep', explained a mother. 'The rest of us are in the streets.' Informal debating societies sprang up with passionate but good-tempered argument. Sending in the troops had for very many people finally tipped the balance against the Communist Party. 'How can the government be so lacking in proper virtue?', asked one worker in Tiananmen Square. 'The people's army belongs to the people!' Li Peng was widely condemned as a 'bastard', Deng Xiaoping dismissed with a grimace. This growing tide of popular hostility towards the Party—no doubt carefully monitored by the regime's plain-clothes spies—must have been a far more powerful argument than the students' weeks of defiance in favour of the use of force. The *shimin* would suffer the heaviest casualties.

Their hostility was fed by an accumulation of grievances against the authorities (particularly the police) for which the ordinary people had pre-viously no outlet. Students on several occasions had to intervene to prevent their citizen supporters from using violence against the (at this stage) passive troops. The students established local headquarters in the buses which had been run across the roads to blockade the advancing convoys, where they could liaise with the local people who brought them food, and check all passing traffic. Activists from the colleges toured the main points of confron-tation in pedicabs, which also served as impromptu platforms from which to deliver rousing messages of support—coupled with appeals for nonviolence. Other messages were carried by members of the 'motorbike brigade'—young men with the funds, sometimes dubiously acquired, to purchase bikes who then joined ranks to cruise the streets in noisy cheerful convoy at night. Students also had to intervene frequently to prevent police spies with cameras from being beaten up. (These were easily identifiable and in some cases must have been sent as a deliberate provocation.) During the two weeks of confrontation, student policy was to 'give ground step by step' if the army resorted to force. When it did so, in the terrible night of 3–4 June, brave students still sought to persuade the enraged citizenry to refrain from violence, rescuing several soldiers from being beaten to death. Even after the massacre, students from Beijing University appealed for a peaceful response to the army:

Our view is that violence must not be countered with violence; the river of blood must not become a sea of blood. Our sacrifice is already grievous; our sacrifice has already clearly demonstrated that Li Peng's government has become the enemy of the people; his last day must be expected soon. But we possess no military strength with which to face modern forces with superior equipment; there is not an inch of steel in our hands. But peaceful struggle is the people's weapon, its strength is immeasurable.

The formation of the Beijing Workers' Autonomous Federation (BWAF), announced in Tiananmen Square on 25 May, was an even clearer signal to the watching authorities that the Party had lost control of the 'masses'. The official trade unions, a recent poll showed, were regarded as either useless or in league with management by 70 per cent of ordinary workers. The authorities issued orders to Beijing factory workers, reinforced by offers of cash, to stay away from the Square. Leaders of the BWAF were already being arrested before the massacre, when it was declared to be a counter-revolutionary organization. It was particularly threatening because of its overtly independent and socialist character. One of its banners carried a quotation from Marx: 'the ultimate goal of scientific socialism is the complete and free development of the human being'. The BWAF's opening statement called for the establishment of 'an autonomous organization which will speak for the workers and bring about workers' participation and consultation in political affairs'. It should not confine itself like the official trade unions to welfare matters, but should address the workers' political and economic demands. It also called for real participation in the workplace:

The organization should have the power, through every legal and effective means, to monitor the legal representatives of all state and collective enterprises, guaranteeing that the workers become the real masters of the enterprise. In other [private] enterprises, through negotiation with the owners and other legal means, the organization should be able to safeguard all legal rights of the workers. (*International Labour Reports,* July–Oct. 1989)

Workers in the Square complained of the loss of job security in the recent economic reforms, particularly affecting the growing millions of casual or contract workers whose migration in search of work had become a national problem earlier in the year. The reforms deliberately encouraged this sort of job mobility while making no provision for its social consequences. The violent demonstrations in April in Changsha and Xian, and in June in Chengdu, officially blamed upon 'hoodlums and unemployed workers', reflected the growing grievance of this newly formed Chinese subproletariat. Beijing workers also complained of widening wage disparities between managers and staff, and of the cuts in real wages forced upon them by inflation. Although the official ban on workers' participation was partly effective, many lorry-loads of cheering workers waving red flags reached the Square. Protest banners in the 17 May demonstration were carried by delegations from Capital Iron and Steel Factory, Beijing Petrochemical Company, Capital Hospital, Xidan Supermarket Workers, Beijing Workers' Union, No. 1 Machine Tool Factory, Pipe Music Instrument Factory, Chinese Heavy Machinery Products Factory, civilian workers of the People's Liberation Army (PLA), the People's Bank of China, Beijing Electric Utilities Co., Ministry of Railways, Beijing Municipal Institute of Labour Protection, and many other similar institutions. After the massacre, the authorities accused the BWAF of seeking to 'take up arms and overthrow the government'. There was no such plan, but militant workers did react violently to the army's use of force, setting vehicles on fire and throwing Molotov cocktails.

The phoney war

For two weeks (24 May–3 June) the Beijing confrontation remained a phoney war while the conservative leadership manoeuvred politically to further weaken the Zhao Ziyang camp and to ensure the army's loyalty before it was called on to wage a real war against the people. Most Beijing students returned, exhausted, to their colleges or worked shifts on the front line in the suburbs. But from all over China more students started to arrive, marching tired but fresh-faced out of the railway station to the applause of shoppers and passers-by who gave them friendly directions on how to get to Tiananmen Square. Many had travelled on the trains without paying—another echo of the Cultural Revolution (when Red Guards 'exchanged experiences'—*chuanlian*—across the country free of charge) to disturb the leadership. Buses started to run again, newspapers reappeared, and as the army failed to materialize, a false but infectious mood of optimism spread on the streets. Exaggerated accounts of army opposition to martial law were pasted on the lamp-posts. Similar stories in the Hong Kong press, suggesting that Li Peng and Deng Xiaoping were in serious political trouble, were faxed directly to Beijing by sympathizers and also displayed in the streets. Many such stories were the result either of wishful thinking or of a last-ditch effort by Zhao Ziyang's own supporters to retrieve the situation. On 19 May—the same day that Zhao privately admitted defeat—his followers circulated reports of the Politburo Standing Committee meetings earlier in the week where he had unsuccessfully called for reappraisal of the student movement and opposed martial law. This divulging of inner-Party argument would be added to the indictment against him. His supporters also helped to mobilize a massive demonstration against martial law on 23 May in which one slogan monopolized the banners and the shouting: 'Li Peng must resign'. In leaflets and posters, the same demand was made of Deng Xiaoping. In the words of a poem displayed in front of the Forbidden City:

> When cult is added to power,
> Even the Chairman makes mistakes.
> Xiaoping suffered criticism [in the Cultural Revolution]
> And the people raised him up.
> Now the country does not want him,
> The people do not want him.
>
> .   .   .   .
>
> The officials eat the food,
> The common people labour all year.
> A small handful get fat,
> A billion are poor.
> To overthrow the old system,
> The people must become the real masters.
> They should elect the good,
> And dismiss the bad!

The street optimism was widely shared by the hundreds of foreign journalists in Beijing, now operating illegally but with apparent impunity in contravention of the newly declared martial law. Chinese newspapers, even including the *People's Daily*, began to publish accurate reports of the demonstrations. When distribution of the more outspoken papers was blocked by the authorities, staff sold copies from vans parked on the roadside. Amazed at the vivid display of people's power on every street-corner, and impressed by the discomfiture of the army, almost everyone overlooked the logical fallacy behind the popular struggle. It could only succeed if the objective for which it was striving—an end to 'hegemonic rule' by the few and the adoption of democratic procedures by the many—had already been achieved. 'Convene the National People's Congress (NPC), Promote Democracy, Dismiss Li Peng, End Military Control', said the banners. Rumours swept Beijing that Wan Li, chairman of the NPC's Standing Committee and currently abroad, would come back to convene a meeting to remove Li Peng and restore normal government. But Wan Li's return was conducted according to older rules of Chinese political culture. Recognizing that the constitutional road had been closed, he arrived in Shanghai and refused to move further, claiming to be suffering from an unspecified illness. Meanwhile the Li–Deng leadership secured pledges of support from every military region in the country, and issued warnings against 'a small group of people who are creating chaos with the aim of rejecting the leadership of the Chinese Communist Party and the socialist system'. The identification of the defeated Zhao faction, by now linked umbilically to the Democracy Movement, as an 'anti-Party' conspiracy was complete. On the popular side, the declaration of martial law had also sharpened perceptions. 'It's not a case any longer of whether we support this government,' said one typical citizen at the barricades. 'We simply do not recognize it. We want to cast it out.' In the Square, students from the Beijing Art Academy erected a seven-metre-high statue called the Goddess of Freedom. The official press fumed that 'This is China, not America' and self-righteously warned the students that Tiananmen Square belonged not to them but to the people of China. In the rural suburbs, a few pro-Li Peng demonstrations were organized among peasants who received cash payments for taking part. Press restrictions on foreign journalists were tightened, and army jeeps cruised openly on the streets to heighten the psychological pressure. The lines of confrontation were now clearly defined and the way was open for the tanks.

The Beijing massacre

The Beijing massacre★ was preceded by a second half-hearted attempt by the army to infiltrate without bloodshed. On the night of 2 June, several thousand young soldiers jogged, unarmed, more than ten miles towards the centre from Tongxian in the east, each wearing running shoes but with a brand new pair of imitation suede boots hanging around his neck. Easily hemmed in by the Beijing residents, they sat exhausted by the roadside in the early morning before shambling back to base, some in tears, several holding hands for comfort. Meanwhile a large number of individual soldiers infiltrated from the west, in plain clothes but easily recognizable because of their trousers and webbing belts. These too were unarmed, but buses carrying their equipment were intercepted separately. It remained unclear whether this was a serious attempt to occupy the Square, or was merely designed to demonstrate that the army had used every peaceful means to reach its objective. The effect was to humiliate the army for the second time in two weeks, and to bring the crowds back to Tiananmen Square for the following day. Both results may have suited the plans of the hardliners who wished to maximize the confrontation.

The crisis now rapidly escalated, although few believed that the army would actually resort to force. In the afternoon of the 3rd, tear-gas was used outside the Xinhuamen entrance to the Zhongnanhai, where the leadership works and resides. More than a thousand troops suddenly emerged from the Great Hall of the People but were hemmed in by the crowd. By 7 p.m. tanks, armoured personnel carriers (APCs), and troop carriers were on the move

---

★ A brief guide to the topography of Beijing will help the reader to follow this account. Tiananmen Square lies in the centre of the city. The entrance to the Forbidden City is due north, across Changan Avenue (Avenue of Everlasting Peace) which runs from west to east along the top of the Square. The students' tents were pitched around the Martyrs' Memorial which stands on a central line near the middle of the Square. Mao's Mausoleum lies due south, and the Square is bounded further south by the Qianmen Gate. The Great Hall of the People stands on the west side of the Square, the Museum of Revolutionary History on the east. Changan Avenue is Beijing's main thoroughfare along which most military activity took place. Heading westwards from the Square, it soon passes the Xihuamen Gate which leads into the Zhongnanhai—the leadership's official work and residence quarter. The next road junction is called Liubukou. Further west, the Avenue passes the Minzu Hotel, then the Yanjing Hotel, and reaches the Museum of Military History in the area called Muxidi. Heading eastwards from the Square, the Avenue quickly passes the Beijing Hotel and, after crossing the Dongdan intersection, the International Hotel slightly north of the railway station. It then heads further east in the direction of Tongxian.

from the western suburbs, meeting fierce opposition from local residents in the area of the Military Museum west of Muxidi. Soon after 10 p.m. some (but not all) army units began to shoot their way through, firing indiscriminately on demonstrators, spectators, pavements, and roadside apartment buildings. An average of two persons was killed in each block, as well as many more on the streets. The local hospital near the Yanjing Hotel would receive sixty-three bodies by the end of the next day. Meanwhile students in the Square, though still unaware of these events, had sworn a public oath to defend it 'to the death'. Soon after midnight two APCs burst into the Square from the south and proceeded west and east, smashing through the barricades and injuring many people before returning to the Square. One was set on fire, its crew dragged out and at least one soldier apparently killed although others were rescued by students.

The APCs' rampage brought even more people flocking towards the Square, cursing the government as 'fascists' and 'heartless dogs'. By 1.30 a.m. on the 4th (when I arrived there, having pursued on foot one APC as it returned from its eastern circuit), the grey shapes of troop carriers were looming up on the western edge of the Square. There was a lull while spectators, including young men and women on bicycles, families with children, even one or two invalids in wheelchairs, strolled excitedly and watched the flames of the APC leaping high near Mao Zedong's portrait above the entrance to the Forbidden City. At 1.50 a.m. a crackle of gunfire to the west of the Square caused a panic. 'Don't be afraid, don't run!', others cried, believing it was only tear-gas canisters. At 2.10 a.m. another burst of firing, and the first casualties were rushed away—a girl with her face smashed and bloody, carried spread-eagled towards the trees, a youth with a bloody mess around his chest. Ambulances began to press with urgent sirens through the crowd. Other casualties were carried off on pedicarts with an escort of cyclists shouting 'Open the way!' A commandeered jeep had one wounded man on the roof, two or three sprawled inside. At 2.40 there was another lull. People streamed back towards the Square past the Beijing Hotel, while ambulances pleaded for a clear path. Some people were just curious to see what was happening, others shouted furiously and called for a general strike. Soon after 3.00, more volleys of sustained semi-automatic fire drove them back with many more casualties. The army now controlled the northern end of the Square, which rapidly filled with tanks and APCs.

Several thousand students huddled around the Martyrs' Memorial in the centre, debating what to do next. Hou Dejian, the pop singer leading four hunger-strikers on the plinth, attempted to negotiate a withdrawal with the army, which offered to let the students retreat via the south-east corner. At 4 a.m. all the lights were turned off. Though expecting an imminent assault, the students stood calmly while their loudspeakers played the 'Internationale'. People began setting fire to the now-abandoned tents and piles of rubbish, although urged not to provoke the army by doing so. The loudspeakers then broadcast two conflicting appeals. A student leader insisted that the Square should not be abandoned. 'We will now pay the highest price possible, for the sake of securing democracy.' But a leader of the Workers' Autonomous Federation then urged withdrawal: 'We must all leave here immediately, for a terrible bloodbath is now about to take place . . . To wish to die here is nothing more than an immature fantasy.' He was supported by Hou Dejian. Soon after 4.30, the tanks to the north started up their engines, conveying the threat that they were about to roll forward. A rather confused voice vote was taken which was interpreted to be a decision in favour of leaving. Between 5 and 5.30 nearly all those in the Square filed out quietly, carrying their banners, while a few spectators applauded. A student picket line guarded the rear, retreating slowly as the tanks advanced. An anonymous student leaflet then describes what happened next:

The citizens and workers of Beijing said goodbye to the departing students with tears in their eyes. The workers shook us by the hand, saying: 'Forgive us, we could not protect you from the army, but you are the real victors.'

The workers and students wept together. The citizens took off their shoes and gave them to those students with bare feet. As we reached the southern gate, we heard the sound of concentrated gunfire behind. A number of students who did not wish to leave were slaughtered there. We called out 'Blood will be repaid with blood: Down with the fascists', and marched ahead. . . .

At 6 a.m. the massacre of Liubukou took place. We were just crossing the road to keep up with the students in front, when nine tanks raced up from the Xinhuamen, belching poisonous gas [probably exhaust fumes] which filled the avenue. Then they opened fire. [It was later established that the students who died were crushed, not shot, by a single APC.]

Two people next to me still had their eyes open but their blood was spattered on my clothes. I tried to support them but they were already dead. I saw another person, a university doctor, whose face was half destroyed by a bullet. Across the avenue were the bodies of many citizens and students who had been crushed by the tanks. . . .

A worker handed over to us another student, saying, 'This is a student from Sichuan. He's gone mad. He saw the tanks crush his fellow-students.' When we finally managed to cross the avenue, we saw the marks of gunfire everywhere, including row upon row all over a four-storey building, and citizens were picking up the bullets.

The army now ponderously and menacingly consolidated its control of the Square and the Avenue to the west and east, not venturing to patrol the side-streets for three more days. On the 4th, groups of citizens still approached the army lines guarding the Square to protest, or out of curiosity. On at least six occasions, the soldiers fired when the crowd became too large or too irritating. From then on until the 7th, squadrons of tanks and APCs cruised east and west by night and day, and some took up defensive positions at key intersections. This gave rise to rumours, magnified in foreign reports, of internal army discord and the possibility of fresh intervention by a 'good' army which would avenge the people's losses. Although there were intra-army tensions, most of the manoeuvres appear to have been part of a sys-tematic plan to 'open the road' by a massive and intimidatory show of force. Beijing citizens soon learnt a new highway code. Anyone who made a threatening or defiant gesture would be shot by soldiers who had been authorized to 'attack those who attack you'. But some trigger-happy sol-diers still fired at random. The young, often frightened, troops had been told that they were facing a revolt by counter-revolutionaries. In some cases, soldiers called out popular slogans in order to lull the suspicions of hostile citizens. Other stories of army units or individual officers genuinely refusing to shoot are better authenticated. Months after the massacre, soldiers who had been involved would invariably insist that their unit had not fired—or only in the air. It also remained impossible to establish just who had given the order to open fire. According to one account, the troops were instructed to use all necessary means to attain their objective. On meeting resistance they sought clarification, but received the reply: 'You have received your instructions. Do not ask again!' If true, this suggests an effort even at the highest level of command to avoid explicit responsibility for the killings.

By far the most severe casualties were suffered by the ordinary citizens of Beijing who sought to prevent the army from entering. Many hundreds were killed during the army's western advance, and dozens more at the top of Tiananmen Square and eastwards as the soldiers 'opened the road'. Most reliable estimates, based on the number of bodies reported in local hospitals, put the total of deaths somewhere below the one thousand mark, with at least three thousand non-fatal casualties. The regime would only admit that 'nearly 300' died including at least 'several dozen' soldiers. It acknowledged that some innocent civilians had died but claimed that hooligans and vicious counter-revolutionary elements among them had started the violence. Their argument assumed it was justified to respond to passive protest or to stone-throwing with automatic weapons. As one eyewitness report describes the fighting outside the Minzu Hotel to the west of the Square:

When after more than an hour the last truck of the convoy had passed by the Minzu Hotel, many hundreds of people (not only students) appeared on the street. They ran after the trucks and shouted protest slogans. A few stones were thrown. The soldiers opened fire with live ammunition. The crowd threw themselves on the ground, but quickly followed the convoy again. The more shots were fired, the more the crowd got determined and outraged. Suddenly they started singing the Internationale; they armed themselves with stones and threw them towards the soldiers. There were also a few Molotov cocktails and the last truck was set on fire. (Amnesty International report, 30 Aug. 1989)

Ultimate responsibility for the killings must rest with the political leadership which ordered in the troops, knowing that this would lead to violence. No effort was made—except briefly on the afternoon of the 3rd—to use more conventional methods of crowd control such as tear-gas. (Li Peng would later claim that the troops ran out of tear-gas and that there were no hydrants near the Square with enough pressure for water cannons.) The use of firepower enabled the hardline regime to intimidate two separate opposing forces: it cowed its critics in the Party leadership, and it taught the people of Beijing who had defied martial law a bitter lesson. Thousands would also be arrested and beaten up (and a number of them executed) in the ensuing repression. The students in the Square suffered fewer casualties, although the eyewitness reports suggest that worse violence was only avoided by their disciplined decision to leave. This picture was blurred by exaggerated claims by student exiles that thousands had been mown down in the Square or crushed by tanks. The regime was able to produce witnesses, including—after a period of hiding in a foreign embassy—the hunger-striker Hou Dejian, to assert that no one had died there. The exact facts remain unclear: some students who refused to leave may have been killed; it is possible although less likely that a few remained in their tents and were crushed when the armoured vehicles advanced. Even if these deaths did not occur, the regime's argument rested on a quibble: many dozens of civilians were shot in the Avenue running across the Square's northern end. Only if that area was excluded could it be claimed that 'no one was killed in the Square'.

★ ★ ★

How is life in Beijing after the 4th of June? You can tell the world two simple things: We have learnt to tell lies, and we are waiting for someone to die!

(A Beijing resident, 1 Oct. 1989)

The repression which followed the events of June 1989, and the nature of the regime which conducted it, were the clearest possible illustration that forty years after the revolution China had lost its way and the Chinese Communist Party had lost its mandate. In night-time searches the martial law troops seized thousands of mostly working-class citizens in Beijing, based on police lists or reports by informers who could phone a special number to give the names of alleged 'counter-revolutionary thugs'. (The usual question among friends was 'How many people have been seized in your street?') A severe beating after arrest and before questioning was routine. Some innocent suspects died in custody or were released with permanent injury. Although violence has always been part of the penal system, and torture was used during the Cultural Revolution, it was quite new for the state apparatus to use these methods of intimidation openly and systematically. In the first weeks after the massacre, arrested suspects were shown on television bearing evident marks of maltreatment—some hardly able to stand. In factories, offices, and other institutions, every employee was required to write a self-criticism, often as long as 3,000 Chinese characters, detailing his or her behaviour in May and June. Some institutions where almost everyone had supported the Democracy Movement tacitly agreed to lie collectively, denying that anyone had visited Tiananmen Square. College heads protected students by giving them sick certificates; hospital chiefs altered records showing how staff had helped the demonstrators. The telling of lies extended to political meetings where participants would stand up and quote the *People's Daily* on the horrors of the 'counter-revolutionary rebellion', knowing that their colleagues knew that they did not believe a word. Yet in some factories militant workers still asked awkward questions: ('If only a "small handful" led the rebellion, why were so many people killed?') Factory cadres clapped loudly whenever Deng Xiaoping's name was mentioned to smother the sound of unfavourable comments. Fewer students were arrested—except the principal leaders whose names were circulated on a wanted list. But Beijing University was punished by a reduction of two-thirds in the size of its student body, while the 1989 intake was required to spend the first year at an army camp in the countryside.

While the people of Beijing 'told lies', they also waited 'for someone to die'. The power struggle which had fatally intersected with the Democracy Movement illustrated yet again how China's political structure was quite unable to solve the succession crisis—of Deng Xiaoping now as of Mao Zedong before. It also showed how Party discipline, backed up for the first time by the open use of force, could effectively cow the majority of Party members who had supported Zhao Ziyang. The situation in the provinces was more complicated: no provincial leader spoke out against the massacre or repression, but many manoeuvred to insulate their own territories from its repercussions, particularly in the seaboard provinces most reliant upon the continuation of good relations with foreign trading partners. Zhao's replacement was not, after all, Li Peng, but the ambitious Jiang Zemin from Shanghai. Jiang had impressed Deng Xiaoping by taking tough preventative measures which lessened the conflict with students in Shanghai. Joined on the Politburo Standing Committee by the successful ex-carpenter Li Ruihuan from Tianjin, both men provided some balance in the awkward gap now widening between Beijing and the provinces.

Jiang attempted to convince foreign visitors privately that he regretted the massacre and was struggling to reduce the influence of the Party elders and the army. The relationship between the Party and the People's Liberation Army (PLA) had significantly altered as a result of the military operation in Beijing. The army had been obliged to intervene during the Cultural Revolution to protect vital installations, but had never turned its guns on the people. To do so now was a blatant repudiation of the Maoist concept (invoked by the citizens and students to some effect although ultimately unsuccessful) that 'the army is the people's army'. A new generation of professional officers could be seen on Tiananmen Square, smilingly explaining how their men had shot no one with a swaggering disregard for the truth. Yet others expressed private anguish at the massacre, while their families far away from Beijing had to fend off angry accusations from neighbours: 'So you brought up your son to kill Chinese!' While waiting for Deng to die, Beijing public opinion tended to agree with foreign observers: another convulsion in the leadership must be expected in which the army could play a larger part. The more optimistic spoke of a cleansing operation by younger officers, appalled by the bloodshed and nauseated by the corruption of their elders. Others feared civil war.

China's incomplete economic reforms were now in suspense. Jiang Zemin moved quickly to appropriate some of the Democracy Movement's objectives. A new campaign was launched against the involvement of senior Party figures and their families in business operations. A wider campaign against corruption found some quick easy targets—private businesses and even a pop star who had evaded paying taxes. Yet there was no indication of any structural changes politically which would enable these campaigns to succeed where others had failed. The November 1989 Party Plenum instead stepped up the attack on political reform as an alleged plot by Zhao Ziyang to restore capitalism. It further watered down the policies of economic reform, saying that 'rectification' must come first and that decentralization should be 'firmly opposed'. Over a million rural factories had been closed in 1989 under the new austerity policies, and China was told by Li Peng to prepare for 'several years of hard living' (13 Oct.). The government now faced a cash crisis. Urban employees were obliged to buy national bonds, and peasants protested when they received promissory notes for the grain they had produced.

China's foreign relations had suffered on a broader scale. France gave particular offence by allowing the establishment in September 1989 of the Front for Democracy in China which sought to unite the various exile movements abroad. Chaired by the scholar Yan Jiaqi, the student leader Wu'er Kaixi (many of whose colleagues were still in hiding in China or had been arrested), and by one of China's new business entrepreneurs, Wan Rennan, it called for the overthrow of the Beijing regime and adopted a new constitution. The presence of Fang Lizhi and his wife in the US Embassy in Beijing where they had taken refuge irritated US–China relations. (Other scholars including Su Shaozhi had managed to leave China.) The pressure for economic sanctions against China, which largely affected sales of military equipment and the provision of soft loans, was not maintained—most Western governments preferred to keep a foot in the Chinese door. But the loss of foreign investment in 1989 was estimated at one to two billion US dollars while tourism revenue fell by one billion.

China was now withdrawing further into ossified reaction, in unhappy contrast to the democratic leap forward in Eastern Europe. East Germany's communist leadership, one of the very few to support China's government after the Beijing massacre, now rejected the 'Chinese solution' of suppressing its own Democracy Movement by force, and flung open the Berlin Wall. (Perhaps those who died in Beijing had demonstrated by their sacrifice that the military route should never be taken again.) On the very same day— 9 November 1989—Deng Xiaoping finally stepped down, handing over to his latest protégé, Jiang Zemin, the chairmanship of the Party's Military Committee. Events in the Soviet Union and Eastern Europe, Jiang claimed defensively, were a 'short-lived phenomenon' and China's current version of socialism would eventually prevail.

The distance between the new regime and the people was symbolized by the fortieth anniversary celebrations in Beijing on 1 October 1989. A picked audience watched the athletic and dancing displays, for which participants had to be paid to induce them to attend. The people of Beijing were kept well away from the Square and fireworks by nervous cordons of soldiers and police. Restrictions on long-distance travel had been imposed to prevent anyone except on official business from travelling to the capital. The gap which this symbolized between the regime and the people could not survive indefinitely.

Contrary to expectations, Deng Xiaoping and his successor Jiang Zemin found ways of bridging that gap over the next decade. But no proper explanation—far less apology—was offered for the massacre. Outside China, the film documentary *The Gate of Heavenly Peace* (1995) sought to offer a more balanced interpretation: It concluded that on both sides, protestors as well as the government, moderate voices were silenced by more extreme arguments. Further insight was provided by *The Tiananmen Papers* (2001), a compilation said to be based on hundreds of documents dating from 1989 which had been smuggled out of China. These revealed that the Politburo Standing Committee, when deadlocked over whether to impose martial law, was obligated by a pre-existing secret resolution to refer the stalemate to Deng and the Party elders. The documents also confirmed that some army leaders were reluctant to intervene, and provided more detail on protests outside the capital. Meanwhile within China, a decade and a half later, the families of those who died still wait in vain for the 'settling of accounts' with those responsible for the massacre.

13

Into the New Millennium
China transformed

A year after the Beijing massacre, a poem with the title 'Deng, where are you hiding?' circulated secretly in the capital. (The author, if caught, would have spent the next ten years in jail.)

'Deng, where are you hiding?
Have you really stepped down?
The state is in crisis by your will,
How long can you dodge the blame?

. . . . .

We call to the mountains:
'Deng where are you?'
The hills and gullies ring back:
'He's just moved on.
He's having a banquet on Mount Emei,
The tables are loaded with maotai spirit, the floor strewn with cigarette
    butts.

. . . .

We return to the heart of the motherland,
And cry out loud before Tiananmen:
'Chairman——Deng!'
The great square replies: 'A little quieter, please,
Don't disturb his inventive spirit.
He's here, working out where he went wrong.'[1]

Deng reinvents China

If Deng had really spent his last years drinking *maotai* and chain-smoking (or playing bridge and appeasing the army as other verses suggested), then the collapse of the Chinese Communist Party predicted by many after 1989 would have been unavoidable. Yet the anonymous poet was after all right: while Beijing stagnated in a gloomy atmosphere of repression, Deng was indeed working out 'where he went wrong'. The result—demonstrating yet again how the Chinese system still required a great leader to make it function—was a qualitative shift of economic gear which over the next decade completed China's transformation into a quasi-capitalist system. Kick-started into new life by Deng in the early 1990s, the economy generated a fever of activity which changed the face of China (at least urban China) by the beginning of the new millennium. In doing so, it promoted social mobility and change on an unprecedented scale to compensate for the survival of a political system which could still be heavily repressive. And it produced sufficient rewards for hundreds of millions of people, and held the possibility of gain for many more, to blunt the edge of dissent—although several more hundreds of millions, particularly in the countryside and among unemployed state workers, were excluded.

The collapse of the Soviet Communist Party in 1991, following peaceful revolutions across Eastern Europe, had seemed for a while to increase the likelihood of a similar demise in China. Old Chinese generals worried about separatism in Xinjiang, calling for the defence of 'socialist unity'. Young dissidents claimed that 'Moscow's today is Beijing's tomorrow' and made defiant phone-calls to fellow dissidents abroad. Yet China was not the same as the Soviet Union, as more thoughtful exiles now including Professor Su Shaozhi presciently observed. The economic reforms had already transformed China into a vast chaotic market where making (or losing) money was a central activity for millions of people who would otherwise be making politics. The sense of national unity was stronger in China, except in its peripheral regions, than in the Soviet Union. Out in the provinces, Chinese public opinion was more likely to remain passive. There was also a widely diffused fear of national upheaval with the historical memory of rebellions, warlords, and civil conflict within the past century. Even those who hoped for the Party's passing feared it might lead to conflict within the armed forces and a violent interregnum.[2]

In retrospect the collapse of the Soviet Union actually gave an impetus to Deng's search for an economic way forward which would buy at least the acquiescence if not the support of the Chinese masses. Already in March 1990 he had outlined his strategy to members of the Party Central Committee:

. . . The political stability we have already achieved is not enough to rely on. And although we have to strengthen ideological and political work and stress the need for hard struggle, we cannot depend on those measures alone. The crucial factor is economic growth, which will be reflected in a gradual rise in living standards. Only when people have felt the tangible benefits that come with stability and with the current systems and policies will there be true stability. No matter how the international situation changes, so long as we can ensure appropriate economic growth, we shall stand firm as Mount Tai.[3]

The fruit of Deng's reflections was harvested early in 1992 when Deng, who had been out of sight for the past year, made a surprise Chinese New Year visit to the Shenzhen Special Economic Zone to deliver the message that 'if capitalism has something good, then socialism should take it over and use it'. His appearance had an element of monkey magic about it: he materialized at Shenzhen's Folk Culture Village—one of China's first theme parks—riding puckishly in a golf buggy escorted by one of his daughters. At first only the Hong Kong press reported his provocative remarks, clearly directed against the conservatives who were thriving in the repressive atmosphere of Beijing. 'Reforms and greater openness are the only way out,' he said, warning that those who stood in the way were 'walking into a dead-end street' and would have to 'leave the stage'. Economic reform should not 'proceed slowly like women with bound feet, but . . . blaze a trail and press forward boldly'. Ironically, the same metaphor was used by Mao in his call to speed up agricultural collectivization in the late 1950s, paving the way for the People's Communes which Deng had already abolished.

   Not for the first time, a Chinese leader had left Beijing to outflank those who remained there (Mao adopted the same tactic when he launched the Cultural Revolution). Deng's journey soon became known as his Southern Expedition—the classical phrase used to describe an emperor's tour of his domains. His enemies in Beijing put themselves in the wrong by at first refusing to publish his endorsement of a market economy and condemnation of 'leftist' opposition. Two months later, both the Party Politburo and senior army leaders pledged their support for Mr Deng when the National People's Congress (NPC) met in Beijing. The National People's Congress Standing Committee chairman Wan Li, who had disappointed the students in 1989 by failing to intervene against the hardliners, found his voice again: 'A ruling party that cannot develop the economy and improve the people's living standards is not qualified [to rule],' he declared.

Deng's startling message was that when it came to developing the economy, the concept which had been regarded as crucial for socialism— the role of central planning—had no magic significance. Conversely, there was nothing inherently capitalistic about encouraging market forces. Equally important, there was nothing wrong with allowing the rich to get richer: they should be allowed to do so and eventually (but not 'too soon') pay more taxes to help the poor. In this way, Deng completed a semantic shift, begun a decade earlier, in the formulaic dogmas which determine policy at every level. At the Twelfth Party Congress in 1982, it was stressed that planning should hold the dominant position while market regulation was supplementary. The Thirteenth Congress in 1987 said that the two should be combined in a 'harmonious whole'. Now Deng said that

The proportion of planning to market forces is not the essential difference between socialism and capitalism. A planned economy is not equivalent to socialism, because there is planning under capitalism too; a market economy is not capitalism, because there are markets under socialism too. Planning and market forces are both means of controlling economic activity. The essence of socialism is liberation and development of the productive forces, elimination of exploitation and polarisation, and the ultimate achievement of prosperity for all. This concept must be made clear to the people.[4]

The focus of argument now shifted from 'planning versus market' to 'public versus private'. The Fourteenth Party Congress later in 1992 endorsed Deng's famous formula of 'building socialism with Chinese characteristics' on the basis of a 'socialist market economy'. It still stipulated that 'public ownership will continue to be the main form of ownership' while adding that other types of ownership (i.e. mixed or private) should be 'jointly developed'. To complete this semantic saga, the Party ventured further five years later at the Fifteenth Congress to declare that 'the non-public-ownership sector is an important component part of China's socialist economy'. It would take another five years before private ownership was fully legitimized—at the Sixteenth Congress in 2002 which allowed private entrepreneurs to join the Party.

The economic fever

With Deng's authority, millions of Chinese now 'plunged into the sea of business' (*xiahai*). In another popular phrase, 'everyone is becoming a businessman (or woman)' (*quanmin jieshang*): this was an updated version of the slogan from the late 1950s that 'everyone should become a soldier' (*quanmin jiebing*). Throughout the mid-1990s, there was a fever of entrepreneurial activity as 'everyone', so it seemed, responded to Deng's renewed invitation to 'get rich first'. Trains, and increasingly passenger planes, were packed with would-be entrepreneurs venturing in every direction, from the north-east to Tibet but especially to the southern coast, to make their fortune. The economic fever became part of a new popular culture in which millions of cadres and their families took part as enthusiastically as everybody else. 'Chairman Mao used to say that Marxism was our magic weapon,' said one Chinese economist. 'Now it is the market.' At the city museum in Zhengzhou, capital of Henan province, famous for its ancient bronzes, an entire wing was turned into a furniture salesroom. 'Ancient things are out of date,' said one salesman: 'Everyone's doing business now.' New catchphrases circulated to satirize the mood: 'Those who wield the scalpel make less than those who use the barbers' scissors; those who make the atom bomb earn less than those selling eggs soaked in tea.' The words for bomb and egg sound the same in Chinese, and opening a barbers' shop was the first step for many ambitious young people up the entrepreneurial ladder.

Behind the often chaotic appearance of this human scramble lay a far-reaching plan, endorsed by Deng against conservative opposition, for a new strategy of market reform designed to revitalize the economy and with it the people. As one Hong Kong observer would put it, 'practically the whole of China would by early next century be turned into one large Special Economic Zone [SEZ]'.[5] Hong Kong and foreign companies were now invited to enter China in far more economic sectors, and far more deeply, than before. For a start, all provincial capitals and some thirty cities along the Yangtze and on the internal borders were allowed to offer preferential policies of the SEZ type. Before long the geographical limitations simply disappeared: even rural counties set up their own 'development zones'— often little more than a patch of empty land with a grand signboard over the road.

During his Southern Expedition, Deng singled out Guangdong province for praise, urging the rest of the country to emulate its success in 'opening up'.

Guangdong province wants to catch up with Asia's four little dragons [South Korea, Taiwan, Hong Kong, Singapore], but it can catch up with them sooner if it speeds up in development. Shanghai is completely capable of achieving faster economic growth, and the four Special Economic Zones, the Yangtze Delta and even the whole country will be different if everyone makes an effort to catch up. We must speed up the reforms, starting now.[6]

Shanghai had long suffered from the central government's reluctance to let it regain its economic dominance of before Liberation. Deng now said that his biggest mistake had been not to include the city in the original list of SEZs. The Fourteenth National Congress now gave the green light: The expansion of the new Pudong zone, across the Huangpu River from old Shanghai, would assist the development of other Yangtze cities and help Shanghai become 'an international economic and financial centre'. The Yangtze was often pictured as a dynamic dragon—with Shanghai as its head. Shanghai's return to favour was no doubt helped by the political dominance of Jiang Zemin and other national leaders—often referred to as the Shanghai clique—who had either originated in the city or made their careers there. The new Pudong, 500 square kilometres in size, moved rapidly ahead. By the end of the century it had 1.5 million inhabitants and its GDP was growing at 20 per cent annually, with an new airport and container ports, new universities, and the country's most advanced electronic industries. US visitors looked at the skyline and enthused that Shanghai had become 'China's Manhattan'.

The key to China's economic growth was . . . economic growth. Against sporadic opposition by Party conservatives and cautious economists, the Dengists believed, in their patron's phrase, that 'the economy should enter a new threshold every few years'. There was a faint echo here, transformed for a different age, of Mao Zedong's belief that China should undergo 'a new political upheaval every few years'. China's real GDP had grown at an annual rate of about 5.3 per cent from 1960 to 1978: in the next twenty years to 1999 the average real rate was 9.7 per cent. The official Chinese statistics on which these averages are based, although accepted by international bodies such as the World Bank, have been challenged but appear to broadly reflect the upward trend. The effect of Deng's Southern Expedition was particularly marked, producing double-digit growth for the years 1992–5. A major reason for this was an inward flood of foreign direct investment (FDI) which grew from US $636 million in 1983 to $45.6 billion in 1998. The distribution remained uneven: by the end of the 1990s, more than a quarter of inward investment went to Guangdong province, and nearly 10 per cent to Shanghai, but the lower labour costs available in inland cities began to offer a more attractive prospect. The mainland benefited enormously from its offshore islands: about two-thirds of FDI came from Hong Kong and Taiwan—(although part of Hong Kong's investment consisted of funds which were illegally exported from the mainland, then reimported to take advantage of tax concessions).

Deng's abandonment of the primacy of state ownership finally allowed Beijing reformers to tackle seriously the problem of the nation's state-owned enterprises (SOEs), although at a high human cost. Once the main motor of economic development in the age of central planning, this sector had also become a guarantee of social stability in urban China. At the start of the 1990s, the largest SOEs (in excess of 10,000 across the country), still produced nearly half of China's industrial output and paid 67 per cent of all tax revenue. Those with a workforce of more than 500 accounted for 41 per cent of all industrial employees. Large or small, a state enterprise took care of all the needs of its workers and dependants, providing housing, schools, and health facilities at minimal cost—the so-called 'iron rice bowl' which the economic modernizers said now had to be 'smashed'. SOE reform in the 1990s became a symbolic measure of the extent to which the government was committed to reform. Western-trained Chinese economists and bureaucrats in key economic ministries mostly shared the sharply negative view of the World Bank, and similar international organizations, as expressed in these words:

A legacy of China's command economy, state-owned enterprises have characterized much of the country's economic landscape until fairly recently. Inefficiency, high debt burdens, an oversized labour force, and costly social services for employees have turned public industries that were once the engine of growth into an obstacle to further modernization of the country's financial and fiscal system (not to say that there haven't also been many successful and profitable state enterprises).[7]

Statistics on the number of SOEs fluctuated widely according to how they were defined but there were probably about 100,000 at the beginning of the decade. (The much higher figure of 300,000 includes thousands of small workshops and factories, many of which had already become privatized informally, with the profits shared by managers and—less commonly—workers.) The number had declined to less than 65,000 in 1998 as a result of conversion to shareholding enterprises, merger, closure, or bankruptcy. The biggest ones—either those which remained profitable or were hardest to reform—were more likely to survive under a policy known as 'releasing the small and retaining the large'. Their output now only accounted for less than

30 per cent of total industrial output, and their profits had declined from 6 per cent to 1 per cent of GDP. Roughly half made an annual loss and many of these would have been bankrupt but for the soft loans which they had secured from state banks. Such loans typically depended upon mutually advantageous 'connections' between cadres and managers.

Urbanization

Mao Zedong had fought a mainly peasant revolution on the strategy that 'the countryside will surround the towns': not a single city was captured from the Guomindang until a year before the 1949 Liberation. China remained predominantly a nation of peasant farmers for the next three decades, and by 1980 81 per cent of the population still depended on the land. Metalled roads were still few in many areas except between county towns; horses and mules were the main form of transport and most rural dwellers lived in mud-built houses with tamped earthen floors and no electricity. Twenty years later, an accelerating process of urbanization had transformed the relationship between town and countryside: 31 per cent of the population were urban dwellers, the number of towns rose from some 3,500 to around 20,000, cities from less than a hundred to nearly seven hundred. Urban planners said that China should aim for an urbanization rate of 40 per cent of its population by 2010, and 50 per cent by 2020. In numbers it meant that another 170 million people were expected in the urban areas in the first decade. This anticipated increase was only partly planned: much of the growth would stem from peasant migration to the towns which could no longer be restrained as effectively as in the past by controls on residency. Besides, the urban sector relied heavily on peasant labour for its workforce. 'A country where most of the population is in poor and remote villages will not be a modern and developed nation,' said State Council minister Wang Mengkui. 'Our urbanisation rate is equivalent only to that of the UK in the 1850s, of the US in 1911 and of Japan in 1950.'[8]

The rapidly expanding city of Changzhou in Jiangsu province, 100 miles upstream from Shanghai on the Yangtze River, offers a good example of China's urban expansion. A medium-sized town with a small textile industry largely dependent on the Grand Canal which passes through it, Changzhou had already began to specialize in electronics in the 1970s. By 1982 it had a population of 370,000 and was designated by Beijing as a 'star city' where the post-Cultural Revolution policy of economic readjustment was being carried out well. Twenty years later Changzhou was a large booming city with a high-technology industrial zone attracting foreign investment, luxury housing estates for its expanding elite, and an ambitious plan to build a huge reservoir of technical skills. Changzhou now had an urban population of 800,000–900,000 but this was swelled by a further 400,000 migrant workers while half a million peasants from the neighbouring rural areas also worked in the city's industries. Changzhou's 'University City' on which construction began in 2002 would, when completed, accommodate one hundred thousand students: City officials said that they wanted 'tens of thousands of qualified professionals to form a strategic resource for our industry of the future'. The rationale for the project, which would cost more than 2.5 billion yuan (£220 million), was that 'the key to effective competition in the new global economy is human knowledge'.[9]

The heavy investment in infrastructural projects, not always based on rational calculation, which was central to China's economic growth in the 1990s, allowed hundreds of towns and cities which did not share Changzhou's advantages to pursue a similar expansion. Typically, Chinese urban development has been extensive, with neighbouring agricultural land annexed often wastefully for new industry, roads, and housing. The old town with its tiled roofs and narrow lanes often remains, obscurely embedded within the urban sprawl, except where space is at a premium—for example on the steep slopes of Chongqing on the upper Yangtze. Nation-wide, an area the size of a medium-sized Chinese county disappears under concrete every year. The amount of land in use for transportation of all kinds, from roads to airports, is expected to double in the first decade of the twenty-first century to an area equal in size to Jiangsu province.

Urban planners in smaller cities pursue the same list of priority projects as those of their provincial capitals: these typically include new high-rise public buildings (particularly the Party, government, and police headquarters), a pedestrian shopping precinct, at least one supposedly hi-tech industrial zone, new schools and colleges, gated luxury housing projects for the local business and political elite, broad highways in the areas of development with carriageways up to twenty metres wide, and an expressway to the airport if one exists or to the next city. Whereas in the Maoist era provincial cities sought to emulate the cold bureaucratic architecture of Beijing, now the more exuberant consumer-oriented style of Shanghai has become the model—especially that of the new Pudong financial district across the river from the colonial-era Bund.

The most dramatic infrastructural change in the last decade affecting hundreds of millions of Chinese has been the expansion of transport by train, road, and air which has transformed the opportunities for travel and boosted social mobility. New rolling stock and faster timetables mean that travel by rail is less likely to be an endurance test except during national holidays (which have been extended to encourage more spending on leisure activities). Ticket purchase has been computerized and it is even sometimes possible to buy return tickets before starting a journey. China built 5,700 kilometres of new line in 1996–2000 of which 80 per cent was double-tracked, and electrified 4,300 kilometres of existing line. A new focus on railway building in backward and remote western China is intended to result in rail links between all the provinces of the region. The star project will be the first ever line into Tibet on which construction began in 2001. Nearly one thousand kilometres of its length is more than 4,000 metres above sea level: the maximum height reaches 5,070 metres when it scales the Tibetan plateau at the Tanggula pass. Meanwhile Shanghai has pioneered the world's first commercially operated magnetic levitation railway between the city and its new international airport. A high-speed rail link from Shanghai to Beijing, possibly also using the MagLev system, is being planned.

The main burden of new passenger traffic, however, was borne by the road system with a rapid expansion of bus services and of private car ownership. Long-distance freight transport by road also grew rapidly as producers sought new markets. In 2002 China's expressway mileage reached 25,000 kilometres, making it second only to the US in the world: the Ministry of Communications forecast it would reach 70,000 kilometres by 2020. The national road network totalled 1.7 million kilometres: this included not only the widening of many trunk roads but hard surfacing for thousands of local roads. By 2000, there were some 15.8 million vehicles on the roads nation-wide compared to 9.4 million in 1994.[10] The sale of passenger cars was expected to treble to 4.2 million by 2008. The image of China as a nation of bicycles was fading: Shanghai banned cyclists from many main roads—forcing the most determined to ride on the pavement while others shifted to travel on the city's new metro system. Mayor Xu Kuangdi even argued that 'bicycles take up more space than cars, because one bicycle behind another one occupies the same room—and the car can carry four people!'[11]

Until the 1990s cars were privately used by cadres or their families who took advantage of their access to a government vehicle and driver, but they were only privately owned by a very small number of entrepreneurs. Within a decade middle-class aspirations to own a private car were no different in China than anywhere else. Many young professionals regarded China's entry into the World Trade Organization as desirable solely because they expected it would lead to lower prices for cars. Some cities sought to contain unrestrained traffic growth by limiting the number of new licence plates issued annually or submitting them to auction, but would-be owners were often prepared to buy plates from other provinces at higher prices.

Air travel was also transformed in the 1990s with total fleet size reaching more than 600 passenger planes, mostly purchased from North American or European manufacturers. By 2000 both Beijing and Shanghai originated more than 700 flights daily, including a growing network of international flights. During national holidays more than 300 extra flights were laid on around the country and to take Chinese package tours abroad. Air tickets could be purchased over the counter without the letters of authorization previously required. Most seats were occupied by business travellers expecting to be delivered on time to their destinations—where many switched on their mobile phones the moment after touchdown to arrange appointments and pursue deals.

Newly affluent entrepreneurs became less cautious about displaying their wealth, building mansions, hiring private guards, and driving in luxury imported cars. The fifty richest millionaires in China were worth more than £100 million each, and the ten wealthiest among them £375 million and upwards, according to the Forbes survey in 2002.[12] One of them was Huang Qiuling, a former farmer who was rated No. 44. Mr Huang who made his career, like most of the seriously rich, through profitable land deals, set up a leisure empire in the ancient capital and popular tourist destination of Hangzhou. At his Song Dynasty theme park, families could dress up in imperial costumes, sit in a buffalo cart, watch Chinese opera, or tour a full-size replica of the White House. Mr Huang had his private office in the Blue Room: there was a scaled-down copy of the Washington Monument at the front of the building, and Mount Rushmore at the back.

Yet while there were no longer political objections to conspicuous wealth, the new millionaires began to find themselves the targets of tax collectors or overreached themselves in other ways. Yang Bin, flower-king of the north-east and number 3 on the same list in 2002, also had a theme park: his headquarters in Shenyang were based on a replica of Amsterdam railway station. Mr Yang overreached himself by entering into a private deal with North Korea to develop a Special Economic Zone on its border without consulting Beijing. He also suffered the misfortune to lose his political backers in the provincial capital who themselves were convicted of corruption, and he eventually received an eighteen-year jail sentence for fraud.

There was a mixture of motives, some less obvious than others, behind the head long pace of China's urbanization and its lavish use of state resources. Some projects, particularly those such as city metros which sought to improve mass transport, were long overdue. Others showed a rather naive hankering for the material attributes of 'advanced' Western society in which the yardstick was too often the four-star hotel, the elevated expressway, and the jumbo-sized shopping mall—and of course city officials also benefited directly from the availability of these new goodies. Some were a mixture of both: every Chinese city had near-slum dwellings in need of demolition but to replace them with luxury villas while decanting most occupants to the suburbs was not the most rational solution. It was also a visible demonstration that China, or at any rate part of the urban sector, could hold its own with the most modernized Western and other Asian cities which many officials, and their families, now had more opportunities to visit and admire. Yet this extravagant emphasis on new urban infrastructure carried an echo too of the earlier conviction, dating back to the 1950s, that the new China could deliver the material goods and 'catch up' with the West with whose superior lifestyle most senior officials and their families, now able to travel freely abroad, had become much more familiar. The largely rural utopia which had been envisaged under the 'three red banners' of the Great Leap Forward found a parallel in the almost entirely urban utopia apparently made possible by the 'economic reform and opening-up' under Mao's successors.

The new society

By the end of the 1990s, a social transformation was well under way, creating a new landscape increasingly autonomous from the Party, with its own aspirations and demands. The most visible signs of this shift were at the material level, as a new middle class expressed its priorities for consumption and acquisition unfettered by any fear of political disapproval. Of equal importance, millions of Chinese now articulated goals and values across a whole range of issues, from sexual relationships to citizens' rights, with a high degree of freedom in their everyday lives. As was often explained to visiting foreigners, especially those with experience of previous decades, 'we can say what we like now—though we can't always put it in print'. On the negative side, the loosening of Party authority together with the spread of corruption encouraged new destructive forces in society, of which the saddest example was a rapid spread of prostitution, human trafficking, and drug abuse.

The outward signs of significant change in the late 1980s had been greeted with a sense of amazement which now seemed quaint. The first public phone boxes in Beijing? Now three rival networks of mobile phones extended to every Chinese province. More than a hundred 'yuan millionaires'? Now there were as many 'dollar multimillionaires'. The reappearance of sexually transmitted diseases in Guangdong? Now the greater worry was HIV-AIDS, nationwide. A new generation of 'strong women' writers tackling controversial themes of loveless marriage and male chauvinism? Now a younger generation wrote semi-fictional accounts of drug-taking and partner swapping.

The gathering pace of reform had led to important economic changes which underpinned the new social structures. The emergence of a housing market encouraged social mobility and the accumulation of wealth. Housing reforms had begun in the late 1980s, initially shifting the burden from the central to local governments. A decade later, the burden had been shifted to a large extent towards the individual occupier. Millions of people in state employment were given the chance to buy, at a discount, the accommodation where they were living. Millions of city residents, obliged to leave public housing due for redevelopment, bought apartments of their own with some financial support depending on eligibility. Mortgages were made available by the state banks or through savings schemes at work. Those who already owned their own homes in the cities were able to sell without incurring official disapproval. If their title to the property was shaky, it could be regularized either through bribery or payment of a recognized fee. With the socialist housing allocation system clearly doomed, there was a strong incentive to buy into the market. New high-rise apartment blocks in the major cities catered for a new market of young professional couples, eager to avoid living with their in-laws and acquire their own home. Their aspirations are reflected in this comment by a young woman working in a public relations office in Shanghai, speaking to this writer on the eve of Chinese New Year:

This year we are not going to spend all the holiday at home with our parents: quite frankly, I find that rather boring now. We'll just spend the first day with them. Then we are going to look for an apartment across the river, somewhere near Century Park. We need a place of our own with enough room for a maid and, later on, a baby, and it's better to start now before prices get too expensive! If there is time, we'll also visit the Home Interiors show at the Shanghai Exhibition Hall.

Reforms in higher education also widened horizons, as universities offered a more diverse range of courses and graduates were no longer 'assigned' compulsorily to jobs by the state authorities. In 2002 more than five million students who had finished secondary school took college entrance exams; more than 50 per cent would be successful, compared with only 2.4 per cent of those who had applied for further education twenty years earlier. Restrictions on independent study abroad were eased. Of more than 120,000 leaving China every year less than ten per cent were state-funded; most were financed by their parents out of savings or often through loans from the wider family and friends. Many Party cadres wished to see their sons and daughters choose a different future from their own, and many young officials sought government scholarships abroad, hoping that they could shift into the private sector after their return. While study abroad in the 1980s had been seen as a way of escape from China—and even more so after Tiananmen Square—by the late 1990s increasing numbers (including quite a few of the 1989 'exiles') planned to return home and make the most of their expertise. The Zhongguancun high-tech park in Beijing, popularly known as China's Silicon Valley, had attracted some five thousand 'returned students', it was reported in 2003, who set up nearly two thousand small businesses (although their survival rate was poor).[13] The Ministry of Education said that more than 160,000 out of the 600,000 thousand students who went abroad in 1980–2000 had returned, most of them in the second decade.

Even the Central Party School in Beijing now adopted the academic trappings of cap and gown for their graduating students and offered a very different curriculum from the one which had once focused on class struggle and the transition to Communism. The new course included subjects such as United States–China economic relations, the environment, and social democratic thought. The students were no longer labelled as 'theoretical workers' after graduation but left with degrees and doctorates: many intended to use their Party connections to go into business.

An 'MBA fever' raged among graduates as China entered the new

millennium—and the World Trade Organization. The first MBA programme in China was introduced only in 1990 when it was officially
decided that the nation was 'in desperate need of high-quality business
leaders'. In that year just 86 students enrolled. By the end of 1999 there were
23,500 students taking MBA courses and 5,000 graduates. The busiest table
in every Chinese bookshop was now laden with MBA course material and
guides on how to win a place at business school—preferably abroad. For
those seeking to gain a BA abroad, the most popular book was *Liu Yiting,
Harvard Girl*, written by ambitious parents who had steered their daughter
towards a Harvard scholarship. It sold 1.1 million copies in the first year of
publication (1999) and was followed by *Harvard Boy* and other imitations.
All MBA courses now required a high degree of proficiency in English,
which was seen as the global business language. Most MBA students were in
their late twenties and had already secured a reasonable job (many institutions offered part-time courses for those in employment) but wished to do
better. The decision to seek a further degree was often a difficult one, as an
MBA candidate from Jiangxi province studying in Shanghai explained to
this writer:

I was going to be the general manager in my company and I was already a key
person, with four hundred people working for me. Business was good, but it was a
small provincial state-owned enterprise, and I had a sense of standing still. After
consulting with two former bosses and my family, I decided to take the plunge and
have not regretted it. Now I have acquired a globalization approach and my ambition
is to become a senior executive in a joint-venture firm with a foreign company.

Changing attitudes towards family and sexual relations also contributed to
the transformation of social attitudes during the 1990s, especially in urban
China. Divorce soared and the annual number almost quadrupled from
319,000 in 1979 to 1.21 million in 2000. Although the national rate of
10 per cent remained below the world average, it was deeply shocking both
for many older Party members as well as traditionalists. However, arranged
marriages—which both groups had favoured—were on the decline as more
young Chinese of both sexes insisted on choosing for themselves while sex
before marriage became widespread.

In rural areas the picture was mixed. Women's inequality had actually
increased during the 1980s when the return to individual family farming
reinforced the traditional patriarchy. In areas of rural Henan surveyed by
Shanghai sociologist Cao Jinqing in the mid-1990s, women were routinely

deterred from remarrying if widowed and denied the right to inherit. Elsewhere the migration of millions of young women to find work in the cities
led to a new assertiveness; millions of others, left at home while the men folk
became migrant workers, effectively became the decision-makers. Yet the
reality was still harsh in more backward areas. The first full-scale survey of
suicide in China showed that the 'rural . . . rate is threefold the urban rate',
and that uniquely in the world, there were more suicide deaths among
Chinese women than men. The report noted a long tradition of rural
women committing suicide by drinking pesticide, and urged more efforts to
'provide basic mental health services to rural areas'.[14]

These contrary trends both indicate a more diverse society and make it
harder to generalize on gender relations in contemporary China. The once
taboo subject of domestic violence generated more concern. A survey in
2001 by the Chinese Women's Federation concluded that this was now a
'significant social problem' which occurred in three out of ten households
and caused the break-up of an average of one hundred thousand families
yearly. On the other hand, a new law introduced in Jilin province which
allowed unmarried women to have a child of their own became a lively
talking point in the media a year later. The Women's Federation itself,
which had represented Chinese women (while deferring to Party requirements) for decades, now found itself criticized for being too conservative in
its approach to women's rights and issues of sexual freedom. On a website
forum in 2002, a Federation official gave evasive answers to questions about
its failure to investigate the problems of rural women or to consider the
rights of sex workers. When she claimed that students who became preg-
nant at college would be 'incompatible with good educational order', she
was accused of advocating 'the order of the monastery'.

The urban–rural divide was most evident in regard to childbearing.
While rural society continued to favour large families in spite of punitive
restrictions (see below), more young urban women favoured late marriage
and wondered whether to have even one child. In the words of one graduate
researcher, 'most of my friends and classmates want to have a marriage at a
late age, and are not so sure about having a kid. I'm not sure myself whether
I can afford it [having a child] in terms of time and energy.'

In Shanghai, where sexual mores were changing faster than anywhere
else, university students were recruited to offer AIDS peer counselling, and
the nation's first sexual health phone hotline provided contraceptive advice
on the web regardless of marital status. Doctors at the Shanghai Institute of

Family Planning Technical Instruction, founded in 1970, which aimed 'to prevent unwanted pregnancy, decrease induced abortion and promote reproductive health', received calls on a wide range of topics previously regarded as taboo. These included concern about failure of sexual performance, lack of enjoyment, and the time taken for intercourse. Others enquired about contraceptive precautions and general sexual health. The institute's website provided information on emergency post-coital contraception, listing several forms of intervention available at its clinic. Anyone who was anxious about unwanted pregnancy was invited to send an enquiry by email on an online form which included a space for the 'unmarried'.

A new youth culture based upon 'romance, leisure and free choice', had emerged in Shanghai according to sociologist James Farrer in a study based on years of fieldwork. Farrer charted a new sex culture dominated by modern transnational values and driven by consumerism, although some elements from the socialist era survived. There was now 'a more nuanced understanding of change in sexual standards and what they mean for individuals, especially for sexually active young women . . .'. Derogatory terms used by young men towards women assumed to be sexually available were also on the decline.[15]

The mobile phone and internet revolutions of the late 1990s became symbols for the transformation of Chinese society. The number of handsets in use exceeded 100 million by the turn of the century and more than trebled again by 2005, reaching double the number of US mobile users. The mobile had bypassed the limitations of the fixed phone in a sensational fashion. Even in the most remote areas there was a mobile network at least within reach of the county town. No Chinese entrepreneur, however small the business, could operate without a mobile: once popular, pagers were soon a rapidly declining market. Almost every driver of every vehicle, from the chauffeurs of the new elite to ordinary bus drivers, used a handset to keep in touch with base. Mobiles were used increasingly among the tens of millions of migrant workers, to search for jobs or call home to families in the countryside. Older Chinese could remember a still recent past when calls could only be made or received at public telephones in shops or at housing gates where neighbours and watch-guards listened in. The young were impatient with these tales of past hardship from their parents. Urban youth were a major target, particularly for value-added services, in advertising for mobile technology which dominated television and public hoardings— rivalled only by adverts for face creams and underwear.

Internet use in China grew rapidly at the turn of the century. By the end of 2002, more than 30 million computers were connected to the worldwide web, with an estimated 80 million users. This put China's internet population in second place in the world, following the US but ahead of Japan. The government had mixed feelings about the internet, and invested heavily in equipment to monitor its usage and block access to offending sites such as the Falun Gong and other dissident groups and foreign human rights organizations including Amnesty International. A number of activists were jailed for disseminating pro-democracy material on their own or other websites. However, it also recognized the global significance of the internet revolution. A *People's Daily* commentary in August 2000 described it as 'great, rapid and extensive' (*dakuaiguang*)—adjectives once used to hail the Great Leap Forward. The internet, it argued, had become a new arena for struggle between the 'correct propaganda' of the government and the 'reactionary, superstitious and pornographic' content of China's enemies. However, the internet was also identified as one of the attributes of modernization and provincial Party bosses sought to attract foreign investors by boasting of the broadband access they could offer. On a more critical note, the *China Daily* warned that the internet was becoming a new religion, and ridiculed the idea that China could use it to 'catch up' with the West. However the wider range of discourse, in spite of restrictions, offered on the web compelled the government to make its own web-based information services more attractive. The websites attached to the *People's Daily* and *New China News Agency* often carried exposés of disasters and policy criticisms which could not appear in the printed versions.

Popular Chinese portals such as Sina.com and Sohu.com were forbidden from carrying 'unauthorized information' whether from home or abroad, on their news websites, and focused mainly on entertainment, lifestyle, and consumer issues. Yu Hongyan, general manager of the Zhaodaola website (the name means 'I've found it') explained its philosophy:

A person has to spend much time looking for something, whether it be a job, a friend, a house or a lover. People in China are aiming for a better life. We are entitled to the quality you get in the US and Japan. We are targeting the 20 to 35-year-olds and trying to attract more women. That's why we have a special channel called 'Real Women' as well as another one called 'Macho Men'.[16]

The farmers' plight

In spite of rapid urbanization, China's rising population meant that the
absolute number of rural dwellers remained as high in 2000 as it had been
twenty years before. The Chinese press habitually referred to '800 million
farmers'—sometimes adding on 100 million more: precise statistics here as
elsewhere were elusive. But for the second time in post-1949 history,
China's farmers were disappointed by the results of a revolution which
initially the vast majority of them had welcomed. In the Maoist period the
benefits of post-Liberation land reform (for all except the landlords who
were expropriated—and often jailed or executed) had been largely cancelled out by the Great Leap Forward and the political struggles of the
1960s. The new liberation of the 1980s which restored control of production to the farmers initially increased incomes and yields almost everywhere,
but by the 1990s hundreds of millions found they were losing out again as
farm prices stagnated, the income gap with urban China widened, yet tax
and corruption pressed heavily on their shoulders. Rural communities often
survived only on the basis of remittances home of the army of migrant
workers (estimated at in excess of 100 million) who fuelled the urban boom
with their hard labour. The new team of leaders under Hu Jintao appointed
in 2002 openly admitted that China was facing a new rural crisis, and there
were calls for a 'third liberation' of China's 'people of the land' (*nongmin*).
The well-known economist Hu Angang argued that

the time has come to effect a virtual 'liberation' of Chinese farmers the third time.
Chinese farmers have to be finally freed from their land, helped to develop and turn
themselves into a non-agricultural population, familiarize themselves with a new
life in cities and become educated, especially those young farmers leaving their
land. . . . Country folk should enjoy the same opportunities and equal rights to
settlement, work, education, voting etc. as their urban counterparts.[17]

For most of the 1990s, attention had focused on the extremes of rural wealth
and poverty while the wider problem of a depressed rural economy was
ignored. The suburban farms bordering railways and roads near provincial
centres and in the coastal provinces often enjoyed near-urban standards of
income. Many original 'farmers' no longer lifted a hoe, but sold part of
their land for development and hired migrant workers to cultivate the rest.
Shenzhen municipal district included more than two thousand villages but
after twenty years of economic development agriculture only accounted
for 2 per cent of total GDP and all the farming was done by migrants. In

semi-urbanized areas around Shanghai and in neighbouring Jiangsu province, rural housing from before the 1980s was a rarity. Only one genuine canal village (Xinchang) survived, although a few more were recreated for tourism. (The most popular, Zhouzhuang, received a million visitors a year.) In Zhejiang around the provincial capital of Hangzhou, farmers built three-storey turreted mansions and put their ancestors' ashes in the turret. In the coastal counties of Fujian province where funds flowed in from migrants—mostly illegal—abroad, communities spent surplus wealth in building new temples or churches.

At the other end of the spectrum were a small number of rural counties with average incomes below the official poverty line (measured as daily per capita income equivalent to less than US $0.66), who received special subsidies and project help. By 2000, Beijing claimed, China's rural poor had decreased from 250 million in the past two decades to only 30 million. Most of the counties still in need of special aid were in remote areas in the southwest and north-west. The World Bank, which had given substantial funding to China's poverty reduction programme, preferred to use the 'international standard' poverty line of below a dollar a day: this resulted in a figure of 100 million rural poor. Yet the real rural crisis lay between these extremes among the majority of farmers who were neither very rich nor desperately poor. The familiar problem of overpopulation was a root cause though by no means the only one. The policy of allowing only one child per family worked unevenly in the countryside and in many villages the extra or 'black' births could add as much as 10 per cent to the officially registered population. Shanghai sociologist Cao Jinqing, who conducted field research in the mid-1990s in densely populated Henan province, was told by officials that 'the power-holders will give [extra] birth just because they have power; those with money will buy their children by paying the fines, and those without power or money will escape to other areas to give birth'. Only an unfortunate minority suffered the draconian sanctions which included compulsory abortion for the mother and destruction of the family home.[18]

By the end of the century, policy had been relaxed to accommodate the real situation: in most rural areas two children were allowed. While population continued to grow, the land available for cultivation continued to be eroded—both by the worsening environment and because of the nation-wide building fever: the total cultivated area decreased by 4.5 per cent from 1978 to 1995. More than a third of the rural population of working age—(150–200 out of 450–500 million according to the usual imprecise figures)—were reckoned to be 'surplus labour', and only half of those found work in the urban sector.

Beijing was only able to claim that peasant incomes continued to rise by calculating the figures on the basis of 'net income', including the discounted value of the food and other supplies the farmers produced for their own consumption. This had made sense in the age of the People's Communes when most services such as education and health were provided free or at nominal charge. In an increasingly cash economy where everything now had to be paid for, it obscured the reality of peasant hardship. The crops might be plentiful but many who harvested them were caught in a trap where they had enough to eat but could not even afford schoolbooks for their children. The rural banks, while happy to lend money for officially backed prestige projects such as hotels, roads, and luxury housing, would not help farmers to invest in higher productivity or processing which could add value to their produce. Li Changping, a former official in rural Hubei who became the country's most outspoken campaigner for farmers' rights, recorded a typical complaint from an elderly farmer's wife in Qipan county:

In the past we just worried about having enough food to eat: that's not a problem now and food is no longer a precious commodity, yet we have many more things to worry about. We worry that our children can't be educated, that we can't afford to see a doctor, that we can't afford new clothes, that we can't pay the taxes.[19]

The farmers' strongest anger was directed at the burden of taxation which often supported a bloated layer of local government and party cadres. Although the abolition of the People's Communes should have reduced the need for bureaucracy, the numbers of officials and their hangers-on increased at every level. Out of China's adult rural population of about 500 million, more than one in twenty—30 million—were on the official payroll. The farmers complained that official appetites had grown in the new society: cadres who once rode by bicycle now had cars and jeeps. Government offices were rebuilt on the edge of the county town with air conditioning and landscaped gardens. No longer obliged for fear of political censure to adopt a simple lifestyle, many cadres indulged in frequent banquets and karaoke sessions with hostesses in attendance at public expense. And all of this had to be paid for. In theory taxation was pegged to a maximum of 5 per cent of farmers' income, but ruthless cadres easily evaded the limit. Either the farmer was over-assessed, or the money was raised by arbitrary 'fees' and 'levies' supposed to pay for public services which might not even exist. Farmers in remote villages without electricity might be forced to pay a 'fee' for the installation of cable television in the county town. Cao Jinqing recorded the complaint of an apple grower in Taikang county, Henan:

The local officials file false reports of the farmers' incomes to the upper authorities partly to show how successful their policies are but also so that they can demand higher taxes. Besides, the taxes are so numerous and heavy, and are levied under so many different names that no one can figure them out. The township and village cadres never explain the system clearly to the farmers and the burden is too heavy for people to bear. Every year as soon as the summer and autumn harvests have been gathered in, the township cadres enter the villages to demand levies, bringing public security police with them. The people are pressed so hard they can scarcely draw breath. Let me put it like this: in recent years the country folk have been living in terror and fear.

The same apple grower described the petty extortion, masked by conventional politeness, which he had to endure every year:

When the apples are ripe, I get visits from the cadres, police, tax and commerce officials, all driving their cars. They say they want to buy apples and each takes two or four or five bags. Am I going to ask them for money? If I do that, you can be sure that next time they will demand an imperial-sized tax payment. Just through this I lose one or two thousand yuan every year, or even more. And when they collect their free apples, I have to escort them with a smiling face and even invite them to come back again. What is the world coming to?[20]

Not all cadres were corrupt: researchers in the field found that the atmosphere from one area to the next could vary significantly depending on the quality of leadership. In one place, the cadres were regarded as parasites who only 'came down' to the villages to 'demand money and lives' (*yaoqian yaoming*). Elsewhere officials could be found who still sought to 'serve the people', throwing their energy into efforts to raise money for rural industry and to persuade higher levels of government to provide more funds. Even honest cadres were unable to provide sufficient services to the rural community, particularly after national reforms in 1994 when the central government shifted most of the burden for welfare, health, and education on to local government. In effect, Beijing squeezed the provincial governments who in turn squeezed the counties who then squeezed the townships and through them the villages: this was the economic basis for the higher taxation passed on to the farmers. One of the most conspicuous results was a general failure to pay teachers and health workers on time. It was common for school or hospital heads, seeking to present the establishment to visitors in a favourable light, to put the claim that 'we pay our wages on time' at the top of their list.

Research in 1994 in village schools in central Sichuan showed that attendance rates were severely affected by increases in school fees, often exacted as payment for 'teaching materials'. Though most children went to primary school, many dropped out in the first year of middle (secondary) school. 'In the past, the motto of schools was "teaching to educate", but it has now become "education to create income", which is desperately frustrating', reported social activist Liu Xianbin. (Liu would be sentenced to thirteen years in jail five years later for advocating democracy in China.)[21]

China's investment in education, at around 2.5 per cent of annual GNP, was exceeded by more than one hundred other countries, and the 1990 census showed marked regional, gender, and ethnic inequalities. Coastal Zhejiang spent over three times more on school-age children than inland Guizhou. Three-quarters of school drop-outs were female. Illiteracy among the Han Chinese population was 17.8 per cent, among the minorities it was 30.8 per cent. Inequality in education, argue two US-based Chinese scholars, 'has created occupational and income gaps between the coastal urban business elites and the farmers of remote areas and inland provinces'.[22]

Rural health in the 1990s showed a similar pattern of diminishing investment from the central government, with sharp regional and local inequalities, and rising costs for rural dwellers who went deep into debt in order to pay hospital fees. Only one-fifth of total government health spending in the late 1990s went to the rural areas (*China Daily*, 17 Sept. 2002). Public health, reported the international NGO Médecins sans Frontières in 2000, had deteriorated since the introduction of the 'socialist market economy' and many people, especially the poorest, '[were] left without basic medical care'. Rural clinics seen by this writer in Anhui province were typically piled high with prescription medicines, including expensive drugs, yet they were often empty of patients. The explanation was that medical workers were underpaid and relied on selling medicines to supplement their income. 'Prices are controlled', a UN health adviser in Beijing explained, 'so the only solution is to over-prescribe. They [village health workers] are using potent drugs like cortisone steroids to remove pain and swelling and increase appetite. They also become victims of aggressive salesmen from the drugs industry.' Foreign UN agencies and NGOs often find that their aid programmes have to supply basic equipment, such as stethoscopes, baby scales, and beds, to rural hospitals which are starved of funds. In some areas the situation had got worse since the collective era. A UNICEF publication acknowledged in 2000 that 'the Mother and Child Health network was greatly weakened after the People's Communes were abolished'. (However, UNICEF also reported a greater willingness by some central officials to acknowledge that there was a large constituency—perhaps as many as 300 million people—who were at risk, and that most of these were women and children.)[23]

With such a wide array of problems facing the majority of China's rural dwellers, it is not surprising that in many areas the reputation of the Communist Party was extremely low. Fortunately for Beijing, farmers tended to blame the local leadership, particularly in the townships—the former People's Commune—although often up to the provincial level, clinging to the traditional view that if the 'emperor in the capital' were properly informed of their plight, he would wield a magic wand to help them. A secret document prepared in Lingxian county, Henan in 1991 (which this writer obtained by chance while visiting the area) set out the situation, from the local Party's perspective, in stark terms:

[Our cadres] do not have a unified approach to tackling these problems and often rely on homemade policies. Some are too slack, others are too strict; some are overbearing, others are indulgent. They do not do enough of what is required, and blithely do what is not required. Worse still, some cadres' families use their power to assign assets to themselves, have surplus children, and occupy housing above the limit, all of which heightens the contradictions between cadres and the common people even to an irreconcilable point. The people have no respect for the cadres and retaliate against them to the extent that some cadres' families are abused or assaulted, their crops are stolen, their trees cut down, and their lives and property are threatened.

Ten years later, the problem of rural instability was openly acknowledged in Beijing. A June 2001 report by the Party's organization department, headed by President Jiang Zemin's top adviser Zeng Qinghong, was revealingly titled '2000–2001: Studies of contradictions among the people under new conditions'. It said corruption had become the 'main fuse' in sparking conflict and that the widening income gap between town and countryside was approaching an 'alarm level'. (In 2000, average rural incomes across the country were measured at US $272 per capita, compared to urban income of $743, and these figures concealed much higher disparities.) There was an

increasing number of cases, rarely reported in the media, where local farmers took direct action to repel the police and tax collectors. A *People's Daily*
editorial in January 2002 said that rural unrest would only be quelled by
raising incomes and lowering taxes. 'Only when there is stability in the
countryside will there be stability in the nation,' it said. The editorial followed a national conference on agriculture which stressed the social dangers
arising from the income gap and warned local authorities to tackle the
farmers' grievances before it was too late. The conference was attended by
Vice-Premier Wen Jiabao who a year later when promoted to Premier would
be quick to demonstrate his concern for rural poverty. His predecessor Zhu
Rongji had addressed the issue using outspoken language in several reports
to the National People's Congress (NPC), and instituted an experimental
rural tax reform in Anhui province.

The rural situation would have been even worse without the growing
demand for migrant labour in the coastal provinces and to a lesser but still
significant extent in inland urban China. Local enterprises at the township
level, hailed as the solution to rural problems in the 1980s, did not do so well
as their goods, often of low quality, faced more sophisticated competition in
the markets, although they still employed 120 million people from the rural
workforce by 2000. At least the same number now left their villages to travel
much further afield, only returning home for the annual Spring Festival. A
figure of 129 million given in 2003 by the Party's rural research department
would mean that one in four of the workforce were migrants.

Mainly female migrant labour had fuelled the export boom from the
earliest days of the new economic zones in southern China. By the mid-
1990s, there were 11 million migrant workers in Guangdong: two-thirds
were women who worked mostly in factories producing toys and garments
or assembling electronic goods for long hours and often in cramped and
dangerous conditions. An increasing number of female migrants were also
employed by the emerging new elite in Shanghai and other cities as child-
minders and domestic servants.

The pattern of migration by the turn of the century has become well
established. The majority of male migrant workers find employment in the
construction industry, typically living in temporary dormitories erected on
the actual site. Others work in service industries, particularly in catering and
food supply. Groups of workers often come from a single village, recruited
by a middleman who himself may originate from the same area. The migrant
flow from labour-rich inland provinces such as Jiangxi, Hunan, Hubei, and

Henan has led to the establishment of regular long-distance bus links. Even a small town may have its own weekly service to Shanghai or Guangzhou. A regular sight at Chinese railway stations are the groups of migrants, with their belongings in cheap holdalls or empty fertilizer bags, sleeping on the forecourt while they wait for a connecting train. The migrants' most frequent complaint is that wages may be paid late or not at all by unscrupulous subcontractors. In 2003 the State Council issued a circular demanding that workers should be paid on time, and the Beijing city authorities later issued special regulations to the same effect. The *China Daily* (24 November) reported that 'the problem of contractors who default on a worker's salary seems to have intensified. Construction workers threatening to commit suicide to recover their earnings are common.' Migrants often complain that they are denied access to medical care or—for those whose families managed to accompany them—schooling for their children. They are subject to harassment by the police who demand papers which they frequently cannot supply: the position of self-employed migrants who collect garbage or offer services such as bicycle repairs is particularly vulnerable. Migrants are also regarded by city dwellers as prime suspects for theft and other urban crimes, which may be true of a minority who fail to find work or who are tempted by the affluent sights of the city.

The economic benefits are still substantial for the majority of peasant migrants who can easily make the equivalent of a year's rural income in one month of urban work. A typical calculation was provided by a farmer from Sichuan province interviewed at Shanghai railway station on his way, with a group of co-workers, to Ningbo on the south-east coast.

If I sell my labour locally in Mianyang city, not far from home, I can earn three yuan an hour: in Ningbo the hourly rate is four yuan. We work ten hours a day, seven days a week [the standard for most migrant workers], so that's about one thousand yuan every month. What would I earn if I worked on the land? Not worth speaking about, if I'm lucky I might get 700–800 yuan cash a year. After my food and lodging in Ningbo, I can earn ten times as much to send home. I can save to get married as well. The extra one yuan an hour makes it worth not seeing my family except at the New Year.[24]

Migrant workers retained their residential permit (*hukou*) from their original home and were given temporary registration in the cities obliging them to live on the premises where they worked. But many moved into slum accommodation illegally or set up clusters of ramshackle houses on the edge of town. Those from the same province would live together, and the informal villages became known as 'Henan Village' or 'Anhui Village' according to their origin. These generated their own informal economy, with private shops, schools, and other services. The argument that migrants should be given proper residential rights began to gain ground, and at the 2002 National People's Congress the delegation from Guangdong staged a lively debate on whether migrants should have voting rights in their place of work. A central planning commission talked of a five-year plan to abolish restrictions. Beijing promised to simplify the temporary registration procedure and China's National Federation of Trade Unions agreed that rural migrants could join urban unions. Concern about migrant conditions began to surface in the more outspoken—or sensationalist—sections of the media. The tabloid *Beijing Star Daily* made its own survey of sexual deprivation among migrants, claiming that some were led by frustration to harass women on buses, to behave rowdily, and even to commit rape (*People's Daily*, 12 Dec. 2003). Combating this familiar stereotype, the economist Hu Angang who has already been quoted said that statistics showed migrants to be more law-abiding than city residents. Writing in the influential journal *Liaowang* (*Outlook*, 25 Feb. 2002), Hu argued that migrants should be allowed permanent urban registration in return for giving up their rights to land in their native village

The workers' plight

The 1990s was a period of rapid growth in output and equally rapid growth in unemployment. While the economy expanded at an annual rate of some 9 per cent, the real number of those in the urban sector without a job grew from around 2 to 10 per cent. Though the claim in previous decades that 'China has no un-employment' had never been entirely true, the vast majority had been assigned to work units which took care of their basic needs. Workers in the state-owned enterprises (SOEs) were regarded as the 'core membership' of the working class and while their wages were low they received significant benefits in kind in the shape of free or subsidized housing, heath, and education. This 'iron rice bowl' came inevitably under threat after the 1992 Party Congress decided that China must 'get rid of a highly centralized planned economy and develop a socialist market economy'. The then Minister of Labour, Ruan Chongwu, declared that China must 'break the iron bowl' though he admitted it would be an unpopular move. A major reform was launched to increase the number of contract workers, thus reducing job security, and to reduce the welfare burden upon the SOEs, often as a prelude to their privatization. Large numbers of workers were 'laid off' (*xiagang*) from their jobs, receiving a reduced wage or basic living allowance but remaining on the factory's books—and thus avoiding classification as 'unemployed'. With enterprises now allowed to go bankrupt (a device often used by managers in order to strip the assets), even these reduced benefits could disappear. By the end of the decade it is estimated that 45 to 60 million SOE workers had been laid off in this way. If their dependants were included, this meant that over a third of the urban population was affected.[25]

Many ex-workers seized the chance, with varying success, to find jobs or create new ones elsewhere. In medium-sized towns in central China, most taxi and pedicab drivers, or those offering roadside services such as clothes-mending or shoe-shining, were former employees of the SOEs. The older ex-workers, over the age of 35, unskilled and relatively uneducated (because they grew up in the Cultural Revolution) found it hardest to adapt. Of those who remained in work, two-thirds were estimated 'to be owed wages, pensions, and compensation for medical expenses as their firms sink deeply into debt'. At first the plight of these urban workers received little notice and was seen in Beijing as an inevitable cost of modernization. In 1998 the Shanghai journal *Xinwen Bao* summed up this attitude in a survey of economic priorities:

With the much stronger push for structural reform that began in 1993, the contradictions inherent in the Chinese employment system have become apparent. Some say that Chinese urban unemployment is actually in the 11 million–13 million range. This translates into an unemployment rate of 6–7 percent—the highest in the fifty year history of the PRC and double what it was in 1980. But China's top leaders are determined to stay the course. [New premier] Zhu Rongji in a May 14 [1998] meeting on assuring the livelihood of laid off [*xiagang*] workers, said that we can't just copy foreign policies and we can't use the methods of the planned economy either. Unemployment will climb still higher during 1999. But as the market economy develops, the private sector will absorb more and more workers so that the unemployment rate will eventually start to fall.[26]

But increasing unrest among the laid-off workers, and fears that the problem would be compounded by the Asian financial crisis of the late 1990s, compelled Zhu Rongji within a year of his taking office to focus more seriously on the problem. At the 1999 National People's Congress (NPC) he announced a huge investment in job creation programmes, asking the Congress to approve a record budget deficit of 140 billion yuan (more than £10 billion). Zhu hoped to create millions of new jobs through infrastructure projects such as bridges, roads, and railways. He travelled widely in the provinces, pledging to tackle the problems of *xiagang* workers, while local governments issued propaganda in praise of those who had found new jobs through their own efforts.

The city of Xian held a conference to honour the stars of re-employment: these included a woman who started a small restaurant by buying food cheaply before the markets got busy, and a factory manager who opened a roadside car repair shop. The plight of those who failed to find work— particularly women who were less likely to benefit from the new investment programmes—began to be examined in the more popular sections of the Chinese press. Guo Xia—also from Xian—had earned 360 yuan (£30) a month in a machinery factory. She was '*xiagang*-ed' in 1998 after nineteen years of employment and would get 155 yuan a month compensation for three years. At present she was lucky to make up the difference babyminding for a local businesswoman. 'But when the child goes to nursery', she complained to the *China Youth Daily*, 'they won't need me. I don't know where I can find anything else.' He Yequn had lost her job in Guangzhou five years ago, and quickly enrolled for a job thousands would now covet. She swept the roads from 5 a.m. to 5 p.m., six days a week. The money was an impressive 1,000 yuan a month but she got to bed at seven every night—and dreaded having to sweep up human ordure.

Far from regarding themselves as a 'vanguard force', most workers were now profoundly alienated from the Communist Party. A survey in 1996 showed that more than half of those polled expressed such critical views as 'I am forced to participate in political affairs' and 'I am disgusted with politics'. Left-wing Party theorists were appalled by the decline in morale among SOE workers. An article in the Party journal *Dangdai Sichao* summed up the dismal situation:

The number of workers laid off by enterprises continues to increase, and the rate of urban unemployment is on the rise. This not only pushes the workers' families in deep water, but also undermines social stability . . .

. . . most of the workers do not regard themselves as the largest beneficiaries of the reform program. During the surveys conducted in March and June 1996, workers believed that proprietors of the non-public economic sector and people who hold power in their hands were the beneficiaries of the reform program. In terms of ranking, private proprietors ranked first, managers and administrators form the next group followed by government cadres, technicians, and peasants. Production workers were at the bottom of the list. Furthermore, most of the workers believe that the gap between the rich and the poor in the society is widening.[27]

The combination of factory lay-offs and increasingly visible corruption—often by the same managers who conducted the lay-offs—led to a surge of labour disputes: the number recorded by the Ministry of Labour grew from 8,150 in 1992 to more than 120,000 in 1999 (a 29 per cent increase over the previous year). Most of these were local protests and were barely reported in the press: those taking part knew that they would be treated more severely if they attempted to link up with other groups. The right to strike had been removed from the Chinese constitution in 1982. While technically illegal, many protests were successful in leading to arbitration awards or promises of cash payments (though these were not always kept) by local authorities anxious to avoid trouble on their patch. It was not uncommon to come across small-scale demonstrations outside Party or government headquarters, regarded by onlookers as 'just another workers' protest'.

In the spring of 2002, a new wave of unrest on a far greater scale broke out, centring on the declining industrial heartland of the north-east. Thousands of laid-off workers protested at the 'restructuring' of the Daqing oilfield—once the industrial model made famous by Chairman Mao's exhortation to 'Learn from Daqing'. Demonstrators here, and at other protest sites including the heavy industry base of Liaoyang, clashed with paramilitary units and many activists were arrested. In Daqing, with vivid symbolism, workers demonstrated in Iron Man Square, in front of the now rusting statue of Wang Jinxi, the idealized worker-hero of the 1960s who in official propaganda had helped make China self-sufficient in oil. Now the country imported 30 per cent of its oil and Daqing had reduced production since 1998 by more than 10 per cent.

The protests at Daqing, typical of many elsewhere, were sparked by attempts to shift the 'laid-off workers' off the factories' books to 'unemployed' status. The plan meant that in an exchange for a one-off payment they would lose the right to continued welfare benefits unless they continued to pay into a pension fund. The workers complained that the lump sum was inadequate for the future, and also protested against alleged corruption by top officials who kept their jobs—and their government cars. The Daqing Oil Company, now owned by PetroChina which was listed on the New York and Hong Kong stock exchanges, admitted that jobs and wages had been 'reformed', but said this was necessary to cope with 'competition on the world market'.

Anger in Liaoyang, which had also pushed through a scheme to make workers accept a one-off severance payment, was targeted at top officials led by Gong Shangwu, the city's Party leader. Workers marched through the streets with banners declaring that 'the army of unemployed want food and jobs', and with the demand 'sack Gong Shangwu and free our city'. Mr Gong had recently made a complacent speech at the National People's Congress (NPC), claiming that Liaoyang under his leadership had 'success-fully realized the goal of pushing forward reform and development amid socio-political stability'.

In a phone interview with Han Dongfang (a labour activist from Tiananmen Square in 1989 who fled to Hong Kong), one Liaoyang worker vented their anger:

> There is no way they [the bosses] can really meet the demands of the workers. Their corruption and embezzlement has led to debts too great to cancel out. They can't arrest all the workers. The people who have demonstrated are on the edge of existence with nothing to lose. There are too many for them to arrest all. These people haven't committed crimes. We are simply asking for our wages so we can carry on living—what's wrong with that? I want to live and eat. I don't want to eat fancy food, just enough to get by. Right now, there are so many laid off workers in Liaoyang with no dole and no wages. We are all being squeezed tight. Think about it, if you're 30 to 40 years old and they pay you off with a few thousand yuan, how long is that cash going to last for?[28]

Disease and disasters

As Chinese society became more diverse in the 1990s, and large parts of it more prosperous, social ills and tensions absent or suppressed in the past also multiplied. The most obvious example was the spread of prostitution, soon evident to any male visitor who stayed in a provincial hotel and was asked within minutes of booking in whether he required 'the services of a young lady'. The burgeoning sex industry contributed to the rapid growth of sexually transmitted diseases and, later on in the decade, was one of several factors in the spread of the HIV-AIDS virus. (The others, discussed further down, were unsafe blood collection and drug abuse.)

Interviewed in 1983, George Hatem (Ma Haide), the American doctor who had worked in Yanan and after 1949 was prominent in disease eradication, said that 'a few cases' of venereal disease had reappeared as a result of 'people coming and going' from abroad under the new Open Door policy.

Our doctors under the age of 50 . . . have never seen venereal diseases and they don't know it . . . so we have alerted our medical profession (and) we have started courses again on teaching VD. I have written to the Atlanta-Georgia Disease Centre and asked for teaching materials on VD and they sent me kits, and boxes and things and they are all labelled STD—and I didn't know what STD was![29]

Within a few years no one could be in any doubt about the meaning of STD: a national surveillance system was set up as early as 1988, and private clinics soon proliferated offering alleged cures—their services were often advertised on street lamp posts. Prostitution was endemic at first mainly in the laxer south where the 'chickens' on offer in tourist destinations such as Hainan island became the subject of lurid newspaper articles. It spread north, bringing STDs with it, along the main transport arteries where roadside restaurants and massage parlours offered a convenient front. In 1996, Chinese police arrested 420,000 prostitutes and their clients, but this was believed to be only one-tenth of the number nationwide, according to a Ministry of Health official (*People's Daily*, 16 Nov. 1999). Society's greater tolerance for sex before and outside marriage was also blamed for the spread of STDs. Official data showed that syphilis increased nearly twenty times between 1990 and 1998 to 4.2 per cases per 100,000 inhabitants, and gonorrhea nearly tripled from 9 to 24 cases.

Acknowledgement of the threat posed by HIV-AIDS was resisted for much longer by health officials particularly at the local level. At first the virus was regarded as a 'foreign disease': foreigners wishing to become residents in China had to (and still have to) submit to a blood test for the virus first. Official concern over the connection with drug use focused mainly on the border areas of south-west China where the virus could also be seen as an import from abroad.

It took the tragedy of tens, perhaps hundreds, of thousands of rural deaths from HIV-AIDS infections to force the Beijing authorities to acknowledge—and then only with several years' delay—that China now faced the threat of a full-scale epidemic. Health officials in the mostly rural province of Henan in the early 1990s had seen commercial blood collection as a revenue earner, in part to compensate for the withdrawal of central financing from the province's medical services. Large profits could be made from selling on blood products (mostly blood plasma-based) to entrepreneurial outfits in the cities. 'There was a mad rush to establish blood collection centres [in Henan]' said a retrospective account in the *Jiangnan Daily*. Unscrupulous 'blood heads' emerged, including government health workers, their friends and relatives, as well as private commercial operators. 'There was no physical examination when blood was sold. There were no tests done on the blood. If you've got blood, they'll take it. No one was refused.'[30]

Poor peasants in an area which grew enough food for subsistence but generated little cash income rushed to sell their blood. This was poured into a vat where plasma was extracted by centrifuge, then transferred back to the donors who had been lured with the promise that 'we'll give it [the blood] back to you, and pay you money too!' A whistleblower, probably from the provincial health department, writing under the pseudonym He Aifang, later described the horrific scene: 'Some blood stations were composed of just a centrifuge, some plastic tubes reused many times and some needles carried on a tractor. They would go into the village to draw blood, bringing blood collection services right to the door and paying on the spot.'

When HIV/AIDS victims began to appear, local officials tried to cover up the disaster. Dr Gao Yaojie, a gynaecologist in the provincial capital, sought to publicize the facts, and distributed medical supplies and educational material in the villages. When she won an international award from the Global Health Council in 2001, the Henan health department prevented her receiving a passport to travel to Washington DC. This clumsy action by the scared bureaucrats finally exposed the scandal which till then had only been reported by a few foreign journalists and by a handful of more adventurous domestic newspapers (all published outside Henan). International HIV–AIDS experts had already noticed a more open attitude among officials in Beijing, and the Henan scandal tipped the balance. By the end of the year warnings were published from Professor Zeng Yi, a leading virologist, that 'even a concerted effort [against the virus] will take eight to ten years to make an impact'. The Henan officials still fought a rearguard action: China's most prominent AIDS campaigner Wan Yanhai was arrested the next year for publishing a confidential document from the province which confirmed the disaster, but was released after international protest. Official estimates of the number infected across China with the virus soon rose from 600,000 to in excess of one million (campaigners claimed there might be one million on Henan alone). In September 2003, the Ministry of

Health reported that there had been 220,000 deaths so far from AIDS, implying that the number of those infected must reach several millions.

Industrial accidents caused by poor maintenance and regulation—particularly in the mining industry—and other disasters blamed on shoddy construction and low safety standards, multiplied in the get-rich-quick atmosphere in the 1990s. Private mines, even if closed down by the authorities, reopened under a different name, hiring contract workers with little or no safety training. Building companies paid off local officials to turn a blind eye to substandard construction, and subcontracted the work to even less competent firms. Buildings and bridges collapsed, chasms opened up in new roads, sleazy karaoke bars and gaming parlours with locked exits to deter detection caught fire, as did shopping centres filled with inflammable material. Fireworks factories run by local governments in defiance of regulations suffered fatal explosions—in one notorious case killing more than forty schoolchildren enlisted by their head teacher to fill firecrackers.

In January 1999 the collapse of a bridge at Qijiang near Chongqing in which forty died triggered vocal public concern: the Chinese media, allowed slightly more freedom by the new government under Premier Zhu Rongji, reported the investigation and trial of those responsible. The Party chief of Qijiang county had been bribed by the construction company, and 'strange sounds coming from the bridge' were ignored when it had opened three years before. At the National People's Congress (NPC) in March, Zhu pledged a new campaign to tackle 'bean-curd construction'. He had coined the term while inspecting a poorly constructed dam at Jiujiang on the Yangtze River which had given way in the floods of summer 1998. Not all disasters received as much attention, and the death of four young women migrants, crushed to death in an overcrowded train at the Chinese New Year was only reported in one newspaper:

The express from Beijing to Shenzhen—the boom town on the Hong Kong border where they sought work—was already packed. At Shangqiu in Henan province, several hundred more migrants struggled to board. The train attendants had only opened the doors to two out of the four 'hard class' coaches, to save themselves the effort of checking tickets. The peasants swarmed, said a witness, like bees entering a hive. Some clambered in through the windows. The [four] girls were crushed in those first few minutes . . . [The sister of one of the girls] struggled free and fought her way towards the attendants, pleading for help. They were drinking tea and ignored her. First aid arrived only at a station down the line two and a half hours later. The four girls, dead or dying, were laid out on the platform.[31]

Disaster horror stories now appeared regularly in the press, although government censors often tried to limit the exposure by insisting that only dispatches from the national media sources should be used. Yet in July 2001 the *People's Daily*'s own national website exposed an attempted cover-up after eighty miners died when a tin mine in Nandan County, Guangxi, was flooded. Mining officials claimed there were no casualties and gave compensation to bereaved families on condition that they 'did not talk on any account to journalists'. The mine owner, who had bribed local leaders with gifts of cars, and employed a small army of hoodlums, was later sentenced to death although his trial received almost no publicity. A year later, a similar cover-up was exposed at the Fanshi goldmine in Shanxi province by the same website, and followed up by Central TV. The mine owner removed thirty-seven bodies from the disaster and buried them at various sites before sealing the mine shaft with truck loads of rubbish to destroy the evidence.

The environmental threat

The surge in Chinese output and consumption in the 1990s, coupled to the demands of an ever-growing population, put further pressure on the nation's natural environment which in many areas had already been undermined by unwise policies in the Maoist era. The basic essentials which support human life—reliable water, sufficient tree cover, and fertile earth—all came under increasing strain. More than 400 out of nearly 700 large cities suffered chronic water shortage. In 1997 the wartime communist capital of Yanan, high on the loess plateau of Shaanxi, had to make do with one and a half hours of running water every three days. The devastating floods of 1998 were attributed to a combination of deforestation in the upper reaches of the Yangtze, and extensive building and overcultivation in the middle valley. In Beijing, the water table was lowered by more than two metres in 2000: levels in the Miyun Reservoir, built in the late 1950s with Mao himself wielding a symbolic spade, were dangerously low. Lakes and marshlands in the Tibet-Qinghai watershed were drying up at an alarming rate. China's deserts, in spite of years of afforestation campaigns, were growing by nearly one thousand square miles a year.

The floods of 1999 were followed by the drought of 2000—the two sides of the same ecological problem caused by excessive exploitation of water resources. The floods in the middle Yangtze valley were attributed to a combination of deforestation in tributary areas upstream and conversion of traditional flood land for new building and agriculture. Much of the urban drought was caused by reckless overuse as China's new consumer society demanded more water. 'Beijingers do not appreciate their precious resource,' said the *Beijing Youth Daily* in a survey of the city's water crisis. The three most wasteful outlets, it concluded, were the 'bottled water industry, on-street car-washes and luxury bathing and beauty salons'. The most tragic stories came, as always, from the countryside. The *Southern Weekend* in a special issue on the 2000 drought found villagers in Henan queueing for a trickle that took half an hour to fill a bucket. Other peasants told of vain attempts to save the lives of thirsty water buffalo by putting damp blankets on their backs. And as fields dried up, desperate farmers were planting their crops in river waterbeds which they knew might suddenly flood when the weather broke. Much damage had been done in the 1950s and 1960s when peasants were mobilized in campaigns to increase immediate crop yields without considering the long term. However, the new economic reforms of the 1980s, which allowed peasants to shift to profitable cash crops, while collective irrigation projects were neglected, also led to overuse particularly in North China where boreholes were drilled ever deeper. In 2001 the Yellow River dried up completely before reaching the sea, for the fourth time in ten years. The Ministry of Water Resources warned that around 50 million people in the Yellow River delta faced chronic water shortages and that the situation would continue to deteriorate, reaching a peak after 2010.

While the dangers were recognized, and a popular environmentalist movement got cautiously under way, some of the proposed remedies—particularly in the shape of huge hydraulic projects—threatened to cause worse damage, while environmental concerns continued to be swept aside by large-scale infrastructural development. For much of the 1990s Beijing had resisted warnings about environmental pollution from high-consumption nations such as the US, arguing that this was sheer hypocrisy at a time when a quarter of China's population still lived on less than $1 a day. While the environment was important, China must 'put development first' and should be allowed more leeway in tackling pollution. However, by the end of the decade, as the signs of environmental degradation became more alarming, Beijing's policy shifted, at least in theory, to 'place equal stress on development and conservation'.

Work on the best-known and most controversial project—the Three Gorges Dam—which creates a 600-km-long reservoir stretching upstream from the gorges on the Hubei–Sichuan border to Chongqing—had finally begun in 1992 under the patronage of Premier Li Peng after he wrested approval for it from the National People's Congress (NPC) in the repression following the Beijing massacre. The Congress had previously indicated disquiet at the project and it was shelved just before the events in Tiananmen Square. The journalist Dai Qing, who had published a book opposing the dam, was accused of 'aiding the turmoil' and her book was banned. By this time, a powerful government lobby had been formed in favour of the project, as Dai has described:

The Ministry of Water Resources not only functions as a government department in charge of the project, but is also what we in China call a 'benefit group.' This means that once the department has won the right to build a project, they can use the project funds any way they want, without monitoring or supervision. Before the Three Gorges project was even approved, people in the department had already used project money to buy fancy cars and to build cottages and houses in Beijing for themselves. They spent about 1/20th of the entire budget even before the project was approved or construction had started. . . . This 'benefit group' seized the opportunity to promote the idea of building this controversial dam. At the same time though, eminent scholars and scientists, the best minds in China, had grave doubts about the technical and economic viability of the dam. They imagined the government would allow an open discussion about the project, but they were wrong. They underestimated the strong resistance the 'benefit group' would put up when facing criticism that threatened to break their 'golden rice bowl.' People in the department saw an opportunity to get money and promotions, so they really fought back. The order came from the top, that no newspaper or magazine was allowed to run articles by scholars critical of the dam.[32]

The world's largest hydroelectric project, the dam would cost an estimated $24bn (£14bn) to hold back its lengthy reservoir and generate up to 18,000 megawatts of hydroelectric power. The dam itself would be 2.3 km wide with a spillway at the centre, powerhouses on either side, and new navigation locks. It was justified both on the grounds that it would alleviate flooding downstream in the central Yangtze valley and that it would generate 'clean' power to satisfy the anticipated growth in demand. Its critics argued that a succession of small dams would be more effective, safer, and less costly and that the environmental consequences of such a vast project were impossible to predict. By 2003, when the river was blocked and the reservoir waters began to rise (although the project would only be complete six years later), more than 640,000 inhabitants had been moved to make way for it and the final total of those displaced was expected to reach well above 1.2 million.

One of the strongest objections to dams of this size is that they are liable to cause rapid silting upstream so that their useful life will be significantly reduced. Although project officials minimized this risk, the go-ahead was given in 2003 with minimum publicity—even before the first stage had been completed—for a new generation of four dams designed to trap the silt much further upstream on the Yangtze River's longest tributary, the Jinsha (Golden Sands) River. Alarmingly, it lies on the edge of a recognized seismic zone, a potential danger not mentioned in the few published Chinese accounts. Xiangjiaba, the site of the furthest downstream of the four dams, was already occupied by a thermal hot springs establishment. The planned height of the dam would be 160 metres: an even larger one upstream at Xiluodu would reach 270 metres.[33]

The tallest dam of all began construction in 2001 on the Lancang River—the main tributary of the Mekong—in Yunnan province. Critics warned that the project that would affect millions of Asian farmers over four neighbouring countries, as well as transforming one of China's most precious ecological zones. The Yunnan government announced with undiluted pride that the Xiaowan dam would stand '292 metres high . . . the equivalent to the height of a 100-storey skyscraper'. Xiaowan is one of eight dams known as the 'Langcang river cascade' designed to exploit the rapid fall in level of the Mekong's main tributary as it flows through Yunnan. These and other projects reflected China's continuing commitment to the 'big dam philosophy'—in which it had the support of the World Bank which had financed a controversial earlier project at Xiaolangdi on the Yellow River.[34]

Water engineers had long been tempted by a simple fact: more than 80 per cent of China's water run-off is in the south and centre but 60 per cent of its cultivated land is in the north. It seemed logical to divert water from the Yangtze and its tributaries to the Yellow River which supplies more than 500 million people. Work on the South–North water transfer project began in 2003: the project was expected to cost at least £11.6 billion over the next ten to fifteen years. It envisaged three separate routes: The eastern route on which work began first would siphon water from the lower reaches of the Yangtze, starting at Yangzhou, in Jiangsu province, to follow the northern route of the old imperial Grand Canal. Experts warned that it would be very difficult to eliminate pollution on this restricted route, and that the intensive canal traffic would suffer. The central route would carry water from the Danjiangkou reservoir in Hubei province north along a

780-mile channel. Raising the level of the reservoir and building the channel would force the 'relocation' of 220,000 people. A third western route
was designed to divert water from the upper reaches of the Yangtze and its
tributaries to the Yellow River in a remote area of Qinghai province, and
was admitted to present daunting engineering problems.

Pollution from industry and increasingly from vehicular transport reached
a crisis level during the 1990s. Tourists on the Yangtze often made the three-
day journey from Chongqing to Wuhan through the Three Gorges without
ever seeing a clear sky. Satellite pictures frequently showed almost the entire
land mass of China covered by a grey cloud. 'The residents of many of
China's largest cities are living under long-term, harmful air quality conditions,' the *China Environment News* reported in 1997. More than half of the
largest eighty-eight cities monitored in 1995 for sulphur dioxide emission
exceeded the WHO guidelines.[35] While tighter regulations and the rundown of old industries led to some improvement in the urban environment,
rural communities were increasingly at risk from poorly regulated small-
scale industries. Many such incidents were covered up when villagers sought
compensation, but in a typical example reported by the *Shanghai Star* half a
ton of arsenic escaped into a river when a truck overturned near Sanjiao in
Guangxi province. The load had come from a factory which had been
banned from producing arsenic in the past but was 'allowed to re-open'.

The Sanjiao Smelting Factory that produced the arsenic is located in a mountainous
area. A pungent odour can be smelt far from the factory and the hill facing the
chimney is bare. . . . The factory has greatly affected the local environment and
villagers' lives, according to the *Information Times*. People in Xinping Village of
Sanjiao County were the first direct victims. Most villagers show symptoms such as
skin cankers as a result of breathing the poisonous air or drinking the polluted water
over a long period. More than 40 cows recently died because of eating poisoned
grass. According to regulations, factories producing poisonous products can't be
opened adjacent to rivers. However, there was a small seasonal river near Sanjiao
Smelting Factory. In spring and summer the water flows into the Sanjiao River,
500 metres away. Villagers said waste from the factory was often found in the river.
Many local villagers use the river water as their water source.[36]

By the turn of the century, more serious efforts were being made to enforce
pollution controls, at least in those cities with healthy economies, and government leaders at the national level warned of a looming ecological crisis.
'It is a long and arduous task for us', said Premier Zhu Rongji in a message
on World Environment Day in 2001, 'to protect the ecology and improve

the environment.' He urged everyone to work for a cleaner China in which 'the sky will be more clear and the landscape more beautiful'. Behind such concerns lay a darker thought that social unrest on a large scale—even the collapse of the Communist Party—might be precipitated if China was allowed to plunge into environmental disaster.

Changing China has always been a truism, even in the long centuries of imperial rule where profound economic and social changes were masked by the continuity of doctrine and tradition. Although the walls and temples of countless Chinese cities and towns remained intact in the earlier decades of twentieth-century China, large parts of the country were already being transformed by new roads, technologies, and ideas. This process was accelerated under Communism although the more remote areas which remained untouched under the Nationalists remained so after 1949 to a greater extent than was understood at the time. However, China began to change more rapidly in the 1980s, mostly because of the post-Mao opening-up to the world (and also the world's opening up to China) but also because more better educated, younger, Chinese were beginning to take over from the revolutionary generation. The process accelerated sharply in the 1990s after Deng Xiaoping gave a renewed impetus to the reform process: large parts of the Chinese land and of Chinese society were being radically transformed rather than merely experiencing change. This transformation contrasted and increasingly jarred with the prevailing political culture of the Communist Party whose bureaucratic and repressive norms often echoed much older characteristics of pre-communist, even dynastic, rule. Even here there was significant change both of generation and ideas in an organization which increasingly defined its role in terms of power rather than ideology and saw its role as that of building a strong and prosperous, not a socialist, China. Much of that prosperity (however unevenly distributed across the country) was generated by China's dynamic participation in the international market. China's strength too was increasingly defined in terms of its ability to play a substantial part on the international stage. By the turn of the millennium, at the end of a half-century which began with more than two decades of partial isolation, the world was now very much with China, and China with the world.

14

China and the World
From Mao to market

In April 1971 the first sign of a thaw between the US and China came when Beijing allowed a team of young American ping-pong players into the country. They were the first group of Americans allowed into China since the 1949 Liberation, and the US responded by lifting a twenty-year trade embargo on China. I was travelling at the time with a young—and extremely Mao-ist—guide: like millions of Chinese, he was amazed by the news that a goodwill gesture was being made to the 'US imperialism' which had isolated China for so long. I suggested that this was only the beginning: the next step would be a visit by a Chinese ping-pong team to the US.

'Never!', he replied passionately, 'that will never happen! They may come to us, but we shall never go to them! The US is still an imperialist country!'

A quarter of a century later, the young guide was a senior official with the China International Travel Service, author of many writings on tourism and also editor of a popular women's magazine. In one of his books he recalls how he 'had the honour' of escorting a former governor of Texas around China. The Chinese people, he says, 'no longer fear or hate foreigners'.

Love and hate in US–China relations

The Beijing massacre, followed two years later by the collapse of the Soviet Union, had a significant impact on the central issue in Chinese diplomacy— its relationship with the US. The rapprochement in 1972 after two decades of cold war hostility had been shrewd and open-eyed on both sides. China used it to lever its way back into the international community, regaining its UN seat and reviving diplomatic and trade relations. The US enlisted an unlikely ally in its contest for world supremacy with the Soviet Union and sought, less successfully, to exploit the new opening in order to outflank Hanoi in the Vietnam War. Public postures of anti-imperialism and anti-communism were no hindrance. Mao Zedong dismissed Beijing's own anti-US propaganda as the firing of 'empty cannons'. President Nixon told Mao reassuringly on his first meeting that 'what is important [to the US] is not a nation's internal philosophy . . . [but] its policy toward the rest of the world and toward us'. After the full normalization of relations in 1979, the US intensified security co-operation with Beijing, even providing military intelligence on Soviet intentions when China invaded Vietnam. China later collaborated in secret efforts to undermine the Soviet occupation of Afghanistan. Throughout the 1980s, as US business welcomed the opening of a new trade frontier which revived century-old dreams of an unlimited market, while US academic institutions revelled in their new access to the mainland, sometimes as uncritically as European Maoists in the past, Chinese human rights abuses were of little concern. As James Mann has written in his exhaustive study of US–China relations, 'human rights was considered a suitable subject for high-level American diplomacy with the Soviet Union, but not with China'.[1]

The televised images of slaughter and repression in Beijing forced the US administration to impose economic sanctions and suspend military and high-level diplomatic contacts. George Bush had headed the US mission in Beijing a decade earlier and claimed Deng Xiaoping as his 'good friend'. He had already been embarrassed in February 1989, during his presidential visit to Beijing, when the Chinese security police prevented Fang Lizhi, the outspoken reformer, from attending a banquet which he was hosting. The White House blamed its embassy for having put Mr Fang on the guest list, not the Chinese authorities for keeping him away! After the massacre Mr Fang caused more embarrassment by approaching the embassy for refuge with his wife. The US could hardly refuse, but spent the next year negotiating a face-saving deal to allow the Fangs to leave the country 'for medical reasons'. The quid pro quo secured by Beijing would be the renewal of access to World Bank funds. More significantly, Mr Bush authorized a secret mission to Beijing by his National Security Adviser Brent Scowcroft only a month after 4 June. Mr Scowcroft paid a second, public, visit, in December: it was intended to send 'a political signal that we are now ready to resume relations on a more normal basis'.[2]

By the end of the next year the ban on high-level contacts had been lifted in spite of the continuing repression and executions in Beijing. China had co-operated in the UN Security Council by abstaining in the vote for US-led military action against Iraq, and in return foreign minister Qian Qichen was granted a symbolic visit to the White House. With Mr Qian by his side, the President blandly declared that 'We have some differences on this whole broad question of human rights, but we have many things in common.' A year later, even Li Peng, the butcher of Beijing, was able to meet Mr Bush, though on neutral ground at the UN in New York. With colossal cheek, Mr Li had told the US secretary of state in Beijing that without the Tiananmen crack-down China would have suffered the same fate as the Soviet Union—as if the US had a shared interest to keep communist regimes in power.

However, the collapse of the Soviet Union would have a far more serious effect on US–China relations than the Beijing massacre, removing the ori-ginal security rationale for rapprochement. The disappearance of the alleged 'Soviet threat' also prompted China to explore better relations with Moscow, conveying a hint of triangular diplomacy. Beijing's decision to purchase SU27 bombers from Russia resulted in a retaliatory decision in Washington to supply F16 fighters to Taiwan. The growing assertiveness of pro-independence sentiment on Taiwan was another complicating factor. China's clumsy attempts to influence the 1996 presidential election on the island by missile-rattling in the Taiwan Straits (see next section of this chapter) also raised the temperature. The mid-1990s altogether were a time of con-flicting trends in US–China relations as both sides tried to decide whether to be friends or foes.

The new impetus given by Deng Xiaoping to China's economic reforms and 'opening up' to the world had encouraged international business to forget Tiananmen Square and vie for new opportunities on the mainland. In 1993 China signed over $110 billion worth of new contracts with foreign companies: most were with businesses belonging to the Greater Chinese community and particularly in Singapore, Hong Kong, and Taiwan, but one in twelve including some of the largest were with US companies. The amount of foreign investment actually used grew six times from 1991 to 1993. Most foreign funding went into the manufacturing sector and the industries which it supported would grow ever more sophisticated. US consumers like those across the world found 'made in China' labels not only on their toys, shoes, and textiles, but on furniture, white goods, and home computers.

The speed with which China was becoming integrated with the world economy should have been reassuring, but it also raised questions in the US about the possible emergence of a world rival. 'No relationship may prove as fateful as that between the United States and China,' argued Richard Haass, one of the most influential foreign policy advisers in Washington. 'Indeed, managing China's emergence as a great power could well prove to be the defining foreign policy effort of this era.'[3] A new set of images now appeared on the front covers of international news magazines, embodying a mixture of approval and fear at the Chinese advance. To quote from the early months of 1996:

> The 21st Century Starts Here: China Booms. The World Holds its Breath (*New York Times Magazine*)
> China: The Next Superpower (*Time*)
> China on the Move (*Newsweek*)
> The Next Superpower: China's return to greatness (*Asiaweek*)

Newsweek's cover story revealed the nagging question behind US admiration for China's economic advance:

Keep that prosperous one-and-a-quarter billion Chinese in mind, with all the goods and services they will produce and consume, and you can see China's rebirth as a blessing to the world. China as friend—there's a comforting thought. . . But a China that saw itself as a natural enemy of the United States—that's another matter.[4]

A year later, a high wire act of international diplomacy dispelled some of the doubts on both sides. The 'Bill and Zemin' show was first staged in October–November 1997 when President Jiang visited the US, followed by a sequel when President Clinton paid his return visit in June–July 1998. Both presidents were free from earlier constraints. Clinton, who had taken a tough anti-China line in 1992 ('We will not coddle dictators from Baghdad to Beijing') in his first campaign for presidency, had been re-elected. Jiang had emerged from the shadow of Deng Xiaoping after the latter's death to oust his principal conservative rivals from the leadership. Both sides now had a realistic view of their top requirements from the other. China sought US assurances that it would not encourage the pro-independence mood on Taiwan, and needed Washington's help to smooth its way into the World Trade Organization. The US required at least the occasional gesture from Beijing in the direction of human rights—the release of a prominent dissident usually did the trick—and sought better access for American business to sell as well as buy in China. Even if these bargains were sometimes difficult to strike, both shared a cosy consensus that US–Chinese relations were of 'strategic importance' to themselves and to the world, though both had to contend with domestic critics—publicly in the US, less so in China—on this subject. (The only problem, though barely noticed at the time, was that the Chinese commitment to this strategic relationship was stronger than that of the US: this disparity would only become evident under the subsequent presidency of George W. Bush.)

Both presidents made full use of photo opportunities and sound bites to portray themselves as successful world statesmen: the audiences they were trying to impress most were back home rather than in the host country. Jiang still had to defuse the opposition of domestic hardliners while Clinton could not ignore the assorted criticism of human rights activists and old-fashioned anti-communists. In both countries, a vigorous campaign by pro-détente scholars and advisers had helped smooth the way. A central figure in Beijing was the influential Academy of Social Sciences adviser Liu Ji who openly criticized Chinese chauvinism of the kind expressed both at the popular level—in books such as the best-seller *China Can Say NO*—and in some sections of the Party and military leadership. Liu argued that the US needed China's markets while China needed US technology—this was where their 'fundamental strategic interest' lay. The Clinton initiative was backed by US think-tanks including the American Assembly which had launched a two-year project in 1995, backed by businesses with a keen commercial interest in China such as Boeing and General Motors, to 'clarify' US policy towards China.

For weeks before Jiang's visit to the US, reported the *New York Times* (31 October 1997), the Clinton administration had put its main energy into preparing the meeting and 'ordering its camera angles in ways that would allow both presidents to look strong to their domestic constituencies'. President Jiang danced the *hula* with students and tried to play the Hawaiian steel guitar during his stop-over in Honolulu. He visited Independence Hall in Philadelphia and rang the bell to start trading at the New York Stock Exchange. He visited the offices of IBM and AT&T and attended a big business banquet. In an address at Harvard University he sought to portray China as standing side by side with the US on the world stage and closely linked by mutual interests.

The US is the most developed country, and China the largest developing country

. . . China holds a huge market and great demand for development, and the US holds advanced science and technology as well as enormous material force. The economies of the two countries are therefore highly complementary with each other . . . China and the US share broad common interests and shoulder common responsibility on many important questions which are crucial to human survival and development, such as maintaining world peace and security, preventing the spread of weapons of mass destruction, protecting the environment for human survival and combating international crime.[5]

The Clinton visit to China was also carefully choreographed to show the president in a favourable light he badly needed at home (where his reputation had sagged in the Monica Lewinsky affair). Clinton was portrayed both as the discoverer of China's rapid economic and social progress and as a missionary preaching the virtues of democracy. His list of Chinese achievements ranged from a village he had visited near Xian that elected its local leaders to the 'explosion of skyscrapers' he saw in Shanghai. He cited the spread of cellphones and computers as evidence of China's 'remarkable transformation' and predicted that the internet would accelerate democratic change. The negative picture of the harassment of Chinese dissidents during Clinton's visit was blotted out—at least for most of the US media— by the regime's willingness to transmit live his joint press conference in Beijing in which he urged Jiang to embrace the virtues of democracy. The *People's Daily* published a round-up of foreign press praise for the debate's frankness—but did not publish a single word of the two presidents' discussion on human rights. In Hong Kong on his way home, Clinton endorsed Jiang as a man of great intellect and vigour who possessed the vision to imagine 'a future that is different from the present'. While acknowledging that there were powerful forces restricting change, he believed that

there is a very good chance that China has the right leadership at the right time, and that they understand the daunting, massive nature of the challenges they face. They want us to understand that there is much more personal freedom now, in a practical sense, for most Chinese than there was when President Nixon came here [25] years ago. But I think they understand that this is an unfolding process they have to keep going. And I hope that we can be a positive force there.[6]

Within a short while the rosy picture conveyed by Zemin and his friend Bill had been badly shaken—though not quite shattered. The momentum was never regained in the last two years of the Clinton presidency, and relations then took a further turn for the worse with the election of President George W. Bush. In December 1998 several leading Chinese dissidents, emboldened by the presidential debate to seek approval for the establishment of a China Democracy Party, were charged with subversion and given harsh sentences (see further below, p. 318). In May 1999, the Chinese embassy in Belgrade was hit by a US missile during the Kosovo war, provoking a wave of genuine anger across China which the Beijing government could hardly ignore. The student demonstrations against US diplomatic buildings in Beijing and other cities would have been more violent if they had not been stage-managed by the authorities. The affair was eventually settled by a half-apology from the US, and talks resumed on China's entry to the World Trade Organization. However, efforts to pick up the threads of the faltering 'strategic relationship' were marred by US plans for a National Missile Defence system which would be offered to Japan—and perhaps even to Taiwan. In January 2001 Bush was inaugurated amid reports that he regarded the relationship with China as one of strategic competition rather than co-operation. Another chance event—the mid-air collision of a US spy plane and a Chinese fighter in April—provoked further outrage on the mainland while Washington claimed, as it had after the embassy bombing, that the incident was being exploited by Beijing.

Yet while the US–China relationship was set back by these disturbing developments, the fact that it survived them was an indication of its under-lying value for both sides—though perhaps more for China than for the US. This was in spite of a widespread feeling among the public that 'China should say no' (the title of the book was often quoted) to the world's superpower. This was apparent after the embassy bombing, and again after the spy plane incident, when the views of Jiang's foreign policy advisers prevailed against those of Party conservatives and senior military leaders. A 'great debate' had taken place after the embassy bombing, said the *China Daily* (6 November 1999), in which some critics argued that China might become the 'next target' for the US. However, China's 'mainstream experts', according to this account, successfully insisted that China should still seek partnership with the US.

By the time of the spy plane incident in April 2001, these divisions in government were matched by those in public opinion as expressed on the street and in internet chat-rooms (although not in the more circumspect print media). The *People's Daily*'s website 'Strong Country' discussion group carried a wide range of views including the following:

- The US government has stamped on our heads but our government is still 'responding with reason'. Our hearts are truly bitter!

- The Americans spoke first [with their account of the mid-air collision] and we had nothing to say. While CNN was reporting the US government version, our television news told us about a tree-planting ceremony in Beijing!

- Blood debts must be repaid with blood! [the Chinese fighter pilot died after crashing into the sea, while the US plane made a forced landing without casualties on Hainan island].

- Calm yourselves! Peace and development is still the main trend today.

- Those who call for action against 'US imperialism' should reflect. Do you really want to goad the US into giving new weapons to Taiwan?

The arrival of the new millennium prompted more thought in Beijing about the longer-term future in a world dominated by one superpower, but it did not alter the commitment to seek a better understanding with the US—if Washington was prepared to play ball. As a commentary in the *Southern Weekend* admitted, 'the importance of US–China relations for Chinese foreign policy exceeds its importance for US foreign policy'. With China militarily so much weaker, and with such huge economic tasks ahead, Beijing could only hope that the US would see the advantage of having China as an ally rather than an antagonist. As Cui Tiankai, head of policy planning at the foreign ministry, put it in an interview: 'Yes, we are asking ourselves about US intentions. We have different systems and cultures, but this cannot justify confrontation. Everyone knows that the US has superiority but it still needs co-operation from other countries.'[7]

In the end it was not Chinese advocacy but the shock of September 11 which persuaded the new Bush administration to set a higher value on its relationship with China. In October 2001 when President Bush attended the Asia Pacific Economic Conference (APEC) in Shanghai, the Chinese ensured that the war against terrorism should figure prominently on the agenda, and declared themselves to be on America's side in what foreign minister Tang Jiaxuan called 'a fight between justice and evil, civilization and savagery'. Chinese commentators, hawks as well as doves, hailed September 11 as a turning-point which gave the US a real enemy to pursue instead of the illusory one that neo-conservatives in the Bush administration had claimed to see on the Chinese mainland. Some doves went further, even finding positive elements in US policy towards China before 1949 which, they argued in terms similar to those of many American scholars, had 'a humanitarian as well as imperialist aspect'. The two countries, argued the *Economic Observer* (14 Oct. 2001) at the time of Bush's visit, should now seek to find 'a common territory of understanding based upon their past history'. With China about to join the WTO, trade was also seen as a unifying factor, and a year later it was described by the *China Daily* (23 Oct. 2001) as 'the driving force in China–US relations'. The Jiang perspective on US–China relations was summed up by the newspaper with unusual clarity: 'What truly matters now for China and the US is a shared political will to anchor what is perhaps one of the world's most influential, yet volatile, state-to-state relationships.' This was an accurate description for a relationship which remained hostage to the unexpected—and not least the unexpected in Taiwan.

Reuniting China

The reunification of China—which meant above all the return of Taiwan and Hong Kong to central rule (Macao followed on from Hong Kong)—was a subject which provoked genuine national sentiment that no leader in Beijing could ignore. 'Who among the descendants of the Yellow Emperor wishes to go down in history as a traitor?', asked Beijing rhetorically in a 1979 statement appealing to Taiwan to embrace the motherland. Throughout the decades of cold war, the central government recognized that no change was possible in the unsatisfactory status quo which saw Chiang Kai-shek and his successors installed in Taiwan, and Britain ruling Hong Kong as a 'crown colony'. The US had extended its protection to Chiang's regime in 1950 when the Korean War broke out: Chinese military action was limited to the largely symbolic shelling of the Taiwan-controlled Off-shore Islands (Quemoy and Matsu). The Offshore Islands crises of 1955 and 1958 which Beijing provoked were intended to embarrass the Soviet Union, not as a prelude to invasion. (Mao feared that Moscow's overtures towards détente with the US would leave China vulnerably alone.)

As China's relations with the outside world were progressively normalized in the 1980s, reunification at last became a practical goal. The original strategy had been to leave Hong Kong—a question in the Chinese view 'left over from history'—to be dealt with after the problem of Taiwan—a more recent and deeper affront to national unity—had been solved. In 1981 Beijing set out nine principles for reunification which guaranteed 'a high degree of autonomy' for Taiwan without any time limit and even allowed the island to keep its own defence forces. However, Taiwan, where the death of Chiang Kai-shek had produced less change than that of Mao on the mainland, failed to respond to what was at least on paper a very generous offer. The Guomindang still ruled the island with an iron grip, suppressing the island's nascent Democracy Movement, and could easily point to the recent turmoil in China, and Beijing's disregard for the human rights of its citizens supposedly guaranteed in the 1954 constitution, to argue that its words could not be trusted. Hong Kong now moved to the top of the agenda because of the need to find a solution ahead of 1997 when the lease on the major portion of its territory would expire. The successful conclusion of the Sino-British Agreement in 1984 (after a bad start following a clumsy attempt by Prime Minister Margaret Thatcher to secure an extension of the lease) seemed to set a hopeful precedent for Taiwan. Events on the island also appeared to weaken the previous rigidity of the Guomindang regime. Martial law was lifted, press restrictions eased, and the Chiang dynasty came to an end after the death of the Generalissimo's son Chiang Ching-kuo in 1988. Indirect trade with China was encouraged and indirect investment—the KMT still banned direct contacts—boomed. Several hundred thousand Taiwanese visited the mainland every year and the KMT's Congress approved sporting, cultural, academic, and journalistic exchanges. In April 1989 the first Taiwan sports team competed in Beijing, and a month later Taiwan officials attended the Asian Development Bank meeting in the capital.

This momentum was brought to an abrupt halt by the events in Tiananmen Square. The KMT government still had to support reunification in theory since its rule was based on the fiction that Taiwan's legislature represented the whole of China. But the idea that the political systems of mainland and Taiwan might become at least complementary was abandoned. As one KMT legislator put it, reunification might take a hundred years, and in the meantime 'what we should do is make Taiwan the hope of China'.[8]

The crackdown in Beijing had an even more dramatic effect on the Hong Kong public where half a million people—one-twelfth of the population—took to the streets. The demonstrations disproved the easy assumption on which Britain had based its undemocratic colonial rule that the people of Hong Kong 'are only interested in making money'. It was an unwelcome lesson too to Beijing which much preferred its diaspora to be affluent and apolitical. Hong Kongers sent money, medical supplies, and messages of sympathy to the students in the square. After the tanks moved in, they donated blood and withdrew their savings from mainland banks in the territory. The reform movement encouraged by Hu Yaobang in the 1980s had encouraged the view that by the time of the 1997 handover China would have moved some way towards a democratic convergence with Hong Kong. After Tiananmen, with the vital Basic Law which would govern Hong Kong still under negotiation, China appeared instead to be going into reverse. In a typical comment published a week after 3 June, the independent Ming Pao wrote:

To the Chinese people at home and overseas as well, the massacre is a horrible lesson. Good will and reasonable hopes have been shattered; confidence in the government is gone. Pessimists may be resigned to the circumstances, while radicals, in desperation, risk arrest or go underground. . . . After the darkest night, we expect the light of morning, the dawn. But are we sure that what we have seen is the darkest?[9]

In Beijing conspiracy theorists in the tight leadership group around Deng Xiaoping saw Hong Kong's support for the student movement as further proof that they were right to take military action. The official line (*Beijing Review*, 11 Sept.) was that

[The] student movement, turmoil and counter-rebellion was orchestrated by a small number of people both inside and outside the Chinese Communist Party who stubbornly clung to their bourgeois stand and engaged in political conspiracy, in collaboration with some anti-communist and anti-socialist forces in the West, Taiwan and Hong Kong, with the aim of overthrowing the leadership of the Party, subverting the socialist People's Republic of China, and establishing in China a completely Westernized bourgeois republic.

Just as the Beijing massacre forced the US government to take account of China's human rights abuses, so Britain was obliged to pay more attention to the democratic aspirations of the Hong Kong people and to their fears of China. The 1984 Sino-British Joint Declaration, based on Deng Xiaoping's formula of 'one country two systems', had guaranteed that Hong Kong's economic, social, and political structures, including the rule of law, would remain autonomous for the foreseeable future. Britain had not consulted the people of Hong Kong before signing the deal but claimed, with some justification, to have achieved some reasonable safeguards in the fine print of the agreement. However the existing structure as of 1984 did not include any meaningful measure of democracy: Britain, which had previously stifled local pressure groups which called for a greater say in their territory's affairs, now had to allow more democracy institutions to emerge at a pace fast enough to satisfy Hong Kongers without upsetting Beijing. The standard view of British diplomats until now had been contemptuous of the democrats, and wary of upsetting Beijing. As expressed by one Foreign Office mandarin before Tiananmen Square changed everything:

They [the Chinese] will be here for ever. I wish the famous champions of democracy would realise that. This talk about political reform is all very well, but how long have we got until 1997? If you've just sold your house, you don't suddenly start redecorating it from top to bottom in a colour which the new owner doesn't like![10]

This complacent view could no longer prevail after 1989, even though British negotiators did their best to 'restore mutual trust' with Beijing. There was immediate pressure, even from pro-British figures of the Hong Kong establishment, for a more rapid pace of democratic change leading towards direct elections of the entire Legislative Council by the year 2003. The best that Britain could achieve, in negotiations with China as Beijing prepared its Basic Law for Hong Kong, was that half its sixty seats should be directly elected by that year, with a vaguer promise of full representative democracy after 2007. This issue would become the central issue in political debate both before 1997 and after. In September 1991, in the first partial elections for the Council, pro-democrats won fifteen out of the eighteen seats available—worrying evidence of potential 'subversion' for Beijing. A year later, the British prime minister John Major who had become impatient with the Foreign Office mandarins, appointed his colleague Chris Patten as the new Hong Kong governor. Patten, equally impatient with the Chinese mandarins, produced a new formula for accelerated democratic change which, while welcomed by the majority of Hong Kong public opinion, quickly enraged Beijing.

The problem for China was that both in Taiwan and Hong Kong new civil societies had emerged with a collective consciousness including complex and articulate feelings about their relationship with Beijing. For the majority of Taiwanese, particularly those whose families had not been part of the 1949 flight from the mainland but had lived there for generations, it amounted to a sense of national identity constrained only by an understandable concern not to provoke the Chinese communist leadership. The

tentative political liberalization of the 1980s had developed into a fully
fledged democratic transition culminating in the first ever direct presidential
election in 1996. Although won by Lee Teng-hui, the Guomindang candidate and successor to the Chiang dynasty, Lee was a native-born Taiwanese
who spoke openly of Taiwan as a nation: while he still professed to look
forward to reunification with the mainland—which remained his party's
official policy—this was predicated on China becoming as democratic as
Taiwan. A year before the election, he had engineered a visit to Cornell
University, his alma mater, for which the US government in spite of angry
Chinese protests gave him a visa, and delivered a speech that caused even
more fury in Beijing.

With the completion of constitutional reform, we have established a multiparty
system and have realized the ideal of popular sovereignty. This has led to full respect
for individual freedom, ushering in the most free and liberal era in Chinese history. . . . In fact, the Confucian belief that only the ruler who provides for the needs
of his people is given the mandate to rule is consistent with the modern concept of
democracy. This is also the basis for my philosophy of respect for individual free will
and popular sovereignty.

   Thus, the needs and wishes of my people have been my guiding light every step
of the way. I only hope that the leaders in the mainland are able one day to be
similarly guided, since then our achievements in Taiwan can most certainly help
the process of economic liberalization and the cause of democracy in mainland
China.[11]

Beijing, still in the grip of intransigent Party and army elders, adopted
heavy-handed tactics to try to intimidate pro-independence voices in the
Taiwan election campaign. The Chinese military staged exercises and tested
missiles in the Taiwan Straits in summer 1995, and again a month before the
elections. The US responded by deploying two aircraft carriers near Taiwan:
senior officials said that the purpose was to remind China that the US
remained 'the premier military power in the Western Pacific' and that military action against the Taiwan Straits would have 'grave consequences'—
although both sides were careful not to provoke a direct confrontation. The
Taiwanese voters, although alarmed, still gave Lee 52 per cent of the popular
vote. Lee said he would work for Taiwan to play a higher international
role and regain its seat in the UN, ceded to Beijing in 1972. Such an
emphatic majority was not much better for Beijing than if the openly
pro-independence Democratic Progressive Party candidate had won.
   No one in Hong Kong called for independence and the majority

accepted that reunification was the only feasible solution, given the territory's location and close ties, while many felt some sense of pride in the mainland's economic progress. Tycoons who had accepted titles from the British Queen now flocked to Beijing to earn credit—and contracts—for patriotism from Deng Xiaoping. Many foreign business interests shared the concern of these 'fat cats' that the British plan to speed up democratic change before the handover would only sour the start of Hong Kong's new relationship. But most ordinary Hong Kongers, who had been politically sensitized by the Beijing massacre, applauded the effort. Anxious not to give the impression of kowtowing to Beijing, Governor Patten announced his plan without prior consultation and was denounced furiously by the Chinese media.

Patten sought to engineer a fully democratic Legislative Council at the coming 1995 elections by changes in the voting system which adhered to the letter of the system laid down in the Chinese Basic Law but subverted its intent. Half the council members would still be elected by 'functional constituencies' but the franchise for these would be extended from small groups of business and professional leaders to the rank-and-file workers and other employees. Another ten seats would still be chosen by a small 'selection committee', but the committee's members would themselves be elected instead of being simply appointed. Though Beijing agreed to negotiate on these points, it saw the plan as a device to ensure a majority for the Democrats and their allies in the Legislative Council. Setting a time limit on the negotiations, Britain carried out the reforms unilaterally after failing to reach agreement with Beijing. China then set up a 'provisional legislature' to take over in 1997, refusing to regard as legitimate the one elected in 1995. In the shorthand terms widely used during the negotiations, 'convergence' between British and Chinese policy had failed, the 'through train' of a smooth transition had been derailed, and Beijing had constructed a 'new kitchen' in which the post-1997 political system would be prepared.

In the end the Patten plan appeared to be a resounding failure which had destroyed any chance of a smooth transition from British to Chinese rule while securing any compensatory gain. In defence it may be argued that it helped nourish a democratic enthusiasm which carried through into the post-1997 era and that by its actions in Tiananmen Square Beijing itself had made it politically impossible for Britain to fudge the issue of democracy in Hong Kong. Finally, there was much truth in the charge frequently levelled from the mainland (and echoed by many Hong Kongers) that Britain had only begun to display an interest in the subject at the tail-end of a century and a half of colonial rule.

Hong Kong returned to the motherland on 1 July 1997, after ceremonies lashed by rainstorms which could be interpreted either as an ill omen for the future or a damp verdict on the past record of British rule. The People's Liberation Army (PLA) crossed the border on the stroke of midnight but then kept to its barracks. The Hong Kong markets continued to function without interference, the container ports were busier than before, the press carried reports on China which would be banned on the mainland, and several human rights organizations operating from the territory also produced highly critical material. President Jiang Zemin and US President Bill Clinton visited Hong Kong a year later for the first anniversary when the new airport, once the subject of controversy between Britain and China, was opened. Although a new legislature was set up on the more restricted franchise which Governor Patten had tried to expand, it seemed for a while to have been a 'smooth transition'.

The successful return of Hong Kong to the motherland, followed a year later by the former Portuguese territory of Macao, was greeted with patriotic enthusiasm across the mainland, but it only focused more attention on the failure to make headway with Taiwan. The frustration showed in Premier Zhu Rongji's impassioned reply to a question at the National People's Congress (NPC), as Taiwan was preparing for its second presidential election.

All the Chinese remember very well that the modern history of China which started with the Opium War in the 1840s is a history of being bullied and oppressed by foreign forces. Taiwan for many years was under occupation and rule of Japanese military forces. Looking back at that part of China's history, we all know China then was poor and weak. However, Chinese people at that time still came up with a strong voice calling for all people not to be slaves. Our Chinese people have been making heroic struggles to make sure that we would not become slaves of others. At that time, I was only nine years old. I still clearly remember all the songs we used to sing; songs that called for the salvation of our motherland. These songs are still clear in my mind today. Every time when I was singing these songs, I became so excited that I was determined to devote all my life to the great cause of our motherland. Today, the Chinese people have stood up. So how can it be possible that we will allow Taiwan—which has been a part of China's territory—to be separated from the motherland? Absolutely, we cannot![12]

This time the Chinese government avoided the military gestures which had proved so counter-productive in the 1996 election, but Zhu could not resist ending with a threat. He urged the Taiwanese to 'make a wise choice', warning that otherwise 'things are hardly predictable because anything may happen'. The people of Taiwan were not impressed and as expected chose Chen Shui-bian, candidate for the opposition Democratic Progressive Party. Only a decade after it began to tolerate democracy, the now-divided Guomindang had lost control of the presidency which it had held since 1927. The only consolation for Beijing was that opinion polls regularly showed a large majority in favour of maintaining the status quo in which Taiwan was independent but did not formally declare it. However, an equally large majority (75 to 85 per cent) rejected the Chinese formula, first coined for Hong Kong, for 'one China, two systems'.

Four years later in 2004, when Taiwan held its third direct presidential election, Beijing showed even more restraint, not even issuing verbal threats and avoiding the usual reminder that the Chinese government reserved 'the right to use force' if necessary. This was in spite of a provocative move by Chen, seeking to rally pro-independence support, who staged a referendum seeking support for increased defence spending to 'consolidate' what he called Taiwan's 'sovereign, independent status'. Standing for re-election, this time against a unified opposition, Chen still gained an outright majority: no major party paid even nominal lip-service to reunification and Beijing was left with the dilemma of what to do next.

However, Beijing's more cautious approach was nullified for many Taiwanese by a steady build-up of mainland missiles located in Fujian province facing the island. These were more a symbolic than actual threat—it was very hard to imagine circumstances in which Beijing would launch missile attacks on their 'compatriots' in Taiwan—which probably reflected frustration by China's military leaders at their inability to take action. Yet it strengthened the argument in the Pentagon as well as in Taiwan for improving the island's anti-missile defences: Taiwanese defence analysts regularly cited the magic figure 'seven'—the number of minutes it would take a Chinese missile to cross from the mainland, and insisted that there was a real and continuing threat. Analysts in Beijing replied that although no one wanted to see military action which would inevitably lead to confrontation with the US, there was a growing danger in the continued stalemate: a conference at Beijing's People's University in 2002 heard the following warnings from Chinese academic participants:

- Among all questions, between China and the US, Taiwan is the most serious.
- If you don't stress peaceful reunification, then the opportunities for mischief will multiply.
- The threat to peace comes from Taiwan refusing to give ground, not from the US or China both of whom want to reduce the danger of war.
- If Taiwan's authorities deliberately build up a social base for independence, it will be even harder to find a peaceful settlement
- Our policy of reunification contains both principles and flexibility, but it cannot be put off indefinitely. Fifty years . . . a hundred years . . . how long do you want us to wait?[13]

The honeymoon in Hong Kong only lasted a year and a half till January 1999 when the territory's Court of Final Appeal upset the Hong Kong government and Beijing by a crucial decision on the 'right of abode'. The court found, on the basis of a provision in the Basic Law, that children on the mainland had this right if one of their parents was now a Hong Kong citizen even if he or she had not be so at the time of the child's birth. The government claimed exaggeratedly that this would result in 1.7 million such children on the mainland acquiring the right to reside in Hong Kong, and, instead of accepting the court's decision, went to Beijing for an 'interpretation'—in fact a reinterpretation—of the relevant clause. The effect was to deny thousands of divided families the right to be united, and to weaken the final authority of the court which now accepted Beijing's new 'interpretation'.

In this and other cases over the next few years, Beijing did its best to avoid being seen to intervene unless invited to by the Hong Kong government. In reality such invitations were triggered by Beijing complaining, in private, first. On the right of abode issue, Beijing had made it clear that it expected the Hong Kong government to order the judges to change their minds—apparently Beijing was unaware that the courts in Hong Kong are different from those in China. In another high-profile case before the courts, local mainland officials were persuaded with difficulty that the government could not guarantee the result in advance.

Senior Chinese leaders seemed unable to realize that interference from Beijing would only alienate Hong Kong opinion further. In doing so they fulfilled the prediction of Martin Lee, leader of Hong Kong's Democratic Party, that 'our ship will not sink but we will die the death of a thousand cuts'. (Mr Lee, and fellow elected democrats on the Legislative Council, were routinely denied visas to visit the mainland.) Chief Executive Tung Chee-hwa, who was handpicked for the job by Beijing and whose family shipping business had been bailed out with mainland help in the past, initially said he would only run for one term. As he became more unpopular, Beijing felt a greater obligation to support him. In October 2000 Jiang Zemin made it clear that he wanted Tung to serve a second term. When asked by a Hong Kong journalist if Tung was 'the emperor's choice', Jiang lost his temper and scolded the territory's media for being 'naïve'. 'When I say what I say [that I support Tung],' he shouted at them, 'it's not because I've chosen him . . . but it must still be done according to Hong Kong's laws.' In July 2002, Tung was elected unopposed for a second term by an 'electoral college' of eight hundred dominated by pro-Beijing and business interests.

Tung announced that he would now rule through a body of appointed but unselected 'ministers', replacing the system of career civil servants inherited from Britain. In 2003, public confidence in him dropped further after his government initially played down the threat of the SARS virus which had spread from neighbouring Guangdong (where news about it was being covered up) into Hong Kong. Imprudently seeking to force through a new security law, he met opposition from liberal and normally pro-Beijing legislators and was forced to suspend it. When the next crisis arose a year later—over whether or not to speed up the pace of democratic reform—Beijing no longer worked behind the scenes but intervened directly.

The Basic Law allowed Hong Kong to initiate moves towards universal suffrage, 'if there is a need', after the year 2007. The wording implied—and was generally taken to mean—that with a sufficient majority in favour, Hong Kong could then change its election law so that the entire legislature was directly elected. It would only have to 'report' the changes to Beijing (although any change to the procedure for choosing the Chief Executive would require Beijing's consent). In 2004 this clause was also submitted for reinterpretation by the Standing Committee of the National People's Congress (NPC). It was for Beijing to decide whether or not there was a 'need' for any change, it concluded in a judgement which gave the central leadership an effective veto. Around this time, Chinese officials also began to express fears that a democratic Hong Kong might seek independence from the Beijing government—an idea regarded as ludicrous by all Hong Kongers who knew very well that they were linked indissolubly to the mainland.

Problems on the periphery

When Chinese officials are sent to serve in Tibet, their colleagues praise them for 'braving hardship' and pity them for having to work in such a 'backward place'. Tibet, with its winter cold and high altitude, has always been regarded as an alien environment and until recently most Chinese have made little effort to appreciate its rich culture and natural beauty. Yet Tibet also arouses patriotic passions which are as vocal as those provoked by Taiwan. Chinese propaganda refers obsessively to the region as 'China's Tibet'; exhibitions of Tibetan art and archaeology always include items 'reflecting historical relations between interior China and Tibet'; and the Western media is denounced for referring to the world's highest mountain as Mount Everest and not Mount Qomolangma. Britain's sporadic efforts to gain influence in Lhasa in the earlier twentieth century are well remembered: so is the CIA's support for the flight of the Dalai Lama to India, and its sponsorship of Tibetan guerrillas in the 1960s. Tibet had been effectively sealed to the outside world—except for a few 'friends of China'—for three decades but when resistance flared up again in the late 1980s, it was witnessed by hundreds of foreign tourists and sympathizers. The US and other Western governments accept that Tibet is part of China but are obliged to put the issue on their list of Chinese human rights abuses. The Dalai Lama has been welcomed to the White House and by other foreign governments as a 'spiritual leader', invariably provoking protests from Beijing.

The huge damage inflicted upon Tibet by the brutal suppression after the 1959 uprising, and by the dogmatic dismantling of its traditional society in the early 1960s—completed in the Cultural Revolution in which Tibet saw some of the worst factional Red Guard fighting in China—was beyond question. The first stage was documented in the '70,000 character petition' confidential report sent to Mao in 1962 by Tibet's second spiritual leader, the Panchen Lama. It described mass arrests, harsh punishments, executions, partial starvation, and the brutal dismantling of monasteries which had led '90 per cent of the Tibetan people to lose heart'. Mao denounced the report as a 'poisoned arrow shot at the Party', and the Panchen spent the next fourteen years in detention.[14] The full tale of the Cultural Revolution in Tibet, which provoked a second smaller revolt in 1969, has yet to be written. Historian Tsering Shakya notes that Tibetans who lived through it 'still express their incomprehension and describe it as the time "the sky fell to the earth" '.[15]

Profiting from the Cultural Revolution and from Tibet's distance from Beijing, ultra-leftist Tibetans rose to the top in Lhasa where some remain in positions of power to this day. Their grip on authority gives them a vested interest in exacerbating local tensions and has been one of the main obstacles to reaching compromise with the Dalai Lama who continues to be regarded by almost the entire population as Tibet's supreme leader. In 1980 the reformist Party secretary-general Hu Yaobang delivered a stern reprimand to the Tibetan leadership. He told them bluntly that Tibet was worse off in many areas than before the revolution and that the Party should 'apologise to the Tibetan people'.[16] Economic conditions now began to improve, tourism to Tibet was encouraged, and negotiations opened with the Dalai Lama abroad.

However, the opening up of Tibet had only increased the desire for independence or at least genuine autonomy. The talks with the Dalai Lama had stalled as neither side was willing to make concessions, and the Chinese position hardened with the political downfall of Hu Yaobang. Beijing was unimpressed by the Dalai Lama's new proposals, in his Five-Point Peace Plan (September 1987) and Strasbourg statement (July 1988) which fell short of demanding formal independence and accepted some form of continued association with China. By appealing for international support—the five-point plan was first announced in a speech on Capitol Hill—the Dalai Lama alienated Beijing further. In any case rank-and-file Tibetans in exile and in the region ignored the nuances of the proposals and demanded independence. The reopened monasteries were filled with a new generation of younger, more assertive Tibetans who led a series of five mass demonstrations between September 1987 and March 1989. Foreign tourists provided the dissidents with a channel for communication with the outside world. Small groups of brave monks and nuns marched around the sacred Barkhor circuit flying the Tibetan flag, with shouts of 'Long live the Dalai Lama' and 'Independence for Tibet'. Civilian casualties mounted till over a hundred Tibetans were killed by the army and armed police in the March 1989 demonstration. Some of the hitherto peaceful demonstrators attacked Chinese soldiers and burned Chinese-owned property: martial law was declared and the Tibetan quarter was surrounded by army checkpoints. The imposition of martial law was an ominous prelude to the crackdown three months later in Beijing: in the nationwide repression which followed, torture and brutality could flourish unchecked in Tibet. Clandestine leaflets, thrust into the hands of rare foreign visitors, hailed the 'heroic nuns' who had demonstrated twelve times in the past two years, and described their suffering:

A list of the fourteen nuns who demonstrated in March this year gives their ages between eighteen and thirty-two, with an average of twenty-three. Four of them were arrested. 'In prison they were intensively tortured, including electric sticks to the breasts and being beaten by rifles, sticks, handcuffs and chains.' It goes on to state that the cell had no electricity and no floor covering, the prisoners were allowed few clothes and they received only two meals a day, one consisting of a single very small momo (steamed bun) and the other of a small cup of wormy vegetables. It also alleges that they were forced to put their heads into a bucket of urine and excrement.[17]

Estimates of the number of political prisoners in Tibet, jailed for offences against 'state security', over the next decade were always in the hundreds (in 1996 an official admitted to two hundred). Occasional visits by international observers were allowed to Drapchi, the main prison in Lhasa. In May 1998, inmates staged protests during a European Union visit and according to unofficial reports some were subsequently beaten to death. Public demonstrations almost disappeared or were staged by only a handful of monks. Dissent was confined to the monasteries which were subjected to tighter controls in the mid-1990s. Strict ceilings were placed on the number of monks in each establishment, the portrait of the Dalai Lama was banned, and a 'patriotic education campaign' required monks and nuns to denounce the Dalai Lama and accept that Tibet was part of China or face expulsion. By the end of the decade, the focus for rectification had shifted from the Tibet Autonomous Region to 'eastern Tibet'—the minority areas of neighbouring Sichuan and Qinghai which were the borderlands of historical Tibet.

After the death of the Panchen Lama in 1989, efforts were made behind the scenes to reach agreement between the Dalai Lama and Beijing on the choice of a young boy to succeed him as his reincarnation. When these broke down in 1995, the Chinese forced the Tibetan abbots to approve their own candidate, while the Dalai Lama's choice, Gendun Choekyi Nyima, was placed in custody together with his family. Monks and nuns were now also obliged to accept the Chinese nominee, Gyaltsen Norbu. The senior lama at Tashilunpo Monastery, Chadrel Rinpoche, who had attempted to negotiate the compromise with the Dalai Lama, was jailed. Asserting a government role in the selection of Tibetan religious figures—just as Chinese emperors had done in those centuries when Tibet submitted to their influence—Beijing looked forward to a time when the Dalai Lama himself would have to be replaced. In June 2002, Tibet's Party establishment turned out to welcome Gyaltsen Norbu, now aged 12, to Lhasa. The scene was rich with political irony as the officials in their dark suits greeted the boy, dressed in robes and flanked by monks. Deputy head of government Ragdi (one of the ultra-leftists who gained power in the Cultural Revolution) congratulated him on his skill in learning the Buddhist scriptures under the guidance of the 'Party central committee and Chinese government'. A year earlier, a statement issued in the boy's name had praised the military occupation of Tibet in 1951.

Despite official tolerance for everyday worship, Chinese officials regard Buddhism as a long-term obstacle to the transformation of Tibet. 'The centre [in Beijing] demands that we should maintain stability in Tibet and weaken the influence of religion,' said Dan Zeng, the region's deputy Party secretary, at an education conference in 1999. Beijing also hopes that the economic transformation of Tibet will lead to a more secular society. The long-planned extension of China's rail network to Tibet, on which work started in 2002, is an important part of this process. The new line, starting from Golmud in the neighbouring Qinghai province, has to climb the 5,000 metre-high Tanggula pass. Four-fifths of the railway will be built above 4,000 metres and half its track will be laid on permafrost: even without any hitches, the 700-mile route would take six years to complete. Track construction began with a ten-thousand-strong contingent of migrant workers from the Chinese interior. Only a few local Tibetans, officials said revealingly, were employed to do manual labour. Thousands of Chinese migrants already in Lhasa mostly ran small shops and restaurants or drove taxis. In the opinion of one taxi driver from Sichuan expressed to this writer, 'Tibet is a good place to come to. There are fewer regulations, and we don't need a residence permit to live here.'

Standards of health and education in Tibet lag far behind most of China, despite fifty years of rule by Beijing. The infant mortality rate for women in one village survey was 12.9 per cent—four times the Chinese average. Schooling also compares poorly with most other parts of China. According to official Lhasa statistics in 2002, only 39 per cent of school-age children attend lower secondary school, with 16 per cent spending two more years at the higher level. Although primary school attendance is claimed to be 87 per cent, foreign aid workers say that the real figure may be as low as 50 per cent in poor areas, with disproportionately few girls. However, allegations of forced abortions and sterilizations in Tibet—often made by critics of Chinese rule—have not been substantiated. Families are now becoming smaller because of new economic pressures rather than compulsion, according to research by a joint US–Tibetan team published in the Australian National University's *China Journal*. Directives to limit births were frequently watered down or ignored at local levels, and fines on families who had four or even five children were usually waived. A shortage of arable land, and competition from incoming Chinese migrants, was a more powerful factor in promoting small families.[18]

In 2003 delegations representing the Dalai Lama again went to Beijing for unofficial talks, although this may have reflected growing Chinese confidence that the changes underway in Tibet were on their side. The task of any serious negotiations would be to find a formula providing genuine autonomy for Tibet which allowed the restoration of religious freedoms. This presented a double risk for Beijing. Autonomy of this kind would set a precedent elsewhere in China—particularly in neighbouring Xinjiang—while a religious revival could rekindle the movement for Tibetan independence. For the Tibetan government in exile, any substantive negotiations would also quickly lead to a difficult decision: should they abandon the claim that a settlement must apply equally to the Tibetan culture zone outside the Tibet Autonomous Region? A statement issued by the Dalai Lama in March 2004, on the thirty-fifth anniversary of the 1959 uprising, reflected the impasse:

For the past fourteen years, I have not only declared my willingness to enter into negotiations but have also made maximum concessions in a series of initiatives and proposals which clearly lie within the framework for negotiations as stated by Deng Xiaoping in 1979 that 'except for independence of Tibet, all other questions can be negotiated.' . . .

I have made it clear that the negotiations must centre around ways to end China's population transfer policy, which threatens the very survival of the Tibetan people, respect for Tibetans' fundamental human rights and entitlement to democratic freedom, the de-militarization and de-nuclearization of Tibet, the restoration of the Tibetan people's control over matters affecting their own affairs, the protection of Tibet's natural environment. Moreover, I have always emphasized that any negotiation must comprise the whole of Tibet, not just the area which China calls the 'Tibet Autonomous Region.'

I must now recognize that my approach has failed to produce any progress either for substantive negotiations or in contributing to the overall improvement of the situation in Tibet. Moreover, I am conscious of the fact that a growing number of Tibetans, both inside as well as outside Tibet, have been disheartened by my conciliatory stand not to demand complete independence for Tibet.

The Xinjiang Uighur Autonomous Region has till recently attracted far less attention although it occupies one-sixth of China's landmass and has 5,500 kilometres of international borders with eight different countries. Subject to Russian penetration in the past, and possessing large oil deposits in the Tarim Basin, it is as strategically important to China as Tibet—with which it shares the same ambiguous past of intermittent control during the imperial period. After 1949, Han Chinese population increased significantly from 6 per cent to 37 per cent four decades later, mainly through the establishment of paramilitary state farms under the Xinjiang Production and Construction Corps, but also through prison camps and other penal centres. The eight million Uighurs, the region's largest non-Chinese minority, comprise 47 per cent of the population: Beijing is concerned that their numbers are growing at a faster rate than those of the Han. Another two million people are Kazakhs or from other Central Asian backgrounds.

The 1990s saw a new burst of Han immigration as migrant workers headed north-west looking for jobs, with encouragement from the Chinese central authorities. More than 70,000 migrants moved into the city of Shihezi and surrounding farms in the single year of 1997. Many found work in state cotton farms as the area growing the crop doubled in less than a decade.

As in Tibet, many younger Uighurs had hoped to benefit from communist reforms in the 1950s, but were alienated by a mix of discriminatory policies and ultra-leftist violence. The Uighurs had suffered grievously under the Cultural Revolution when all mosques were closed and use of the Arabic script was banned. In the 1980s younger Uighurs again hoped to benefit from the post-Mao modernization drive, but instead met with discrimination in education and employment. Most Uighur schoolchildren studied in separate classes from the Han—and even played in separate sections of the school yards. Only a small number—mostly the offspring of party members or government officials—were educated in the Chinese mainstream. By the mid-1990s, Beijing acknowledged the emergence of a 'separatist threat' in Xinjiang. Many young Uighurs, frustrated by these disadvantages, were influenced by radical ideas elsewhere in the Islamic world. There were serious riots in Yining in 1997, several bombings in the capital Urumqi, and more than seventy incidents were recorded in the following year. As in Tibet, the authorities responded with a 'rectification' campaign in which many innocent people became the victims of human rights abuses, thus provoking more resistance. In 1999 Amnesty International recorded 190 executions of Uighurs in the past two years. It also protested over the bizarre imprisonment of Rebiya Kadeer, a Uighur businesswoman who had previously been praised in the Chinese press for her entrepreneurial success in founding a large trading company. Kadeer's husband worked for the US-based Radio Free Asia and she was given an eight-year jail sentence for sending him copies of the official Party newspaper the *Xinjiang Daily*: the indictment described this as 'giving information to separatists'. (Kadeer was finally released in 2005.)

The September 11 terrorist attacks in New York City were seized on by Beijing which quickly claimed that Xinjiang separatists had been 'trained by the Taliban', and used the 'war on terrorism' to claim exemption from censure for its repression in the region. Uighurs in exile protested in vain that Western media was taking the Chinese claims too much at face value. While a few still clung to the memory of the short-lived Eastern Turkestan Republic established in 1944, most ordinary Xinjiang Muslims were resigned, however unhappily, to the prospect of continued Chinese rule.[19]

Human rights and international pressure

In what has become a ritual, the US State Department, in its annual human rights country report, regularly condemns Chinese failings and China responds by denouncing the US for its own human rights violations. The curtailment of human rights in China was endemic, the State Department said in 2001, listing abuses such as 'extrajudicial killings, torture and mistreatment of prisoners, forced confessions, arbitrary arrest and detention . . .', the detention and torture of unofficial church leaders and the death in custody of scores of adherents of the banned Falun Gong sect. The Chinese State Council's Information Office replied with a paper condemning the US for 'escalating violence, unfair judicial practices, the widening gap between rich and poor, widespread gender discrimination . . .', and cited statistics on illiteracy, lack of access to social security, human trafficking, and other social ills.

In a similar ritual, conducted at the UN Commission on Human Rights in Geneva, a resolution condemning China has been tabled every year, almost always sponsored by the US. China regularly succeeds in securing a majority decision that the resolution should not be discussed. International human rights organizations complain that the US makes little effort to lobby support for its own resolution, while many Western countries refrain from co-sponsoring it in order to protect their own relations with Beijing.

More positively, China has entered into a dialogue on human rights with the international community which includes visits by UN officials, joint training and seminars on issues of legal reform, and a limited willingness to discuss individual cases. A small number of high-profile dissidents over the years have had their sentences reduced, or have been allowed to go abroad on the pretext of needing medical treatment, as a result of international pressure. However, such releases are often made for tactical purposes to defuse criticism on the eve of an important diplomatic event, and may be followed by increased repression.

The 1989 Tiananmen affair has remained an exceptionally neuralgic spot for the Chinese leadership: brave dissidents who called for it to be reappraised were punished severely and security was stepped up at every anniversary. In 1990, the entire square was sealed off, watched by a sullen crowd which had been forced back to its outer boundary. On the tenth anniversary in 1999, the square was conveniently closed for relaying and renovation. Before the fifteenth anniversary, police harassed Ding Zilin, leader of a group of 'Tiananmen mothers' who has painstakingly gathered information and sought publicity abroad on the deaths of her son and many others killed in 1989. (Her list contains the names of 155 dead and 63 wounded.) When foreign journalists have the rare opportunity to ask questions about the massacre, Chinese leaders reply in almost identical terms as in this explanation by Premier Wen Jiabao:

In the last century, at the turn of the 1980s and 1990s, drastic changes took place in the Soviet Union and countries of Eastern Europe. In China, a political disturbance occurred. At that time, the party and government of China adopted resolute measures in a timely fashion to safeguard social stability and became more determined to press ahead with China's reform and opening up.[20]

Safeguarding 'social stability' has been the mantra under which any form of human rights violation is justified, and the target of official oppression has shifted as Chinese society has changed in the decade and a half since 1989. At first the authorities focused their efforts on rounding up the alleged 'black hands' behind the pro-democracy movement who were then convicted on charges of 'counter-revolution'. Typically, trials were held before hand-picked audiences after the accused had been held incommunicado for months, their lawyers were banned from entering 'not guilty' pleas, and official media pronounced them guilty before sentence had been passed. In a typical case, marine biologist Chen Lantao, born in 1963, was sentenced to eighteen years in Qingdao, eastern China, for 'counter-revolutionary incitement and disturbing traffic order'. Outraged by the news from Beijing in June 1989, Chen had made speeches at a bus terminal in Qingdao and outside two factories denouncing the massacre. (Chen's sentence was later reduced to thirteen years and he was finally released with two years' remission in 2000.)

I was just 25 years old, full of vigour to get started in life, when this ill fortune struck me. I would make up for lost time if I get the chance to regain my freedom. The only reason I have been jailed for 18 years is that I was frank and outspoken about the June 4 massacre in Tiananmen Square. My defence counsel was going to argue that I had no counter-revolutionary aims . . . to my great distress, the court did not allow him to defend me from the basis of my innocence. (letter to Amnesty International)

Two years after Tiananmen, the US-based Asia Watch compiled a list of more than one thousand detainees identified by name, and noted that many provinces had reported arrests of several thousand unnamed individuals. Provincial courts, anxious to prove their zeal, were often harsher than those in the capital. Yu Dongyue and two other young men from Hunan province had defaced Mao's portrait in Tiananmen Square by throwing eggs at it filled with ink. A Hunan court found them guilty of 'counter-revolutionary sabotage' and gave them sentences of twenty, nineteen, and sixteen years. All subsequently spent time in solitary confinement, under conditions described by a former prisoner as 'just over two square metres in area [with] no ventilation or heating . . . and almost pitch-dark'.

The deposed Party Secretary-General Zhao Ziyang disappeared from sight after the massacre, under a form of house arrest which was sometimes relaxed but never lifted. He was occasionally seen playing golf or moving around the country, but never allowed to return to politics. Several letters were circulated unofficially in his name, including one before Preisdent Clinton's 1998 visit to China, urging his successors to admit that the 1989 suppression had been a grave mistake. Zhao's personal secretary Bao Tong was jailed for seven years for 'counter-revolutionary propaganda and incitement' and after his release provoked official wrath by continuing to call for a 'reversal of verdicts'. In a letter which Bao copied in 2000 to the UN High Commissioner for Human Rights, he described his treatment:

. . . During these twenty-two months, I have been warned eight times by agents of the Public Security Bureau. They said that my actions constituted 'endangering state security.' I was told that the reporters who interviewed me were 'punished' or were going to be 'punished.' Whenever any important political anniversaries came along, my telephone line had technical difficulties such that I would have no phone service for days.

. . . Since the beginning of the year 2000, my personal freedom has been limited and violated. Day or night, whenever I step out of my home, there are always six people closely following me. They come with me when I accompany my grand-daughter to school, and when I go to the hospital, bank or shops . . . In addition, it has long been a practice of the security agents to prevent guests from seeing me . . .

I am an old man, and I have neither fear nor illusions, but I feel obligated to confront such violation of a citizen's civil rights, even if that means my own imprisonment.

Several prominent dissidents from the pre-Tiananmen generation continued to speak out, knowing that they would risk punishment: their courage also demonstrated an essential continuity with earlier dissent. In 1996 Wang Xizhe (co-author of the 1973 'Li Yizhe' manifesto) joined literary critic Liu Xiaobo in a statement calling for the impeachment of Jiang Zemin and talks with the Dalai Lama on Tibetan autonomy. Wei Jingsheng, famous for his 1979 essay on 'Democracy: The Fifth Modernization', was rearrested in 1995 after attempting to form a political discussion group. Another Democracy Wall activist, Fu Shenqi, had earlier been sent to re-education camp for speaking to foreign journalists. By this time, the Chinese government was using exile abroad as a supplement to harsh imprisonment and as a token of 'moderation' which could also earn foreign approval. Wang fled China in circumstances which suggest that the police made no effort to stop him. Fu was allowed to leave after completing three years' detention. Wei was brutally treated in prison and then released in 1997 in response to international pressure and as a goodwill gesture after Jiang Zemin had visited Washington. The 1989 student leader Wang Dan was released into exile shortly before President Clinton's return visit in the following year. By the end of the decade most of the original dissident leaders were abroad, though there were some exceptions. Liu Xiaobo, also prominent in 1989 after serving three years for his joint manifesto with

Wang Xizhe, remained in Beijing and has written extensively on China's new society. The two chief 'black hands', Wang Juntao and Chen Ziming, identified by Beijing were released on so-called 'medical parole' in 1994 after pressure from Bill Clinton: Wang left for the US but Chen stayed in Beijing, and was returned to prison after staging a one-day protest on the 1995 Tiananmen Square anniversary.

The overall lesson of the 1990s was clear: Beijing preferred to see its dissidents living abroad where they would have little influence on the domestic scene and easily succumbed to factional arguments among themselves. Those who stayed on knew the consequences of renewed dissent. The most vocal—and the bravest—were a loosely connected group, including some veteran dissenters, who attempted to establish a China Democracy Party (CDP) in 1997–8. They took advantage of a brief political thaw, referred to optimistically as the 'Beijing Spring', after Deng's death and the Hong Kong handover, during which the Jiang Zemin regime made several gestures—which included its decision to sign the International Covenant for Civil and Political Rights—to create international goodwill.

The CDP founding members issued their first 'open declaration' in Hangzhou on the eve of the Clinton visit, hoping to take advantage of the democratic breeze which the US president briefly brought to China. Their manifesto declared that 'a government can only come into being according to the wishes of the public. . . . A government is the servant of the public and not the one which controls it.' Although their leader, Tiananmen activist Wang Youcai, was soon arrested, CDP members in several provinces flummoxed the authorities at first by applying for official approval. However, Beijing soon issued instructions that the CDP was an 'illegal organisation' and launched a crackdown. With nonchalant disregard for international concern, Li Peng himself declared that 'if [a group] is designed to negate the leadership of the Communist Party, then it will not be allowed to exist'. This was followed by two waves of arrests: Wang Youcai was sentenced to eleven years in jail: his 'crimes' included seeking to hold a CDP meeting under the pretext of a tea party. After more harsh sentences had been handed down, Jiang Zemin reiterated Li Peng's hard line against 'subversive and splittist activities by international and domestic hostile forces'.[21]

Yet the growing diversity of Chinese society in the 1990s, as the socialist ethic faded while market forces gained power, created new challenges to the Party's authority. This may partly explain its overreaction in the case of the

Falun Gong sect, banned in 1999, whose members were cruelly persecuted and attracted sympathy from abroad. Religious and mystical sects had gained ground in the early 1990s: people talked of a 'religion fever' which took many forms. Heterodox religious sects—Christian, Buddhist, and Daoist—which had re-emerged in the previous decade grew in numbers, particularly in disadvantaged rural areas, and also suffered persecution. In urban China, many people turned towards spiritual health cults in what became known as a 'Qigong [art of qi] fever'. The qi represents the body's vital energy which according to its practitioners can be harnessed by physical or mental exercises. Chinese army leaders were intrigued by the possibility of utilising its apparent paranormal powers, and stories circulated that even Deng Xiaoping had been impressed by the performance of popular qigong 'masters'. One such performer, Zhang Baosheng, was said to have staged a demonstration in which he moved a pair of jade balls from one room to another: the former general Wang Zhen expressed the hope that Zhang could one day 'steal some nuclear secrets for us from the Russians or Americans'.

The Falun Gong sect was founded in north-east China by Li Hongzhi, a 40-year-old grain store clerk who had previously played the trumpet in an army band. Mr Li claimed to have learnt his art from a Buddhist master at an early age: when he was eight years old he 'already understood the past and future of the human race'. Like other Masters, he taught a combination of spiritual meditation and breathing: he also propounded a philosophy which borrowed from the more mystical elements of Buddhism and Daoism. The exercises were supposed to enable the practitioner to cultivate his or her Falun (wheel of law). Installed in the lower abdomen, this rotated clockwise and absorbed energy from the universe.[22]

In common with other popular cults in the 'religion fever', the Falun Gong was financed by contributions paid by the faithful to attend the Master's lectures or to buy his publications. But Li had higher ambitions than other self-styled 'masters' which led him into trouble. He altered the date of his birthday to coincide with that of Buddha (though he claimed to be merely adjusting an erroneous record), and his teachings assumed an increasingly messianic tone. Unwisely, he withdrew from the state-sponsored Qigong association (perhaps in a dispute over finance) and quarrelled with some of his own disciples. Concerned by the spread of a sect now operating outside the bounds of official control, the authorities banned several of its publications and encouraged criticism of it in the media. The Falun movement was also unusual in its militant response to interference from the state:

this was perhaps partly because its membership included a number of mostly retired Party officials. In April 1999 Falun Gong protestors picketed a magazine in Tianjin which had published a critical article: several of the protestors were arrested. Li had emigrated to the US but returned secretly to China and (although he later denied responsibility) appears to have ordered a much larger demonstration in Beijing. Several thousand of the faithful mounted a silent picket around the Zhongnanhai on 25 April, alarming the regime and infuriating Jiang Zemin whose limousine had to drive to his office through the demonstrators. Three months later the movement was banned as an 'evil cult' and a warrant issued for the arrest of Master Li— who claimed that the ban had been predicted by the sixteenth-century French astrologer Nostradamus.

Police and other authorities throughout China acted with special zeal in implementing a ban which had the personal authority of the president. Local neighbourhood and street committees pressurized known believers to recant: many who refused to do so were sent to labour camp. Falun Gong activists were prosecuted on retrospective charges of having organized a heretical cult or written material for it. From New York Master Li urged his faithful to resist: on the first anniversary of the ban, sect members appeared on successive days in Tiananmen Square, unfurling banners and trying to practise ritual meditation. Most were middle-aged and some called out 'Falun Gong is good' as they were dragged along the ground and shoved into police vans. Master Li wrote a poem to rally the spirits of his followers, part of which read 'With the teacher (Li) at the helm, the Fa (law) saves all beings; one sail is hoisted, 100 million sails follow.'

Beijing's overreaction alienated many Chinese people who had no particular sympathy for the Falun Gong and stimulated opposition abroad. In March 2000 Amnesty International reported that

Tens of thousands of Falun Gong practitioners have been arbitrarily detained by police, some of them repeatedly for short periods, and put under pressure to renounce their beliefs. Many of them are reported to have been tortured or ill-treated in detention. Some practitioners have been detained in psychiatric hospitals. Those who have spoken out publicly about the persecution of practitioners since the ban have suffered harsh reprisals . . . According to Chinese official sources, by late November 1999, at least 150 people, officially described as 'key' members of the Falun Gong, had been charged with crimes. . . . In addition, hundreds, possibly thousands, of other practitioners have been assigned, without charge or trial, to serve terms of 'administrative' detention in forced labour camps for up to three years. Unfair trials have continued and arrests and detentions of practitioners continue to be reported every day.

Entering the world

The Chinese phrase for joining the World Trade Organization—which finally took place in December 2001—was *rushi* or 'entering the world'. After more than twenty years of economic reform and 'opening up', China had completed the journey from which it had been previously excluded by US isolation plus Maoist chauvinism. The *People's Daily* (13 November 2001) hailed it as 'a major historic event', the biggest revolution since 1949, a triumph for Chinese diplomacy—and for Jiang Zemin:

Joining the WTO is a major strategic decision taken by the Central Committee of the Communist Party of China and the State Council after making a correct assessment of the situation and taking a broad and long-term view about the matter. It fully demonstrates the farsightedness of the third generation collective leadership with Comrade Jiang Zemin at the core who assume responsibility for controlling the whole situation and advance with the time, and their firm confidence in deepening reform and expanding opening, it also fully displays China's active posture in conforming to the trend of economic globalization and actively participating in international competition and co-operation. Over the past 15 years, the tremendous achievements gained in China's reform and opening up have provided condition and possibility for China's participating in the multilateral trading system; China's unremitting efforts for joining the WTO have also forcefully promoted the whole process of China's reform and opening up.

But officials were at pains to warn that China would not have an easy transition: there would have to be radical changes to commerce, agriculture, and the legal system. 'Most people in the cities just hope that prices of imported goods will get cheaper,' a WTO researcher in Shanghai said. 'Everyone's waiting for the day when they can buy a car. They don't think about what the effect may be on workers' jobs or on peasants in the countryside.'

Beijing hoped that more investment and more exports would flow from WTO membership, as foreign manufacturers were lured by cheap labour and the country's vast internal market. In return, China is meant to open up its financial, retail, and telecommunications markets during the following five years and to cut tariffs. Beijing also hoped that WTO entry will force a massive shake-up in inefficient state industries, announcing a plan for fifty new state-owned companies to seek capital overseas and compete in the world market. 'China has a lot of work to do: government and industry will have to learn new rules,' said Tong Zhiguang, one of the chief negotiators for WTO membership. 'We have obligations to honour as well as rights to enjoy. Companies will have to meet world standards: it won't be enough just to cut prices.'[23]

Foreign banks would be allowed to conduct domestic yuan business without restrictions within five years, and foreign insurers would be able to operate freely within the same period. The move was expected to shake up China's inefficient banking sector and to provide foreign know-how for insurance and the securities business. Oil quotas would be scrapped and foreign companies able to set up their own petrol stations. Foreign department stores, till then operating in a grey legal area, would be freed from restrictions. The agreement would phase out Chinese tariffs in sectors such as the automobile industry where cheap, low-quality, domestically produced cars are expected to suffer from competition. Telecom charges, till then among the highest in Asia, were expected to fall.

Economist Hu Angang offered a long-term prediction of the kind to make Chinese nationalist hearts swell with pride. If China maintained its post-1980 rate of development it would 'catch up with the US in terms of total GDP' in the next two decades, and its total trade volume will only be slightly lower than that of the US. The forecast was predicated on China developing 'without social unrest, a split in the country, or major mistakes in important economic decisions'. However, Hu spoke for a strong body of technocratic opinion which has no doubt that entry to the WTO—described by him as the world's 'economic Olympics'—is essential for China.

The world needs China and China needs the world even more. The long-term advantages of a liberal trade system and more-transparent market competition to China's economy will far surpass the short-term cost adjustments of open trade.[24]

The vision was shared by the new generation of young professionals, many of them trained abroad or working for foreign companies, who already regarded themselves as part of a global community. 'The WTO is only a symbol for the change that China is making,' said a high-flying MBA student at the China–Europe International Business School in Shanghai: 'Every industry will have to compete globally, and human resources will also become part of the market. We know we have to fight for our jobs: that is why we are here.' Some hoped for a political dividend: 'The threat of unrest is there, but WTO entry will help the system change faster, politically and socially. It will be a good way to anchor China to the world,' said another student.

It was admitted that many people, particularly in the rural areas, would suffer in the short term. 'China's [agricultural] producers will be major losers,' said an official Chinese summary of losses and gains. 'Tariff cuts and freer imports will mean domestic grains like corn and soybeans must compete with higher quality imports. Cheaper meat imports will threaten the domestic livestock industry.' Even the popular lychee fruit grown in southern China, would be threatened by earlier-maturing crops from south-east Asia. Premier Zhu Rongji, who had brought the fifteen-year long negotiations to a successful conclusion, also acknowledged the dangers of an unequal contest between mainland agriculture, where the average farm size is just half a hectare, and the vast expanses of US agribusiness, backed up by extensive farming in countries such as Argentina and Brazil. However, pro-WTO modernizers regarded entry as a lever which would open the long-blocked door to further agricultural reform, as Zhu spelled out to the 2002 National People's Congress (NPC):

We need to adopt measures that conform to the WTO rules and effectively safeguard the interests of Chinese farmers. We should increase investment in agriculture and rural infrastructure to improve production and living conditions in the countryside and the ecological environment there. Emphasis should be placed on support for projects of water-conserving irrigation, drinking water, production and use of marsh gas, hydroelectric power generation, rural road building, and grazing land fencing. Support for agriculture should be strengthened in the fields of agroscientific research, dissemination of agricultural techniques, prevention and control of plant diseases, pest control, information consulting and farmer training . . .

Only a few voices managed to challenge the pro-entry consensus, although they spoke for millions more who would never be heard. The popular press had for some years given space to complaints from the emerging consumers' lobby (sometimes covertly backed by Chinese companies) that foreign producers were dumping substandard goods or providing poor after-sales service. Such complaints often had a strong anti-Japanese or anti-US tinge. In 1997 a department store in Haikou, capital of Hainan island, 'removed all Sony products from its shelves when the nearest Sony branch refused to replace a burnt-out TV tube within the officially prescribed three-year warranty period'. At a demonstration in Guangzhou against the US bombing of China's Belgrade Embassy in 1999, one placard read 'I'd rather die of thirst than drink Coca-Cola; I'd rather starve to death than eat McDonald's.' Foreign manufacturers found ways to defuse such crude protests: Chinese instead of Western models were used to advertise foreign lingerie; fast-food chains 'sinified' their décor and even some menu items; brand names of electronic goods were changed to sound indigenous.[25]

Outright opposition to WTO entry—against the official Party line—had more difficulty in securing media attention. Economist Han Deqiang, one of the few critics to find a publisher (and labelled as a 'leftist' for his views) complained of the imbalance:

China's mainstream media pour all their enthusiasm to praise WTO . . . But no voice from businesses directly faced with international competition appears on media . . . Although these small businesses feel vaguely the threat from foreign goods, they have little information about the whole situation, no organization, and no representation in political affairs.

Most big enterprises still belong to the state, leaders of which are appointed by central or local government, and don't bear final responsibility of the enterprises. If the government is dedicated to join in WTO, they will raise their hands automatically. For the sake of personal income, these leaders will have the possibility to enjoy as high salary as their foreign counterparts, which far outweighs their concern for the overall interest of the enterprises.[26]

The growers of tobacco, soya, fruit, peanuts, even everyday vegetables, who now faced more foreign competition, had even more difficulty in getting heard. Only one Chinese newspaper reported a campaign launched by Greenpeace in Hong Kong, in collaboration with Shanghai agronomists, against a patent claim by the international agribusiness Monsanto for a molecular marker in wild soya beans which had originated in China.[27]

China had, after all, joined the world and there was no going back. It was more than half a century since Mao Zedong, seeking (without success) US support in the coming civil war with Chiang Kai-shek, had held out the tempting prospect of China's potential market. 'America needs an export market for her heavy industry and these specialized manufactures. She also needs an outlet for capital investment,' he told the American diplomat John S. Service in 1945.[28] Mao had lived long enough to see the American economic blockade lifted and China able to open the door to Western goods and finance. Mao did not spell out the advantage this would give China in time to turn the tables and dominate the world market, but he would have appreciated the dialectical logic. Perhaps after all the Chairman would not have been so dismayed to see China, a quarter of a century after his death, 'enter the world' and exploit its own labour market to engage in global competition, but he would have warned that the struggle was far from over.

China was always too complex a society to allow for any definitive summing up of its current state, or for any reliable forecast of its future trajectory, but because our knowledge of what was happening in the decades of isolation was so limited it was tempting to try to do both. Now with better access at all levels to a society which has grown even more complex, and with China scholarship no longer subject to the distortions (whether pro or anti) imposed by the cold war, we are less likely to risk simple conclusions. The same goes for the Chinese themselves: it is almost impossible to find anyone on or outside the mainland who will offer any confident prediction if asked where China may be heading. Outside concern with this question has also been overshadowed in the first decade of the new millennium by mounting catastrophes elsewhere, particularly in the Middle East, which in journalistic terms have most of the time driven the Beijing dateline a long way down the news list. China's appeal is diminished too because it appears to be (and to some extent actually is) less 'different from us' than before. This process of what might be called 'de-sinicisation' gathered pace dramatically in the decade after Deng Xiaoping's second reform initiative in the early 1990s. It was speeded by new technologies (the mobile phone and, later, the internet), by the spread of Western or pan-Asian consumer values (fast food and soft furnishings), by a new migration of 'educated youth' to study abroad and then return home, by the success of China's export-led manufacturing industry and its entry into the WTO, and less obviously but crucially by the Communist Party's ideological shift away from socialist goals (however flawed in practice) towards capitalism or something very like it.

Nevertheless the question of 'Whither China?' which has been raised at critical moments over the past century is still as important and perhaps even more so. China, with the world's largest population and fastest growing economy, is in rapid transition from the status of a developing to a developed country, however uneven the process. Deprived in the 1950s and 1960s of the opportunity to play its legitimate international role, it was then slow to seize the opportunity when it became possible, but has now become a much more significant actor on the world stage. Its relationship with the US will become critical as China acquires yet more economic and military strength and the potential to oppose more effectively the frequently over-bearing policies of the world's sole superpower. The model of development which China provides to the developing countries is very different from the 'self-reliant' alternative it presented in the past, but allowing for disparities of size it is still worth their study. China also has an opportunity, in spite of or indeed because of its headlong rush to modernization, to learn from the huge mistakes that the advanced economies of the world have already made, and to pay more respect to the protection of the environment and to main-taining established structures of society. Finally for all the rapid changes of the past decade and a half, Chinese civilization still retains many of its previous characteristics, presenting at its best a set of values in which the quest for harmony, a respect for human sensibility, and a profound historical awareness all offer lessons to be learnt.

None of this is going to happen if the doomsday predictions of China's future turn out to be correct and if, in their language, this vast nation 'collapses' or 'falls apart'. My own view, argued in this book both explicitly (in Chapter 1) and implicitly in the way that I have presented China's modern evolution, is that there will not be such a disintegration unless it is part of a much larger process such as widespread environmental disaster. The analogies with the past which cite inter-dynastic interregnums, peasant rebellions, and warlord separatism are now anachronistic. China's strong sense of national unity (at least in China proper excluding the minority provinces on the periphery) is now reinforced by vastly improved physical connections and social mobility and there is no space left for 'independent kingdoms' such as those of the 1920s and—in a less obvious form—during the upheavals of the 1960s.

I am aware that we—those observing China from outside who, however well informed, are looking through what I have called a 'sliding door' which can be passed through but still presents a barrier—have often got the task of predicting China's future spectacularly wrong. Few believed that Mao Zedong would sweep up the country as rapidly as was achieved in the civil war. Even fewer foresaw the radical shift to the Great Leap Forward or the rapid escalation of the Sino-Soviet dispute. The Cultural Revolution was a baffling phenomenon at first and yet we also failed to anticipate how quickly and thoroughly it would be repudiated after Mao's death. To complete the list, Richard Nixon's opening to China took nearly everyone by surprise. Some of these failures can be explained—the last in particular—by the pernicious influence of the cold war agenda on Western attempts to understand China—but it is still not a record of which to be collectively proud.

I still believe that China is now in a very different situation from the era when, as Mao observed with a fair degree of chronological accuracy, one could expect 'a great upheaval to occur every six or seven years'. The weakest and most worrying area, which imposes a necessary caveat on any confident prediction, is the inability of the political superstructure to evolve in pace with the nation's rapid economic and social transformation. Too often the machinery of state repression still operates with its traditional clumsiness and cruelty, and while no one expects China to adopt Western democracy, the refusal to allow even partially democratic elections above the village level is unnecessarily restrictive. All thinking Chinese (many of whom are now willing to talk in public on such matters), and most Party officials (who will only talk in private), agree that China has to move forward if not to a pluralistic democracy then to a greatly modified system in which the 'ruling party' seeks its mandate from the public and submits to genuine scrutiny of its behaviour and performance, especially over the crucial issue of corruption. Yet decades of centralized rule have created too many vested interests in preserving the Party (and its affiliated organizations) as a bastion of privilege, where the fortunate can now enjoy much larger economic rewards than before, and where it is always safer to be inactive than to take the initiative. In many areas outside that of formal institutions the political climate has improved markedly: there is more scope for discussion of sensitive subjects and more room, though still circumscribed, to organize social activities and protest. Huge quantities of information and argument circulate compared with the past, and determined journalists are pushing to the limits and beyond. There are reasonable grounds to hope for further progress under the new leadership—representing the first post-revolutionary generation—chosen in 2003 and headed by Hu Jintao and Wen Jiabao, especially after the final retirement a year later of Jiang Zemin. While there is still a tendency to revert to default positions of intransigence if national sovereignty or the primacy of Party rule is seen to be under threat, the new leaders appear more aware of the need to bridge social divisions, to tackle environmental blight, to tackle bureaucratic obscurantism and encourage more open communication. Admittedly this progress is fragile but the best hope is that the current leadership will keep moving slowly forward while the real China of 1.3 billion people continues to evolve and until another more decisive generation of leaders will emerge.

This is an undramatic scenario which is more credible in my view than any of the doomsday alternatives but it cannot be an excuse for inaction. For the longer that the leadership marks time, the greater the risk of the unknown. The main threats are likely to come less from political unrest than from the deteriorating environment which is visible now even to the casual visitor and from the uncertainties of the world trade system on which the health of the Chinese economy increasingly depends. There is always a danger too of international conflict particularly over the unsolved issue of Taiwan for which outside powers also share historical responsibility. Nuclear problems in the region, with continuing tension in the Korean peninsula and US plans for an East Asian system of missile defence, add another dangerous area of uncertainty. For all these reasons we may conclude that China and its leadership have a window of opportunity in the immediate years ahead through which they can move safely, but that an unexpected storm could blow it shut at any time.

By the middle of the first decade of the new millennium, China's government and people can look forward to an array of red and black letter dates which symbolize both the successes and weaknesses of this hugely important and increasingly diverse society. The year 2008 will see the staging of the XXIXth Olympics in Beijing—an event greeted with national rejoicing when the venue was awarded by the International Olympics Committee seven years earlier. It was the first time that spontaneous crowds had headed for Tiananmen Square since 1989, and was in sharp contrast to China's failure, a decade earlier, to secure the Asian Games. Yet the Olympics will be a serious test for the new, new China in several significant ways. In a city chronically short of water and often choked by vehicular pollution, it will be a practical test of China's ability to tackle the growing environmental challenge. Nor will it pass the test simply by, as in the past, banning traffic and closing down local industries for the duration of the Games. It may also have become clear whether the prospect of the Olympics has compelled China to significantly improve its human rights record, as many foreign advocates of the award to Beijing argued, or whether, to the contrary, awkward dissent will once again be swept off the street or banished to the countryside.

Soon after the Olympics the final stage of the Three Gorges Dam is scheduled to be completed when the reservoir is filled to its highest level. By the end of the decade the railway line from Golmud to Lhasa which scales the heights of the frozen Tibetan plateau is also scheduled for completion.

Both projects are feats of engineering and symbols of a continuing belief, based in the Maoist past, that 'human beings can triumph over nature'. Yet they also raise difficult questions both at a technological and political level: Will the dam wreak unanticipated damage on the water systems of the middle Yangtze River? Will the engineers manage to build the railway across the permafrost as successfully as they claim, and if so what will be the environmental cost? The human cost of both projects remains to be calculated too. More than a million residents in the new reservoir area upstream will have been relocated, many of them hundreds of miles from their homes, while the railway will accelerate the colonization of Tibet with Chinese migrants and their values.

A year before the Olympics, the Communist Party will hold its Seventeenth Congress at which the leadership of Hu Jintao and Wen Jiabao chosen in 2002 will doubtless declare that China has made great progress in the past five years and will seek a second term of office. Will this be merely a formality, or will the Party have moved at last in the direction of at least some degree of internal democracy? Will a new echelon of leaders have begun to emerge, holding out some promise of breaking the routine bureaucratic mould? Hu and Wen will be judged (whether or not the Chinese people have an opportunity to express their views) by their success or failure in tackling corruption, unemployment, the income gap, in improving health services and education, and minimizing the downside of China's entry into the WTO. Another important yardstick will be the progress made in curbing the growth of the HIV-AIDS virus which according to some estimates could reach 20–30 million cases by the end of the decade. The 2007 Congress will also mark nearly sixty years of the rule of the Communist Party—a considerable achievement in spite of the cold war and Western hostility in the earlier years, and the tragic and largely self-inflicted disasters inspired by Mao later on. Most recently under Deng and Jiang it has carried out the remarkable manoeuvre of switching tracks from the socialist to the capitalist road. It is an epic story and there is much more to come.

Notes

1. The new 'New China'

1. Xie Chuntao, quoted in John Gittings, 'Lichee economics', *Guardian*, 4 July 2001.

2. On state capitalism, etc. see Nigel Harris, *The Mandate of Heaven: Marx and Mao in Modern China* (London: Quartet, 1978); Jean C. Oi, 'Fiscal reform and the economic foundations of local state corporatism in China', *World Politics*, 45/1 99–126.

3. Liu Xiaobo, 'The rise of civil society in China', *China Rights Forum*, no. 3 (2003). See also Wang Yizhou, 'Civil society in China: concept and reality', *Global Thinknet* (Tokyo: Japan Center for International Exchange, n.d.).

4. Wen Jiabao, speech at Harvard University, 10 Dec. 2003.

5. Wang Meng, talk to Transnational China Project (http://www.ruf.rice.edu/~tnchina/) at Rice University, 11 Mar. 1998.

6. Colin Mackerras, *Western Images of China* (Hong Kong: Oxford University Press, 1999), 183.

7. Robert Kapp, speech at Xiamen Investment Fair, *People's Daily*, 9 Sept. 2003.

8. Gordon Chang, 'Chang's reply, China's critical moment', *China Brief*, 1/8 (Jamestown Foundation), 25 Oct. 2001.

9. Minxin Pei, 'Is China unstable?', *CERN Web Notes*, no. 11 (July 1999) (Carnegie Endowment for International Peace).

10. Liu Qing, 'Human rights, democracy and China', *Journal of International Affairs* (New York: Columbia University), 49/2 (Winter 1996).

11. Li Junru, speech of 15 July 2002 to conference at People's University (author's notes).

12. Deng Xiaoping quoted in Lena Sun, 'China's peasants hit back: rising rural unrest alarms Beijing', *Washington Post*, 21 June 1993; Hu Angang et al., 'Sounding the alarm: the social instability behind the economic prosperity', *Strategy and Management* (Beijing) (Apr. 2002); Chen Guide and Wu Chuntao, *Zhongguo Nongmin diaocha* [*A Report on the Conditions of China's Peasants*] (Beijing, 2003).

13. Shalendra D. Sharma, 'Stability amidst turmoil: China and the Asian financial crisis', *Harvard Asia Quarterly* (Winter 2000).

14. Feng Jianhua, 'Energy crisis?', *Beijing Review*, 47/3 (15 Jan. 2004); Wang Yichao, 'China's energy woes', *Caijing English newsletter* (online), 10 Dec. 2003.

15. Shanghai conference on poverty reduction: Jonathan Watts, 'Chinese lesson in how to put food in the mouths of millions', *Guardian*, 27 May 2004.

2. Search for Socialism

1. North-west China Party propaganda dept., *Gongchandangyuan biaozhun de baxiang tiaojian tongsu jianghua* [*Eight Popular Lectures for a Model Communist*] (Xian: North-west People's Press, 1952).

2. E. H. Carr, *The Bolshevik Revolution 1917–1923*, i (Harmondsworth: Penguin, 1966), 238–56; Carr (ed.), *Bukharin and Preobrazhensky: The ABC of Communism* (Harmondsworth: Penguin, 1969), 16–17.

3. On Kang Youwei and Mao, see Frederic Wakeman, *History and Will* (Berkeley and Los Angeles: Univ. of California Press, 1973), 99–102. Mozi's text in Joseph Needham, *Science and Civilisation in China*, ii (Cambridge: Cambridge Univ. Press, 1956), 167–8.

4. Soong Ching Ling (Song Jingling), 'Shanghai's new day has dawned', 26 May 1950, in *The Struggle for New China* (Beijing: Foreign Languages Press, 1952), 245–9.

5. Shirley Wood, *A Street in China* (London: Michael Joseph, 1958), 175.

6. For everyday life in the early 1950s see Ralph and Nancy Lapwood, *Through the Chinese Revolution* (London: People's Books Co-operative Society, 1954); Rewi Alley, *You Banfa!* (Beijing: Foreign Languages Press, 1952); Wilfred Burchett, *China's Feet Unbound* (Melbourne: World Unity Publishers, 1952).

7. Chin Chao-yang, *Village Sketches* (Beijing: Foreign Languages Press, 1957), 169–71.

8. Hu Yu-chih, 'Publications that serve the people', *People's China*, 16 Dec. 1952.

9. Yudin's appointment is described in Wu Xiuquan, *Eight Years in the Ministry of Foreign Affairs* (Beijing: New World Press, 1985), 40.

10. On Five-Year Plan see Mark Selden, *The People's Republic of China: A Documentary History of Revolutionary Change* (New York: Monthly Review Press, 1979), pt. 1.

11. Chen Han-seng, *China Reconstructs* (Beijing), no. 10 (1955).

12. William Hinton, *Fanshen* (London: Secker and Warburg, 1983), 161–3.

13. Michael Schoenhals, 'Original contradictions—on the unrevised text of Mao Zedong's "On the correct handling of contradictions among the people" ', *Australian Journal of Chinese Affairs*, no. 16 (July 1986).

14. Hsiao Ch'ien (Xiao Qian), *Traveller Without a Map* (London: Hutchinson, 1990), 191.

15. Alan Winnington, *Breakfast with Mao* (London: Lawrence and Wishart, 1986), 180.

16. For Mao Zedong on Confucius, see *Selected Works*, (Beijing: Foreign Languages Press, 1977), v. 273–4; for his 'study tour', see ibid. 222.

17. The 'poor and blank' metaphor was first used in 1955; see *Mao Zedong sixiang wansui* [*Long Live Chairman Mao Thought*] (Beijing, 1969), 34.

18. Zhou Libo, *Great Changes in a Mountain Village* (Beijing: Foreign Languages Press, 1961), 220–1.

19. Mao's editorial notes to *Socialist Upsurge in China's Countryside* (1957), 250 included the reference to 'demons and monsters'.

20. Reports on water conservancy campaign in *Peking Review*, 4 Mar. and 1 Apr. 1958.

21. *Songs of the Red Flag*, compiled by the scholars Guo Moruo and Zhou Yang (Beijing: Foreign Languages Press, 1961), 88.

22. 'The Girl Checker', *Peking Review*, 13 May 1958.

23. 'Greatness from small beginnings', trans. in *Peking Review*, 3 June 1958.

24. For Chen Boda on 'brand-new man', see *Hong Qi [Red Flag]*, no. 3 (1958); on the 'primary unit', see ibid. no. 7 (1958) (also probably by Chen). Chen's significant role is discussed in Roderick MacFarquhar, *The Origins of the Cultural Revolution*, ii (Oxford: Oxford University Press, 1983), 78–82.

25. For the Anhui photograph, see Ministry of Agriculture, *People's Communes in Pictures* (Beijing, 1960).

26. Wang Meng, 'The Barber's Tale', *Chinese Literature* (July 1980).

27. Passages cited from Mao's *Notes* are found in Moss Roberts, *A Critique of Soviet Economics* (New York: Monthly Review Press, 1977), sections 14, 23, 25, 29, 32, 41, 43, 49, 66.

28. Su Shaozhi, *Democratization and Reform* (Nottingham: Spokesman, 1988), 108.

29. *Nine Critiques*, trans. as *The Polemic on the General Line of the International Communist Movement* (Beijing: Foreign Languages Press, 1965).

30. Quotations from fifteen-point statement, 'On Khrushchev's phoney Communism and its historical lessons for the world', ibid. 441–2, 471, 478.

3. Mao Zedong versus the Party

1. The leadership clashes of 1967 are summarized in an important study of Party history since 1949 published by the Central Committee documentary research office, *Guanyu jianguo yilai dang de ruogan lishi wenti de jueyi: zhushi ben [Explanatory Volume on the [1981] Resolution on Several Questions in the History of the Party since 1949]* (Beijing: People's Press, 1985), 406–11.

2. Edgar Snow, *The Long Revolution* (Harmondsworth: Penguin, 1974), 18; Yan Jiaqi and Gao Gao (his wife), *Zhongguo 'Wen Ge' shinian shi [History of the Ten Years' 'Cultural Revolution']*, 2 vols. (Hong Kong: Dagongbao, 1987).

3. Robert Payne, *China Awake* (London: Heinemann, 1947), 326–7; Edgar Snow, *Journey to the Beginning* (New York: Vintage, 1972), 166–7.

4. Theodore White, *Thunder out of China* (New York: Sloan, 1946), 230. For the early cult of Mao see Raymond Wylie, *The Emergence of Maoism* (Stanford: Stanford Univ. Press, 1980), ch. 8. Mao's cult in the late 1950s is discussed on pp. 462–8 of the 1985 Party research volume cited in n. 1, above.

5. Mao Zedong, *Selected Works*, v. 141.

6. ibid. 344–5.

7. Wang Meng, 'The Young Man who has just arrived at the Organization

Department', trans. in Kai-yu Hsu, *Literature of the People's Republic of China* (Bloomington, Ind.: Indiana Univ. Press, 1980).

8. Liu Binyan, 'On the Bridge Site', ibid. (Liu recalled its fate in a famous speech to the 1979 Writers' Congress).

9. Quoted in Chi Hsin, *Teng Hsiao-ping* (Hong Kong: Cosmos, 1978), 80–1.

10. Quoted by *People's Daily*, 16 May 1986.

11. The Foreign Ministry takeover is described in K. S. Karol, *The Second Chinese Revolution* (London: Cape, 1975), 267–9; the junior diplomats' complaint is in *Survey of the Chinese Mainland Press* (Hong Kong: US Consulate-General), no. 4004.

12. Jiang Qing, speech of 12 Apr. 1967, *Hongse Wenyi* [*Red Literature and Art*] (Beijing), 20 May 1967.

13. Deng Xiaoping, *Selected Works, 1975–1982* (Beijing: Foreign Languages Press, 1984), 329–30.

14. *People's Daily*, 6 Jan. 1986.

15. Percy and Lucy Fang, *Zhou Enlai: A Profile* (Beijing: Foreign Languages Press, 1986), p. 134.

16. Zhou Enlai, *Selected Works* (Beijing: Foreign Languages Press, 1900), i. 370–2.

17. See n. 1, above.

18. Quoted in Chi Hsin, *Teng Hsiao-ping*, 54–64.

19. Chi Hsin, *The Case of the Gang of Four* (Hong Kong: Cosmos, 1977), 146–8.

20. Yan Jiaqi and Gao Gao, *Zhongguo 'Wen Ge'*, ii. 507–10.

4. The Rebel Alternative

1. Documents on Chen Lining in *Survey of the China Mainland Press (Supplement)*, no. 225; ibid. no. 4159; *BBC Summary of World Broadcasts, iii. The Far East*, no. 2765. Chen's case is discussed in Robin Munro, 'Judicial psychiatry in China and its political abuses', *Columbia Journal of Asian Law*, 14/1 (Spring 2000), 30–1.

2. For a discussion of Red Guard rhetoric, see Elizabeth J. Perry and Li Xun, 'Revolutionary rudeness: The language of red guards and rebel workers in China's Cultural Revolution', *Indiana East-Asian Working Paper Series on Language and Politics in Modern China*, no. 2 (July 1993), 1–18.

3. Stuart Schram, *Political Thought of Mao Tse-tung* (Harmondsworth: Penguin, 1969), 152–60.

4. Li Jui, *The Early Revolutionary Activities of Comrade Mao Tse-tung* (New York: M. E. Sharpe, 1977), 30, 84–5; Mao's Hunan report, in Schram, *Political Thought of Mao*, 250–9.

5. E. J. Hobsbawm, *Social Bandits and Primitive Rebels* (Glencoe: Free Press, 1959).

6. Jean Chesneaux, *Peasant Revolts in China 1840–1949* (London: Thames and Hudson, 1973), 21.

7. Quoted in John Gittings, *Role of the Chinese Army* (London: Oxford Univ. Press, 1967), 66–7.

8. Rewi Alley, *Man Against Flood* (Beijing: New World Press, 1956); Lapwood, *Through the Chinese Revolution*, ch. 6.

9. Reports of the revival of 'evil tendencies' are documented in C. S. Chen (ed.), *Rural People's Communes in Lien-Chiang* (Stanford: Hoover Institution, 1969).

10. Gu Hua, *A Small Town Called Hibiscus* (Beijing: Panda Books, 1983), 16–17.

11. 'The Gourmet' in Lu Wenfu, *A World of Dreams* (Beijing: Panda Books, 1986), 136.

12. Rene Goldman, 'Rectification campaign at Peking University', *China Quarterly* (London: School of Oriental and African Studies), no. 12.

13. Dennis Doolin, *Communist China: The Politics of Student Opposition* (Stanford: Hoover Institution, 1964), 27, 34–50. Imprisoned 1958–83, Lin recalled her experiences in *Lin Xiling zixuanji [Lin Xiling's Selection]* (Hong Kong: Wide Angle, 1985).

14. Yue Daiyun and Carolyn Wakeman, *To the Storm* (Berkeley and Los Angeles: Univ. of Calif. Press, 1985), 120–1, 155.

15. Anna Louise Strong, *Letter from Peking*, no. 49, 30 May 1967.

16. On Red Guard movement, see John and Elsie Collier, *China's Socialist Revolution* (London: Stage 1, 1973), 87–92; Jean Daubier, *A History of the Chinese Cultural Revolution* (New York: Vintage, 1974), 70–87; Karol, *Second Chinese Revolution*; Michael Schoenhals (ed.), *China's Cultural Revolution, 1966–1969* (New York: M. E. Sharpe, 1996); Elizabeth J. Perry and Li Xun, *Proletarian Power: Shanghai in the Cultural Revolution* (Boulder, Colo.: Westview Press, 1997); among many others.

17. The Shanghai Commune is discussed at length in Karol, *Second Chinese Revolution*, pt. 3.

18. On the *Shengwulian* and the principal author of its manifesto, see Klaus Mehnert, *Peking and the New Left* (Berkeley: Center for Chinese Studies, 1969); Jonathan Unger, 'Whither China?: Yang Xiguang, red capitalists, and the social turmoil of the Cultural Revolution', *Modern China*, 17/1 (Jan. 1991), 3–37; Yang Xiguang and Susan McFadden, *Captive Spirits: Prisoners of the Cultural Revolution* (Oxford: Oxford University Press, 1998).

5. Second Cultural Revolution

1. *Liaoning Daily*, 23 Apr. 1975.

2. Mao's talk with Red Guards, 28 July 1968, in *Miscellany of Mao Tse-tung Thought* (Arlington: JPRS, 1974), ii. 469–96.

3. The 'revenge cannibalism' carried out at the height of the factional violence (mid-1968) in Wuxuan and several other Guangxi counties was researched by the poet Zheng Yi who managed to acquire internal Party documents detailing the events. It is still officially denied by the Chinese authorities. Zheng Yi, *Scarlet Memorial: Tales of Cannibalism in Modern China* (Boulder, Colo.: Westview Press, 1996); John Gittings, *Real China: From Cannibalism to Karaoke* (London: Simon and Schuster, 1996), ch. 8.

4. Peter Worsley, *Inside China* (London: Allen Lane, 1975), 248; Karol, *Second Chinese Revolution*, 141–2; John Gittings, 'Pine and willow pattern', *Guardian*, 30 Apr. 1971, repr. in Gittings, *China through the Sliding Door* (London: Touchstone, 1999), 37–40.

5. Mo Bo, 'I was a teenage Red Guard', *New Internationalist*, Apr. 1987. A fascinating wide range of views from former Red Guards is found in Yarong Jiang and David Ashley, *Mao's Children in the New China* (London: Routledge, 2000).

6. John Gurley, *China's Economy and the Maoist Strategy* (New York: Monthly Review Press, 1976), 5.

7. For Mao on education, see 'Spring Festival remarks' and 'Hangzhou speech', in Stuart Schram, *Mao Tse-tung Unrehearsed* (Harmondsworth: Penguin, 1974).

8. In 1983 Zhang Tiesheng was sentenced to fifteen years in jail on charges of 'counter-revolution'. He was released ten years later and became a successful rural businessman, *Chen Bao* (Beijing), 11 Dec. 2003.

9. 'Spring Shoots' was praised in *China Reconstructs* (Aug. 1976), and denounced by Beijing radio, 29 June 1977. Text of 'Loyal Hearts' in *Chinese Literature*, no. 10 (1978).

10. S. Hillier and J. Jewell, *Health Care and Traditional Medicine in China 1800–1982* (London: Routledge, 1983), 108–11, 123.

11. Four conditions quoted in H. V. Henle, *Report on China's Agriculture* (Rome: UNFAO, 1974), 180.

12. *Hunan Daily*, 24 Dec. 1974.

13. John Gittings, 'The great walls of China', *Guardian*, 30 July 1974; *China Quarterly*, no. 59: 626.

14. Stephen Andors, *China's Industrial Revolution* (New York: Pantheon, 1977), 234–5.

15. The Fengqing affair is related in Yan Jiaqi and Gao Gao, *Zhongguo 'Wen Ge'*, ii. 499–502.

16. Zhang Chunqiao, 'On exercising all-round dictatorship over the bourgeoisie', *Red Flag*, no. 4 (1975) (trans. in *China Quarterly* (June 1975), 360–3); Yao Wenyuan, 'On the social basis of the Lin Piao anti-Party clique', *Peking Review*, no. 10 (1975).

17. Peter Moller Christensen and Jorgen Delman, 'A theory of transitional society: Mao Zedong and the Shanghai School', *Bulletin of Concerned Asian Scholars*, 13/2 (1981); Christensen, 'The Shanghai School and its rejection', in Stephan Feuchtwang and Athar Hussain (eds.), *The Chinese Economic Reforms* (London: Croom Helm, 1983).

18. On the 'revolutionary tide', see *Issues and Studies*, no. 3 (1972); Li Chien in *Peking Review*, 34 (1976).

19. Deng's polemics with the ultra-left in 1975–6, discussed in Merle Goldman, 'Teng Hsiao-p'ing and the debate over science and technology', *Contemporary China* (Columbia University), 2/14 (Winter 1978).

20. Foreign trade debate: Deng's speech of 18 Aug. 1985 in Chi Hsin, *The Case of*

the Gang of Four (Hong Kong: Cosmos, 1977), 273–6; ultra-left position in *Peking Review* (27 Aug. 1976), 9.

6. Economics in Command

1. This opening analysis has relied heavily on Cyril Lin, 'China's economic reforms II: Western perspectives', *Asian-Pacific Economic Literature*, 2/1 (Mar., 1988); also Feuchtwang and Hussain (eds.), *Chinese Economic Reforms*.

2. See analysis of the underlying problems of the Four Modernizations in Liu Suinian and Wu Qingan (eds.), *China's Socialist Economy: An Outline History* (Beijing: Beijing Review, 1986).

3. Chen Yun speech, trans. in *Inside China Mainland* (Taipei: Institute of Current China Studies) (Apr. 1980).

4. Xue Muqiao, *On Socialist Economy* (Beijing: Foreign Languages Press, 1981); addendum in *Beijing Review*, no. 49 (1981); 'Socialism and planned commodity economy', ibid. 33 (1987); 'Away with dogmatism and ossified pattern', ibid. 4 (1988).

5. John Gittings, 'Wages and management in China', *Journal of Contemporary Asia*, 9/1.

6. Yu Guangyuan (ed.), *China's Socialist Modernization* (Beijing: Foreign Languages Press, 1984), 594–617; Liu Guoguang, 'Socialism is not egalitarianism', *Beijing Review*, no. 39 (1987).

7. Liu Guoguang, 'Unifying planning and marketing', *Beijing Review*, no. 41 (1987).

8. David M. Bachman, *Chen Yun and the Chinese Political System* (Berkeley: Center for Chinese Studies, 1985), 152.

9. Yu Guangyuan (ed.), *China's Socialist Modernization*, 84–101, Gao Shangquan, in *Beijing Review*, no. 15 (1988).

10. Quoted by Reuters, 4 June 1987.

11. For the Shenzhen experiment see *Ta Kung Pao* (Hong Kong), 17 Sept. 1987.

7. Peasant China Transformed

1. Fei Xiaotong, *Small Towns in China* (Beijing: New World Press, 1986), 28–36; *Chinese Village Close-up* (Beijing: New World Press, 1983), 200–1.

2. Wang Weizhi, *Contemporary Chinese Population*, ed. Xu Dixin (Beijing: Chinese Social Sciences Publishing House, 1988), cited in Jasper Becker, *Hungry Ghosts: China's Secret Famine* (London: John Murray, 1996), 270–1. According to Vaclav Smil, 'We will never know the actual toll because the official Chinese figures for the three famine years greatly underestimate both the fall in fertility and the rise in mortality and because we cannot accurately reconstruct these vital statistics' ('China's great famine: 40 years later—Education and Debate', *British Medical Journal*, 18 Dec. 1999).

3. Peter Nolan, *China Now* (London: Society for Anglo-Chinese Understanding), no. 108.

4. This account of the origins of the responsibility system is drawn from material in *China Quarterly*, no. 81, p. 163; no. 83, p. 615; *Beijing Review*, nos. 3, 11, 17, 34 (1981); 24 (1982), 4, 7, 22, 33, 44–50 (1983).

5. John Gittings, *Guardian*, 12 and 15 Mar. 1982.

6. Quoted by Lin Zili in *Social Sciences in China* (Beijing: Academy of Social Sciences, 1983), i. 65.

7. *Beijing Review*, no. 46 (1984).

8. Material on rural reforms in *BBC Summary of World Broadcasts*, iii. *The Far East*, nos. 7556, 7669, 7671 (1984); *Beijing Review*, no. 14 (1985), 49 (1986).

9. Deng Xiaoping, *Selected Works 1975–1982*, 297 ff.

10. Gittings, 'From blossoms to bricks?', *China Now*, no. 109 (Summer 1984), 3–5.

11. Quoted from *Rural Economic Questions* (Beijing, 1984), no. 1, in *Inside China Mainland* (Taipei) (Aug. 1984). On the 1979–84 rural reforms, see further Justin Yifu Lin, 'Rural reforms and agricultural growth in China', *American Economic Review*, 82 (1992), 34–51; Carl Riskin, 'Chinese rural poverty: marginalized or dispersed?', ibid. 84 (1994), 281–4.

12. On rural industrialization see Robert Delfs in *Far Eastern Economic Review*, 4 June 1987; *Rural Economic Questions*, no. 12 (1985) (*Inside China Mainland*, Apr. 1986).

13. See articles by Fei Xiaotong in *Beijing Review*, nos. 20–2 (1984); 14, 17, 21 (1985).

14. Gittings, 'From blossoms to bricks?', 3–5. Peasant extravagance was criticized in *China Daily*, 29 June 1987, and in *Jingji Xiaoxi* [*Economic News*], no. 116 (1985), trans. in *Inside China Mainland* (Apr. 1985).

15. Report in *People's Daily*, 2 Mar. 1987.

16. William Hinton, *Guardian*, 27 Aug. 1984; see also Hinton's detailed argument that the collective achievements of the model Dazhai Brigade were falsely disparaged, in *Monthly Review* (New York) (Mar. 1988).

17. *China Daily*, 24 Sept. 1987.

8. The Growth of Dissent

1. Wei's 1966 journey quoted in Roger Garside, *Coming Alive!: China after Mao* (London: Deutsch, 1981), pp. 268–71.

2. Gordon Bennett and Ron Montaperto, *Red Guard* (New York: Doubleday, 1971), 215; Liang Heng and Judith Shapiro, *Son of the Revolution* (London: Chatto and Windus), 207; Anita Chan, *Children of Mao* (London: Macmillan, 1985), 187; Yi Ming in Gregor Benton, *Wild Lilies Poisonous Weeds* (London: Pluto, 1982), 44: student's poem recorded at Xiamen University by Charlotte Shalgosky.

3. Xiao Lan (ed.), *The Tiananmen Poems* (Beijing: Foreign Languages Press, 1979) describes how the poems were hidden. The books sold from the bus in Tiananmen Square included Tong Huaizhou (ed.), *Tiananmen geming shi wen-xuan, xu bian* [*Selection of Poems from the Tiananmen Revolution: Supplement*],

published in Apr. 1978. Tong Huaizhou (ed.), *Tiananmen shichao* [*Copies of Tiananmen Poems*] was published officially in Dec. 1978 by the People's Literature Press and carries Chairman Hua's calligraphy. 'Tong Huaizhou' is a pseudonym, conveying the sense of 'A son who remembers Zhou [Enlai]'.

4. The text of 'We want real Marxism-Leninism', trans. here by Beth McKillop, is included in *Tiananmen shichao*. An illustrated volume also titled *Tiananmen shichao* (Shanghai: People's Arts Press, 1979), carries the text of 'With head high . . .' and a heroic woodcut of Wang Lishan.

5. Texts from *Beijing Spring* [*Beijing zhi chun*], trans. in Claude Widor (ed.), *Documents on the Chinese Democratic Movement 1978–1980*, ii (Hong Kong: Observer Publ., 1984), with a well-informed introduction.

6. Guo Lusheng (pseud. Shi Zhi), poems trans. in Widor (ed.), *Documents*, ii. 233–4 and 348–50; ibid. 83 for his membership of United Action group whose attack on Lin Biao is recorded in Jean Daubier, *History of the Chinese Cultural Revolution* (New York: Vintage, 1973), 104; Guo's first poem, trans. in David Goodman, *Beijing Street Voices* (London: Boyars, 1981), 130–1.

7. Bei Dao, 'Answer', in *Shikan* [*Poetry*] (Mar. 1979); translation and critical discussion, in Bonnie MacDougall (ed.), *Notes from the City of the Sun: Poems by Bei Dao* (Ithaca, NY: Cornell University Press, 1983), and MacDougall (ed.), *Waves* (London: Heinemann, 1983).

8. Ai Qing, 'The *Red Flag*', in Kaiyu Hsu (ed.), *Literature of the People's Republic of China* (Bloomington: Indiana Univ. Press, 1980), 917–18.

9. For Yu Luoke see Gordon White, *Politics of Class and Class Origin* (Canberra: Australian National Univ., 1976); his sister's novel, *A Chinese Winter's Tale* (Hong Kong: Renditions, 1986); her article about him in *Siwu Luntan* (Sept. 1979); extract from his diary in *Zhengming* (Hong Kong), no. 3 (1980); poem by Bei Dao is dedicated to Yu (in *Notes from the City of the Sun*, 58–62); a semi-fictional play about Yu by Wang Keping published in *Beijing zhi chun* (Widor (ed.), *Documents*, ii. 410–28); the dissidents Xu Wenli ('My self-defence', 9, 16) and Liu Qing ('Prison memoirs', 901) (see below) both take Yu as a model for their own later imprisonments.

10. Zhang Zhixin's essay 'My views remain unchanged', in *Beijing zhichun*, no. 8 (1979); prison doctor exposed in *Zhengming*, no. 8 (1979), 32–3: Ren Zhongyi's views published in *Beijing Review*, 30 (1979).

11. Benton, *Wild Lilies*, 122–7. Fu Shenqi would himself be arrested in the great round-up of Apr. 1981. Liu Binyan, speech at Tongji University, Shanghai, 6 Nov. 1986.

12. Anita Chan, *Children of Mao*, 87; Liu Guokai, *A Brief Analysis of the Cultural Revolution* (Armonk, NY: M.E. Sharpe 1987).

13. The name of Li Yizhe attached to the manifesto was taken from those of its three principal authors, LI Zhengtian, Chen YIyang, and Wang XiZHE; trans. in Christian Bourgeois (ed.), *Chinois, si vous saviez* (Paris: Bibliothèque asiatique, 1976), and excerpted in Benton and Hunter, *Wild Lily, Prairie Fire* (Princeton:

Princeton University Press, 1995), 134–45. This account is based largely on Benton's earlier *Wild Lilies*, 16–38.

14. Chen Erjin, trans. by Robin Munro as *China: Crossroads Socialism* (London: Verso, 1984), esp. 2, 192. See also Munro's 'China's Democracy Movement: midwinter spring', *Survey*, no. 121 (1984).

15. Quotations from 'Single Spark' exhibition recorded by the author; see Gittings, 'Not just a pretty picture', *New Internationalist* (Apr. 1981).

16. Fu Yuehua was released from labour camp in 1984 but was still in detention in 1986 and her current fate remains unknown.

17. Wei Jingsheng, texts in Widor (ed.), *Documents*, i; trans. (also Fu Yuehua) in W. Sadane and W. Zafanolli, *Procès politiques à Pékin* (Paris: Maspero, 1981). See also his letters from prison and other writings, trans. in *The Courage to Stand Alone* (New York: Viking, 1997).

18. Liu Qing, 'Notes from Prison', trans. in *Chinese Sociology and Anthropology* (Autumn–Winter, 1982–3). Liu spent ten years in jail before being expelled to the US where he is president of the New York-based group Human Rights in China. 'Repression in China flows in and out like the tide', he told *Time* (31 July 2000). 'It's always present. It's just that sometimes it's enforced gently and sometimes severely.'

19. Extracts from Xu Wenli's 'Self-defence' were published by Amnesty International in Feb. 1986. Xu was released in 1993, but jailed again in 1998, and was forced to accept exile in the US in Dec. 2002.

20. Andrew Nathan, *Chinese Democracy* (New York: Knopf, 1985), ch. 10; Liang Heng and Judith Shapiro, *Return to China* (London: Chatto and Windus, 1987), 35–55.

21. Demonstrations of 1985 reported in *Zhengming* (Nov. 1985); Bo Yiho called for a stable political environment, complaining that if senior officials had to busy themselves morning, noon, and night dealing with unexpected incidents, the reforms would never take place (Beijing radio, 28 Nov. 1985).

22. Quoted in *Zhengming* (Jan. 1987).

23. Quoted in *Inside China Mainland* (Mar. 1987).

9. The Party under Pressure

1. Hua's alleged mandate is examined in Andres Onate, 'Hua Kuo-feng and the arrest of the "Gang of Four" ', *China Quarterly*, no. 75 (Sept. 1978).

2. Wang Hongwen's challenge is recounted by Deng Xiaoping, *Selected Works, 1975–1982*, 218, 265–6.

3. A typical hagiographic essay, *Hua zhuxi zai Hunan* [*Chairman Hua in Hunan*] (Beijing: People's Press, 1977), was prefaced by a probably bogus 'quotation' from Mao: 'We must create public opinion, we must publicize Comrade Hua Guofeng, we must make the whole people gradually get to know him.'

4. Argument with Hu Qiaomu in *Zhengming* (Nov. 1982).

5. Hua's self-criticism (3 Aug. 1982), trans. in *Inside China Mainland* (Dec. 1982).

6. Deng's comments on drafts of the 1981 Resolution in *Selected Works 1975–1982*, 276–96; see also the lengthy gloss on the Resolution: *Guanyu jianguo yilai dang de ruogan lishi wenti de jueyi* [*On the Resolution on a Number of Historical Questions since 1949*], produced by the Central Committee's Documentary Research Office (Beijing: People's Press, 1985 rev. edn.).

7. *A Great Trial in Chinese History* (Beijing: New World Press, 1981). Professor Zhang's interrogation is transcribed at p. 45.

8. Trans. in *Inside China Mainland* (June 1982).

9. Wang Renzhong, *People's Daily*, 1 July 1982.

10. For the 1986 Party reforms, see Robert Delfs in *Far Eastern Economic Review*, 29 May 1986; *Wen Wei Po* (Hong Kong), 21 and 22 July 1986.

11. *Zhengming* (Apr. 1984).

12. Li Ruihuan profiled in *Beijing Review*, no. 40 (1984); *Jiushi niandai* [*The Nineties*], no. 2 (1987).

13. Li Peng profiled in *Guangjiaojing* [*The Mirror*], no. 4 (1987).

14. Hu Qili's speech, trans. in *BBC Summary of World Broadcasts*, iii, *The Far East*, no. 8225.

10. The Scholars Speak Out

1. Fang Lizhi's speech of 4 Nov. 1985 summarized in *Zhongguo zhichun* [*China Spring*] (New York) (Feb. 1987); a digest of it circulated by internal *Cankao xiaoxi* [*Reference News*], trans. in *Inside China Mainland* (Dec. 1986).

2. Yue Daiyun: *To the Storm* (Berkeley and Los Angeles: Univ. of California Press, 1985), 23.

3. Lu Dingyi's self-criticism in *Minzhu yu fazhi* [*Democracy and the Legal System*], no. 4 (1983).

4. Ding Ling, interview in *People's Daily*, 31 Oct. 1983.

5. Proceedings of the 1979 Seminar summed up in *Zhongguo gongchandang liushinian dashi jianjie* [*Introduction to Main Events in Sixty Years of the CCP*], (Beijing: National Defence Univ., 1985), 604–6. Su Shaozhi recalls the debate in *Marxism and Reform in China* (Nottingham: Spokesman Books, 1993).

6. For Su Shaozhi on class, see *Selected Writings on Studies of Marxism (SWSM)* (Beijing: Institute of Marxism-Leninism-Mao Zedong Thought), i. 6 (Feb. 1981); see generally Stuart Schram, *Ideology and Policy in China since the Third Plenum, 1978–1984* (London: School of Oriental and African Studies, 1984).

7. Wang Ruoshui, 'On alienation', *SWSM* i. 12 (May 1981).

8. Li Honglin, 'The authority of democracy', *SWSM*, ii. 4.

9. 'Political restructuring of socialist states', *Social Sciences in China*, no. 3 (1988); also *Beijing Review*, no. 39 (1987).

10. Seminar on 'Socialist spiritual civilisation and theoretical work', *Red Flag*, 16 July 1986.

11. Li Honglin, 'Modernization and democracy', *Shijie jingji dabao* [*World Economic Herald*], (Shanghai), 8 June 1986.

12. Fang Lizhi's writings from this period, trans. in *Bringing Down the Great Wall* (New York: Knopf, 1991).

13. Criticism of Wang Ruowang in the 1950s in Hualing Nieh, *Literature of the Hundred Flowers* (New York: Columbia Univ. Press, 1981), ii. 385.

14. Wang on zest for life, in *Qingnian yidai* [*Youth Generation*], no. 4 (1986).

15. For Wang's argument with Deng, see *Jiushi niandai* [*The Nineties*] (Hong Kong), no. 2 (1987).

16. Liu Binyan on the danger from the left, in *Jiushi niandai*, no. 2 (1987).

17. Remarks at Shanghai conference, *Zhengming*, no. 1 (1987).

18. Liu's pre-1949 recollections, in 'The call of our times', *Wenyibao*, nos. 11–12 (1979); tale of Liu Shulan, ibid. 6 (1979), both trans. in Lee Ou-fan Lee, *Chinese Literature for the 1980s* (Stanford: Stanford Univ. Press, 1985).

19. Conservative reactions quoted from *Xinhua* commentary, 28 Jan. 1987, in *BBC Summary of World Broadcasts*, iii. *The Far East*, no. 8480; *Henan Ribao*, 19 Jan. 1987, ibid. 8472; Shenyang radio, 2 Feb. 1987, ibid. 8485; Bo Yibo, ibid. 8494; high-class hotels, *Xinhua*, 21 Jan. 1987, ibid. 8474; *Beijing Daily* on Western evils, 4 Feb. 1987.

20. Zhuozhou conference: *Guangming Daily*, 21 Apr. 87; *Asiaweek* (Hong Kong), 10 May and 7 June 1987.

21. The 'five gentlemen' affair in *Jingbao* [*Mirror*] (*Hong Kong*), Sept. 1987.

11. The Door Opens Wide

1. Deng's National Day speech, 1 Oct. 1984: 'The desire for peaceful reunification of the motherland is taking hold in the hearts of all descendants of the Yellow Emperor.'

2. Hu Yaobang on Taiwan, in *Beijing Review*, no. 42 (1981).

3. Sun Yat-sen, 1924 lecture, in N. Gangulee, *The Teachings of Sun Yat-sen* (London: Sylvan Press, 1945), 65.

4. Author's interview at ACFTU headquarters, Apr. 1984.

5. Yue Qingping, 'Opening up: The lessons of history', *Beijing Review*, no. 39 (1987).

6. Mao's view, in Moss Roberts, *A Critique of Soviet Economics* (New York: Monthly Review Press, 1977), 103.

7. Huan Xiang, undated speech and 7 June 1984 report, trans. in *Inside China Mainland*, nos. 4 (1983) and 2 (1985).

8. Alec Nove, *Economic History of the USSR* (Harmondsworth: Penguin, 1969), 89.

9. *China Daily*, 9 Nov. 1987.

10. Reuters, 22 May 1986.

11. Xue Muqiao, Symposium on western China, *Xinhua*, 10 Aug. 1984.

12. Ji Chongwei, in *China Reconstructs*, no. 9 (1984).

13. Gu Mu on wavelike development, in *China News Agency*, 24 Feb. 1985

14. Xu Shijie's report, in *BBC Summary of World Broadcasts*, iii. *The Far East*, no. 0017.

15. Reports from Guangdong, ibid. 8717 and 0005.

12. Tiananmen Square, 1989

1. See Select Bibliography for more material on the Beijing massacre. Specific sources for quotes are given in the text and *BBC Summary of World Broadcasts*, iii. *The Far East* is abbreviated as *FE*.

13. Into the New Millennium

1. Poem trans. in 'Tiananmen one year on', *Guardian*, 31 May 1990.
2. On public opinion after Tiananmen see 'Two years after Tiananmen'. *Guardian*, 4 June 1991; John Gittings, ibid. 31 Aug. 1991.
3. Deng Xiaoping, *Selected Works*, iii. *1982–1992* (Beijing: Foreign Languages Press, 1994), 342–3.
4. ibid. 361.
5. Willy Wo-lap Lam, *China after Deng Xiaoping* (London: John Wiley, 1995), 77.
6. *BBC Summary of World Broadcasts*, iii. *The Far East*, 11 Mar, 1992.
7. World Bank external news service, 'China sheds iron rice bowl, advances reforms', Feb. 2002.
8. 'China encourages mass urban migration', *People's Daily* website, 28 Nov. 2003.
9. Detlev Rehn, *The Electronics Age Comes to China: The Case of Changzhou City* (Bonn: Ostasien-Institut, 1984); John Gittings, 'Yangtze's pearl has new lustre', *Guardian*, 30 May 2002.
10. 'Road work stressed at meeting', *China Daily*, 8 Aug. 2000.
11. Mayor Xu was briefing foreign journalists in February 2001 on Shanghai's new modernization plan; see John Gittings, 'The city at the dragon's head roars into the future', *Guardian*, 3 Mar. 2001.
12. Forbes Global 2002 list at http://www.forbes.com/2002/10/24/chinaland. html
13. China's Silicon Valley, discussed in Xinhua News Agency, 17 Dec. 2003.
14. Michael R. Phillips, Xianyun Li, Yanping Zhang, 'Suicide rates in China, 1995–1999', *Lancet*, 359/9309; 835
15. James Farrer, *Opening Up: Youth Sex Culture and Market Reform in Shanghai* (Chicago: University of Chicago Press, 2002).
16. Gittings, 'Communists caught out by net revolution', *Guardian*, 17 May 2000.
17. 'China needs a third "liberation" of farmers', *People's Daily* online edn. 12 Aug. 2002 [edited].
18. Cao Jinqing, *Huanghe bian de Zhongguo* [*China beside the Yellow River*] (Shanghai: Literature & Arts Press, 2000).
19. Li Changping, *Wo xiang Zongli shuo shihua* [*I tell the Premier the truth*] (Beijing: Guangming Daily Press, 2002), 9.
20. Cao Jinqing, *Huanghe bian*, 355–7.
21. Liu Xianbin, 'The farmers need democracy: an investigation of rural problems in Sichuan', *China Rights Forum* (Spring 1997).
22. Rong Xuelan and Shi Tianjian, 'Inequality in Chinese education', *Journal of Contemporary China*, 10/26 (2001).

23. Gittings, *Guardian*, 4 Sept. 1999; *Guardian Weekly*, 11–17 May 2000.

24. Gittings, 'To get rich is glorious, for some', *Guardian*, 19 Mar. 2002.

25. Dorothy J. Solinger, 'WTO entry: will China's workers benefit from this "win-win" deal?', *China Rights Forum*, 1 (2002).

26. Wang Anwen, 'The ten top Chinese economic issues of 1998', *Xinwen Bao*, 28 Nov. 1998, trans. in http://www.usembassy-china.org.cn/sandt/econ98.html

27. *Dangdai Sichao*, no. 2, 20 Apr. 1997, trans. in Hartford Web Publishing World History Project, http://www.hartford-hwp.com

28. 'Over 30,000 Liaoyang workers demonstrate to demand Yao's release', Radio Free Europe, 18 Mar. 2002.

29. George Hatem, author's interview, Nov. 1983.

30. *Jiangnan Daily*, 2 Mar. 2001, trans. in 'Recent Chinese reports on HIV/AIDS and sexually transmitted diseases', US Embassy Beijing website, 1 July 2001.

31. *China Youth Daily*, 15 Mar. 1989, as summarized in Gittings, '800 million suffer as Beijing miracle turns into mirage', *The Observer*, 21 Mar. 1999.

32. Dai Qing, 'Human rights abuses and the Three Gorges Dam', speech at University of Toronto, 26. Feb. 2004, text on www.ThreeGorgesProbe.org

33. Gittings, 'Hidden danger behind Three Gorges Dam', *Guardian*, 30 May 2003.

34. On Chinese dam thinking, see especially Gavan McCormack, 'Water margins: competing paradigms in China', *Critical Asian Studies*, 33/1 (Mar. 2001).

35. World Resources Institute, 'China's health and environment: Air pollution and health effects', text on www.wri.org

36. 'Arsenic pollution scare', *Shanghai Star*, 19 Dec. 2002.

14. China and the World

1. James Mann, *About Face: A History of America's Curious Relationship with China* (New York: Vintage Books, 2000), 103.

2. For Brent Scowcroft's visit, see *New York Times*, 10 Dec. 1989

3. 'Starting over: foreign policy challenges for the second Clinton administration', *Brookings Review* (Spring 1997), 15/2.

4. 'China on the move', *Newsweek*, 1 Apr. 1996.

5. Jiang Zemin, 'Enhance mutual understanding and build stronger ties of friendship and Co-operation', speech of 1 Nov. 1997.

6. Bill Clinton, Hong Kong press conference, 3 July 1998.

7. Cui Tiankai, author's interview, July 2000.

8. Simon Long, *Taiwan: China's Last Frontier* (London: Macmillan, 1991), 224.

9. Ming Pao, *June Four: A Chronicle of the Chinese Democratic Uprising* (Fayetteville: University of Arkansas, 1989), introd.

10. Quoted in Gittings, 'High wire in Hong Kong', *Guardian*, 31 Oct. 1992.

11. Lee Teng-hui, 'Always in my heart', speech of 9 June 1995, Cornell University.

12. Zhu Rongji on Taiwan, press conference after NPC, 16 Mar. 2000.

13. International symposium on political science and China in transition, People's University, Beijing, 15–16 July 2002, author's notes.

14. Panchen Lama's report, in *A Poisoned Arrow* (London: Tibet Information Network, 1997).

15. Tsering Shakya, *Dragon in the Land of Snows* (London: Pimlico, 1999), ch. 12; John Gittings, 'Sound and fury in Tibet', *Far Eastern Economic Review*, 12 Sept. 1968.

16. Hu Yaobang report, text in *Zhongguo Shidai* (Hong Kong) (Apr. 1998).

17. 'Tibetan nuns defy might of China', *Guardian*, 8 Nov. 1989.

18. Melvyn Goldstein et al., 'Fertility and family planning in rural Tibet', *China Journal*, 47 (Jan. 2002), 19–39.

19. See further Nicolas Becquelin, 'Xinjiang in the Nineties', *China Journal*, 44 (July 2000), 65–90; Amnesty International, 'Arbitrary detention of Rebiya Kadeer—a women's human rights defender and prisoner of conscience', 17 Apr. 2000.

20. Wen Jiabao on Tiananmen, press conference after NPC, 14 Mar. 2004.

21. China Democracy Party, *Nipped in the Bud: The Suppression of the China Democracy Party* (New York: Human Rights Watch, 1998).

22. Maria Chang, *Falun Gong: The End of Days* (New Haven: Yale University Press, 2004).

23. Tong Zhiguang, *Guardian*, 12 Dec. 2001.

24. Shuxun Chen and Charles Wolf, Jr., *China, the United States, and the Global Economy* (Santa Monica: Rand corporation, June 2001), ch. 6.

25. Resistance to foreign goods discussed in Beverley Hooper, 'Globalisation and resistance in post-Mao China: the case of foreign consumer products', *Asian Studies Review*, 24/4 (Dec. 2000).

26. Han Deqiang, 'Free trade means free war—A discussion on China's accession to WTO', Presentation to Thirty-third Conference of Union of Radical Political Economics.

27. For Monsanto campaign, see Gittings, 'China faces agricultural revolution', *Guardian*, 13 Nov. 2001.

28. Mao invites US investment, quoted from talk with John S. Service, 13 Mar. 1945, *Foreign Relations of the United States, 1945* (Washington DC: US Government Printing Office, 1969), 272–8.

Chronology 1949–2004

1949–51: Communist 'Liberation'
Civil War ends with collapse of Nationalist armies.
Chiang Kai-shek and Guomindang flee to **Taiwan**.
Mao proclaims **People's Republic of China** (1 Oct. 1949).
People's Liberation Army (PLA) occupies **Tibet** (1951).
US rejects **diplomatic relations** with China unless it remains neutral.
Sino–Soviet Treaty (Feb. 1950) provides economic aid, defence guarantees.

1950–2: Social and Economic Reform
Land reform redistributes to poor peasants, punishes landlords.
Marriage Law (1950) abolishes 'feudal practices'.
Unemployment, prostitution, and inflation tackled.
Literacy and health campaigns launched.

June 1950–July 1953: Korean War
China intervenes when US forces approach Yalu River (Oct. 1950).
US imposes economic blockade, 'interdicts' **Taiwan Straits**.
China excluded from the **United Nations**.
Armistice agreement signed at Panmunjom (July 1953).

1953–6: Normalization
First Five-Year Plan (1953–7) stresses heavy industry.
First National People's Congress (NPC) (1954) adopts state constitution.
Eighth Party Congress (1956) pronounces end of 'class struggle'.
People's Liberation Army (PLA) becomes conscript force.

1954–7: Attempted opening to West
More equal relationship with Soviet Union after **Stalin's death**.
Zhou Enlai plays peacemaker at 1954 Geneva **conference on Indochina**.
China supports peaceful coexistence at Bandung **Non-aligned Conference** (April 1955).
US–China **Warsaw Talks** (1955–7), US rejects Chinese overtures.

1955–7: Mao begins to take radical road
Agricultural Co-operatives set up to collectivize land (1955–7).
Hundred Flowers movement (1956–7) invites intellectuals to speak out.
Anti-rightist campaign (1957) launches crackdown, thousands sent to countryside.

1958–61: Great Leap Forward

People's Communes replace agricultural coops, communal messhalls, rural steel-smelting.

Mao quells criticism led by Defence Minister Peng Dehuai at **Lushan Plenum** (July 1959).

Famine causes estimated twenty million premature deaths.

Temporary retreat as communes scaled down into **brigades and teams** (1961).

1958–63: Sino-Soviet dispute

Khrushchev visits Beijing, alarmed by **Offshore Islands crisis** (July 1958).

Soviet Union remains neutral in **Sino-Indian border dispute** (1959).

China criticizes Soviet détente policy with the US at 1960 **Moscow Conference**.

Moscow rejects Chinese demand for **nuclear weapons** help, ends economic aid.

China refuses to sign 1963 **test-ban treaty**, explodes **atom bomb** (Sept 1964).

1962–5: Internal Party struggle

Mao warns 'never forget class struggle' at 1962 **Tenth Party Plenum**.

Jiang Qing (Madame Mao) organizes **ultra-left criticism** of Beijing city leaders.

Socialist Education Movement targets alleged capitalist revival in countryside.

Defence Minister Lin Biao circulates Mao's '**little red book**' in armed forces.

1966–8: Cultural Revolution (1)

Beijing leadership overthrown as **Red Guards** emerge (summer 1966).

Eleventh Plenum (August 1966) endorses Cultural Revolution.

Liu Shaoqi and **Deng Xiaoping** demoted, **Lin Biao** proclaimed 'chosen successor'.

Rebel groups '**seize power**'; factional violence reaches peak (1967).

Red Guards sent to countryside, '**Revolutionary committees**' take power (1968).

1966–73: China breaks out from isolation

Mao claims '**we have friends all over the world**'.

China aids **North Vietnam** in war with US, blocks Soviet aid.

Sino-Soviet **border clashes**, Soviet threatens nuclear strike (1969).

Henry Kissinger pays secret visits, seeking new ally in cold war.

President Nixon visits, acknowledges Taiwan part of China (February 1972).

China regains **UN seat** from Taiwan, recognized by two-thirds of its members.

Foreign trade doubles from 1965 to 1973, Western technology imported.

1969–76: Cultural Revolution (2)

Schools and colleges reopen with new '**revolutionary education**'.

Workers share control of factories, **material incentives denounced**.

'**Barefoot doctors**' and rural medical co-operative schemes promoted.

Lin Biao dies in plane crash over Mongolia (Sept. 1971).

Zhou Enlai restores state administration, sets modernization goal.

Deng Xiaoping returns as Zhou's deputy, new ultra-left offensive.

Death of Zhou (Jan. 1976) mourned in **Tiananmen Demonstration** (5 April).

Deng dismissed again, **Hua Guofeng** becomes acting premier.

1976–84: Rejection of Cultural Revolution

Mao dies (9 Sept. 1976), **Gang of Four** arrested (6 Oct.) after national mourning.

Hua Guofeng claims succession, announces '**Four Modernizations**'.

Third Party Plenum (Dec. 1978) endorses Deng's policy of '**seeking truth from facts**'.

Democracy Wall in Beijing and **unofficial magazines** briefly encouraged.

Free markets opened in towns, peasants allowed to farm **individual land**.

Mao's mistakes condemned at Eleventh Party Plenum (July 1981).

Hu Yaobang replaces Hua, Deng calls for '**reform and opening up**'.

1979–88: Open Door policy

China signs **US trade agreement** (1979), allows **joint ventures** (1980).

China rejoins **IMF and World Bank**, oil prospecting begins.

Special Economic Zones and **Open Cities** set up.

Zhao Ziyang calls entire seaboard China's '**gold coast**'.

Chinese **arms sales** expand to Gulf and Middle East.

1983–8: New thinking versus reaction

Campaign against '**spiritual pollution**' (Dec. 1984).

Hu Yaobang encourages **rethinking of Marxism** (Sept. 1985).

Scholars call for **reform of political structure** (1986).

Student demonstrations (Dec. 1986); **Hu Yaobang** resigns (Jan. 1987).

Zhao Ziyang becomes Secretary-General, **Li Peng** Premier.

1988–9: From crisis to massacre

Price reform postponed as **inflation** tops 20 per cent.

Martial law declared in Lhasa (March 1989).

Scholar–student coalition petitions for **political amnesty**.

Death of **Hu Yaobang** (Apr. 1989) inspires **Democracy Movement**.

Martial law declared in Beijing by **Li Peng** (19 May).

Armed forces shoot their way into Tiananmen Square (3–4 June).

Jiang Zemin replaces **Zhao Ziyang** as Secretary-General.

Fortieth anniversary celebrated under armed guard in Beijing (1 Oct.).

1990–2: Stagnation and repression

Hundreds jailed, dozens executed, in post-Tiananmen **crackdown**.

Deng Xiaoping warns of need to **resume economic growth** (March 1990).

China abstains on UN **Iraq war** vote, **Li Peng** meets Bush (Oct. 1990).
Growth of **Falun Gong** and other cults, spread of '**Mao fever**'.

1992–7: Reforms move into higher gear
Deng's **Southern Expedition** kickstarts the economy.
Fourteenth Party Congress endorses **socialist market economy** (Oct. 1992).
Double-digit **GDP growth** in 1992–5; massive urban reconstruction.
Farmers' incomes become static, **rural taxation burden** rises.
Death of **Deng Xiaoxing** (Feb. 1997); **Hong Kong** handover (July 1997).

1997–2001: China becomes a global power
Jiang Zemin, Bill Clinton, exchange visits (Oct. 1997, June 1998).
US plane bombs China's **Belgrade Embassy** (May 1999).
Hainan **spy plane** incident (April 2001).
China awarded **2008 Olympic Games**.
George W. Bush visits Shanghai, China joins '**war on terror**' (Oct. 2001).
China completes entry to **World Trade Organization** (Nov. 2001).

2001–4: New millennium, new problems
Sixteenth Party Congress: **Hu Jintao** becomes Secretary-General (Nov. 2002).
Tenth National People's Congress (NPC): **Wen Jiabao** elected Premier (Mar. 2003).
Henan province **HIV-AIDS scandal** revealed.
SARS epidemic: cover-up and exposure (Dec. 2002–July 2003).
First stage of **Three Gorges Dam** completed, project launched to 'transfer water north' (July 2003).
Hu, Wen, tackle problems of **rural poverty** and **migrant workers**.

China's Political Leaders

Chen Yun Born 1905, Shanghai, typesetter in youth; Long Marcher, joins Politburo 1934; post-1949 economic affairs expert; critical of 1980s reform; favours limited space for market; backs Tiananmen crackdown 1989; dies 1995.

Deng Xiaoping Born Sichuan 1914; Long Marcher, political commissar in anti-Japanese war; Party General Secretary 1954–66; purged in Cultural Revolution, struggles against Gang of Four 1975–6; gains paramount power 1978; launches economic reforms 1980; approves Beijing massacre 1989; restarts economic reforms 1992; dies 19 Feb. 1997.

Hu Jintao Born 1942, first Party leader to join after revolution; trained as hydraulics engineer: serves in rural hinterland, Tibet; youngest member of Politburo Standing Committee 1997; Party Secretary-General 2002; shows more concern for rich–poor divide.

Hu Yaobang Born 1915; youth leader and protégé of Deng; becomes General Secretary 1980; criticizes ultra-left excesses in Tibet; says Marxism cannot solve all China's problems 1984; forced to resign by Party conservatives 1987; death in April 1989 sparks Tiananmen Square demonstrations.

Jiang Qing Born 1914, film actress in Shanghai; reaches Yanan and begins living with Mao 1937–8; after Liberation barred from political role; begins attack on 'feudal and bourgeois' culture 1962–5; forms Cultural Revolution Group 1966; promotes 'revolutionary operas', elected to Politburo 1969; arrested Oct. 1976; convicted of 'counter-revolutionary crimes'; dies in jail 1991.

Jiang Zemin Born 1926, student activist; joins Party 1946; trained as engineer in Soviet Union 1955; plans Shenzhen Special Economic Zone 1979; Mayor of Shanghai 1985; replaces Zhao as Party Secretary-General June 1989; stresses 'national dignity' and material progress; US presidential visit 1997; propounds new theory of 'Three Represents' 2000; steps down but retains influence 2002.

Li Peng Born 1928, orphaned, becomes adopted son of Zhou Enlai; trained in Soviet Union 1948; minister of power 1981; appointed Premier 1987; declares martial law in Beijing May 1989; launches Three Gorges Dam project; chairman of National People's Congress (NPC) 1998–2003; known as butcher of Beijing.

Liu Shaoqi Born 1898, studies in Moscow; appointed Party Secretary-General 1943; Vice-Chairman 1949; succeeds Mao as head of state 1959, criticizes Great Leap; attacked in Cultural Revolution; resigns Oct. 1968; banished to Henan, dies of medical neglect 1969; rehabilitated 1980.

Mao Zedong Born 1893; founding member of CCP July 1921; leads Red Army on Long March 1934–5; develops theory of peasant-based revolutionary struggle; dominates Yanan wartime regime 1937–45; proclaims People's Republic 1949; aligns with Soviet Union and intervenes in Korea 1950; speeds up socialist change in countryside 1954–6; launches Great Leap Forward 1958–61; condemns Soviet 'revisionism' 1960–3; launches Cultural Revolution against critics 1966–8; welcomes Richard Nixon to Beijing 1972; dies 9 Sept. 1976.

Peng Dehuai Born 1898, Long Marcher; guerrilla warfare leader in anti-Japanese war; commander of Chinese troops in Korean War 1950–3; Minister of Defence 1954–9; dismissed after criticizing Great Leap at Lushan Plenum; early target of Cultural Revolution; arrested 1967 and dies of medical neglect 1974.

Wen Jiabao Born 1942, trained as geologist; joins Party 1965; reputation as strong administrator, avoids political conflict; Premier of State Council 2003; stresses social goals, tackles SARS and HIV-AIDS crises.

Zhao Ziyang Born 1919, met Deng in 1938; after Liberation tackles land reform in south China; protected by Zhou Enlai in Cultural Revolution; appointed Premier 1980; replaces Hu as Secretary-General 1987; opposes martial law, dismissed May 1989; under house arrest or silenced by Party discipline until his death in Jan. 2005.

Zhou Enlai Born 1898, forms Party branch in France 1921; supports Mao on Long March; negotiates with Nationalists 1937–45;. Premier and Foreign Minister 1949; keeps government functioning in Cultural Revolution; negotiates thaw with US in Nixon visit 1972; target of Gang of Four attack; widely mourned when dies Jan. 1976.

Select Bibliography

History

Cohen, Paul, *China Unbound: Evolving Perspectives on the Chinese Past* (London & New York: RoutledgeCurzon, 2003).

Fenby, Jonathan, *Generalissimo: Chiang Kai-shek and the China He Lost* (London: Free Press, 2003).

Jung Chang and Halliday Jon, *Mao: The Unknown Story* (London: Jonathan Cape, 2005).

Lawrance, Alan, *China since 1949, Revolution and Reform: A Sourcebook* (London & New York: Routledge, 2004).

Mackerras, Colin, *The New Cambridge Handbook of Contemporary China* (Cambridge: Cambridge University Press, 2001).

Mitter, Rana, *A Bitter Revolution: China's Struggle with the Modern World* (Oxford: Oxford University Press, 2004).

Cultural Revolution

Jiang Yarong, and Ashley, David, *Mao's Children in the New China* (London: Routledge, 2000).

Li Zhensheng, *Red-Color News Soldier* (London: Phaidon, 2003).

Perry, Elizabeth, and Li Xun, *Proletarian Power: Shanghai in the Cultural Revolution* (Boulder, Colo.: Westview, 1997).

Schoenhals, Michael (ed.), *China's Cultural Revolution 1966–1969* (New York: M. E. Sharpe, 1996).

Zheng Yi, *Scarlet Memorial: Tales of Cannibalism in Modern China* (Boulder, Colo.: Westview Press, 1996).

Reminiscences

Ch'ien, Hsiao, *Traveller Without a Map* (London: Hutchinson, 1990).

Liu Binyan, *A Higher Kind of Loyalty* (New York: Pantheon, 1990).

McGivering, Jill (ed.), *Macau Remembers* (Hong Kong: Oxford University Press, 1999).

Wu Ningkun, *A Single Tear* (London: Hodder & Stoughton, 1993).

Zhang Lijia, and Macleod, Calum (eds.), *China Remembers* (Hong Kong: Oxford University Press, 1999).

Zhang Xianliang *Grass Soup* (London: Secker & Warburg, 1994).

—— *My Bodhi Tree* (London: Secker & Warburg, 1996).

The Beijing Massacre

Benton, Gregor, and Hunter, Alan (eds.), *Wild Lily, Prairie Fire: China's Road to Democracy 1942–1989* (Princeton: Princeton University Press, 1995).

Black, George, and Munro, Robin, *Black Hands of Beijing: Lives of Defiance in China's Democracy Movement* (New York: John Wiley, 1993).

Han Minzhu (ed.), *Cries for Democracy: Writing and Speeches* (Princeton: Princeton University Press, 1990).

Hinton, Carma, and Gordon, Richard, *The Gate of Heavenly Peace* (film documentary) (Brookline, Maine and Boston: WGBH and Long Bow Group, 1995).

Zhang Liang, Nathan, Andrew, and Link, Perry (eds.), *The Tiananmen Papers* (New York: Public Affairs, 2001).

Economy and Reform

Chan, Anita, *China's Workers under Assault: Exploitation and Abuse in a Globalizing Economy* (Armonk, NY: M. E. Sharpe, 2001).

Chang, Gordon, *The Coming Collapse of China* (New York: Random House, 2001).

Croll, Elisabeth, *From Heaven to Earth: Images and Experiences of Development in China* (London: Routledge, 1993).

Khan, Azizur, and Riskin, Carl, *Inequality and Poverty in China in the Age of Globalization* (Oxford: Oxford University Press, 2001).

Kjellgren, Bjorn, *The Shenzhen Experience or City of the Good Cats* (Stockholm: Stockholm University, Department of Chinese Studies, 2002).

Nolan, Peter, *China and the Global Economy* (Basingstoke: Palgrave Macmillan, 2001).

Solinger, Dorothy, *China's Transition from Socialism: Statist Legacies and Market Reforms, 1980–1990* (Armonk, NY: M. E. Sharpe, 1993).

Studwell, Joe, *The China Dream: The Elusive Quest for the Greatest Untapped Market on Earth* (London: Profile Books, 2002).

Rural Issues

Becker, Jasper, *Hungry Ghosts: China's Secret Famine* (London: John Murray, 1996).

Cao Jinqing, *Huanghe bian de Zhongguo [China beside the Yellow River]* (Shanghai: Literary and Arts Press, 2000).

Gao, Mobo C. F., *Gao Village: Rural Life in Modern China* (London: Hurst, 1999).

Garnaut R., Gao Shutian, Ma Guonan (eds.), *The Third Revolution in the Chinese Countryside* (Cambridge: Cambridge University Press, 1996).

Li Changping, *Wo xiang Zongli shuo shihua [I Tell the Truth to the Premier]* (Beijing: Guangming Press, 2002).

The New Society

Chang, Maria Hsia, *Falun Gong* (London: Yale University Press, 2004).

De Burgh, Hugo, *The Chinese Journalist: Mediating Information in the World's Most Populous Country* (London: RoutledgeCurzon, 2003).

Evans, Harriet, and Donald, Stephanie, *Picturing Power in the People's Republic of China: Posters of the Cultural Revolution* (Lanham: Rowman and Littlefield, 1999).

Farrer, James, *Opening Up: Youth Sex Culture and Market Reform in Shanghai* (Chicago: University of Chicago Press, 2002).

Gittings, John, *Real China: From Cannibalism to Karaoke* (London: Simon & Schuster, 1996).

Hessler, Peter, *River Town: Two Years on the Yangtze* (London: John Murray, 2001).

Jones, Stephen, *Plucking the Winds: Lives of Village Musicians in Old and New China* (Leiden: CHIME Foundation, 2004).

Perry, Elizabeth J., and Selden, Mark, *Chinese Society: Change, Conflict and Resistance* (London and New York: Routledge, 2000).

Sun Shuyun, *Ten Thousand Miles without a Cloud* (London: HarperCollins, 2003).

Weston, Timothy, and Jensen, Lionel (eds.), *China Beyond the Headlines* (Oxford: Rowman & Littlefield, 2005).

Xinran, *The Good Women of China* (London: Chatto & Windus, 2002).

Literature

Dai Sijie, *Balzac & the Little Chinese Seamstress* (London: Vintage, 2001).

Gao Xingjian, *Soul Mountain* (New York: HarperCollins, 2000).

Goldblatt, Howard, *Chairman Mao Would Not Be Amused: Fiction from Today's China* (New York: Grove Press, 1996).

Ha Jin, *The Bridegroom* (London: Vintage, 2001).

Liang Xiaosheng, *Panic & Deaf: Two Modern Satires* (Honolulu: Hawaii University Press, 2001).

Liu Sola, *Blue Sky Green Sea & Other Stories* (Hong Kong: Renditions, 1993).

Mo Yan, *Red Sorghum* (New York: Penguin Books, 1994).

Wang Shuo, *Please Don't Call Me Human* (London: No Exit Press, 2000).

Wei Hui, *Shanghai Baby* (New York: Simon & Schuster, 2001).

Yang Lian, *Notes of a Blissful Ghost* (Hong Kong; Renditions, 2002).

Zhang Kangkang, *Living With Their Past: Post-Urban Youth Fiction*, ed. King, Richard (Hong Kong: Renditions, 2002).

Politics and Protest

Dillon, Michael, *Xinjiang: China's Muslim Far Northwest* (London and New York: RoutledgeCurzon, 2003).

Fewsmith, Joseph, *China since Tiananmen: The Politics of Transition* (Cambridge: Cambridge University Press, 2001).

Gilley, Bruce, *Tiger on the Brink: Jiang Zemin and China's New Elite* (Berkeley and Los Angeles: University of California Press, 1998).

Human Rights Watch and Geneva Initiative on Psychiatry, *Dangerous Minds: Political Psychiatry in China Today and its Origins in the Mao Era* (New York: Human Rights Watch, 2002).

Lam, Willy Wo-Lap, *The Era of Jiang Zemin* (Singapore: Prentice-Hall, 1999).

MacFarquhar, Roderick, *The Origins of the Cultural Revolution*, i–iii (Oxford: Oxford University Press, 1974, 1983, 1997).

Nathan, Andrew, and Gilley, Bruce, *China's New Rulers: The Secret Files* (New York: New York Review of Books, 2003).

Unger, Jonathan (ed.), *The Nature of Chinese Politics: From Mao to Jiang* (Armonk, NY: M. E. Sharpe, 2002).

Yang, Dali L., *Beyond Beijing: Liberalization and the Regions in China* (London: Routledge, 1997).

Hong Kong

Blyth, Sally, and Wotherspoon, Ian (eds.), *Hong Kong Remembers* (Hong Kong: Oxford University Press, 1996).

Hung, Eva, *City Women* (Hong Kong: Renditions, 2001).

Tsang, Steve, *A Modern History of Hong Kong* (London: I. B. Tauris, 2004).

Xu Xi, and Ingham, Mike, *City Voices: Hong Kong Writing in English, 1945 to the Present* (Hong Kong: Hong Kong University Press, 2003).

Tibet

Batt, Herbert (ed.), *Tales of Tibet* (Oxford: Rowman & Littlefield, 2001).

Goldstein, Melvyn, *The Snowlion and the Dragon: China, Tibet and the Dalai Lama* (Berkeley and Los Angeles: University of California Press. 1997).

Hilton, Isabel, *The Search for the Panchen Lama* (London: Penguin Books, 2001).

Norbu, Dawa, *Tibet: The Road Ahead* (London: Random House, 1997).

Shakya, Tsering, *The Dragon in the Land of Snows: A History of Modern Tibet since 1947* (New York: Columbia University Press, 1999).

Tibet Information Network, *A Poisoned Arrow: The Secret Report of the 10th Panchen Lama* (London: TIN, 1997).

Environment

Donald, Stephanie, and Benewick, Robert, *The State of China Atlas*, 2nd edn. (Berkeley and Los Angeles: University of California Press, 2005).

Elvin, Mark, *The Retreat of the Elephants: An Environmental History of China* (New Haven: Yale University Press, 2004).

Shapiro, Judith, *Mao's War Against Nature: Politics and the Environment in Revolutionary China* (Cambridge: Cambridge University Press, 2001).

Intellectual Debate

Davies, Gloria (ed.), *Voicing Concerns: Contemporary Chinese Critical Enquiry* (Oxford: Rowan & Littlefield, 2001).

Wang Chaohua (ed.), *One China, Many Paths* (London: Verso, 2003).

Zhang Xudong (ed.), *Whither China? Intellectual Politics in Contemporary China* (Durham, NC: Duke University Press, 2001).

China and the World

Chen Jian, *Mao's China and the Cold War* (Chapel Hill, NC: University of North Carolina Press, 2001).

Lampton, David, *Same Bed, Different Dreams: Managing U.S.–China Relations, 1989–2000* (Berkeley and Los Angeles: University of California Press, 2001).

Long, Simon, *Taiwan: China's Last Frontier* (London: Macmillan, 1991).

MacKerras, Colin, *Western Images of China* (Oxford: Oxford University Press, 1999).

Mann, James, *About Face: From Nixon to Clinton* (New York: Vintage, 2000).

Sinha, Radha, *Sino-American Relations: Mutual Paranoia* (Basingstoke: Palgrave Macmillan, 2003).

Westad (ed.), *Brothers in Arms: The Rise and Fall of the Sino-Soviet Alliance* (Stanford: Stanford University Press, 2000).

Index of Names

General Index

Plenum 122–3, 165, 168, 192, 193;
Sixth Plenum 168; Twelfth
Congress 165, 169, 181, 184, 253;
Thirteenth Congress 116, 169,
176, 181, 206, 253; Fourth Plenum
229; Nov. 89 Plenum 248;
Fourteenth Congress 253, 276;
Fifteenth Congress 253; Sixteenth
Congress 2, 253; Seventeenth
Congress 329
criticism of 149, 153, 246, 247
discipline 48–9, 174–7, 247
elders 225, 227, 234–5
and intellectuals 189–90, 191–3,
199–203
membership and organisation 94,
169, 170–1, 176, 179–80, 186
as 'ruling party' 2–3, 13, 252
1981 Resolution on Party History
41, 80, 108, 168, 194
1989 crisis 224–5, 233, 234–5, 239,
247
in the 1990s and 2000s 7–8, 12–13,
289, 329
Communist Youth League 66
conservatives 180–3, 190–1, 203–5
constitution 28, 89, 158
contradictions, theory of 27, 36, 46, 50
corruption 3, 15, 172–7, 180–1, 226,
231, 248, 273
Cultural Revolution 28, 42, 44, 59,
228–9, 234
Group (CRG) 33–4, 51, 54, 58, 70, 74
martyrs of 146–9
origins of 51–4, 67–9
'socialist achievements' of 80, 85, 88,
93
in Tibet 308–9
verdicts on, 17, 44–5, 80–1, 167,
169–71, 194–5, 202
violence in 78–9

D
Daqing, labour unrest 279–80

Dazhai Brigade 81, 90, 127
dazibao (big character posters) 69, 89,
153–4, 158
democracy
demonstrations for 155, 160–1, 223,
230–1
'The Fifth Modernization' 141,
156–7, 195
Mao's view of 45–7
and political reform 195–6, 197–8,
318
Democracy, Front for (1989) 248
Democracy Movement (1957) 66–7
Democracy Movement (1978) 144,
154–5
Democracy Wall 141, 154, 155, 158,
160
development, strategy for 219–21,
253–5
drought 284–5

E
East is Red, The 43
economy, political 35–8, 93
education
debate on (1957) 66–8; (1970s) 77–8,
95–6
reforms (1970s) 82–5; (1990s) 263–4,
271–2
egalitarianism 34, 37, 81–2, 105, 107,
121, 139, 231
enterprise, private 3, 116–17, 129–130,
253
entrepreneurs 112, 131–2, 254, 260
environment 15–16, 284–9
Exploration 141, 156

F
Falun Gong 11, 267, 314, 318–20
Fanshen 26, 63
farmers, *see* peasants
Fengqing debate 91–2
Fengyang County 119–20, 125–8
feudalism 22, 174, 218, 222